2 — Govt

WITHDRAWN
UTSA LIBRARIES

PRICE MAKING IN
A DEMOCRACY

BY
EDWIN G. NOURSE

WASHINGTON, D.C.
THE BROOKINGS INSTITUTION
1944

THE BROOKINGS INSTITUTION

The Brookings Institution—Devoted to Public Service through Research and Training in the Social Sciences—was incorporated on December 8, 1927. Broadly stated, the Institution has two primary purposes; the first is to aid constructively in the development of sound national policies; and the second is to offer training of a super-graduate character to students of the social sciences. The Institution will maintain a series of co-operating institutes, equipped to carry out comprehensive and inter-related research projects.

The responsibility for the final determination of the Institution's policies and its program of work and for the administration of its endowment is vested in a self-perpetuating board of trustees. It is the function of the trustees to make possible the conduct of scientific research under the most favorable conditions, and to safeguard the independence of the research staff in the pursuit of their studies and in the publication of the results of such studies. It is not a part of their function to determine, control, or influence the conduct of particular investigations or the conclusions reached; but only to approve the the principal fields of investigation to which the available funds are to be allocated, and to satisfy themselves with reference to the intellectual competence and scientific integrity of the staff. Major responsibility for "formulating general policies and co-ordinating the activities of the various divisions of the Institution" is vested in the president. The by-laws provide also that "there shall be an advisory council selected by the president from among the scientific staff of the Institution and representing the different divisions of the Institution."

BOARD OF TRUSTEES

DWIGHT F. DAVIS, *Chairman*

ROBERT PERKINS BASS

DAVID K. E. BRUCE

VANNEVAR BUSH

KARL T. COMPTON

HAROLD W. DODDS

MARSHALL FIELD

JEROME D. GREENE

AMORY HOUGHTON

DEAN G. ACHESON, *Vice-Chairman*

ROLAND S. MORRIS

HAROLD G. MOULTON

JOHN LEE PRATT

LESSING ROSENTHAL

LEO S. ROWE

EDWARD R. STETTINIUS, JR.

ANSON PHELPS STOKES

HARRY BROOKINGS WALLACE

JOHN G. WINANT

HAROLD G. MOULTON, *President*

EDWIN G. NOURSE, *Vice-President*

Copyright March 1944 by The Brookings Institution

Second printing September 1944

PREFACE

This volume has had a distinctly unusual, if not unique, publication history. The first chapter appeared as a pamphlet in January 1942; between then and July 1943, the eleven chapters of Parts I and II, together with Appendixes A, B, and C appeared in a series of twelve pamphlets. Now, after a lapse of more than two years since the beginning of serial publication, this material (with all the chapters revised and some of them extensively rewritten) together with three additional chapters and four additional appendixes are presented in book form. Three chapters have been dropped from the original list but the length of the treatment extended some 50 or 75 pages beyond what was planned in the early stages of the work.

The reasons for serial publication were stated in a prefatory note in the first pamphlet of the series. The decision grew largely out of a belief that there was an "active and steadily mounting interest in the modern workings of the private enterprise system, approached from the standpoint of price and production policies." There was doubt in the writer's mind, however, as to when business thinking would be most keenly alert to the issues involved or able to devote attention to them. It seemed, therefore, that it might be wise to begin presentation of the material at an early date but to defer the appearance of the final volume until a time not much in advance of the beginning, at least, of post-war re-conversion activities.

Other reasons for adopting the pamphlet form of

pre-publication were stated in the prefatory note to the first chapter as follows:

"We believe that this procedure has two advantages besides the earlier presentation [of part of the material] which it makes possible. The final volume will extend to some 375 or 400 pages and, in view of the character of the subjects discussed, may prove a somewhat formidable reading assignment in these busy days, even for those who are particularly interested in the problems with which it deals. But anyone can find a period of leisure sufficient to read a pamphlet of 25 to 40 pages. Furthermore, the interval between pamphlets gives the reader time to turn over in his mind each section of the argument and define his own degree of acceptance or points of dissent. Thus he can mature his own thinking as he moves from one chapter to another over a longer period than is ordinarily devoted to the reading of any particular book.

"From the standpoint of the author also, this extended contact with the reading public has marked advantages. It is hoped that many readers will write the author with reference to points at which they find the argument unclear or in their view faulty as to its statement of facts or the reasoning based upon them. Many of these comments will undoubtedly contribute to clearer statement and a more close-knit argument as the text is revised for presentation in ultimate book form, Some of these reactions, too, will no doubt prove highly illuminating and entitled to consideration as alternative interpretations even where the writer does not find himself able to accept them."

The response to this invitation for readers' criticisms and suggestions has been gratifying. The written communications and oral comments which have come to the author during the ensuing months have been both interesting and enlightening. They have shown an extreme range of agreement and dissent, both on particular details of the analysis and on the underlying postulates and major conclusions.

To all who have contributed to this running forum, the author expresses his deep appreciation mingled with regret that he could not agree with all the divergent views presented. In "signing off," a final invitation is extended to all readers of the book for new or supplementary comments. Possibly some who have been moved to criticism or suggestion with reference to earlier chapters have reserved judgment until they could see the concluding chapters, whereas others may find doubts they have already expressed somewhat removed by the rewriting of passages in the earlier preprinted chapters or by the supplementary discussion of Part III. Others may have had their dissent strengthened or new grounds for divergent views raised in this finishing process. Whether by way of disagreement, acceptance, or supplementation all such commentary will be cordially welcomed.

Edwin G. Nourse

The Brookings Institution
February 1944

The study upon which this book is based was made possible in part by funds granted by The Maurice and Laura Falk Foundation of Pittsburgh. However, the Falk Foundation is not the author, publisher, or proprietor of this publication and is not to be understood as approving or disapproving by virtue of its grant any of the statements and views expressed herein.

CONTENTS

PART III. PROSPECTS

PART I
PRINCIPLES

CHAPTER I
BETWEEN AUTOMATIC AND AUTHORI-
TARIAN PRICE MAKING

The coming of world war forced most businessmen to concentrate their attention sharply on short-run problems of getting maximum output in accordance with specifications and schedules drawn up for them by the military experts. The public, too, has become preoccupied with immediate questions of jobs gained or lost, of high taxes, war-bond buying, and consumer deprivations. For managers, workers, consumers, and legislators alike, ordinary economic issues, even those of the most fundamental sort, have been pushed into the background by zeal to serve a common cause in the hour of crisis.

But though this war activity and war psychology may dim our recollection of the economic problems we were wrestling with a few months or a few years ago, it has by no means blotted them from our minds or furnished solutions for them. Nor does the war bring any comforting assurance that there will not be a sharp resurgence of these same problems a year or a few years hence, after the guns cease firing.

In fact, in the minds of many, the war actually heightens the tension of our thinking as to the long-run future of economic life. It is easy to detect an almost desperate sense that this war is a sort of "last chance" for economic civilization. As to its military aspect, there is a widespread feeling that the war must eventuate in some form of world-embracing delegation of police power adequate to keep the peace. With that assured, economic men might in future devote their efforts consistently to the tasks of producing material well-being, their lives no longer mortgaged to the dirty business of destruction. On its economic side, we hope peace will forward or at least not impede institutions and practices of economic life in which strong incentives, skillful technical direction, provident handling of property, and efficient organization may be effectively combined. Only so can the mass of citizens find the dark days of "sweat and blood and tears" ushering in a new day of work and abundance and harmony.

During the depression of the 1930's, and particularly after the advent of "the New Deal," our minds were directed with new energy to re-examining—and often challenging—the economic system under which we lived. Fresh attention was given to the age-old problem of how men can most effectively organize themselves for making a livelihood. And, as generally happens in such cases, opinion divided. There were conservatives who emphasized, and perhaps exaggerated, the virtues of ancient business forms and practices. There were radicals who were excited, and perhaps intoxicated, at the prospect of revolutionary changes—Communist or Fascist—which were being experimented with in other countries. And there were moderates of many varieties who thought that peaceful progress could best be found in some eclectic combination of old-fashioned individualism, newly awakened government responsibility, and large-scale voluntary co-operation—perhaps after the manner of Sweden's "middle way."

Whatever the division of thought, such objectives of mass well-being were, as a practical matter, coming to be approached through more vigorous measures of political leadership and through the more active intrusion of government into the economic sphere. This very fact has led to no little apprehension among businessmen. Many of them fear that further centralization of effort under government agencies, inevitable in the war period, may furnish both the occasion and the means for putting government permanently in charge of economic life. They fear that "the American way" of business is seriously threatened, that possibly an economic system which we had been wont to consider an integral and essential part of our democratic heritage may now be doomed. They foresee the end of free business enterprise under private capitalism, coming either in a single swift stroke at the end of the war or in a few long strides rapidly timed. Even in the latter case, they see but a few more years left for the system in which they have been reared and to which they are still devoted.

The quotations presented on pages 6 and 8 give a representative sample of the views which prominent American business executives entertain both as to the virtues of our traditional system and as to the dangers by which it is now beset. Though obviously these men have vested interests, it would be cynical to doubt the sincerity of their belief that what they refer to as "the American way" of private capitalism, with free enterprise and the profit motive, is a sound and productive system for the conduct of our joint economic effort. But neither these quotations nor the general run of similar discussions make very clear the precise nature of these institutions as conceived by their proponents or the exact process by which national well-being is to be achieved. Different spokesmen use the terms in different senses, but they give a broad impression that these are simple, absolute, and permanent facts of economic life. In fact, however, they are complex and changing.

IN THAT DAY when our Constitution was written and the principles and concepts of our young nation established, business leadership was sought as a matter of course. Today business leadership should again be looked to for guidance when those principles and concepts are under fire. The Constitutional Convention of 1787 dedicated our nation to individual freedom, to free enterprise and to democracy. This Congress should resolve itself into a rededication of those principles. . . . Conflicts abroad emphasize to Americans the priceless value of our way of life. To understand . . . and protect [it] against today's onslaughts of alien philosophies, demands a thorough understanding of our basic political and economic concepts. . . .

Our convention program will discuss the accomplishments and opportunities of private enterprise with emphasis on that system as a force for social progress, the creator of high living standards, the stimulant to cultural advancement, the mainstay of national defense and the path to, and through, new frontiers. . . . What were the specific advantages and benefits strikingly apparent in countries where democracy and private enterprise flourished? Economically, standards of living were raised. More of the world's goods were made available to more people. The invention and creation of new commodities, new processes, new services enriched the lives of many instead of only the few. . . .

The doubts of our generation concerning the capacity and function of private enterprise . . . today root in the departures we have made from our true course. It is the fundamental necessity of a return to our original concepts of the democratic way of life.

Howard Coonley, Chairman, Walworth Co.
Congress of American Industry, Dec. 1939.

Economic life is a social process in a continuous state of evolution. Exploration, science, the technological processes of production, corporate structures, commercial procedures, the legal mandates and prohibitions, even the intellectual atmosphere within which men conduct business affairs—all these have greatly changed during the last fifty, twenty, even ten years. Under a system still eligible in 1941 to be called private capitalism, the private capitalist is a quite different functionary than he was in 1787. The free enterprise that campaign orators defended in the autumn of 1940 was not conceived in the same terms nor buttressed by the same property rights and codes of practice as those established by the Founding Fathers.

It is important, therefore, that, well in advance of the return to peace and its opportunities, we re-examine the character of our economic institutions and our past business practices. We must analyze the changes which have been taking place—or the lack of change—to discover whether steps have been taken, adjustments made, which would keep the process of economic life active and healthy under private management.

If capitalism and private enterprise are to be maintained or in some sense restored after the war, the general public will have to be satisfied that this system furnishes them as high a measure of material well-being as can reasonably be expected under any practicably attainable alternative. Both the businessman and the citizen should consider with open mind the principles upon which a system of free enterprise operates and the conditions which must be met by those who seek to live under it if it is in fact to bring about for all parts of our economy the largest degree of success and satisfaction of which it is inherently capable.

OUR TASK [is] to save free enterprise . . . to *prove* what America has always known in its deep folk-mind to be true—that a free economy is the base and bulwark of all the freedoms which the common people wisely demanded be defined in the United States Constitution's Bill of Rights. What the people want is definition. Facts and figures and blueprints, an argument as obviously truthful as the hole-proof pattern of two-plus-two-make-four, and as simple as A-B-C, and as dependable as the multiplication table. Give America that, in human terms it can trust, and it will have no time for unsound teachings and purple promises. . . . Industry is no longer on the defensive. We are not cowering in the shadows of a forgotten doorway of the temple of American life. The soldiers in the cause of a free economy and free enterprise are marching men. We are moving to the defense of America. The thump of our drums is the steady beat of the American heart. Industry's defense of private enterprise today is the defense of all the American freedoms. . . . Events in Europe demonstrate that when private enterprise is replaced with political control, free government and human freedoms fail inevitably.

> C. M. Chester, Chairman, General Foods Corp., Congress of American Industry, Dec. 1940.

THE AMERICAN Federation of Labor supports our American capitalistic system and free enterprise (as the labor men wished to call the system) just as vigorously as we support trade unions and the right to organize and bargain collectively. We regard both capitalism and trade unions as essential factors in the maintenance and perpetuation of our democratic form of government.

> William Green, president A. F. of L., interview in Washington *Sunday Star*, Nov. 24, 1940.

This understanding can be attained most readily through analysis of the price-making process.

PRICE MAKING A KEY TO ECONOMIC ANALYSIS

Our modern economic world is organized and conducted primarily in terms of money exchanges.[1] The results of our economic management, private and public, express themselves primarily in prices of goods and services and in the money incomes of the various participants in the economic process. If business organization or practice is bad, the ill effects are seen in prices; if prices are unconsciously distorted or purposely manipulated they lead to demoralization of markets and eventual decline of production and consumption. Pointing the way to maximum efficiency in price-making institutions and practices is the goal of economic science in a free economy.

Prices fall conveniently into three classes, according to the processes by which they are arrived at. At one pole is the simple, natural, flexible kind of prices that emerge spontaneously in free markets patronized by individual unorganized producers and buyers. These we shall call "automatic" prices, since no individual or agency assumes any particular responsibility for them. At the opposite pole lies "authoritarian" price-making. Under it, prices do not emerge spontaneously in free markets but are registered by a formal procedure of "price-fixing." Public control undertakes to direct the course of prices as part of a planned economy. This centralizing of power and responsibility holds a strong appeal for some minds, but many turn from it with grave apprehension.

Between these two extreme types of price-making lies the middle ground of "administered prices"—those

---

[1] This "price system" will be discussed in more detail in Chap. 5.

to be found in situations in which the seller is a sufficiently important factor in the market and has sufficient control over productive resources to make it possible for him to adopt and carry out a price-and-production policy.[2] This area embraces the major part of modern industrial life[3] with its large corporate producers, chain stores, trade associations, collective bargaining unions, and co-operative organizations. And yet the peculiarities, possibilities, and demands of this kind of price-making have by no means been mastered by businessmen or adequately examined by economists. We can best approach its description and analysis by examining briefly the characteristic features of the systems which flank it on either side.

AUTOMATIC PRICES UNDER SIMPLE COMPETITION

The essence of automatic price-making is to be found in the process of individual bargaining. Economics got its start as a branch of formal learning at a time when the tide of individual freedom of productive effort and bargaining activity was just beginning to rise or to reassert itself. Serfdom and feudal obligations had been largely done away with. Exploration and colonization

[2] To a lesser extent, the administrative control of prices vests not in the seller but in the buyer, who occupies a similarly strategic control as large-volume productive consumer or distributor.

[3] This statement would be challenged by some in the ranks both of businessmen and of economists. There is division of opinion between those who ascribe much importance in the price-making process to the policy factor in executive action and those who concede it only slight influence. The former attribute great significance to the making of choices, including the choice to alter situations. The latter argue an extreme deterministic philosophy and reduce the businessman, no matter how large his firm or how impressive his nominal authority, to the position of economic automaton. My own views as to the scope and nature of price policy (linked with the various aspects of production policy) put me in the former group. They are set forth in general terms in App. A. The grounds for my position are explained in more detail in subsequent chapters of this book.

had increased the mobility of labor and the activity of trade. The medieval guild had passed; the labor union had not yet emerged. Money exchange was highly developed, but financial controls had not grown much beyond individual or family limits. While handicraft had begun to yield to factory methods, establishments were small and largely personal in both ownership and management. From top to bottom of society, the individual was released from old obligations and endowed with new rights and resources. Personal competition had not been absent before this time, but it had been much in the manner of animals struggling over an inadequate "kill." The new competition which emerged in the late eighteenth and early nineteenth centuries took on a more dynamic quality as increases in productive efficiency, derived from new explorations and techniques, became more and more available.

The times begot their relevant philosophy. Adam Smith gave it classic expression. The heart of his doctrine was that if the individual was left free to exert himself in the midst of opportunities and was given responsibility for his own well-being, self-interest would produce results better than could be achieved under any program of official direction. Prices, reflecting the actions of economically free men, could not be quarreled with any more than one could quarrel with the thermometer for registering the temperature. Moreover, this free price system would, like a thermostat, be not merely a recording device but also one of control. If prices went up sharply, production would be stimulated to reduce the shortage; if down, it would be checked until the glut was relieved.

Under such conditions, it was reasoned, the seller, if his sales returns do not permit him to recoup costs, will shift his effort to some more promising line of endeavor. This will keep labor and capital always moving away from the spot where production is relatively overdone and, since everyone is free to enter any business, toward the places where production is so scarce as to cause product to command a premium over costs, that is, profit above the normal. Thus the nation would benefit from sound direction and co-ordination of activities as well as from the greater stimulation derived from the freeing of individual enterprise.

In this remote and somewhat idealized situation, prices will be registered automatically as the expression of the balance which spontaneous supplies and demands strike in the market. The "economic man," using only common sense in the pursuit of the individual interest or advantage which he can see just beyond the tip of his nose, may be relied upon to keep supplies constantly adjusting themselves to demands. *Laissez faire* becomes the almost obvious rule of conduct for government in its relation to economic life. There are no unemployed workers since everyone accepts the best employment that is offered, no idle funds since capital is saved only under the spur of an adequately rewarding price or interest rate, no persistently unutilized plant capacity since an "economic man" will accept a lower rent in preference to disuse.

While it was the professional economist who elaborated this theory of automatic price-making, the businessman has been quick to admire the picture and accept it for himself. He has indeed been prone to put it forward as an explanation of price movements even today, although conditions are quite different from those to which the original theory was applied. The major point in that difference is that economic life is no longer dominated by the business operations of individual producers and traders. Great blocks of capital, management, and labor having crystallized in modern business, the flow of automatic price-making and its accompanying economic adjustments gives place to consciously previewed and purposely directed group operations.[4] To facilitate these developments or to remedy defects in the economic society thus evolving, government has piled up enabling acts and regulatory acts until the automatic price-making process of laissez-faire theory (and partial application) has largely disappeared. While some people take alarm at this change and seek the restoration of the automatic system, others place their hopes in the elaboration of fuller and better controls.

THE FACE AND FORM OF AUTHORITARIAN PRICE FIXING

In our own country, we have had a small but growing amount of price-making by government authority. In the main it has been limited to public regulation of prices charged by private producers, the object being to protect consumers by setting maximum prices or to protect producers by setting minimum prices. Examples include public utility regulation, railroad rate control, the Guffey coal acts, and both federal and state milk controls. More general schemes of price-fixing reappear perennially as proposals for dealing with the agricultural prob-

[4] In this connection, it is of course worth remembering that in the earlier days when firms were small, markets also were severely restricted in size by the lack of easy means of transportation and communication. Competition in these markets was also inhibited by the lower level of public education and the stronger hold of habit and custom. In appraising the situation of a century ago and that of recent decades, therefore, it is easy to exaggerate the force and flexibility of competitive forces then. But, by the same token, it is easy to underestimate the extent to which similar forces operate in the altered situation presented by large-scale industrialism in a world of cheap transportation, swift communication, and better education.

lem, and the ultimate scope and character of price control under the war influence is yet to be seen. Abroad, we see comprehensive systems of authoritarian price-fixing under Communism, Fascism, and the National Socialism of the Third Reich. Many of them go beyond the regulation of prices and rates charged by private business to include prices fixed by government agencies which are themselves producers.

It is indeed a striking feature of experiments which begin with mere price regulation that they rapidly spread to ever wider controls over the field of business. Once a price or group of prices has been formulated and promulgated, the control agency may find itself called upon to take active steps to support and effectuate it in the market. The productive system, bereft of the former free price guidance, however perfect or faulty, must be directly controlled as to its technique, volume and timing of investment, choice of goods to be produced, and their volume and quality. The ultimate end toward which such a development tends is a planned economy in which production must be scaled, supplies rationed, priorities established, techniques adjusted, capital channeled, labor mobilized and controlled to put the public's consumption and the business world's system of production in working harmony with the official price structure. Some directive agency as national brain must supervise the beating of the nation's heart, the breathing of the nation's lungs, the functioning of organs of secretion and excretion, and the co-ordination of muscular activity. It is no longer left to the nervous reflexes of price response. While it may be convenient for purposes of business and domestic management to retain the mechanism of money wages and price exchange, this is only a nominal price system, an administrative convenience rather than a significant factor in economic organization or a vital element in social functioning.

Many, perhaps most, of our citizens would hesitate to embark on so sweeping a program of politico-economic change as is here sketched[5]—all the more since they have witnessed various types and stages of its experimental development abroad. Some of them, in despair over the shortcomings of our present price-and-production situation, look longingly toward partial or complete restoration of the low-level safety of spontaneous price-making under small-scale competition. Others, who feel that such a return to a small-unit system of organization would entail too great a check to technological progress, still believe that economic direction cannot be left to either individuals or groups. They discuss a goal of high-level safety and efficiency conceived in terms of "the general welfare" as formulated by a headquarters staff and effectuated through "the provident state." The milder types of "economic planners" think in terms of merely advisory economic guidance, complementing a system of business operation still predominantly private. The more ardent planners show a clear distrust of the ability of private agencies to function for the public good.[6]

[5] Instead of starting with price-fixing, authoritarian incursions into the economic field may, of course, start with measures which act directly upon scale or direction of productive effort, investment, market exclusions or diversions, credit extension, or the mobilization of labor. These are likely to affect prices indirectly. On the other hand, non-price controls by government may be of kinds which alter income distribution or allot goods and services to consumers in ways that change the pattern of economic welfare with little change in the price structure.

[6] Though strong in their confidence as to the ability of commissars, bureau chiefs, and professionally trained administrative agents to discharge the weighty duties of directing such a system with the skill, firmness, flexibility, and vision as to technical and organizational progress which would assure maximum satisfaction of the material wants of the population as a whole. See "Collective Bargaining and the Common Interest," *American Economic Review*, Suppl., March 1943, p. 1.

"Parity prices" under the Agricultural Adjustment Act, coal prices under the Bituminous Coal Act of 1937, and various minimum wage and rate schedules are fragments of a conceivable system of general authoritarian price-making. With the success of one fixation depending on other prices being brought into consistent relationship, there is discernible in these separate attempts to remedy specific price ills a gathering momentum toward comprehensive price control, and its attendant production and consumption control.[7]

No doubt the faults in our price structure which prompted these regulatory devices were real. Relief of specific difficulties has unquestionably been afforded under some of the regulatory devices applied. But before we commit ourselves to an enlargement of these efforts or elaboration of the parts into an all-embracing plan of economic organization under authoritarian price-making, alternative possibilities should be intensively studied. This turns our attention to the prevailing scheme of price-making in American business. In spite of remnants of automatic price making and some intrusion of authoritarian price making, our system is largely in the hands of private businessmen, but with considerable centralization of control over both prices and the productive operations related to them. It is a system of "administered prices" or "monopolistic competition," whether among few or many competitors.

THE DUAL NATURE OF "ADMINISTERED" PRICES

Administered prices, though clearly distinguished from either automatic or authoritarian prices, partake of the nature of both. They are like automatic prices in that producers with great freedom to make whatever

---

[7] This excludes from consideration special wartime controls and the possible retention of some of them after the war.

product they like on such a scale as they see fit trade in
an open market for any price that they find acceptable.
Administered prices depart from the theory of automatic price-making in that producers are differentiated
as to product, location, or other significant factors and in
that the individual concern makes a sufficiently large
percentage of its distinctive articles (with attached services) so that it can exercise a price policy and give the
policy some degree of force through its control of the
volume of output. This ability to administer a block of
resources of significant size under an integrated production and price policy gives many large industrial executives a power of control akin to that of a public agency
engaged in authoritarian price-making.

On the other hand, price administration by private
firms is unlike authoritarian pricing in that the corporate
executive must operate within the limits of a price
system in which he must pay wages and salaries that will
attract the necessary kinds of workers and charge prices
which will permit the absorption of his product and
maintain earnings which will preserve his capital, provide for its necessary growth, or so fortify his credit
rating as to permit necessary borrowings. That is to say,
he must face the responsibility for his own acts within
the bounds of his company rather than absorb them in
a total economy as a political regime may do.

Corporate price administration is unlike authoritarian
price-making also in that the policies of the several
executives do not ordinarily become parts of a conscious
program of general economic welfare.[8] It is a common
fear, based on a considerable body of experience, that

___

[8] This perhaps implies unduly that general welfare is the objective of
authoritarian regimes. Nationalist aims are generally in fact paramount
but likely to be qualified by some group or class bias—proletarian, religious, or racial. Authoritarian economic and social planning as it approaches the totalitarian stage sets national growth and power more and

such solidarity of action as is developed, such planning as rival concerns in an industry do exercise, seeks only to advance the common interest of the particular group and tends to exploit the public. Whether this tendency is inevitable and perhaps cumulative or whether there is any factor of self-correction is a matter of great importance to the future of private economic enterprise and one which will be examined in some detail in succeeding chapters. Clearly, however, the administrative price and production actions of the executives of large manufacturing and commercial corporations do not unconsciously but dependably achieve the stimulation of progress and co-ordination of effort for the nation's economic life. If such results are to be attained, it must be through conscious purpose and a sound grasp of the nature of economic forces and the business institutions through which they operate.

Executive responsibility is the keynote of the "administered price" situation. This is in sharp contrast to the automatic system. There, however egregious the blunders of the individual enterpriser, the general tide of business would not be appreciably disturbed, and to its onward march he could promptly readjust his private affairs. Since the structure of small business organization does not rise very much above the ground, the danger of any catastrophic collapse is precluded. Under authoritarianism, on the other hand, responsibility is centralized in the "provident state" much more fully than under our scheme of private but large-scale enterprise. Labor is assigned to its task and shunted to its place of

---

more as its goal. While logically these objectives call for maximum development of productive resources, such an outcome is not compatible with superior economic status for "party" members or unfavorable status for despised minorities.

work.[9] Capital is abstracted from private income or property and committed not to such enterprises as appeal to the wish or judgment of its erstwhile holders, but to such as conform to the economic plan of the nation's economic leader. If his judgment proves fallible, a single mistake may entail collapse of the whole towering structure of the controlled economy.

The dangers incident to power are, however, not absent from the régime of "big business." So long as technological necessity and organizational efficiency dictate the retention of large-scale business units, responsible executives, courting opportunities for business development and personal emolument, draw down upon themselves a very substantial measure of economic responsibility. They become trustees for the preservation of large blocks of capital; for furnishing employment for substantial groups of working people identified with that province of the economic domain which they undertake to administer; and for the purveyance to consumers in general of various goods and services in measure compatible with the richness of our natural resources, our working capacities, and our willingness to exert ourselves in the supplying of our wants. "Big business" presents opportunities for the skillful direction of the economic life of principalities which may be very large as compared with the economic enterprise of an individual but each of which is small as compared with the economic life of the nation.

The economic self-interest of universally free individuals no longer acts as an Invisible Hand to guide business on the right way. This guiding hand is stayed when the free individual enterprise of the masses is

[9] L. Hamburger, *How Nazi Germany Has Mobilized and Controlled Labor*, Brookings Institution Pamphlet No. 24 (1940).

superseded by the group enterprise of corporate industry, trade, and finance. Responsibility for determining
the direction of the nation's economic life today and of
furnishing both opportunity and incentive to the masses
centers upon some 1 or 2 per cent of the gainfully employed.[10] It becomes necessary, therefore, to ask what

[10] Of 56 million gainful workers in 1939, there were 43.7 million in
the ranks of industrial and commercial employment, chiefly corporate.
Of those so employed, 3 million are classed as "managerial" employees,
most of them routine supervisors rather than responsible directors of
business affairs. How many of the latter are there?

Since there are approximately 500,000 active corporations in the
country, we might, if we assume that each corporation had a single
directive head, take that figure as measuring the group responsible for
the tempo and efficiency of our industrial, commercial, and financial
life. Obviously, most corporations have a group frequently running to
scores and occasionally to hundreds who have some real voice in making
policies and affecting the character of business enterprise within their
respective concerns. On the other hand, the nominal heads of many
small corporations have so little scope of discretion, so little capacity
for exercising it, or the companies may be such virtual subsidiaries of
or tied to larger concerns that they do not in fact exercise a directive
function in any real sense. Probably it would be an exaggeration to
say that a million executives (an average of two per active corporation)
directed 40.5 million workers. This would center economic enterprise in
2.5 per cent of the working force of organized business.

These figures are based on estimates presented in Spurgeon Bell, *Productivity, Wages, and National Income* (1940), p. 10 and App. B.
Fortune (February 1940, pp. 58 ff.) derived a figure of "30,000 managers" of United States business by crediting "four or five top executives"
each (together with a few outside lawyers, engineers, and other specialists) to the 5,650 corporations of 5 million dollars or more which
account for 75 per cent of all corporate assets. This estimate of "30,000
managers" checked by comparing it with "the government's list of
those receiving $15,000 a year or more from corporations." It is clear
that many corporations below the 5 million dollar level are significant
factors in determining the character of national enterprise, and executives below the $15,000 salary bracket are often important executives
in these or even the larger concerns. *Fortune* itself suggests that "judgment" begins at $6,000 in the corporate hierarchy. Unfortunately, there
is no government figure for this salary group comparable to the one
quoted for $15,000 and above. Undoubtedly the group multiplies rather
rapidly between $15,000 and $6,000, but even if it increased nearly
ten-fold, it would still appear that the real directive function converges
upon an administrative group which makes up less rather than more
than 1 per cent of the business population.

principles of economic organization and direction the members of this small group are actually applying to this great task and what in fact are the fundamental principles which must be relied upon to guide them to the goal of success for both themselves and the economy.

In a preceding volume,[11] we examined numerous concrete price policy situations in which reduction of price (or comparable improvement in quality) translated efficiency advances into consumer gains. This study pointed out how "pacemakers" of American business had in fact passed the gains from technological progress on to the consumer to a degree which has permitted considerable rise in living standards of our people, and it argued that if such policies were "generalized" over industry and trade, much further economic progress could be made. Some critics have maintained that, however true the logic of this statement, it is essentially unreal. They have asserted that situations in which progressive price reduction is possible are rather sharply limited, and the possibility of generalizing such a course remote or nonexistent. This objection in fact rests upon a faulty analysis of some of the basic factors entering into many of these situations which are regarded as impregnable to the general principle of price adjustment.

We shall examine this issue further in the present volume. In so doing, we shall divide our inquiry into two clearly distinguishable questions. (1) Is the following of a low-price policy inherently unsound or unworkable? This question is explored particularly in Chapters VI to XI,[12] after certain premises and lines of approach have

[11] Edwin G. Nourse and Horace B. Drury, *Industrial Price Policies and Economic Progress* (1938).

[12] Chap. 10 extends the argument of the previous volumes in this series so as to include certain time considerations of a relatively short duration. In those studies, emphasis was on the long-run economic process, post-

been analyzed in Chapters II to V. (2) Is such a course unlikely to be followed because of psychological, organizational, or legal difficulties in the way of putting it into practical operation? This question is analyzed in Chapters XII, XIII, and XIV.

DOES THIS APPROACH REVEAL A BIAS?

Since *Industrial Price Policies and Economic Progress* was not a forthright denunciation of current business practices, a plea for "trust-busting," or a brief for increased governmental regulation, some readers were disposed to interpret it as a complacent eulogy of business as it operates today—particularly "big business." There was, however, no thought on our part either of "painting the lily" or of formulating a scheme of apologetics for things-as-they-are. But any attempt at constructive criticism of human institutions that fails to discover and properly evaluate the elements that are sound and useful is as unsatisfactory and untrustworthy as one which ignores those with harmful tendencies.

Our studies led us to believe that many students of economic problems had become unduly preoccupied with the abuses of the past or with examples of current industrial management which have not yet outgrown the older patterns of shortsighted behavior. We thought we

---

poning so far as possible any consideration of cyclical disturbances. It is obvious, however, that as long as we have such disturbances, every price must be made in one phase or another of some kind of business cycle. Any practical application of a general principle of price adjustment must include careful consideration of the time at which such action may or should be taken. In order both to continue the orderly examination of the ramifications of our general argument and to correct confusion to be noted in some quarters between this and the argument for "price flexibility," Chap. 10 will be devoted to discussion of "the timing of price changes."

discerned numerous and significant instances of spontaneous action by industrial price-makers who aggressively utilize the powers of large business organization to accelerate the rate of technological progress and to employ varied devices of benefit-sharing in a price structure which serves to enlarge volume, maintain employment, and make for continued industrial prosperity. We believed that the analysis of how such practices were related to the continuance of economic progress should be carried through with great thoroughness by businessmen and economists working together in mutual understanding and respect. We reasoned that *if* such price-making policies and practices as some firms have developed could come generally into vogue, our business system would be well on the road to achieving the level of general welfare demanded of it.

This, of course, simply raises the corollary question: Can such a generalization of the constructive methods of the leaders become the dependable practice of all or most of our business executives? The fact that this question is taken for examination rather than the question of how to "restore competition" in the old-fashioned sense, or introduce "plan economy," socialism, or authoritarianism in some new order, reveals an acceptance of certain postulates, predilections, or—if you prefer— bias. If such a bias there be, readers should be informed of it at the beginning that they may be at once aware of the foundations upon which the argument of the book is based.

Our approach presents two aspects, both of them resting upon what we believe to be sound economic grounds. The first is a belief in the wisdom and economy of evolutionary growth or institutional modification and educational adaptation rather than sharply disruptive revolutionary change. Revolutions have appeared from time to time to be socially necessary. But they involve too high a social cost to be undertaken except in truly exigent situations after all practicable means of evolutionary development, guided by the minds and hands of intelligent men, have been tried or at least thoroughly examined and found inadequate. Obviously, we must not prejudge the magnitude of the costs of even drastic change. On the other hand, we must not overestimate the thoroughness or rapidity with which improvement can be attained through adjustment and modification of existing institutions and the education and stimulation of human behavior within that institutional structure.[13]

We have a great investment in the present system. Not a material or financial investment alone, but a great spiritual investment—the traditions, acquired aptitudes, habits of life, psychologic responses, and political shibboleths which have evolved out of many generations of building such a structure. Mere thrift in management demands that we try to conserve this investment if, within a reasonable time, we can learn to operate and adjust this machine so that it will produce the output of which it is theoretically capable.

In subsequent chapters I shall seek to explore frankly the difficulties as well as the possibility of such evolutionary change. The ultimate outcome of this line of effort must still remain in doubt until more actual experimen-

---

[13] Evolutionary modification of institutional structure is mentioned here as essential to the completeness of the thought. It embraces regulatory devices and agencies, property rights, and the like. These large and complicated issues do not come within the scope of the present study. This volume limits itself to the thought and action of the men who attempt to operate a machine of the basic design that we have today.

tation and demonstration have been recorded. But as a matter of economic engineering, I am convinced that a business system dominated by private corporations, some of them of great size, with less rather than more participation by government than now obtains, *could* be made to function efficiently in the public interest.

The writer's second bias is a belief in the long-run superiority, in terms of high efficiency and lower social cost, of democratic private enterprise as against plutocratic or bureaucratic centralization of power. The economic argument for democracy and decentralization is too lengthy to be undertaken here. Part of it, however, will emerge in connection with the discussion of particular points in several subsequent chapters. Here we are simply concerned that the reader be made fully aware that a belief in the economic superiority of democracy is a postulate of our whole study.

All who share a belief in the *capacity* of private enterprise to achieve national well-being should be ready to turn to the task of studying anew its operational requirements—to see what private capitalism must do to realize its full potentialities. The next three chapters begin this task by reviewing popular and professional ideas about "free enterprise," "competition," and the "profit motive."

BY THE BILL OF RIGHTS, guaranteeing the liberties of the individual, a "new social order" . . . was created, establishing the American system of free enterprise. It relied not on the wisdom and initiative—or lack of it—of rulers, but tapped instead the limitless resources of all the people's enterprise and the inborn desire of every individual to achieve economic sufficiency for himself and family. . . . It was not in the power of government or of a ruling class to tell anyone what he might do with his own.

Frank E. Gannett, President, Gannett Newspapers, "Dangers to the Free Enterprise System," in The New Outlook in Business, Bronson Batchelor, ed.

OUR AMERICAN SYSTEM of free enterprise is far more than just a way of doing business. It is a system which at its best comprehends good sportsmanship; gives free play to the laws of supply and demand and of competition; produces an ever-improving standard of living; develops initiative, character, and discipline; and in many ways goes far toward improving the morale and bettering the lives of our people. When I speak of free enterprise at its best, I mean when it is free of monopoly, private or governmental; free of government control or intimidation; free of trade agreements that would control prices and production after the manner of the European cartel system, and after the manner too, if you please, of the late and unlamented N.R.A. For a democratic government to destroy free enterprise, is for that government to destroy itself. Your great association [N.A.M.] has no higher duty than that of inculcating in the public mind an understanding of what the American competitive system of free enterprise is and what it means to the American people.

J. Howard Pew, President, Sun Oil Co., Congress of American Industry, Dec. 1940.

CHAPTER II

FREE ENTERPRISE AND *LAISSEZ FAIRE*

In the preceding chapter, it seemed permissible to speak in terms of "private capitalism," "free enterprise," "the profit motive," and the "prevailing economic system" with substantially the same freedom that these phrases are ordinarily bandied about in popular conversation. These are expressions which occupy a prominent place in businessmen's discussions of the economic system, but in large part they were borrowed from the jargon of the economist. They are defined and subscribed to by members of both economist and business groups in quite divergent ways. Generally speaking, however, it seems fair to say that the majority of businessmen believe that the writings of the classical economists enunciated an economic creed which expressed fundamental truth with reference to free enterprise under private capitalism, and that all that is needed for economic sanity and safety in the present disturbed world is a popular understanding of those basic principles and a return to their consistent practice.

On pages 26 and 28 there are presented several representative expressions of such views as voiced by distinguished American businessmen. Three similar quotations appeared in the preceding chapter. As was there remarked, the persons from whose discussions these quotations have been culled do not ordinarily seem to consider it necessary to be very precise as to the sense in which the term "free enterprise" or related concepts

THE POWER which individuals as citizens entrust to government is being used to hurt individuals as workers, earners and savers, to undermine the American system of economic freedom which is inseparable from political and personal freedom under the American way of life. Americans must make up their minds whether they want to restore the capitalistic system. Don't we still have this system today? In theory, yes. In practice, no. Under a capitalistic system the individual must have freedom of economic action. This freedom can be taken away quite as effectively by establishing conditions which make its exercise impossible as by governmental edicts which expressly prohibit it.

> Ernest T. Weir, Chairman, National Steel Corp., Economic Club of Detroit, Nov. 1939.

THE MAINSPRING of the American incentive system of private enterprise is the hope of reward it extends to every individual. Not always does he attain his goal; not always does he realize his hope. But it is his vision of a future reward that keeps him working, saving, striving; keeps our system moving forward and bettering the lot of everyone who lives within it.

> Charles R. Hook, President, American Rolling Mill Co., Congress of American Industry, Dec. 1939.

THE GENERAL MOTORS scheme of administration is founded upon the principle of free enterprise. Important as a comprehensive scheme of organization may be, the administration of the plan involves the human equation. That means men—aggressive men—of experience and ability. There were many such among us. Manifestly, in any organization men should move from the bottom up to the top. That develops loyalty, ambition and talent, because there is a chance for promotion.

> Alfred P. Sloan, Jr., and Boyden Sparkes, *Adventures of a White-Collar Man*, p. 137.

are intended. Apparently it is assumed that the phrases are self-explanatory. As a matter of fact, however, all such general terms may be given considerably different interpretations by different speakers and their several listeners or readers.

In this chapter and the two which follow, therefore, we shall proceed to a brief examination of the somewhat divergent and frequently vague ideas which cluster around these useful but often ambiguous phrases. This review exercise should help us to get more sharply in mind the issues we are talking about, and enable writer and reader more easily to keep in intellectual step throughout the remainder of the book.

FREEDOM OF ECONOMIC ENTERPRISE—THE SPIRIT OF '76

Language is a growing thing, and words have current meanings as well as traditional definitions and etymological explanations. Before considering present concepts of free enterprise, therefore, we may profitably go back to note the origins of the idea. By a curious coincidence, the great economic classic, Adam Smith's *Wealth of Nations*, and the American Declaration of Independence were brought forth in the same year. Both, in their particular ways, reflected an upheaval in human thought and action which had been gathering force for decades, even centuries, as expressions of a doctrine of "natural liberty" which grew up in Western Europe and, when transplanted to the colonies, took on even more vigorous growth. It expressed itself in many ways, notably in the passing of slavery, serfdom, and feudal labor relations, and in the popularization of the right of individual ownership of property. When men acquired the right to their own persons and labor power and secured command of natural resources, they demanded as a corollary the right to engage in any kind of business for which they had a liking or which promised the greatest return. The masses, having won freedom, wanted to use that freedom for their own advancement.

The American Declaration of Independence, therefore, and our Constitution expressed not merely a desire for political independence and religious toleration but reflected also a demand for freedom of economic enterprise under which every man should be given the opportunity to pursue his own economic advantage as he saw fit. It is thus quite proper to regard "free enterprise" as a distinctive feature of "the American way." Adam Smith's book at the same time explained with great care the economic logic of the system of free enterprise as he preached it and as the colonies and young republic practiced it. He undertook to show why individual freedom could be relied upon as the most effective way of promoting the wealth of nations and the need to break down the commercial restrictions which had become so prevalent. His explanation became the brief for a doctrine of "*laissez faire*" still widely held, sometimes in forms that would have shocked the good Dr. Smith.

The doctrine of free enterprise was a sort of white man's "Emancipation Proclamation." It noted that under the feudal system a man's chances of being productive largely depended upon where he happened to be born, on what kind of land, and under which particular feudal lord. There was no effective device for making new and better combinations between labor and resources. But while this rule of status still persisted, opportunities for something more than traditional methods of self-subsistence had been developing. First came the process of exploration and discovery, which brought new countries into the network of commercial relation-

ships. This was soon followed by the rise of new techniques of production, the invention of the steam engine
and various types of mechanical equipment, and a general acceleration of scientific discovery. These developments gave rise first to the domestic system of manufacture and then to the early factory system.

Now the factory employer wanted to be free to
recruit labor among those who, by law or custom, had
been attached to the land or controlled by the guild, but
their labor utilized with only indifferent efficiency.
The new *laissez-faire* doctrine argued that laborers
should be free to shift their domicile and to seek employment wherever it was offered. Likewise, every man
of unusual capacity should be free to enter the ranks of
employers and to engage in any business in which he
saw an opportunity. This done, the incentive to gain by
intensifying activity and changing its direction in quest
of new opportunities and in response to new knowledge
would mean greater productivity all around.

It is notable in this connection that up to that time the
field of "business" had been largely confined to commercial and financial pursuits. The major area of economic life was under a self-subsisting agrarian and
handicraft regime, and chances for making a profit were
sought chiefly in driving sharp bargains in areas where
prime producers were little aware of the value of their
own goods. This applied conspicuously to the trade between England and her less industrial neighbors, and
the Orient, South America, or other backward regions.
Under this mercantile capitalism, the businessman was
not essentially engaged in increasing productive efficiency, but in scalping profits from trading disposable
surpluses of commodities he might find here, there, and
elsewhere.

The coming of the Industrial Revolution and the birth of the factory system greatly altered this situation. It gave a new emphasis in business life. Besides seeking a trading differential between purchase in one market and sale in another, businessmen became concerned in exploiting new lines of production and new processes. New bargaining and contractual relationships developed which enabled them to profit from increases in productivity they themselves could effect by expanding volume and enhancing efficiency of production.[1]

Thinkers of Adam Smith's time were familiar in retrospect with a world which had moved along at snail's pace under the numbing effects of status and special privilege. But about them they saw the possibilities of accelerated progress in proportion as the door was opened to the new dynamic forces of technological and organizational improvement. Their *laissez-faire* doctrine argued that the door should be equally open to capitalist-employer, worker, and consumer if all parts of the process were to adjust themselves one to another so as to facilitate this forward march.

Under free bargaining, the laborer would get his share of increasing productivity by driving as hard a bargain as he could for the sale of his labor, his bargaining position steadily strengthened through the expansion of new employment.[2] The consumer likewise would get

[1] In emphasizing at this point the constructive aspect of the new situation, we do not forget its seamy side. The fact that under the new factory system manufacturers sought profits by using this organizational power to force down wages or prices of raw materials is dealt with later in this chapter and in Chap. 4. In the blind early days also profits were sought by skimping quality or even quantity of goods, but this was the sort of abuse which tended most strongly to bring its own penalties and cure, though by no means yet eradicated.

[2] Adam Smith's rather optimistic outlook soon gave way to the pessimism of Malthus and Ricardo. The highly elaborated argument that an "iron law of wages" would hold the standard of living of the

his share by freely following his own self-interest and purchasing in that market where he could find the most satisfactory goods at the lowest possible price. Since free markets would keep prices as low as permitted by the state of the arts, real wages would improve with the march of technological progress, and pressure for increase of money wages would largely be limited to adjusting differentials. The employer, in his turn, would share in the expanding community income by constantly discovering new ways of cheapening or improving his product and thereby holding or expanding his consumer market. He could not, however, be ground between labor on the one side and the consumer on the other, because he would have to be given a living wage for his personal and property services or else he would be forced to pass out of the picture, leaving the laborer without any plant or employer, and the consumer without a source of goods.

As was observed in Chapter I, price-making under such conditions becomes an automatic function of a free market. Government is relieved of its immemorial task of trying to promulgate "just" or "fair" prices. It is deprived of its opportunity to engineer exploitative prices based on trade restrictions or monopolies set up by

masses at a bare subsistence minimum was seized by English factory owners as a welcome rationalization of practices which conformed to their narrow interpretation of the *laissez-faire* principle. In America the high ratio of unappropriated natural resources to available labor supply conduced to a more optimistic interpretation of labor productivity and a high general standard of living. "The American school" of economists from Henry Carey to Simon Patten not merely repudiated the simpler formulations of the Malthusian doctrine but often went so far as to deny the existence of a principle of diminishing returns. The great body of American economists have been more "orthodox," and in time we began to hear of "neo-Malthusians." Recently, "national maturity" has come to be interpreted by some in terms of economic stagnation and chronic unemployment.

royal franchise, which had been a recurrent abuse of autocratic regimes. The doctrine may be briefly summarized as follows: (1) As to government, let its activities in the field of business be limited to the very minimum necessary for the maintenance of property rights and peaceful life. (2) As to business, let the system of private capitalism grow naturally under free enterprise, and the law of supply and demand will operate automatically to establish the right prices. Commodity and service prices will reflect the lower costs resulting from progress in technique and organization. As for wages, they will reflect the productivity of each worker. Economic activity will be guided by such prices into the most productive channels and thus promote to the fullest possible extent the national prosperity. These principles were conceived as embodying universal truth capable of achieving "the wealth of nations" and the welfare of the masses.

Little fault can be found with the logic of classic free enterprise and *laissez faire* in the simplified situation which it assumed. The credit which has been given to it for the economic progress in Great Britain, in the gradually industrialized areas on the Continent, and in the United States during the larger part of the nineteenth century must go in part also to technical factors. (1) This was a period of extremely rapid settlement of new lands and exploitation of their virgin resources. Hence opportunities of enterprise suitable for the individual laborer and his family, possessed only of freedom and the right to amass for himself and his heirs whatever wealth he could appropriate and create, were abundant. (2) Besides this *extensive* expansion of opportunity, mechanical invention and scientific discovery were pushing out the bounds of economic opportunity *intensively*.

Freedom of enterprise accelerated the exploitation of these possibilities. Though the rate of population growth was rapid in the areas of quickened industrial and commercial activity, the labor force, instead of tending as it had before to outstrip production, now could barely keep up with new demands for labor and enterprise.

Adam Smith started from the premise that the majority of human beings were sufficiently industrious and ambitious, or sufficiently avaricious and sensual, to respond to such opportunities to increase the product on which they depended for material satisfaction.[3] Some might deplore, and many did, the good sense or the good taste of the free and democratic masses in selecting for consumption the particular objects they did and toward which they thereby directed the productive efforts of the community. But unquestionably this freedom did make for great acceleration of business activity and the enlargement of material well-being as the ultimate consumer elected to enterpret it.

FREE ENTERPRISE AND CORPORATE GROWTH

Early economic writers did not perceive any inherent conflict between the idea of free enterprise for the economically liberated individual worker and free commercial or industrial enterprise for the capitalist employer. The latter was just emerging at that time and Adam Smith was quick in his appreciation of the potential usefulness of such capitalist enterprisers and em-

[3] "It is not from the benevolence of the butcher, the brewer, or the baker that we expect our dinner but from their regard to their own interest." (*Wealth of Nations*, Bk. 1, Chap. 2.) "The natural effort of every individual to better his own condition, when suffered to exert it with freedom and security, is so powerful a principle that it is alone, and without any assistance, not only capable of carrying on the society to wealth and prosperity, but of surmounting a hundred impertinent obstructions with which the folly of human laws too often incumbers its operations." (*Wealth of Nations*, Bk. 4, Chap. 5.)

phatic in his belief that they should not be "cabined, cribbed, or confined" by any kind of government-fostered monopoly or privilege. For a century and more, the businessman reveled in his new-found sense of leadership, and the less able or enterprising workers were not unwilling to commute their individual opportunities for wages in steadily expanding and more productive group operations.

Capitalist leadership grew by what it fed on—complete freedom of business enterprise. It explored and exploited new technical methods, new commercial opportunities, new schemes of economic organization; it accelerated wealth creation and amassed in relatively few hands the reserves of capital necessary to keep this enlarging plant and advancing technique in a condition of vigorous growth. But the very freedom which favored the triumphal march of capitalist enterprise came in time to trench on the domain of individual enterprise.

This restrictive tendency was linked with the growth of the business corporation. Certain among the most ambitious spirits saw new possibilities of getting a still more productive organization of human effort if they could secure for themselves certain rights of leadership beyond those possible in an individual undertaking or a partnership. These larger rights they had conferred upon them by the state, first as particular individuals specially chartered to embark on specific corporate undertakings, later under general incorporation laws which permitted any group to launch almost any business by meeting a few formal requirements. Whereas business had up to that time been organized on two levels—those of the individual and (in a limited sense) of the government—it thereafter showed a third clearly defined level —that of the impersonal business institution exercising a directive role for large blocks of the working and capital-accumulating population.

From our vantage point in time, we can readily see the double stream of consequence that flows from the complete freeing of capitalistic enterprise and its institutionalizing in large impersonal corporations vastly above the individual in power and resources and strongly influential over, if not at times actually controlling, government itself. Clearly this development of capitalistic enterprise as a high command in business has accelerated productive efficiency in ways which we can be quite sure would never have been attained if each worker had, during the last century and a half, been limited to the results which he could accomplish under complete self-direction, with no benefit and no compulsion from outside leadership. But while we recognize this gain and admit the desirability of equipping natural leaders with organizational devices, such as the business corporation, to facilitate the exercise of that leadership, we cannot blind our eyes to the fact that this development has definitely circumscribed the current realization of completely free economic enterprise by the individual worker or saver or by the relatively small firm. And we must not overlook the possible danger in case leadership either falters or degenerates into oppression.

Over the pioneer and developmental period of industrial capitalism and free corporate enterprise—roughly from the Industrial Revolution to the end of the nineteenth century or even the onset of the First World War—capitalistic business leaders and corporate executives manifested little doubt of themselves or hesitation in the exercise of their role of specialized enterprisers. In the swift, forward surge of economic life as new lands were explored, new techniques of production

developed, and the new pattern of business organization elaborated, they were able to achieve brilliant suc-
cesses and were willing to accept the no less spectacular
personal defeats that were an incidental feature of the
process.

By and large, also, the mass of the follower population seemed reasonably content to accept the fruits of
this leadership in the form of a rising standard of living,
even at the expense of such mild frustrations of the yen
for individual enterprise as might be entailed. They
could put up with wages which looked small as compared with promoters' profits and executives' salaries
and bonuses so long as business was kept active and jobs
were plentiful. They could transmute the free enterprise of individual wage bargaining into collective bargaining as a means of exacting a larger share of industry's
rewards. They could resort to political and legislative
action as a means of curbing particular practices of corporate enterprise even while its general directive role was
left intact.

But as the decade of the 1930's drew on, it began to
appear to many that business enterprise had been stricken
with a strange paralysis or that it suffered from inherent
weakness of leadership[4] rather than a mere tendency to
be greedy or domineering in its conduct of activities
which were highly productive for the people as a whole.
Thereupon misgivings arose as to the long-run accept-
ability of the private business corporation as the custodian and executor of economic enterprise for the mass
of the people. Compromise between much individual
and a little public enterprise had been easy as long as the
proportion of urban wage earners was not very high, and
workers not promptly reabsorbed in industrial employ-

[4] This issue is examined further in Chaps. 4, 12, and 14.

ment after the introduction of labor-saving devices could generally find subsistence through self-employment. But as these early phases of capitalistic development were rounded out after the turn of the twentieth century amidst the disturbing and distorting conditions of wide-spread and recurring military conflict, it became evident that more severe criteria of performance might in the longer run be imposed on the system. It might be held responsible for the level of employment as well as skill in operation. Idle men unable to secure access to idle plant capacity, and funds saved but unable to find a place of investment represent, if the condition persists, a definite impasse between the claims of free corporate enterprise and free individual enterprise, both of which appear to be inherent and vital elements in modern industrial society.

SELF-RELIANCE VERSUS ADMINISTRATIVE RESPONSIBILITY

If we are to keep our ideas of the evolution of free enterprise in correct perspective, we must remember that when the concept emerged in the early days of the Industrial Revolution it connoted not a single change in the situation of the economic man but two changes. One of these—the gain in freedom—has been steadily emphasized; the other—a shift in responsibility—has been frequently overlooked.

When men passed out of the old feudal relationship into a new condition of freedom and democracy, they were emancipated from the claims of a feudal lord upon the disposal of their time, the direction of their activities, the quality of their subsistence, and their freedom of residence and movement. In emphasizing the personal satisfaction and the economic stimulus which derives from this emancipation, it is easy to forget that, with this new-found opportunity, there went also a new responsibility. In claiming freedom from their erstwhile lords, these freedmen also relieved the lords of their former responsibility. This now developed upon the individual himself.

Balancing the claims to labor that the feudal lord had possessed and exercised, responsibility also had rested upon him for giving his dependents military protection and economic support. This obligation he had exercised with varying degrees of faithfulness and success. Free laborers acquired the opportunity of employing their talents and increasing their industry so as to provide themselves with a higher standard of living than had previously been provided for them. But they also took full brunt of responsibility for seeing that, owing to their individual weakness of mind or body, their natural indolence, or the blows of outrageous fortune, this should not result in their having a lower standard than before or no subsistence at all.

A large number of them at once commuted this responsibility by accepting a new dependence. They entered a wage relationship in lieu of the risks and opportunities of self-employment. To be sure, a measure of individual enterprise was retained in this new relationship, since it was not one of status but of contract, based on a price bargain at least nominally free. Now when labor in large measure passed over from self-employment to wage employment in groups by capitalist enterprisers, a new situation developed. Dependence on others, to which the workers thereby returned, was not matched in any high degree by employers' assumption of responsibility for them in season and out and after, as well as during, their most productive period, which was characteristic of the feudal relationship.

A phrase which gained considerable vogue as a description of the industrial wage system was that the laborer "contracted himself out of risk." He no longer had to make himself a job, but had his income underwritten for the contract period by the capitalist enterpriser. There is an obvious measure of truth in this expression. But it would be hard to imagine one more blind or more cynical as to the measure of risk which was still left in the hands of the laborer who could be discharged on short notice if business were slack or who could be thrown on the scrap heap at middle age.

In other words, private business did not undertake much corporate responsibility for maintaining employment, productivity, and subsistence for the group attached as laborers to its plant or line of production. This statement carries no implication that they should have done so. We are not concerned here in ethical judgments but simply in tracing the realities of an economic process. We recall that, partly on the initiation of employers themselves, partly at the insistence of union organizations, and partly through general public sentiment expressed in legislation, there has been an attempt to readjust this balance between enterprise and responsibility. This has taken the form of unemployment insurance, retirement annuities, or old-age benefits. But these are largely compensatory devices, not a functional adjustment within the operative structure of industry itself. We shall have occasion in Chapters V, IX, and XI to note how this matter is related to the general propositions of labor price policy and the policy of industrial and commercial firms in making up the schedules of prices of the goods and services which they sell.

In setting out this issue, we do not overlook the difficulties in the way of carrying responsibility for employment and subsistence, which had been an inherent feature of the feudal system, into the technological and commercial situations of modern industry. Such responsibility constitutes an element of inflexibility fundamentally at war with the principle of technical efficiency and the adjustment of labor to the needs of rapidly changing techniques which lies at the heart of modern industrialism. We should not, however, overlook the nature of the underlying economic factors involved in the change from self-employment to corporate freedom of enterprise, individual bargaining, and the wage contract. This poses for us a new question which needs to be asked with reference to the meaning of free enterprise, namely, its possible limitation under highly developed industrial conditions.

CAN THERE BE TOO MUCH FREEDOM OF ENTERPRISE?

In all this evolution of the principles and practices of economic enterprise, there have been not merely ambiguities of definition as to the meaning of enterprise and the nature of its freedom but also considerable doubt as to whether it is *per se* the most desirable condition for business to attain. For example, free enterprise, taken literally, means types of business organization which sharpen competition to such a degree as constantly to eliminate the less efficient producers and progressively transfer business into the hands of the most efficient. Quite aside from the frowns of antitrust laws and regulatory agencies and the complaints of laborers or suppliers of other services or wares, producing enterprisers themselves have revolted against so heroic an interpretation of the principle of free enterprise. The weaker brethren have objected to elimination in this battle of efficiency, and even the strongest have at times found the pace so hot that they were willing to participate in some general scheme of abatement. This is notably true of Judge Gary's policy of "friendly competition," the trade associations' attempt to "civilize competition," and a whole flock of price maintenance measures which have been vigorously pushed, particularly from NRA days down to the present.

Corporate enterprise that has demanded the greatest freedom internally has at the same time demanded tariffs to keep foreign enterprise from free access to our markets. It frequently supports laws designed to prevent businesses from crossing state lines or from simplifying productive or distributive methods. It has resisted laws designed to check combinations in restraint of enterprise and has fought for laws to "freeze" undertakings that become too aggressive. Clearly its answer is, yes, enterprise can be too free. This matter will be examined further in the succeeding chapter.

On the side of labor, also, the ideal of complete freedom of the individual has been discarded. The agglomeration of individuals into groups for the purpose of preventing their individual enterprise from being cramped by the disproportionate bargaining power of large corporate employers called for internal regulation which abridged the "natural" rights of the free individual. Group discipline meant that marketing of the individual's labor had to be circumscribed by the group policies of the organization. The strongest and most skillful are not allowed to exercise their free enterprise to the extent of securing a differentially higher wage as compared with those at the bottom of the scale who just meet the minimum required for union membership. Flat wage rates (even with broad classifications) are certainly a compromise with the simple principle of free individual enterprise. Furthermore, the union's control of entrance to the trade and the partial accomplishment of the closed shop impose a still more severe limitation on the enterprise of those regarded by the union as too numerous or for other reasons unsuitable for inclusion within the collective bargaining group.

Labor union officials, no less than executives of industrial and commercial corporations, become trustees of the private enterprise of a large number of individuals within their respective organizations. Unions conduct a scheme of administered prices whose wisdom or unwisdom has profound repercussions on the functioning of the whole economic system. We shall, therefore, have occasion throughout the book to refer to union officers along with corporate executives as price administrators whose policies must be considered in the light of the basic principles which we are analyzing.

PRIVATE ENTERPRISE AND PUBLIC ENTERPRISE

The discussion of these issues leads us inevitably over into that shadowy borderland which divides economics from or unites it to the realm of political science. We have been talking about free enterprise as a right of the citizen and about his delegation of this right to business leaders who subsequently organize and, for operative purposes, govern a substantial part of the lives of their workers and to a lesser extent of investors and consumers. If we accept the democratic concept of free enterprise as implying a "natural" right of every man to use his labor and any capital he may possess to satisfy his wants and provide for his family, we must still bear in mind the fact that this right cannot be exercised by the individual alone. Under modern technological conditions, it must be in essence delegated to leaders who organize the production of automobiles, the construction and operation of railways, or the joint production of a complicated array of paint, plastics, explosives, and medicines in a chemical industry.

So long as the enterprise of most workers and savers finds ready outlet through the organized channels of industry and trade furnished by private corporate units, the system of private group organization will be found acceptable as an interpretation of free enterprise. But once the channels of private industry become clogged in serious degree over any long period of time, it is inevitable that enterprising men will reassert their right to turn to some other agency or organization conceived to be stronger or to reflect more truly the aspirations of the mass of the people rather than any class—even a class which represents the greatest technical skills and the profoundest human wisdom. If such a demand gains full momentum in a democracy, it means the substitution of public enterprise for private enterprise.

When, as was noted in the preceding section, economic men have recognized the necessity of exercising their economic freedom through organized groups—corporations, unions, co-operative associations, and various others —we are brought to grips with two major questions as to the relative desirability of alternative patterns of group organization for the conduct of economic activity. One of these questions is essentially administrative or one of political science. Will individuals find their demand for personal opportunity and a voice in control more fully satisfied through the comprehensive group organization of government ownership and operation of business than through so-called voluntary and private relations or organizations of corporate management, union-company labor ties, and bank and investment house financial controls.

It is not within the province of this book to explore
questions of political philosophy and the mechanisms
by which large numbers of men can be organized with
greatest administrative effectiveness under so-called private or public agencies.[5] There would seem to be no
inherent reason, however, why the machinery of private
business organization should not provide at least as good
a means of registering and weighing the varying tastes
and desires of individuals and of satisfying their sense
of "rights" in matters touching the conduct of their
economic life as could be furnished through more cumbersome and remote machinery of government.

But the politics of group effort in the business sphere
is inseparable from the economic issues which it raises.
However well the political aspects of the question
of public versus private enterprise may be settled on
grounds of personal predilection, traditional sentiment,
or scientific knowledge, we must ultimately come to a
reckoning with basic economic considerations in deciding

[5] It must be obvious that the line between these two provinces has
steadily become less clear in recent years. This is due not alone to the
growth of large-scale corporations and nation-wide unions and federa-
tions of unions but to the organization also of half-public, half-private
irrigation, drainage, or other "district" improvement undertakings, of
port or other "authorities," and in recent years a veritable flood of
operative government corporations. Certain aspects of the political
science of the labor movement—"labor jurisprudence"—were dealt with
exhaustively by Sumner Slichter in an earlier publication, *Union Policies
and Industrial Management*. The political structure and functioning of
the large corporation are dealt with in a forthcoming volume *Business
Leadership in the Large Corporation*, by R. A. Gordon. Pioneer work
along the political frontier of the economic field was done by Gardiner
C. Means. (See "Financial Control of Large-Scale Enterprise," *American Economic Review*, Supplement, March 1939, pp. 110 ff., and "The
Distribution of Control and Responsibility in a Modern Economy,"
address delivered at the twenty-ninth annual meeting of the American
Political Science Association, Philadelphia, Dec. 27, 1933.)

the terms upon which human beings can work effectively with each other. Within the setting of personal and social psychology, there is a hard core of organic principles of economic functioning which will broadly condition the ultimate efficiency of an economic system.

If corporate enterprise is directed with a maximum understanding of and conformity to these principles on the part of its responsible executives, the transferring or trusteeing of a substantial part of what was individual enterprise under simpler conditions of technique and organization will be made with a sense of safety and satisfaction by the mass of worker-consumers. Likewise, if these functions are adequately and intelligently performed by locally autonomous business units, the residual task of economic regulation or operation left over to demand the attention of centralized group action, organized as government, will be reduced to its minimum. Government can let business most severely alone when business is embodying and achieving most freely and fully the enterprise of all potential workers and aspiring consumers.

We are here undertaking to explore objectively what practices and philosophies of corporate executive performance would promise most toward reducing to the lowest possible level the popular demand for government intervention in the economic activities of its citizens. But this does not mean that we accept the interpretation of free enterprise urged by many businessmen that makes it synonymous with exclusive *private* enterprise. In such a view government must not enter any field in which private interests see a prospect of profit. Even if we admit a first right of private business leaders to organize the use of all the economic resources which

THE ACHIEVEMENTS of American industry command the admiration of the civilized world. These achievements derive from a system of free enterprise founded on the bedrock of a constitutional government designed to protect the individual in his right to life, liberty, and the pursuit of happiness. The essence of this system is the right of citizens to pursue their individual likes and interests, including the right to acquire, own, and use property, all within the restraints of good citizenship. . . .

A fundamental requirement for the successful operation of the free enterprise system is that each individual business shall pursue its own course on a plane of enlightened self-interest. . . . Our American industrial system makes possible the kind of management that can secure a coordinated use of the combined character, intelligence and intimate understanding of the men and women who know most about their own individual jobs; management capable of giving balanced consideration to the many interrelated factors involved in business decisions; management that commands the confidence of employees; that affords the opportunity for individual leadership at every organization level; that leads, rather than drives; that manages from the bottom up, as well as from the top down; that gives human ability, wherever found, its full chance. . . .

The contribution that American industry can make to the national welfare depends upon the preservation of free enterprise and individual initiative. Laws to protect society from abuses are necessary and desirable, but in the public interest it is essential that any law, or any other process affecting industry, shall not [so] limit the authority of management as to render it unable to fulfill its responsibilities. . . .

Declaration of Principles, adopted in Congress of American Industry, Dec. 1939.

48

they are capable of putting to profitable employment, we cannot grant that this precludes the right of workers or owners of other resources to avail themselves of public organization as a means of salvaging what has been rejected by private organizers.

The situation here is quite different from that which furnished the background of Adam Smith's formulation of the principles of free enterprise and *laissez faire*. Businessmen in the late eighteenth century sought to eject government from large areas of business life not merely because they objected—and rightly—to the quantity of its activities but because also of their quality. That is, the *laissez-faire* movement was in considerable measure a protest against aristocracy, special privilege, and court corruption[6]—and abuses which in England led a little later to the Liberal Reform movement and in France to the revolutionary overthrow of the Bourbons. Common men of enterprise wanted to share in expanding commercial and industrial opportunities rather than to have them monopolized under royal franchise, distributed frequently through the intrigues of a corrupt court.

Whatever the shortcoming of modern proposals for experiments in the exercise of government business control or operation, they must be recognized as the democratic expression of a demand for economic well-being for the masses which has not been achieved by the prevailing system of private enterprise. Hence the issue between individuals in their private business capacity and individuals united in a public capacity is joined on grounds which permit of intellectual analysis and ex-

[6] Compare Alfred Marshall, "The Social Possibilities of Economic Chivalry." *The Economic Journal*, Vol. 17 (1917), p. 18.

perimental demonstration as to the reality of abuse and the attainability of reform.

It may quite possibly be that many of the current demands or even expectations are beyond the limits of reasonable fulfillment. It may be that popular thinking has been beguiled by naïve faith in "the provident state." But if the American businessman is to retain his present territory of free action or to regain for his own some of the lost provinces of recent years, it must be on the basis of a convincing demonstration that he is accomplishing the maximum material satisfaction for the mass of consumers on a self-sustaining basis. The major goal for the proponents of private enterprise must be the same as that of those who would enlarge public enterprise, namely, the fullest satisfaction of the wants of all our citizens that can be permanently attained within the limits of the nation's resources, material and personal. Under our democratic system they have the power to choose between private and public enterprise as means of securing the satisfaction of their material wants.

Wise men still differ as to where to draw the line between those things which free economic enterprise can best accomplish through individual efforts, those which can be attained (best or only) through group undertakings based on the principle of private bargaining, and those which require the complementary organizing and administering facilities of democratic government. The point we want to underscore here is that all three are indispensable, interrelated, and mutually helpful expressions of the great basic economic force of individual free enterprise. The problem is to develop both the highest quality of performance in each area and at the same time the functionally best proportioning among them.

In conclusion, we may well remind ourselves that the politico-economic doctrine of *laissez faire* anticipated Darwin's formulation of the evolutionary principle of "survival of the fittest." Such a setting forth of objective principles of an evolutionary process marked a new line of approach as compared with Smith's subjective philosophy of "natural rights" and the Invisible Hand. But both had, as a common factor, a reliance on an underlying natural process of mere adaptation to an environment that was "given." Later thought in biology has built forward from the general concept of natural evolution to the analytical and purposive evaluation of "fitness" (for what?) and the devising of practicable modifications of environment. It is similarly true in economic thinking that we have shown sufficient confidence in our powers of appraisal, diagnosis, and constructive imagination so that we interfere actively to modify old or create new institutional devices through which elemental economic forces may express themselves in new ways to promote ends that we regard as desirable.

Leaving the individual free to exercise his enterprise gives scope to competitive urges that will produce their best results only if they operate in a business environment which is designed with skillful regard to both the strengths and the weaknesses of these inborn qualities of men. In the next chapter, therefore, we shall try to get a more adequate understanding of the nature—the rich and varied nature—of competition as a factor in human life and its relation both to freedom and to progress.

CHAPTER III
COMPETITION AS METHOD AND AS GOAL

The concepts of free enterprise and of competition have a substantial area of overlap. If freedom of economic enterprise means anything as an operating principle of business, it means competition among individuals or organized groups. It is a trite old phrase that men do not go into business "for their health" but to get ahead, to make gains. To do this in any vigorous or adequate way they must reach out to experiment with any new means of appealing to or of creating consumer demand and with more efficient and hence more economical means of supplying that demand. Each enterpriser must be free to take his opportunity where he finds it, not stopped by the fact that it may happen to lie in territory formerly cultivated by another individual or corporation.

But merely to say that business enterprise is by its very nature a struggle among business units competing to outdo each other tells us very little about the nature of competition as a determining force in economic life. What are the ends we believe to be served by competition and by what means does it attain those goals?

THE IDEALIZED PICTURE OF COMPETITION

No maxim has been more freely repeated in the modern business world than "Competition is the life of trade." If those who use this phrase mean merely that competition makes business lively, that it quickens the tempo of commercial effort, they thereby set up a goal that, though entirely proper and laudable, does not envisage competition as a great constructive goal of economic life. Others see competition not as a short-run stimulus to acquisitive activity, which in the long run may prove wasteful or economically destructive. They think of it as a means to "the good life" in the economic sense. Besides "needling" enterprise to greater activity, competition is widely credited with giving it guidance toward ever greater efficiency in the work of production.

Economists have given extended and intensive attention over the years to the examination of these constructive goals of competitive enterprise and to the processes by which they are approached.[1] Seeking to discover fundamental laws of economic causation, the economist has proceeded, much after the manner of the natural scientist, to reduce his analysis to simplified situations. He could not control the phenomena he was studying and isolate areas of "pure" competition for purposes of experiment or demonstration. But he has formulated definitions to cover such hypothetical conditions. "Pure competition" implies a product that is uniform or highly standardized and that is exchanged from many sellers to many buyers in a market free of controls over the individual producer, merchant, or purchaser. This simply means competition "unalloyed with monopoly elements."[2] Under such a set of conditions, it was argued, each buyer, operating in pursuit of his own interest, would be a positive force toward economic efficiency by seeking out the most economical sources for the satisfac-

[1] Attention has focused primarily on individual competition. The nature and results of group competition have had much less adequate consideration. This aspect of the matter will be dealt with later in the present chapter.

[2] Edward Chamberlin, *The Theory of Monopolistic Competition* (1933), p. 6.

tion of his wants. The producer or seller likewise would, in pursuit of his own interest, be seeking out the most economical source of materials and the most efficient means of assembling and fabricating them. Only by doing so could he hold or enlarge his market and maintain or increase his profits.

But it was recognized that mere individual freedom and the absence of monopoly would not insure prices and a direction of economic effort which were economically correct or ideal. Hence the process of economists' thinking went a step farther to formulate the terms of "perfect" competition. These included not merely the ideal of a free and open market and a completely standardized product. Idealized also were the persons who produce for that market or who bring their patronage to it either as buyers or as sellers. These persons were assumed to have adequate information as to production or marketing alternatives and the intelligence and mobility which make it possible for them to act promptly and surely in the pursuit of their own self-interest. In "perfect" as in "pure" competition, it is assumed that the units of supply of or demand for goods shall be very numerous and each unit so small as to have no appreciable effect on the general market situation.

No one need quarrel with the proposition that perfect competition thus defined would furnish a theoretically perfect mechanism for turning out prices and would supply automatic guidance to the production process. The individual producer would have a powerful motive to introduce improvements, and the individual consumer would, in the disposal of his patronage, have a powerful means of converting these technical improvements into larger consumer satisfaction, that is, into economic progress. Free-wheeling common sense rather than scientific direction would be the method for attaining general well-being.

But no person of normal intelligence could be unaware of the fact that "perfect competition thus defined . . . does not exist, never has existed, and never can exist."[3] It was perhaps approached most closely under the simple conditions of pioneer agriculture and pre-industrial handicraft and trade that characterized America in the late colonial and early national period. The people of that time and place were select as to their mental alertness and their physical energy and daring. They had freed themselves to a high degree from home ties and the yoke of custom, resources were unusually accessible, and native shrewdness of the horse-trading variety quite commensurate with the simplicity of the individual business decisions needing to be made. A great deal of the business and economic thinking which is still current had its origin or finds it background amidst such surroundings. Hence there has been a strong tendency to go on emphasizing the virtues of competition as such, without very close scrutiny of its limitations even in simple situations and its still greater practical shortcomings in the vastly different situations presented by modern industrial organization.

It is not surprising that businessmen of the early days were delighted to accept classical economists' explanation —and justification—of the system under which they operated.[4] They have been eager to carry the econo-

---

[3] Clair Wilcox, *Competition and Monopoly in American Industry*, TNEC Monograph No. 21 (1940), p. 3. The word deleted from this quotation was "probably." Professor Wilcox's reason for inserting it is not clear to the writer.

[4] "The impact of the *Wealth of Nations* upon business men and politicians alike was very great. But although the apostle of economic liberalism spoke in lucid and persuasive terms, his success would not have been so great if he had not spoken to an audience that was ready

mists' eulogies of ideal competition over into the world of real business regardless of its wide departure from the conditions which the economists assumed. They have often tried to draw the cloak of virtue around their most dubious operations by saying, "You can't beat the law of supply and demand"—which is used as a synonym for competition among, and between, producers and consumers. What *is* surprising is that among economists there should be so many who seem to take the view that a mere subdivision of modern industrial and commercial units, which would not materially reduce operating efficiency, would bring our system reasonably close to the condition of sound guidance and maximum progress set forth in the theory of perfect competition.

In this chapter, therefore, we shall briefly examine: (1) some of the shortcomings of small-scale "pure" competition even under simple economic conditions; (2) certain changes in the concept of competition that must occur as we pass to the complex operational situation created by the growth of modern industrial technique and business organization; (3) the potential economic gains as well as losses that may grow out of this change.

---

to receive his message. He spoke with their voice, the voice of the industrialists who were anxious to sweep away all restrictions on the market and on the supply of labour—the remnants of the out-of-date régime of merchant capital and the landed interest. Moreover, the class of industrial capitalists was not yet matured enough to have acquired respectability. Smith presented this class with a theory which supplied what was still lacking. By analysing economic activity against a background of naturalist philosophy, this theory gave to the conduct of the prospective leaders of economic life an imprint of inevitability. They recognized in the self-interest which he put at the centre of human conduct the motive which inspired their everyday business life. And they were delighted to know that their pursuit of profit was now to be regarded as unselfish . . . the business man now became in theory what he already was in practice—the leader of the economic and political order." Erich Roll, *A History of Economic Thought* (1939), pp. 151-52.

This done, we shall, in later chapters, consider whether or how we could make as large as possible the area of such gain and reduce the losses to a minimum through better understanding of the nature of the business process and through business practices.

SOME PRACTICAL SHORTCOMINGS OF COMPETITION

The high regard that has been paid to competition as a guiding force in economic life rests on two premises: (1) that the individual is the best judge of how to attain his own interest, (2) that all persons can simultaneously attain their individual interests. Neither of these propositions is fully tenable in the modern business world.

In terms of psychology, every man must say for himself what he wants or what, in any field, he conceives to be to his advantage. In this sense he is the best, indeed the only competent, judge of his interest in his business relations. But this merely defines his superficial interest—the thing he thinks he wants. It may prove ultimately to be something quite different from or even in conflict with what the attainment of his more ultimate aspirations would require. Common experience refutes the claim that the rank and file of "economic men" really know what is good for them in the sense of choosing those lines of action that will satisfy their wants most fully. In an environment of "pure competition," surrounded by the facilities of a "perfect market," enabled and encouraged to stand up and make their own decisions, they would still be far from having the intellectual or moral qualities or the facilities for decision which would enable them to choose their courses well. Most of the time men are careless in examining or they vacillate in pursuing what in their more studious moments they themselves conceive to be their real interests.

They are easily misled by appeals to jealousy, pride, or avarice to act as individuals or groups in ways that present little or no chance of really promoting the ends they actually desire.

In the nature of the case, the individual can be informed as to only a very narrow range of choices—those that lie close to his immediate sphere of observation and action. Unless the technique of the business is very simple, most individuals will prove poor judges of even these near-at-hand choices. Competition, when it becomes a race or a struggle between units of enterprise to outdo each other becomes, in terms of the bargaining process, a race in which they try to outbid each other. This very process modifies the price relationships on which each of the contenders relies for guidance of his subsequent action. To a certain extent, this process is constructive or correctional, but it does not carry within itself safety devices that prevent its running to excess, and thus distorting a process that began as one of sound and wholesome economic adjustment. The very fact that the individual is free to express his personal judgment means that he is not protected against himself—from possible *mis*judgment. He may fall victim to mass hysteria, speculative mania, or the obscuring of ordinary economic landmarks by the very acceleration of the process of change.

An auction sale, a rate war, and a business boom represent outstanding examples of unfettered competition, but outstanding examples also of its shortcomings as a fool-proof device for the regulation of economic activity. Unrestricted competition among the ill-informed or the naturally incautious invites a dangerous stampede toward the fad in design or style, the creation of excess productive capacity, the ill-advised shift of population, the wild bidding up of market prices, or the feverish liquidation of property regardless of longer-run value. This is illustrated by a thousand well-known competitive episodes, such as the Florida land boom of the recent past, the notorious South Sea "bubble," or the "tulip mania" of the seventeenth century in Holland. In fact, competition is the life of any boom or bubble as also of any depression or business crisis. As such, it is an undisciplined force that operates to enhance the amplitude of the pendulum's swing away from its equilibrium point quite as truly as it operates to pull the pendulum back from the farthest swing of its aberration toward the point of best adjustment.

This brings out a curious contradiction in the whole concept of competition. If we attempt to give every man complete purity of competition; standardize the goods in which he deals; make his market free, open, and continuous; give him the fullest possible access to accurate and adequate information; and give persons and goods and capital maximum opportunity to move to their most advantageous place of use, we have in a formal sense magnified and perfected competition. But in a deeper, more vital sense we have shrunk it to the disappearing point. We have reduced the economic process to a purely automatic response to economic environment. Such a response is the antithesis of competition in the aggressive, innovating, adventurous sense in which that term is ordinarily used. The only real expression of business enterprise is imperfect competition. Its essence is found not in the standardization of goods but in their differentiation, not in the complete mobility of market situations but in certain non-fluid or not immediately transmissible characteristics. These may be availed of by one individual or company as a protective, retarding, or defensive device, but by another as an opportunity for outdistancing his competitors through developing superior techniques or creating or exploiting new areas of demand.

Economists from time to time, for more than a hundred years back, have recognized this real or imperfect competition along with the theoretical or ideal competition to which they as a group gave their major attention. Professor Marshall employed the illuminating expression "interpenetration of competition and monopoly," and more recently Professor Chamberlin has popularized the phrase "monopolistic competition."[5] This term is not altogether acceptable to businessmen because it seems to tar many of them with the opprobrious brush of monopoly. As a matter of fact, monopoly, if precisely defined as full or perfect monopoly, is as theoretical and unreal a term as "perfect competition."[6] Monopol*istic*, on the other hand, simply means having some measure of control, and when the word is combined with "competition" the phrase reflects very clearly and usefully the fact characteristic of much of modern business, namely, that it is conducted under conditions in which some measure of competitive freedom and some degree of control are actively blended.

In other words, it describes the situation of administered prices of modern industrial organization and practice.[7] Is this kind of competition capable of producing

---

[5] Chamberlin, *The Theory of Monopolistic Competition.*
[6] Frank H. Knight, "Imperfect Competition," *The Journal of Marketing*, April 1929, p. 360.
[7] Economic theorists are prone to refer to agricultural prices en masse as illustrating a competitive price-making process. As a matter of fact, however, they do not approximate "pure" competitive price—to say nothing of "perfect" competition—much if any more closely than do non-agricultural prices as a whole. They do not even meet the conditions laid down in the definition of pure competition. Farm products are

prices adjusted with refinement and skill to the objective of securing high efficiency in the use of the nation's economic resources and a rapid rate of progress in technique and organization? Many economists seem to assume that it cannot, simply because it is not competition in the classic sense. Many businessmen seem to assume that it does or can, without their giving any

---

notoriously not standardized in character and quality, though in some cases they are handled under "official grades." While farmers as a class are numerous and are in most cases small-scale producers, buyers are characteristically large-scale or operate in small numbers or singly at original transaction points.

Differentiation of product as to quality is characteristic even of the so-called "staples." (Cotton has 48 federal grades, besides 13 "half grades," and wheat 35 grades besides "sample grades" and special premiums for protein content.) They are differentiated also as to market situation. Thus certain markets are able to maintain rather permanent aberrations of price from other markets for similar products while for shorter periods both large and small markets get "out of line" with the customary price structure in ways that show clear evidence of local factors impeding the flow of competitive adjustment.

Even the increased flexibility and comprehensiveness of price relations introduced by the evolution of organized exchanges, future trading, and short selling did so much to facilitate or so little to prevent or preclude price manipulation or trading abuses that public control under the Commodity Exchange Administration was demanded and has largely displaced private trading according to strictly free market policies.

The agricultural co-operative movement arose as a protest against buyers' monopolies at local points and restraints on competition at central markets. In a few cases before 1921 and in many instances thereafter it "came of age" as a move to secure centralized or federated monopolies of agricultural sellers. Relatively small "pools" and the "orderly marketing" movement led to the legalizing of large distributive controls under the Federal Farm Board and its "stabilization corporations." Up to 1933 the monopolistic aspect of agricultural competition did not go beyond the point of manipulation of supplies produced individually, while control of production did not go beyond the advisory influence exercised by government. With the passage of the first Agricultural Adjustment Act in May 1933, government influence over the scale and direction of productive effort became a positive factor of some significance. (See Edwin G. Nourse, *Government in Relation to Agriculture*, Brookings Institution Pamphlet No. 25 (1940); William H. Nicholls, *Imperfect Competition within Agricultural Industries* (1941); and Geoffrey S. Shepherd, *Agricultural Price Analysis* (1941).)

particular attention to guiding its operations or scrutinizing their objectives.

A major purpose of this book is to press the analysis of this twilight zone between economists' theorizing and businessmen's practice. In consideration of the premise noted at the beginning of the previous section to the effect that pure competition furnishes the best guide to economic life because the individual is the best judge of how to promote his own interest, we have examined some shortcomings of unorganized individual guidance of economic activity. We shall look next at the tendency throughout business life to introduce elements of control as a means of increasing the efficiency of economic action even at the sacrifice of some measure of individual freedom.

Here we pass to the second question posed on page 56. What changes in the character of business competition occur as the complex operational situations of modern industrial techniques and business organization and their collective bargaining agencies largely supersede individual and small-scale business units?

COMPETITION AND SIZE OF THE BUSINESS ENTERPRISE

Economists and reformers often argue that growth in size of business concerns inevitably means growth of monopoly and increasing failure to achieve the goals of general welfare that competition was assumed to attain. Businessmen, on the other hand, have sought to direct attention to gains of efficiency as the motive and the result of larger-scale business organization. This would mean not merely increase in technical efficiency but also the more efficient allocation of resources to productive effort and guidance of such effort to the realization of larger consumer values in the market. These differences of interpretation do not present the antithesis of black and white; they cover a wide range of possible shades of gray.

Let us recall the simplified case of pure, individual competition, agricultural or handicraft, discussed in the preceding section. If individuals are to attain to perfect competitive functioning, they must have full knowledge of the range of productive possibilities and market opportunities within which they are operating. They must know the alternative sources of materials and the relative transportation, trading, and financing costs of assembling these materials. They must know what technical production possibilities are made available by science and engineering. They must understand how to adapt their activities efficiently to those of the productive and distributive system.

But no individual *can* know all this. The mere statement of requirements points at once to the impossibility of attaining them within the structure of individual or extremely small-scale business organization. The individual must identify himself with some larger form of business association as a means of ascertaining what these possibilities are and of availing himself of them as they become known. Capital requirements characteristically transcend those of the individual enterprise and often assume colossal proportions. If productive and commercial efficiency is to be enlarged by the evolution of techniques and the broadening of market horizons, the individual cannot long retain the purity of his individual competitive situation.

In American agriculture, this obvious paradox has been met to an infinitesimal extent by corporation farming, to a small but significant extent through co-operative associations,[8] and to a larger extent through the participation of the federal government in the business of farming. Begun as a purely educational and advisory supplement to individual enterprise, recent "action" programs have made this the closest approximation to "plan economy" to be found among American industries.

It is, however, the evolution from small-scale handicraft to modern industrialism in which we are particularly concerned. Progress from shop to factory, from partnership to small corporation, and from local corporations to national and international industrial systems has brought the organization of more and more individuals into larger and larger group enterprises. Probably no one would deny that this combination of individuals into organized enterprises has put at the disposal of such groups of workers greater power to acquire the broader information that is pertinent to their activities. It also provides specialized expertness for dealing with technical and business situations of increasing complexity and wider scope.

But when the erstwhile competitive power of individuals is thus delegated by them (under whatever degree of pressure) to some group enterprise, this new power of competition becomes an attribute of the organization as such or of certain individuals holding executive control in it. Instead of practically equal competitive power among individuals of only moderate inequality in economic strength, we get the greatest inequality between certain individuals within organizations and between organized business units. This brings

[8] The manner in which local and federated shipping co-operatives may bring a comprehensive and analytical market service to the aid of the individual farmer is presented in some detail in Sam H. Thompson, *Economic Trends in Livestock Marketing* (privately processed, 1940).

us back to the second assumption of idealized competitive theory, namely, that everybody could simultaneously attain his individual economic interest.

Power, in all situations, may be applied in different ways and directed toward different ends. It may be used clumsily or adroitly, stupidly or wisely, beneficently or harmfully. When the competitive struggle between individual and individual is mitigated by all members of the group becoming employees or officials of a joint enterprise, the individual *may* secure better facilities, superior training and direction, and larger opportunity to apply his productive efforts to his own advancement. If such be the use made of the power derived from organization, the competitive strength of those individuals against outsiders is preserved or even enhanced, though the pattern of competition is transformed.

On the other hand, the transition to group enterprise *may* be marked by suppression of individual competitive effort among workers reduced to a wage or salary basis. The enhanced competitive strength of new business organizations has at times taken the form of a local employers' monopoly, used to depress wages and curtail opportunity for advancement. Such a course leads inevitably to the counter-organization of workers and a new competitive struggle—now on the basis of collective rather than individual bargaining.

Under simple conditions of individual enterprise or self-employment, there is no conflict of interest between the businessman and the business. They are one; hence their interests are identical. But with the development of large-scale organization this identity disappears. There is competition not only among individuals within the group and among the groups—corporate producers, financial agencies, and trade unions—but also competition between the executive agent in any of the organized units and the organization itself. It is notorious that corporation officials have sometimes exploited their companies to enrich their personal fortunes. It is equally well known that some labor union officials have used their positions to advance their personal wealth and prestige at the expense of members. No picture of competition as a significant force in modern business is complete unless it recognizes these later derivative types of competition as well as early simpler forms.

It is individual business interests of this acquisitive character that (as intimated on page 57) cannot be fully attained simultaneously, since attainment by one is at the expense of others. But all productive interests of individuals may be simultaneously attained on a competitive basis through a properly designed economic structure run under scientifically conceived policies. As the word "policies" implies, however, it would not be an automatic but a highly sophisticated system. There is no reason why intelligent men should not use and shape their institutions—including the giant corporation, the big union, and the nation-wide co-operative—so as to gear the best skill and greatest industry of the varied mass of economic men to maximum joint productivity and individual reward in approximate conformity with the productive value of individual participation. This is what is called "professional management" in the later chapters of this book.

As to external relations—with rivals and with the public—the dictum that the growth of big business means by equal steps the death of competition is based on the consideration of particular instances and a relatively short time span rather than a comprehensive view of long-run trends. Facts plainly visible show that market competition between giants in a given line of industry far exceeds anything seen in the competition among business pygmies.[9] True, the reduction in number of administrative units creates possibilities of gains through abstention from competition if a substantial measure of monopoly could thereby be maintained. But the growth in variety in consumers' wants and the increased versatility of scientific techniques in meeting them persistently "leaks" competition back into each new monopolistic situation that is devised.[10]

Many large corporations have ceased to be specialized concerns for making a particular product or class of

[9] This point was developed at some length in E. G. Nourse and H. B. Drury, *Industrial Price Policies and Economic Progress* (1938), particularly pp. 220-21, 265-70. Persons entertaining the more sentimental and less analytical view of competition seem to feel that any large area of control or high state of organization among industrial and distributive interests precludes the continuance of a state of competition that may be effective and highly satisfactory as measured by either of the major criteria. It might as well be argued that valor and military virtue disappeared with the end of individual hand-to-hand encounter. Certainly there was more spirited individual muscular activity, probably more signs of emotion, more puffing and blowing, more sound and fury when cavemen fought with clubs and claws or even when foot soldiers contended with long sword and dagger. But surely no one would say that war has abated, skill waned, or valor departed when gigantic, highly mechanized, and perfectly organized armies are joined in trench or blitz warfare or when navies maneuver a complicated attack and defense between surface squadrons of battleships, cruisers, and destroyers in an environment of floating mines, aerial scouts and bombers, and powerful but elusive submarines. The time and space aspects of the process are changed, but its grim determination and ultimate effectiveness are not thereby abated.

[10] Of course a considerable amount of this is non-price rather than price competition. The former may be of equal advantage to the consumer if it takes the form of improvements in quality or design for which the purchaser has a desire at least equivalent to his desire for lower price. Where it takes the form, however, of changes or additions significant as selling points rather than as real utilities, it may have little or no consumer value, or become a positive detriment. Service and salesmanship as types of non-price competition may similarly range from high utility to acute disutility. The point is discussed further in Chap. 8.

products and have become unspecialized concerns for making money. For example, a modern chemical corporation is, in its own words, engaged in the business of "tearing down and building up molecules." Though its initial field of competition was limited to explosives, it is now a large factor in the field of fertilizers, paints, rubber, plastics, textiles, and what not. Another concern that began with paints now runs a wide gamut, including even food products. The household refrigerator became a common denominator of competition between two of the automobile companies (one large, one small) and two leaders in the electrical field. The latter have a relatively secure hold on certain lines of production that require powerful and highly specialized plant, but for other items on their list they have to meet the competition of the "shop around the corner." On the other hand, one of these companies has been known to launch a competitive foray into an entirely foreign field of heavy construction, simply because it was one of a handful of concerns equipped to do very large-scale electric welding.

Futhermore, large concerns are buyers as well as sellers, and it is frequently to their interest to maintain a number of suppliers capable of meeting their needs for equipment or materials and competitively eager to preserve this market. On the other hand, the large corporation has a potential ability itself to enter many underlying fields of production and, by this process of vertical integration, see that it shall not itself become the victim of a monopolistic situation. The Ford Motor Company's entrance into the steel business is a well-known example. Similarly, the California Fruit Growers Exchange, when it considered itself to be exploited by sellers of box shook, purchased timberlands and mills.

It operates them only on a skeleton basis as insurance of the maintenance of a competitive market in which to buy.

Finally, it may be recalled that one of the causes that led to the growth of the large corporation was elimination or reduction of "the wastes of competition." It was recognized that considerable savings were to be made by strategic location of plants of maximum technical efficiency, by integration of processes that would greatly reduce the cost of purchase and transportation of supplies and duplication of sales effort in the marketing of the product. The mere fact that there were other and less beneficent or even justifiable aspects of the consolidation movement should not blind us to the very real wastes into which business organized on the basis of small-scale competition may fall. The point, as stated before, is that competition is not a single, easily distinguishable economic force that always and necessarily operates to the good of the country. Whether on the plane of individual effort or of large-scale corporate business, it has the "defects of its qualities," and these we need to distinguish with care rather than to indulge in undiscriminating praise or blame of competition as such.

THE QUALITY OF COMPETITION

Even on the plane of individual competition in business that employs simple techniques, the question arises as to what constitutes proper or fair methods of competition and what patterns of conduct are to be barred by voluntary code or by legal and administrative authority. It is no part of our present purpose to enter into discussion of the rules of the game which have come to cover the most obvious forms of disapproved conduct, such as misrepresentation of quality, bribery, secret rebates, malicious interference, and collusive agreements. More difficult has been the definition of types of competition which, though not based on deception or "strong-arm" methods, yet are to be regarded as predatory or "cut-throat" competition. Under the automatic price-making in which no producer's product is of sufficient volume to be a significant factor in supplying the market or determining price, this issue could hardly arise. But as units of enterprise grew in size, it became possible for a large or financially strong firm to reduce price for the direct and recognized purpose of eliminating a competitor. The large firm's greater resources would enable it to outstay its smaller rival through the period of cutthroat competition, after which it could restore the price or even enhance it as a means of recouping losses incurred during the price-cutting period. To some extent, regulatory legislation or courts acting under common-law principles have discouraged such types of competition by requiring that price reductions made in one territory must be extended to the whole area served by the company and that, once a price was cut, it must remain at its reduced level until enhanced costs or some other clear reason could be adduced for its restoration, other than the mere collapse of the rival at whom the cut was aimed.

But the members of given lines of business have frequently sought to go much beyond this point and establish protective devices that would define cut-throat competition and outlaw any competitive practice falling within this definition. Obviously, defining what is "cutthroat" is difficult when the relative strength of competitors rests not on deceit or brute force but on differentials of efficiency. There is a strong tendency, when any large number of persons are hard-pressed in the competitive struggle, to define as unfair anything that produces the elimination of some or trenches seriously on their prosperity. The first connotation of cut-throat is, obviously, that it removes a competitor and removes him by somewhat violent means. But it is fair to assume that no enterpriser ever welcomes being eliminated in the competitive struggle. This would be equally true under the small-scale competition of Adam Smith's day. If efficiency in given cases derives from large size, and this mere fact of size is made the basis of a prohibition to the low-cost producer against passing on the benefits of his enhanced efficiency to the consumer, the very essence of constructive competition is lost.

Pondering the unfortunate results of the competitive struggle between Cain and Abel and the hard bargain between Jacob and Esau, society has been trying over the ages to find a way to preserve competition as the life of trade without allowing it to be the death of any tradesman. Generally speaking, such attempts tend to reduce the struggle for efficiency as a basis of price to mere shadow-boxing and make price-maintenance the rule of administered prices.[11] Without attempting to pass judgment upon the merits of any particular piece of legislation of this general character, we may group the whole body of "unfair trade laws," "fair trade laws," chain store taxation, and price maintenance legislation, whether state or federal, as belonging to this class of competition-attenuating devices. The movement came to its height in the industry codes of the NRA, whose influence has not yet disappeared from many fields of

[11] That this protective sentiment and effort should have become so widespread is first-hand evidence of the stepping up of the potential of competition that comes from the transition from individual or small-scale business to that which involves large-scale enterprise.

WE SHOULD fight against any effort of the government to help us make profits—that's our job. We should fight to the death against legislation which has as its objective taking competition out of the competitive system, for in free competition lies the force which will operate inexorably to bring down costs and thus expand markets.

Where has articulate business stood on the maintenance of open competition? Business has had several clear-cut chances to express itself on this issue. One of the first was when NRA's Blue Eagle went on the hunt.

The NRA was an experiment in fascist control of business. It was deliberately designed to control competition—not to promote it. If there ever was a time when every believer in the free competitive system should have shouted to high heaven, it was when that law was proposed. Actually the businessmen who did oppose it were conspicuous. Henry Ford stood out to the last. The Automobile Manufacturers Association, which includes all manufacturers except Ford, accepted a code for labor standards but refused, in spite of all kinds of pressure, to adopt a trade practice code. Here and there throughout industry arose other last-ditch fighters for free enterprise, protesting because they knew that free markets and free thought were inseparable; that political liberty could not survive alongside economic regimentation.

Today the NRA is a dead issue. But its spirit lives and stirs and rises again in hydra-headed persistence. Since its demise, the Miller-Tydings Act has legalized price maintenance and price fixing. State fair trade

Continued on page 74

business. That business itself is not unanimous in approval of this as a general program of business effort is indicated by a quotation from an official of a concern that has pushed a small automobile corporation into vigorous price and quality contests with the Big Three of the automotive world. (See pages 72 and 74.)

Large producers and small producers have been about equally concerned in abating the pace of competition. As a means of "protecting the little fellow," we have had not only the legislative measures just mentioned but the considerable organizational effort embodied in the trade association movement. The father of this movement deprecated the application of the theory of survival of the fittest in the world of business, saying: "The human law should be not the survival of the strong, but *the survival of all*, of the best there is in all, and oftentimes, there is more of good, more of real value to humanity in the weak than in the strong."[12] He therefore proposed "associations of competing manufacturers and dealers to lessen competition and advance prices."

Anyone at all familiar with the trade association movement in its present form will recognize that it is not to be fully and clearly characterized by this exhortation of its founder. Trade associations have become agencies of research and education, designed to increase the efficiency of the laggards and, in drafting and inculcating codes of trade practice, designed to keep any mem-

[12] Arthur Jerome Eddy, *The New Competition* (1912), p. 16. He observed further: "While the large corporation and the trust are the natural results of competitive conditions, each is simply a more powerful competitive unit; competition, if curtailed at all by the organization of a trust, is curtailed only for the time being, soon it is keener than ever, and consolidation may follow consolidation to lessen its disastrous effects, or producers, large and small, may form associations to control in a measure the competition." (P. 51.)

practice acts have been passed in 44 states. Laws to license business leap from the floor of every state legislative session. This year in the state of Michigan alone twenty-six licensing bills were proposed by twenty-six business groups, all aimed at throttling free and open competition, all designed to put some competitor out of business. . . .

Have businessmen condemned and fought against these attacks on our American system of free competitive enterprise? The answer must be a reluctant "no." The fact is that the state capitals and Washington, D.C., have been infested with businessmen seeking licensing laws or some other form of special privilege all aimed, as they put it, "to civilize competition." . . .

Granted that these business seekers after special privileges are in the minority. The great majority of businessmen have given tacit consent to such activities by their silence. They have not even been articulate in their recognition of the Federal Trade Commission as Public Friend Number One of free competitive enterprise. Charged with partial responsibility for maintaining open competition and with full responsibility for protecting business against unfair competitive attacks, this great agency has not always had the vigorous support of business. Minority groups have attacked it unfairly; there has been resentment of its so-called interference with business. These attacks have missed the main point. The Federal Trade Commission makes no attempt to control or manage business, but merely to police business to its own advantage. . . .

Paul G. Hoffman, President, Studebaker Corp.,
American Petroleum Institute, Nov. 1939.

ber—large or small—from using methods of deception, bad faith, fraud, or oppression in his dealings. However, the concept of "oppression" simply brings us back to the original issue as to what kind or intensity of competitive effort is stimulative and useful and when or how it may become harmful.

Even the biggest business units have at times decided that the pace was too hot and have announced a policy or adopted a practice of "friendly competition." This phrase was employed by Judge Gary in enunciating a policy for the United States Steel Corporation. Abatement of competition under a rule of "live and let live" is not essentially different from the situation when a trade association (or trade union) "sets the pace." Its only distinctive feature is that, instead of the common denominator between most efficient and least efficient being worked out through a somewhat democratic association of many firms, the tempo is decided upon aristocratically (however benevolently) by the leader, and the rest of the industry "gets on the bandwagon." In the case of U. S. Steel, the trade association machinery of the Iron and Steel Institute was a convenient means for carrying out the program of "follow the leader."

Whether such measures are promulgated by the "big business" leader or the "little business" rank-and-file, the essential question is the same. Is the particular kind of competition outlawed because it threatens to harm the firm? The industry? The economy? Does the attempt to erect protective devices mean that in their absence, though business survives, profits disappear or are reduced to some harmfully low level? To this question, we shall return in the following chapter, in which we examine the nature of the profits issue. At this point, it is enough to observe how widely competition as an element in any workable system of administered prices that may be devised differs from competition under the regime of automatic price-making.

The competition on which automatic pricing relied was of a spontaneous, adaptive, and generally short-focus sort. The individual reacted to his environment much like an animal following his sense of sight or smell or his still less tangible "instinct" to the best feeding grounds. But the competition of executives in organized and directed business enterprise characterized by administered prices calls for quite different qualities—those of reasoned and intricately purposive action. Such a system aspires to move beyond the law of the economic jungle and seeks to find ways of organizing men in teams of most effective sizes for exploring new types of productive effort and for executing progressively improving techniques so as to enlarge our sustained flow of material well-being.

Orderly effort of this sort can be achieved in a society of free men only if price relations provide suitable incentive and reward for suppliers both of productive property and of productive labor. Instead of being "each for himself and the devil take the hindmost," it would be a cross between sportsmanship, with its rules of the game, and military discipline, with its desire to conserve the straggler at the rear. In terms of sportsmanship, it would mete out punishment or contempt if the fight is "fixed." In terms of military discipline, it would seek to conserve resources and effect a solidarity of group aim and effort.

COMPETITION, CO-OPERATION, AND CO-ORDINATION

In popular speech the words "competition" and "co-operation" are commonly thought of as antithetical.

However, we have already noted that the attempt to succeed in the competitive struggle leads to group action and organized effort. Competition and co-operation thus appear as obverse and reverse of the same basic pattern of conduct. We co-operate with others to build a group strong enough to compete effectively with others likewise organized for competition. To say this is simply to apply to the economic aspect of society principles long ago formulated in general terms by the sociologist. As one of them puts it:

The social process is a reaction between persons each attempting to satisfy his own interests. If we look into the different modes of this reaction, we find that they reduce to two; viz., *conjunction of interests and conflict of interests*. . . . The social process could not occur at all if a certain measure of the conjunction of interests did not exist among the earliest specimens of the human species. Such community of interests as that between parent and offspring, children of the same family, members of the same clan or tribe, may contain little that is clearly different from the community of interests in a pack of wolves. If the latent community of interests among primitive men had been no greater than that among other animals, their descendants would not have developed the contrasts that now exist between human individuals and their societies, on the one hand, and brute individuals and their societies, on the other. . . . In general, conflict is the obvious phase of association in earlier stages of the social process, while conjunction of interests grows more evident in later stages.[13]

Herbert Spencer saw the "social organism" as following one of two types, the militant or the industrial. In the former, co-operation is aristocratic or compulsory. In the latter, it is democratic or voluntary. This type of organization is much the newer, and we are still trying to understand its nature and requirements and to

[13] Albion W. Small, *General Sociology* (1905), pp. 203, 205. This general view is elaborated in detail in Pts. 4 and 5 of the book.

devise workable relations of free enterprise and contracts achieved through individual and group bargaining under which all individuals may most effectively apply their talents in joint enterprise to attain the greatest wealth for everyone.

The introductory chapter of this book called attention to that small group of business executives, 1 or 2 per cent of the industrial and commercial working force, who today furnish its responsible directive agents. It is their task so to resolve the conflicts or personal competition of individual employers among themselves or as groups and the group competition between workers and "owners" that the company may be able to compete successfully with rivals for the patronage of the market. But this external competition of corporations internally co-operating under a scheme of mitigated but active competition must itself attain a high degree of collaboration among independent parts of the economic system if we are to achieve the technologically possible level of prosperity for the nation—that is, its people.

This whole book is devoted to expounding the thesis that such a scheme of business organization can be based on a philosophy of direction that appeals to the enterprise of the management group as well as the masses, and appeals to a robust spirit of individual enterprise, not a mere vague and unreliable altruism. Though it would repudiate mere individual acquisition as the goal of business, it would incorporate a lively spirit of rivalry in promoting the distinctive ends of economic life.

FRUITS OF COMPETITION FROM OTHER ROOTS?

No doubt some will say that our discussion has proceeded to a point where it has robbed the term "competition" of that precise and profound meaning with which economists have labored to invest it. This is perhaps true as to those economists who seek to limit use of the term to a so-called "perfect competition" and to set up canons of perfection which permanently abstract the concept from the actualities of the business world.[14] Those who argue that approach toward such competition is necessary to keep prices in an industrial society as low as they could and should be are proposing to drive a tractor with an ox-goad. We, on the other hand, argue that the driver of the tractor must use different tools, follow different procedures, and master a science and art fundamentally different from those of ox-cart days.

But, even among those who perceive these differences, there are many who seem convinced that such newer processes of price-making must be directed from outside, that is, from government. We for our part are not ready to concede that it cannot be developed—and developed better—from within. That would simply mean that scientifically equipped group competition was showing a capacity to deal with the more complicated problems of industrialism as well as or better than blind atomistic competition dealt with the simpler problems of a primitive economy.

No attempt need be made here to set forth in terse and categorical form a new definition or design of business competition appropriate to and most serviceable in the modern industrial situation. It must be left to emerge from our discussion of a series of aspects of the evolving business process. Here, we merely observe that the significant question is not the form of competition, but the results it produces.

[14] See F. H. Knight, *Risk, Uncertainty, and Profit* (1921), pp. 76 ff., and *Journal of Political Economy*, Vol. 49 (1941), pp. 821-25; also G. F. Stigler, *The Theory of Competitive Price* (1942), p. 24.

Amid the simple individualistic conditions of handi-craft and early industrial society, the competitive effort of economically untutored men hustling to look out for themselves might produce full and progressively more efficient utilization of resources. This spells national prosperity. Planned economy under authoritarian government should seek similar goals of public well-being but without the mediation of free business competition. If we are to preserve private enterprise on the plane of industrial technique to which we have evolved, we must perfect and demonstrate its ability to attain the goal of full and efficient use of national resources. Under atomistic competition, individual prosperities add up to national prosperity; under industrial competition, prosperity for the economy must be co-operatively engineered and its co-operative achievement allowed to subdivide into the welfare of firms and individuals.

Here lies the core of professional business management. If we are to make free enterprise work in an industrial age, we must learn that professional competition and co-ordination are something different from trade competition and behavioristic adjustment. Co-ordinated competition must be based on policies scientifically derived.[15] Its goal must be similar in kind to that automatically approximated in primitive economics but should be as much above it in level of achievement as scientific technology surpasses primitive arts.

Competition—struggle—is not something demanded for its own sake, either by the individual or by society. What is wanted is the ends which competition is supposed to promote. The individual desires that quality and degree of competition which will permit him the greatest opportunity for self-expression and still yield

[15] See Chaps. 10, 11, and 12.

him the maximum of immediate well-being and long-run security. Society, like the individual, wants results. This means growth of national wealth, and toward such growth competition at particular places and in particular concentrations, dilutions, and combinations has been found to be a useful means.

The goals of traditional competitive business must be served; it is not necessary—not indeed possible—that they be served by methods that in outward form preserve the aspect that we have been accustomed to describe as competition. Instead of personal struggle, there must be economic statesmanship at the centers of control which are inevitably thrust into being by the development of our technological processes. This shifts competition from the unorganized spontaneous response of the masses to the organized but locally autonomous direction of a relatively small executive personnel. The real need is that businessmen shall accept these objectives and set about perfecting processes compatible with modern industrial requirements through which they can be attained.

CHAPTER IV
PROFITS AND THE PROFIT MOTIVE

Starting, in Chapter II, with an examination of the meaning—or meanings—of free enterprise, we proceeded in the next chapter to that corollary of free enterprise which is most dear to the public—namely, competition. Now we turn to study the corollary of free enterprise most dear to the heart of the businessman—namely, profits or the "profit motive." Freedom of enterprise has little meaning unless those who exercise initiative and industry are recognized as claimants to the wealth which they create. But this merely outlines a principle of reward. The devices by which the principle may most effectively be carried into practice are still in process of experimental development. As one of several methods of reward, profits have been long and widely regarded as a sort of mainspring of any practical system of private business.

No particular problem as to the meaning of profits or the operation of the profit motive arises so long as business is conducted on the basis of individual enterprise. It hardly occurs to the "family" farmer, the self-employed artisan, or the small shopkeeper to split up his total income and credit the parts to separate sources of productivity. His prime concern is to utilize all his labor supply and direct it as effectively as possible, with the aid of such capital as he can accumulate specifically for the purpose of having something on which to apply his labor or with which to increase his labor power.

But when many workers, lenders, investors, and managers come to be organized in great group undertakings, there develop rather elaborate devices for determining how the total product—in value terms—shall be allocated to or divided among the several participants. With our American devotion to the principle of free enterprise, these devices have very largely taken the form of individual and collective bargaining. Many persons try to make this bargaining as free and flexible as possible and thus an automatic system for the determination of individual incomes on a basis approximating objective valuation of productive contributions. Others have sought to exercise and expand individual or group controls so as to enlarge their own incomes, regardless of whether or not this made reward correspond to productive values. The question arises then whether such elements of control or such economic "administration" within our highly organized system add to or detract from the efficiency of business operations themselves. Does this way of rewarding participants furnish a more or a less powerful motivation toward full use of productive resources and improving productive techniques?

Seeking light on these questions, we shall in the present chapter review briefly the characteristics of the several major kinds of income disbursed in the ordinary processes of business, and inquire how these kinds of income are related to each other and to the idea of profit motivation.

THREE TYPES OF INCOME

Reference has already been made to individual and collective bargaining as the process by which the great majority of individual incomes are determined. This is the process by which wages and salaries (except those of top executives) are arrived at, as are also commercial rents and market rates of interest. All these make up the class of incomes which are stipulated in advance of a given period of operation and whose payment is a fixed obligation of the corporate or other group enterprise regardless of the ultimate outcome of the firm's operations as a whole. They are commonly referred to in economic discussion as "contract shares" in income distribution.

Profit, on the other hand, falls into a distinctly different class of income, commonly referred to as "residual." It constitutes what is left to the proprietary interest after the many-sided bargains with workers, landowners, lenders, and managers have been completed and the payments stipulated under these contracts have been made. Its amount reflects bargaining skill or forbearance (as to what is sold as well as what is bought), the strength of organizational position, shrewdness or luck—good or bad—in being at a particular spot in the business process at times when particular situations develop. Profits differ—nominally at least—from the contract shares in that they may be either positive or negative.[1] That is to say, the contract shares may absorb more than the net return from a given period of business operation so that the proprietary interest suffers a loss instead of receiving a profit. For this reason, the capitalistic organization of business is often referred to as a "profit-and-loss" system.

A third type of income falls between these two major classes. It is not distinct from the other two but furnishes a bridge between them. It is highly important for our present analysis. We shall call it "contingent" income. It is in the nature of a premium added to contract salaries

[1] See pp. 94n, 97n.

or wages, interest, and occasionally even to rent.[2] Its nature and the role it plays in our business life will appear as we discuss the relation of interest and dividends, wage payments and bonuses, and the growing practice of "profit-sharing."

Interest and dividends. A modern business ordinarily includes capital of two orders of participation: (1) loan capital and (2) equity capital. The former is "hired" at contract rates of interest. In general, these are the competitive rates established by bargaining in the money market—or markets. We do not say "rate" because it is evident that even contract interest arrived at competitively will be set at different levels according to particular circumstances and conditions, with higher rates to cover risks and possibly servicing costs. But interest charges constitute the contract type of income on capital.

Equity capital, on the other hand, participates in the ultimate fortunes of the company. Traditionally, it stands first in line as claimant to the surplus of revenue above contract costs—that is, the profit of enterprise as such, over and above the cost of materials and the payments going to labor and to loan capital. Since the enterprise function and the "venture capital" with which it is linked bear certain risks of business, this share includes also negative profits. As was said before, the capitalistic system is not merely a profit system, but a profit-and-

[2] From this point forward, I shall not differentiate land from other classes of productive property. The distinctive position of rent as a residual claimant was early emphasized by Ricardo and long followed by the great majority of economists. Later, however, theory was rounded out by more careful examination of the analogous premium payments to other types of scarce capital goods and to rare labor and managerial abilities. Such differential payments, however, like commercial land rent, rise out of specific types of productivity and can be priced fairly well in the competitive market. They thus fall outside the inquiry with which this chapter is concerned, namely, proprietary profits and salary or wage bonus.

loss system.[3] Equity capital, in this view, receives the "residual" profits or suffers the ultimate losses of capitalistic enterprise.

There is some blending of contract and residual incomes to contributors of capital. Junior bonds often carry a higher coupon rate, which reflects a possible sharing in risk. Preferred stocks have a claim (often cumulative) on profits prior to common stock, but they forego any claim to enjoy the full profit rate of a very successful period in exchange for some measure of security (in the case of cumulative preferreds) against reduction or cessation of income during unprofitable periods or for a prior claim to assets in case of liquidation. Occasionally, however, preferred stocks or even bonds may be given a contingent claim to income by being allowed to participate in profits after the dividend rate on common stock attains a certain figure. Such a contingent claim is

[3] There is, of course, a certain amount of business which is, somewhat pridefully, described as "non-profit." From time to time, men in larger or smaller areas of business have found it relatively feasible to dispense with the entrepreneur in the ordinary sense and to supply both the exploratory and directional function and the necessary equity capital direct from the ranks of the active participants in the enterprise itself. Sometimes this has been done at the initiation of a user interest, as in the case of co-operative associations, or sometimes by buying out the original entrepreneur interest, as in the case of concerns that are mutualized. Such a procedure is particularly adapted to a line of economic activity in which the need for service is strongly felt and clearly defined in the minds of the group (farmers, consumers, insurers, or others) and where marked changes in the character of the service performed are not anticipated, or where the participants themselves are likely to be the best judges of the kind of service needed. (See E. G. Nourse, *The Legal Status of Agricultural Co-operation*, particularly Chaps. 1 and 2.) The fact that there are such fields does not point to the conclusion that all economic activity could be most satisfactorily organized on this basis but rather suggests a differentiation between areas in which public enterprise is, or could be, organized on a satisfactory basis, areas in which private co-operative business is feasible and perhaps superior, and still other areas in which the more aggressive and speculative types of profit-seeking entrepreneurship promise the most rapid rate of development.

supposed to bring a somewhat speculative profit motive to bear upon investors in such a way as to secure capital at a lower contract rate or to secure it more easily and abundantly at any given rate. The question of how profit motivation operates in the case of common stock will be deferred until we have looked briefly at the three types of income paid for personal rather than property participation in business.

Wages and salaries. The practice of paying contract wages and salaries is too universal and long-standing to require much comment. The wage contract secured by the worker, the cost contract entered into by the employer ordinarily covers the unit price without commitment as to total amount, that is, the maintenance of employment. Differences occur, however, as we move from unskilled to skilled classes of workers, to scarce personal qualifications and to persons who, though employees, are also executives of the company. We pass from piece, day, or weekly wages to annual or, in effect, permanent salaries. Thus the cost of maintaining a skeleton force of indispensable technicians and managers is "frozen" into the overhead cost structure of the typical corporation in a way somewhat similar to that of fixed charges for bond interest and cumulative preferred stock dividends in the case of capital.

But is the contract income position of one particular class or certain classes of workers in the business to be contrasted with a residual claim of other workers comparable to that noted in the case of capital? In a general way, the answer is "no." I am not aware of any situation in which the president, board chairman, or other individuals or groups have as persons been made residual claimants to the profits of the company, with capital reduced to the position of receiving a purely contract share.

On the other hand, the tendency of modern business practice has been to enlarge the contingent claim of wage and salary receivers in ways and to a degree which cause contingent labor income to appear as a perennial and vigorous competitor with capital as a claimant for the residual share of company income.

As the progress of corporate evolution has brought the separation of ownership and management functions, it has magnified a new class of employed personnel—the professional manager group. Their income has been put on a contract basis similar to that of salaried technical and clerical employees and somewhat less similar to that of wage workers. But the managerial group have carried over some of the perquisites of the owner role in that they have often been rewarded with blocks of stock or, because of their relatively ample income and closer knowledge, have often had opportunities to acquire equity holdings under conditions which gave them important sources of income from the corporation in addition to their salaries. It appears to have been the belief that such retention of profit-making opportunities by active executives after management and ownership had been differentiated was important as a means of attracting the ablest men to the places of largest opportunity and of stimulating them to their best efforts.

The same philosophy has extended the system of participation in profits still farther down in the ranks of workers.[4] This has taken the form of labor bonuses and profit-sharing plans. To the extent that schemes of bonus

[4] It is true of contract wages and salaries, as we saw it to be of contract interest, that frontiers are both indistinct and fluid. When the gap between interest rate and profit realization remains wide for a considerable time, workers are likely to seek by individual or collective bargaining to transfer this premium to their contract wages. Some of the results of this procedure will be discussed in Chap. 9.

payment or of profit-sharing have been generalized throughout the salary and sometimes the wage structure, the profit motive is restored to the individual worker in business on some basis designed to equalize the claims, responsibilities, and incentives of all those who contribute to the prosperity of the joint enterprise. If this process of diffusing increased productivity is carried out so fully as to embrace officials, scientific staff, white-collar workers, and wage earners as well as owners of equity capital, obviously long-time loan capital may stand out as the one participant which is excluded from all claim to surplus return at the same time that it protects itself (largely but not fully) from possibility of loss through a mortgage on physical property.[5]

MOTIVE TO WHOM?

Our brief survey of types of income brings us to consideration of profit as a motive in business. Are profits most potent as an economic motive if localized and concentrated or if widely diffused? And does their "sharing" with certain classes of executives and other workers do

[5] Employers who have not been friendly to the profit-sharing idea as applied to workers have based their objection to a considerable extent on the fact that under such a system labor "claims a share in profits but does not shoulder a responsibility for losses." It is true, of course, that labor does not risk loss of capital, but, as pointed out in our discussion of free enterprise, it continues to bear the risk of loss of income through unemployment even when it does not accept wage adjustments during periods of less profitable operation. It is the upper-salaried executive and technician group whose tenure is permanent and who have a bonus arrangement, who share most fully in profits while still being relatively well protected against loss.

Those who are philosophically inclined may indeed think it worth while to push farther than is ordinarily done the analysis of the concept of loss as the counterpart of profit. One can lose not merely what one already has; quite as real is the loss of opportunity to utilize productive capacities to get greater output. It is sometimes said that capital is in a distinctly different situation than is labor because it runs the risk not merely of receiving no income as recompense for its use but may

violence to the concept of profits as a residual income to certain capitalists or classes of capital?

In raising the question of the relation between profit and some particular economic function whose performance is essential to the healthy life of business, we encounter a considerable ambiguity which has always hung about the profit concept. Is profit merely a residual claim of impersonal capital or in some measure a claim of the capitalist as a personal participant in business? It is sometimes spoken of as a function of entrepreneurship or business enterprise. But this simply raises the question whether the essence of entrepreneurship consists in saving capital, in deciding when and where to invest it, or in managerial direction of the undertaking to which the capital has been committed.

Our ideas of the nature of capitalism and the science of its functioning grew up under the relatively simple conditions of owner-management in which the proprietor supplied both capital and the active direction under which it was used. But with the institutionalizing of corporate business, the equity capitalist has been removed from active management about as completely as the

---

actually be impaired or completely destroyed in the process. This difference, however, is more apparent than real. Honest and valuable work has at times been done, for which the worker was not able to collect his stipulated salary, wage, or fee because of the unfavorable outcome of the enterprise. Furthermore, even where labor income has been paid as nominated in the bond, the conditions of employment have not infrequently been such that what the worker received was less than what he gave in the form of impairment of health or (for professional technicians and managers) prestige or professional standing which might lower his subsequent earning power. In extreme cases, both contract and self-employed workers have so thrown their physical resources into unfavorable situations as literally to "work themselves to death" or to complete physical and mental breakdown. This would seem to be a pretty close equivalent to the extinguishment of capital assets. If anything, the capital situation is less dire. Complete loss of capital may mean its dissipation rather than its destruction. But the health lost by one worker is not transferred to others.

lender capitalist. This has caused economists to make sharp differentiation between capitalist profits and the income of management. With the growth of large industrial and financial units, the accumulation of capital reserves, the development of both technical and commercial research, and the high degree of training and specialization in executive personnel, a great deal of what once was business uncertainty and uninsurable risk has been removed through professional foresight and scientific prevention. Some of the residue has been insured by special companies of risk equalizers for small concerns or has been self-insured by concerns large enough to do so economically under the law of averages. This means that the major uncertainties, both potentialities of gain and risk of loss, are handled for society by professionally trained and selected specialists, whose earnings tend in the long run to reflect the competitive cost of such service. The relatively high payment going to them serves as a stimulus to the development of protective and progressive devices for reducing wastes and conserving capital in the most productive lines of use.

Under modern corporate organization and practice, plans and decisions which result in the venturing and channeling of capital are very largely made by professional (salaried) managers. This change of roles in the business cast has led some economists to differentiate a concept of "pure" profits, which they identify with the "venture" function, defined as mere abstract willingness to commit funds to undertakings whose outcome is shrouded in inescapable uncertainty. Here, as in the case of "pure" competition, we find the process of refinement carried so far as to reduce the concept to a faint scholastic ghost on the outermost rim of the real business world.

It is true that proprietary capital has the final de-

cision as to whether it will commit itself to an active
investment, which promises profits (in excess of mere
interest) but at the same time entails hazard of loss.[6]
Such, however, is not the role of capital that most clearly
distinguishes it as a claimant to profits. Nor is it the role
that gives the profit motive its greatest significance in the
economic process. Quite the contrary. It is this ownership right to give assent for use of capital or to withhold
it which in the last analysis links the equity capitalist
most closely to the role of mere lender, whose active
connection with his capital ceases with the committing of
it to a loan.[7] On the other hand, it is the active, personal

[6] The theory that profit derives from or redounds to capital as such
is weakened by a practice that businessmen themselves devised in the
most intensive period of development of the corporate institution. This
practice consisted in using loan capital to finance all or a major part of
fixed capital, issuing bonds up to approximately the value of physical
plant; using equity capital represented by preferred stock to finance
highly specialized machinery, inventory, and general working capital;
and issuing common stock to the promotional group. Such stock carried
a claim to all residual income above the contract shares (and semi-contract
claim of preferred stock). Whatever dividends might be derived from
such common stock would not be a return to actual capital but to the
promotional labor or acumen of those who developed the enterprise.
It might be due either to efficiencies brought about under the new (often
consolidated) company or to a monopolistic strengthening of its bargaining position—both as buyer of services and materials and as seller
of product. While such procedures have been considerably curtailed under
modern regulatory agencies, their emergence in business practice emphasizes the promotional rather than property aspect of profit motivation.

[7] Nor is this similarity destroyed by the fact that equity capital exposes
itself to the hazard of loss at the same time that it enters its claim to
residual profits. The lender at interest accepts a ceiling on his capital
return in exchange for some sort of a floor of security against loss. But
the bald record of "bad debts," mortgage foreclosures, and bond defaults
is ample evidence that loan capital operates on a basis of interest-and-loss
quite as truly as equity capital operates on the basis of profit-and-loss.

　　Furthermore, it is a very tenuous line which divides contract interest
payments from profits secured by the holder of equity or proprietary
capital. Contract rates on loans of this character are not uniform, reflecting a general supply-and-demand price for funds. Instead, they
adjust themselves to the degree of financial risk involved or supposed to
be involved in the several enterprises. Since some lenders are in a

phase of proprietorship or managerial direction that not only creates proprietary profits for capital but does most to substantiate the claim that capital also creates benefits for all other participants in the business process.

Productive goods and producing persons work together in a great economic partnership. Capital as such is the "sleeping partner," and the active role of proprietary enterprise under modern industrial conditions is exercised by the professional executives who "administer" business. It simply is not possible to talk in any fruitful way about "pure" profits on capital, about capital as a creator of income, or about the profit motive as a vital factor in the operation of our economic system except in terms of the persons who give life to the business enterprises in which capital is used, once it has been accumulated, and the decision to venture has been made by the investor on either a proprietary or a loan basis.

The managerial policies which business executives formulate and put into execution largely condition even

---

position to judge the actual magnitude of such risk better than others, they may in their very selection amongst a variety of different lending opportunities secure for themselves a premium above the general lending rate. This process is itself a return for the exercise of a certain amount of individual financial enterprise.

Beyond this, of course, the field of industrial and commercial finance itself becomes an area of business enterprise. On the one side equity commitments are selected, averaged, and constantly shifted so as to maximize returns and minimize losses. On the other side, better placing of investments tends to stimulate a clientele whose capacity to save is not matched by skill or confidence in choosing investment outlets.

Some economists shrink from so frank a re-examination of traditional views of profit motivation. One suggests that my treatment "gives inadequate attention to the enormous risks of the true 'new venture' which initiates a new enterprise or a new form of activity. I doubt whether capital on an interest basis could be secured for such activities, and yet they are at the heart of progress under free enterprise." But a great insurance company recently broke through conventional business practices to put hundreds of millions of dollars to work in the housing field to earn 5 per cent when "venture" capitalists thought the field too hazardous.

the decision of capital to commit itself or withhold itself from business enterprise—to venture or not to venture. This makes the corporate manager (or management hierarchy) much more really the custodian and strategist of business enterprise than is the owner of any class of capital, even equity capital.

The almost revolutionary change of American business from an "ownership" basis to a "management" basis has been widely and somewhat plaintively recognized by holders of both loan and equity capital, who have seen themselves pushed into the background by a new type of "inside" management. Berle and Means[8] were particularly assiduous and successful in calling this change to the attention of the public, or at least exposing the mechanics of the process. Objection to this development was based on the fact that it caused an aristocracy of management dominated by entrenched and often interlocking groups of manipulative financiers and legal Men Friday to supersede a democracy of control by all contributors of capital, however small. That the change has been accompanied by abuses, no one can doubt. But it has also involved the emergence of a salaried and highly specialized group of professional managers[9] whose constructive possibilities should not be overlooked.

[8] A. A. Berle, Jr., and Gardiner C. Means, *The Modern Corporation and Private Property* (1932). More intensive examination of the economic character and consequences of these organizational changes has been made by Dr. R. A. Gordon in a study, *Business Leadership in the Large Corporation*, which will appear as a companion to the present book.
[9] The reader should be cautioned not to confuse the expressions "business manager" and "professional management" employed in this book with the terms "manager" and "management" as used by James Burnham in *The Managerial Revolution*. He specifically defines the managerial group as "the operating executives, production managers, plant superintendents, and their associates [who] have charge of the actual technical process of producing. It is their job to organize the materials, tools,

As to how the profit motive operates in actual business affairs, we must look at both the capitalist and the manager aspects of entrepreneurship. It is frequently asserted that the profit motive acts as a mainspring in causing the private enterprise system to "tick" by stimulating savers and active users of capital. "The profit motive," it is said, "is essential to private enterprise. It is the hope of profits which leads investors to put their money into new undertakings and to expand existing ventures. The ability of private enterprise to attract the savings of investors has made possible increased production, lower prices, and a higher scale of living for all."

As a matter of fact, these are the distinctive roles of interest, and are adequately served under a schedule of interest rates that reflects the several grades of risk after these have been reduced by managerial specialists and specialized investment institutions. The really crucial area of economic motivation capable of being importantly stimulated by extra gains is that which is covered by the exploring, experimenting, innovating activities of that

---

machines, plant facilities, equipment, and labor in such a way as to turn out the [physical product or service]." (p. 82.) This identifies managers with the group commonly referred to by economists as "technicians." Burnham's displacing of the business manager by the technical director is, of course, to be explained by the fact that his "managerial" society is not a "business" world. Even so, the separation of these rival schemes of social organization is not clear in his treatment. When discussing capitalist society he is vague and frequently confused as to the function of business management and its relation to the work of the technician. This lack of sharp differentiation carries over into his exposition of a society considerably advanced toward the managerial type. Here, both in operational and in regulatory roles, government officials would combine many functions of the technician and of the business manager. The implication in Burnham's treatment that the enlargement of a managerial type of social organization involves the disappearance of pecuniary relationships is at least debatable. But so long as money incomes and market exchanges are retained, the role of business management will persist under either private or state business.

part of the working force of business which is placed in the position of managers and technicians. Since these skills and aspirations are widely distributed through the working force, it would appear that the practice of bonus payment and profit sharing already discussed under the head of "contingent" labor incomes constitutes a very effective application of the profit motive. A still wider circle of influence resulting from the way in which the gains of business are allocated or distributed concerns the price at which product is sold.[10] We shall touch on that matter later in this chapter and develop it at some length in the following chapter. Here, however, we need to note that there are two somewhat divergent objectives currently set up in business as ends to be attained or ministered to by the profit motive.

MOTIVE FOR WHAT?

One of these ends may be called "acquisitive," the other "constructive." Thus the profit motive may animate a struggle to take away from others wealth they already have or constrict their income so as to enhance

[10] Thus it may be argued that there is no reason why any residual "pure" profit which can neither be professionally dealt with nor institutionally insured should inure to capital or to any other active participant as such. As we have just seen, these functionaries are both protected and stimulated by the interest and wage rates accruing to them through their respective market machineries, and any remaining "pure" profit, being general rather than specific in its origin, should in terms of optimum operational requirements be general in its distribution; that is, should be passed on to consumers.

Under modern corporate practice, it is quite as likely that the responsible executive would, as a professional worker, drive as hard bargains as he can with all classes of capital so as to enlarge the profit residue to himself or to some official group designated as recipients of "bonus." If, however, his mind tended to run to the achieving of prestige through the growth of his company rather than to the increase of his personal income, he might regard such company revenue, unallocated under any existing distributive arrangement, as a free fund which he could use to enlarge the company's market through price reduction.

the profit residue of the enterpriser who deals with them. This situation has been notably illustrated when size or strategic position has been used to hold down or force down the price paid for materials or the wage paid for labor. It is equally illustrated when the same methods are used to hold up or force up the price of product.[11] If the wealth thus amassed is needed for and is actively employed in the expansion of output and reduction of its costs, the benefits, instead of going in any restrictive way to a single individual, will, with only brief deferment, be passed on to the general public either in the form of better wage or other contract incomes or as lower prices and a better standard of living. Such amassing may, however, be carried to a point where it produces great concentration of control, and this control may be directed to hoarding or the tardy and partial application of capital to the enlargement of product or increase of efficiency. If so, the profit motive, so potent for the gratification of the individual or class, may become a means of clogging the economic process and prejudicing the interests of the public at large.

A considerably different interpretation of the profit motive is, as set forth in our discussion of the nature of private enterprise in Chapter II, a desire to make profits through the introduction of better techniques, better organization, or whatever may enhance efficiency and lower costs of production. The profit motive thus utilized creates new sources of income and means that profits are derived from the enlargement of total product, not from subtractions from the incomes of other participants in the economic process. Instead, such profits may be linked with

[11] From a quite different approach C. J. Foreman has developed an illuminating and useful classification of profits in his *Efficiency and Scarcity Profits* (1929).

simultaneous enlargement of the real incomes of others.

The problem of prices and income shares is not one simply of dividing up a predetermined flow of wealth but of so organizing the whole scheme of pecuniary relations as to stimulate technological and organizational improvement and enlarge the total flow of economic production. Inasmuch as every income group is by nature a pressure group, each tries to divert the lion's share of the gains of progress to itself. But those who formulate and administer business policies have a responsibility to promote the kind of distribution which assures further progress.

What interpretation and application of the profit motive the businessman makes depends somewhat on his background, training, and personal characteristics, but also to some extent on the character of the business organization of which he is a functional part. We shall look briefly, therefore, at the role played by the professional manager in the industrial corporation, which typifies so large and so strategically important a part of our modern business system.

THE PROFIT MOTIVE AND PROFESSIONAL MANAGEMENT

Both the background and the outlook of salaried professional management today are very different from those of the older owner management. In so far as managers are chosen from among persons who have an investment in the business or in so far as they acquire such an interest out of income, professional management, to be sure, retains a trace of the traditional capitalist owner motivation. This is in general, however, overshadowed by a dominant salary (and bonus) motivation. But there is also a third part—like but also unlike the spirit of the owner-operator. It may be called professional pride, artistry, or the instinct of workmanship. As an overtone to the last two—or even all three—there is a vague something known as "prestige." To a considerable extent, though varying with different people, the prestige attaching to the businessman varies directly with his income and thus becomes practically identified with the profit motive in the general pecuniary sense. But it would be a mistake to suppose that the professional manager is rated in the business community merely by the size of the salary which his services command.[12]

His standing will be based also on evidence of the profitableness of the company's operations while under his management or on professional estimates of his skill in guiding the company through periods of financial difficulty. Finally, it may reflect in part his reputation as an able manager in some technological or engineering sense. In any of these ways he may be contributing to the success of the company and may be given credit for this contribution. In the last analysis, however, the motivation which guides the professional business manager in his career of management must depend on the criterion of success which he holds before himself as the objective of his efforts. What, then, is the criterion of profit-seeking enterprise which determines the choice

[12] In practice, of course, the market for executive talent is so narrow and so non-fluid that measurement of the competitive return on such services is difficult or subject to manipulation. It may become a question of how large a figure the manager dares to write in the budget for himself and can persuade his executive or finance committee or his board of directors to confirm or keep his stockholders from attacking. The large corporate executive may honestly feel that the true value of his services is the whole of the difference between all other contract costs and total revenues, determined though they are by a variety of external factors as well as by the skill of his internal management, including his skill in picking subordinates. The question which concerns us is whether this interpretation of profits as an adjunct of professional management promotes or retards the long-run prosperity (activity) of the system.

which corporate management makes from among many alternatives?[13]

The simplest and most widely prevalent impression of this criterion is, in ordinary parlance, that he shall seek to "make as much money as possible" for his company. Essentially the same criterion is widely used by economists under the phrase "maximization of the profits of the individual firm."

Some businessmen repudiate the view that they are out for maximum profits. One of this group challenges even my somewhat milder statement that "in broadest terms, it may be said that businessmen have only one policy, and that is to make money."[14] He says:

While this is in general true, I would list the entrepreneur's aims as follows:

1) He seeks to make a living and to obtain economic security for himself and his dependents.

2) He seeks to make his business strong and likely to endure.

3) He seeks to make his business grow both in size and influence, not only for the strength itself but also as a matter of pride and of achievement.

4) He desires the approval of his employes and associates in the business as well as the approval of his neighbors and friends. He wishes to be regarded as a successful, enlightened, and decent citizen.

Other business spokesmen on their own initiative have made similar declarations as to the broader and more diverse criteria of executive policy.[15] In general, how-

[13] Many writers are content to show the nature of the environmental limitations under which the business manager operates. But our analysis is directed primarily toward discovering how achievement may best be enlarged within the ultimate boundaries set by those conditions.

[14] App. A., p. 454.

[15] Edward A. Filene and Charles W. Wood, *Successful Living in This Machine Age* (1931); Tom M. Girdler, "Industry and Labor," *Fortune*, January 1938; Lewis H. Brown, "A Common Ground for Management and Labor," address at the Seventh International Manage-

ever, their qualification of the idea that profit maximization is the chief end of the businessman tends to introduce moral or other non-economic considerations. But a correct understanding of the true nature and function of profit and the most skillful utilization of the profit motive in the conduct of business affairs need not, in fact should not, rely upon these extraneous considerations. Business decisions are sound and correct only as they are based on strictly economic criteria. (See Chapters XI and XIV.) It behooves us therefore to examine the profit motive in its time perspective.

THE MAGNITUDE AND DURATION OF PROFITS

We may best begin with a very simple situation. The small trader, with a stock of goods already bought, may face potential buyers in the market with the thought that, surely, the higher the price he can exact, the greater will his profit be. He soon finds that this is not necessarily true. If he waits all day before he can find a high-price buyer or if during a day he sells only one unit at a high margin, instead of ten at a margin half as great, he has not maximized profit on his capital or return on his time. Furthermore, if he expects to stay in business, he may have lessened his chance of future profit by showing himself to be a hard man from whom to buy. Or, on the cost side, he may, by keeping his

---

ment Congress, Washington, D.C., 1938; Paul G. Hoffman, "The Corporation as a Social Instrument" in *The New Outlook in Business* (Bronson Batchelor, ed.); Charles E. Wilson, "Progressive American Industry," address at 28th annual meeting of the Chamber of Commerce of the United States, April 1940.

For a quite different approach to the whole problem, however, see Ernest T. Weir, "Profits and Patriotism," an address at the annual meeting of the American Institute of Steel Construction, (p. 329 n.) and Enders M. Vorhees, address before Controllers' Institute of America (p. 446 n.).

volume low, cut himself off from the most favorable quantity discounts in procuring his goods for sale.[16]

If now we take the typical industrial situation—a concern carrying on a continuing process of manufacture and sale to the trade or to users of the product—we find the problem of defining profit objectives projected into a much longer time dimension and into more and more complicated situations. Certainly it does not mean the widest margin per unit of product regardless of the volume of output. In so far as any producer or trader has a measure of control over his business situation, he will seek to do that volume of business with that surplus of income over costs which will give him the maximum total net return. This statement is engagingly simple in form but it merely moves us from one slippery phrase to another. How is "total profit" to be measured in an organic and continuing economic society in which it is not possible to isolate one set of business transactions from the whole scheme of business relations of which it is a part, nor to cut off one time period from the stream of time on which it rides and to whose future character and direction it contributes?

These issues arise in connection with all our business transactions, but they are particularly pertinent to those of large business organizations which—as they always do—occupy positions of strategic importance in the industrial and commercial structure. If, as we said in our simple illustration, the trader at his market stand cannot

[16] The very illustration from which we start serves notice that the discussion proceeds in terms of producers individualized as to their productive technique, organization, and management and likewise differentiated as to the character of product, market location, and personal relations to buyers—in other words, under a situation of administered prices. The concept of profit maximization under "pure" competition and "perfect" competition would have to be analyzed in quite different terms.

afford to reach for the largest possible margin on a single transaction or on a single day lest he thereby spoil his market in the future, this is still more true of the enterpriser with substantial investment in a producing plant—infinitely more true in the case of a large integrated corporation in a key industry. By and large, such corporations have a pretty lively sense of the necessity of using whatever power they may have in such a way as to retain present market outlets and develop additional ones.[17] This is evidenced by their deep faith in the power of research as a means of cultivating their market and of improving techniques in the interest both of better product and of lower cost. This might be called a *lineal* extension of their concept of maximizing business profits or the introducing of a long-time perspective instead of a short-run view of the operating problems of a particular line of production.

But mere extension of management's time objective may lead to an interpretation of the concept of maximum total profits which, though long enough, is dangerously narrow.[18] Management may shape its policies to a time perspective so long as to contemplate changes in population, taste, techniques, and government policy and yet follow policies inadequate to the task of bringing profits

[17] A rather conspicuous exception no doubt was to be found in the case of the Aluminum Company of America, which over a considerable period of time was satisfied to do a moderately expanding business on a high profit margin rather than seeking to exploit fully the industrial possibilities of the outstanding "light metal."

[18] While economists have given much attention to the problem of "maximizing the profits of the firm," the tools of analysis that they have developed have been inadequate or ill adapted to the needs of the businessman. Being the only ones at hand, however, they have sometimes been employed by economists in academic theorizing or by others in industrial or governmental advisory or regulatory positions to suggest or justify harmful courses of action. This matter will be alluded to further in Chaps. 7, 11, and 12.

to their long-run maximum. Executive authority may not be sufficiently concerned about producing in the present those cross-section relationships that will promote profit-making conditions in the future. Not only *lineal* extension of the businessman's view but *collateral* broadening of his efforts toward economic adjustment is necessary. He must consider not merely how to adapt himself to his market and how to exploit his market most fully, but also how he and his fellows must mutually create the kind of market within which they can severally thrive.

As a matter of fact, there is no external economic world that provides a market into which large business enterprises can enter and live on the principle of extracting as big a profit as possible from a situation for whose creation or maintenance they have no responsibility. No general market exists except as a creature or a synthesis of all the business enterprises that seek to operate within it. Obviously a small amount of parasite business could exist indefinitely. But as for the major industries that make up the body and bones of our economy, they must create the conditions of prosperity out of which profits are to be derived. "Maximum profits" in the long run mean therefore that moderate interpretation of unit profits in the single instance that promotes continuous harvesting over the years, that careful plowing back of gains into the economy which insures future yield. Such a conservation movement involves maintaining the flow of consumer purchasing power quite as definitely and consciously as it means maintenance of plant capacity or more generalized capital reserves.

The growth of the corporation in size commensurate with whatever technological and organizational needs industry develops and the emergence and education of an elite corps of professional managers at its head have institutionalized business. The corporation is chartered for long or even perpetual life. It has a flexibility of purpose and organization which permits it to press its activities into new fields, however remote. Its research departments, set up for the purpose of developing new techniques, new organization, new means of creating, stimulating, directing, and satisfying human wants, orient it to an outlook considerably different from the trading or short-run producing profits of small personal enterprise. The office of its chief executive is comparable to that of president or chancellor of a great university or research institute. It does not so much offer a personal chance to make a financial "killing" as it imposes a period of arduous administrative work, at whose end the executive hopes to hand the office over to his successor with the company's resources intact or enlarged and with its role of public service clarified and expanded. If this promise of corporate management is to be realized, we need a much wider understanding of the several planes upon which profit motivation can be understood and can operate in the process of formulating business management policies and administering prices.

ENTERPRISE, PROFIT, PROGRESS

We have in this chapter sketched a background of profit motivation within the general structure and practice of income distribution. That structure and practice are not rigid and predetermined by natural laws but are subject to purposeful modification by administrative policy and group bargaining. In drawing our discussion to a close, we should distinguish two broad classes of profits and two significant ways of dealing with them in business practice. First are those profits that are "freak," casual, or fortuitous. Second are those that are contrived, scientific, functional—the distinctive fruits of enterprise.

Casual profits are of relatively little importance for our analysis. The fact that a windfall gain sometimes falls into the lap of the businessman or that a cyclonic disaster sometimes inflicts a loss upon him or even "takes his shirt" is important chiefly by reason of the means we take to see that such good fortune contributes as much as possible to, and such bad fortune detracts as little as possible from, the aggressiveness and efficiency with which our productive operations move forward. Business experience has taught us the wisdom of treating such vicissitudes of business life under the law of averages so that the inescapably fortuitous element in business may as largely as possible cancel itself out from operative programs. But this wisdom is not always followed.

The larger and more diversified the unit of business organization, the easier it is to effect adjustments to extraordinary gains and losses through the standard device of corporate reserves. Small or highly specialized companies, if they happen to be lucky in the matter of profits, may have their management led into economically unhealthy practices by the accrual of sudden wealth. Others may be put out of business by sudden losses disproportionate to the size of their reserves, the financial resourcefulness of their management, or the availability of a source of outside funds willing (and legally permitted) to tide them over an emergency period. This has led to perennial consideration of the possibilities and limitations of government agencies as proper and useful means of equalizing such random factors in business on a scale beyond that practicable for even the most widely integrated corporations or for commercial insurance agencies.[19]

If such a profit comes only once in the lifetime of a business or "once in a blue moon," it does not constitute a profit *motive* significant for the practical conduct of business, though it may occasionally influence some "long-shot" gambler. Nor can its sharing have much effect as reward on managers or workers or on markets as a means of lowering prices. In fact, such a gain may quite possibly derive from some sudden upshoot of demand which raises prices. Since the casual profit has no continuous and operational relation to the normal conduct of business, it does not become a factor in policy making and may be dismissed from our further analysis.

But when we consider the other class of profits—contrived, scientific, and functional—the story is quite different. Such profits lie close to the heart of the problem of promoting economic progress through our business institutions and the economic policies of the responsible business leaders, with which this book is concerned.

Free enterprise, as we have seen in Chapter II, is the gateway through which human effort reaches out to new lands, new products, new methods from whose introduction into business a profit may be made over and above the wages and interest customarily paid for traditional types of business effort. It is the distinctive function of business enterprise to discover productive opportunities, to develop cost-reducing improvements of technique and organization, and thereby to create or enlarge a margin between costs and pre-existing prices.

[19] In the small-scale business of agriculture, federal crop insurance, the stabilization corporations of the late Federal Farm Board, and various farm credit and agricultural marketing activities under a succession of "adjustment programs" are cases in point.

Here is the point at which profit is introduced into business. But this is not enough. Management must also know what to do with profits once they have been secured. It is fatal to try to "freeze" or hoard them at their place of entry. They must go some place to complete their fructifying service.

We expect the new improvement to be copied by others, and anticipate that competition will thus disseminate it into general service. But under conditions of large-scale corporate competition, such dissemination takes place in response to conscious policies and through institutionalized methods. Our earlier discussion of the corporation practice of profit-sharing dealt with one creative or re-creative method of handling profits. In our next chapter we shall examine more particularly the methods by which profits are dispersed in the form of lower consumer prices. Here we wish merely to outline a general point of view as to the nature of "cultivated" profits and the relation of cultural methods to the richness and permanence of harvests.

In dealing with this issue, we must consider the particular business in its setting as a part of business in general or the economic system. While the individual firm has at any moment of time to accept the conditions of the commodity market, the labor market, the money market, and all other parts of the business environment as it finds them, these several markets are themselves in the wider perspective and in the long run determined by what all firms taken together are doing. The income that the various business concerns put into the hands of workers, the amount of employment they offer, the kind and quantity of raw material they take and the prices they pay for them, and finally the quantity and prices of the products they offer the public all go to determine the character of the infinitely interrelated stream of business and whether it shall be a deep, strong, and steady current, or be erratic, scant, and sluggish. It is not a stream which exists because of some internal force or external control by act of God, with economic men having merely to come and dip their buckets. It is created or consummated out of their own acts, wise or foolish, stimulative or restrictive.

The combination of free enterprise in "the spirit of '76" and business strategy in the modern industrial manner puts major stress on the time perspective in which choices are made and to which policies are adjusted. It contemplates changes in market technique along with promotional or adventitious alterations in market demand of the most sweeping sort. It recognizes the repercussions on the profit-making position of the business which result indirectly from modification of the purchasing power of the public through alterations in wage rates, volume of employment, dividend disbursements, tax burden created by relief needs, and other of the broader factors which enter into the complex interrelations of an economic society. Attempts to "maximize the profits of the firm" ultimately defeat themselves if management closes its eyes to roundabout effects and ultimate consequences of its policies and procedures.

All this may involve some reinterpretation of the profit motive. But it does not involve its abandonment. Profit-making opportunities appear with every new discovery, invention, or successful reorganization of business structure or practice. But in order that the stream of profit-making may be maintained at full tide, it is necessary that the specific profits that emerge from each successive step in technological progress shall be passed on democratically to the body of society that is, the mass of consumers—rather than being monopolized by any particular group.

The fundamentally important questions that need to be answered by the statesmen of an economic society in this connection are two in number. First, how rapidly should the premium to the enterpriser who discovers or creates the new improvement or to the capital which is ventured in the untried undertaking be passed on to the mass of workers and consumers who are general rather than specific factors in the realization of this profit? Second, by what scheme of allocation and through what distributive devices should such dissemination take place?

We shall, no doubt, have to continue to ponder, and sweat, and quarrel over practical solutions to these problems in the future as we have so often during the past history of private enterprise. One point, however, seems to have been made pretty clear in this school of experience; that is, that it is quite possible to have the rate of profit so high that the maintenance of profits and of the basically more important wage and salary payments may be seriously impaired. Shrewd businessmen are quite aware of the possibility of "pricing themselves out of a market." A few enlightened labor leaders are beginning to see that it is quite possible to price their followers out of employment. It is no less important for the business enterpriser to realize that he can "profit" himself out of business opportunity. The attempt to maintain high rates of profit kills the goose that lays the golden eggs.

This is due to the fact that business life is an organic social process. The attempt to maintain and capitalize each new gain in the form of permanent profit is like trying to achieve physical immortality rather than the constantly rejuvenated stream of racial life, where children move on to years of productive and reproductive life and in due time pass individually from the picture, while the society and its culture continue their forward march. The particular technological achievements that give birth to profits must be promptly passed on if they are to become fully fruitful. Only as such general progress is made do we have a healthy, growing economy out of which new profit-making opportunities can arise.

Such a disciplined, far-seeing employment of the profit motive will be further examined in the chapter which follows.

CHAPTER V

FREE ENTERPRISE, PRICE POLICY, AND DEMOCRACY

In the preceding chapters we have briefly reviewed the three major areas of concept and practice generally regarded as making up "the American way" of business life. It was noted that *free enterprise* starts as a demand for self-direction and personal income, made by men freed from feudal or mercantilist control. As society reaches an advanced stage of corporate organization, this becomes a three-cornered struggle between the individual, the business institution, and the state. *Competition* was seen to be an ever-present force that animates the body of free enterprise and takes on many forms. From mere personal endeavor to excel, it branches out to become a pervasive bond of organization that brings men together in groups for greater strength—strength which may be used for the constructive ends of greater efficiency or the destructive ends of predatory conflict. The comparative violence, discontinuity, and concentration of collective bargaining supersedes the close-grained flexibility and diffusion of individual bargaining. *Profit,* accepted as the goal that free enterprise seeks through the method of individual and group competition, likewise is susceptible of varied interpretations. Manifestations of the profit motive range all the way from the most primitive forms of destructive acquisition to the most sophisticated long-range processes of continuously expanding productivity as a dependable series of ever-richer harvests.

So wide is the range of these different interpretations

of enterprise, competition, and profit-seeking capitalism that many men of many tastes and beliefs can select and combine them in a score of significantly different pictures, each put forth by its proponents as the "American way" of economic life. Is there then no common denominator of these divergent and, in their extreme range, warring philosophies?

The basis for reconcilement is to be found in two common requirements or objectives, on which all or nearly all thoughtful people would agree. The first is that the American way must be one that produces maximum product or material well-being. The other is that it must be voluntary; that is, the individual must be free to make his own choices as to where he will live, how much he will work (and at what calling), and what kinds of goods and services he will exchange his income for. When the two objectives involve a measure of conflict, some would compromise chiefly from one side, some from the other.

We turn, therefore, to consider whether the combination of interpretations of free enterprise, competition, and the profit motive prevalent in business circles today are mutually consistent or will in fact fit together into a working economic process capable of attaining the dual —but related—goals of prosperity and freedom. Or, from the other approach, are there any broad fundamental principles according to which the process of everyday business can or must be conducted if the institution of free, competitive, profit-seeking enterprise is to operate in such ways as to gratify most fully the tenacious aspirations of economic men?

The brief résumé of preceding chapters presented in the opening paragraph of this chapter points out that the harvests to be won by profit-seeking enterprise may be envisaged in cramped or in expansive terms. It is peculiarly the function of the economist to consider the way in which the magnitude and certainty of these harvests year after year depend upon the procedures according to which they are currently distributed as private money income. Division may be in almost any proportion among the "hands" who have labored and the "masters" who have planned and financed the process of production. But it is not a matter of indifference or a matter merely of taste or of ethics what division is in fact made. This distribution of the benefits is simply one step in a continuous process of economic life, a phase in a cycle which must be correctly adjusted to the other phases—production, consumption, saving, and investment—if our economic life as a whole is to attain "health" or make business prosperity greater and more dependable.

In our search for the principles through whose application free enterprise can most effectively approach the goal of national welfare as maximum mutually consistent prosperity of its citizens, three lines of analysis are to be followed. First, we shall look at the technological requirements within which our economic system must operate. Second, we must consider the complex system of interrelated prices under which technological activities are organized. Finally, this techno-economic process must be related to the organizational setting provided by a democratic philosophy of life.

TECHNICAL PRODUCTIVITY AND REALIZED PRODUCTION

Expanding power to discover and utilize productive resources may be set down as a basic feature of worker-and-capitalist enterprise as it has operated since the dawn of the Industrial Revolution. It is significant that the period of industrial capitalism and the period of modern science and engineering have been concurrent. If one turns to metaphor, he is in doubt whether to call them parents or twin children of the Industrial Revolution. There are relations of both cause and effect.

While science and engineering as such lie outside the domain of economics, they are the soil in which our economic life is rooted, and it is only through some properly conceived scheme of economic husbandry that they can be brought to full fruitage as realized technological progress. Science made its own answer to the question of how its life must be lived, its work done. This was in terms of absolute freedom of thought and action, of adventure and experimentation. Freedom of business enterprise represents the analogous demand of the progressive human spirit for freedom to apply in the area of human action the useful knowledge derived from free-ranging scientific thought. Free enterprise as a doctrine of high technical efficiency includes high efficiency in the human arrangements by which all the forces of nature are harnessed in productive work. Business enterprise is itself a laboratory of social science, in which freedom of thought and action are quite as imperative, if progress is to be made, as is the freedom of science in the older and simpler fields of nature.

The essential problem of the natural sciences has been to gain such insight into the forces and processes of nature as to achieve predictability and gain control. The essential problem of economics is so to employ these controls and so to apply these techniques as to enable men to get the maximum of return from the minimum expenditure of effort on their part. To attain this end, each person in the process must (as was shown in Chapters II and III) be as free as the conditions of group effort will permit to direct his effort and talents to whatever place he deems most advantageous and to employ whatever technique and equipment he finds most suitable or can devise by way of improvement.[1] This has meant the venturing of effort and capital to explore and develop new lands, the free movement of consumer masses nearer to new resources, and the improvement of transportation facilities to bring raw materials and finished products readily to markets wherever they may be found. It has meant the right of the consumer to select for purchase whatever goods best suit his taste or his evaluation of their usefulness.

It was against the background of unhappy experience with authoritarian direction of labor force and consumption patterns that men of the eighteenth and nineteenth centuries agitated and even fought to get the right of self-direction and individual bargaining. But they could not fully foresee the difficulties in appraising and pursuing their own advantage that would develop as the process of free bargaining passed farther and farther from the conditions of direct barter. The abstractions and complexities of a highly developed pecuniary exchange and credit economy held future difficulties undreamed of at the early or even the middle stages of its development. Recognized to the extent that they are today, we are confronted with assertions that the money economy or the system of pecuniary capitalism has broken down. The next step of those who leap to this conclusion has been to urge "technocracy," the more extreme forms of economic planning, Fascism, or Com-

---

[1] Thus, for example, patent laws may be used to stimulate inventive effort, but also to retard the widest use of the new productive power discovered or harnessed; labor union organization may be used to get better working conditions and improve the wage structure, but also to distort wage relations or to prevent introduction of more efficient methods of production.

munism to modify drastically or completely to supersede the system of price-organized society that has evolved during the last few hundred years.

Cues to the difficulty that led to the partial breakdown and the alleged unworkability of the system of capitalistic enterprise and price-bargaining are readily to be found in the way in which concepts of technological efficiency have been translated into cost, costs related to price (and prices to cost), and these in turn related to profits, capital accumulation, and the maintenance of production. These institutions and practices constantly challenge our most searching study.

We have called attention to the relationship of natural science as handmaid to economic life. Science and engineering, by gaining new knowledge of the secrets of nature, showed us how to apply our efforts to or with natural resources so as to produce greater utilities for a given outlay or to produce given utilities with less effort or material. This aspect of modern economic life is well epitomized in the famous slogan of the du Pont Company, "Better things for better living through chemistry," and is typified by the great expansion of technological research in industry during recent decades. But the natural scientist in his laboratory has his attention focused primarily on the mere technical possibility of bringing a certain product out of his test tube. Even when questions of cost in relation to volume are forced upon his attention, the terms of the problem are laid down by the particular assumptions set up by his industrial employer or by possible users of his technique under conditions, either of small-scale or of mass production, that they may envisage. When we observe these businessmen, weighing the possibilities and selecting from the range of techniques available for commercial application, we find horizons sometimes broader, sometimes more narrow. A broad view is suggested in General Electric's slogan, "More goods for more people at less cost." The significant point for our purpose is that, by and large, businessmen have not taken a view of the economic application of possible techniques which was broad enough to attain the maximum of operational efficiency for the economy.

This brings us to consideration of the relationship between technical and economic efficiency or between qualitative efficiency and quantitative efficiency. As our section title suggests, we need to distinguish between productivity and production. Thus chemist, physicist, metallurgist, engineer, and business technician[2] can go only a certain distance in bringing about the betterment of our economic life. Their programs of action are subject to fructification or to sterilization by the control of top executives who operate in the higher realm of strictly economic forces. It is they who must harness technical powers so as to yield their potential economic product.

If, in his selection among price alternatives, the executive does not harmonize his cost factors with the possibilities of market absorption—if he does not "make money"—he breaks the circuit that furnishes the motive force on which business runs. But the mere fact that he does at a given moment effect a workable adjustment and make money does not mean that he has arrived at the right answer to his ultimate problem. If he merely keeps his prices in line with such costs as have obtained in the past or is guided by such a picture of costs as his cost accountant may paint or such interpretation of the profit motive as his banker may urge, this is likely to mean the

[2] The bookkeeper, the paymaster, and (as to their routine activities) the salesman, purchasing agent, and others below the policy level.

introduction of better techniques at the expense of employment. If, on the other hand, he follows the course dictated by labor union executives, he is likely to maintain employment at the expense of better techniques or perhaps increase the pay of some at the expense of others' employment. Only when the highest technique is combined with full employment is the problem of national prosperity and progress solved.

A failure of production to increase in full proportion to the growth of potential productivity has resulted from the divorce of institutionalized business enterprise from the enterprise of individuals. The latter may, by the very existence of large business concerns, be shorn of the opportunity for personal initiative which they had in a more simply organized society. The corporate executive may be able to utilize for his firm the teachings of high efficiency production even in an economy in which a substantial fraction of the labor force is unproductive. Such a society attains high specific productivity for certain individuals, for certain firms, or even for certain industries, but drops to a much lower efficiency for the economy as a whole. Perhaps it does not average lower than the same society would attain if fully employed but using methods of less specific efficiency. But still it fails to advance by an amount commensurate with its technological possibilities. Furthermore, the reduced prosperity of large segments of the society puts a "ceiling" on the success and growth of even those concerns which, because either of favorable location or of superior internal management, are able to "get by."

As proof of the superiority of the prevailing system of private capitalistic enterprise, its defenders point to the high rate of productivity or specific efficiency of that part of the system which is active. Critics of the private capitalistic system, on the other hand, point to long-continued non-employment of some 10, 15, or other per cent of the labor force as evidence of the system's breakdown or even its inherent unworkability. This charge must be answered, this situation must be remedied, if private capitalism is to be fully accepted as a satisfactory scheme of organization of modern industrial life. The fact that locally and temporarily successful operation has not been so fully generalized as to give us high production and not merely high productivity prompts us to try to envisage the broad principles upon which the productive potentialities of a capitalistic system could be fully attained. This leads us to consider the nature of the price system within which the price-making executive has to function.

PRICE SYSTEM AND PRICE POLICY

Nearly 30 years ago Professor Mitchell, in attacking the problem of the business cycle, found it useful to start with a general exposition of the "system of prices" whose relationships in part condition and in part result from the actions of businessmen.[3] He classified prices broadly as those of consumers' commodities, of producers' goods (including raw materials and labor), of business enterprises (and securities), and of services of persons. He disavowed any intention of trying to establish categories. Instead, he sought merely to emphasize the "organic" interrelations of prices. This included the idea of a structure of prices such as the cross-section pattern of retail and wholesale prices, prices of finished goods, and prices of the ingredients that enter into them.[4]

[3] Wesley C. Mitchell, *Business Cycles* (1913), p. 27.
[4] Mitchell also showed wages, salaries, and fees as a system of prices related both to each other and to prices of commodities. He did not, however, go on to elaborate the idea of interest rates as prices of capital use,

He emphasized the time flow of prices, saying, "Present prices are affected by prices of the recent past and also by the anticipated prices of the near future." Whether in cross-section or in time sequence, "the price system," he said, "has no logical beginning or end. At whatever point analysis may begin tracing the interlocking links of the price chain, to that point will it come round again if it proceeds far enough."

The same general point of view had been earlier advanced by the Swiss economist, Walras, and has been developed in many ways by others, while it is constantly implied in the action of men in their business arrangements. Mitchell referred to business enterprisers as all the time selecting and combining priced goods in such a way as to "squeeze money profits out of these price margins."[5]

Economists of the price interrelationship school have been concerned primarily in developing techniques for tracing out these interactions to a final state of "equilibrium," thereby discovering laws of price determination. While these methods have had considerable analytical value, they may readily be the undoing of anyone who directs his attention exclusively along this line. Such methods of analysis lead the student to consider the way

which in another aspect become the connecting link between market values of current goods or services and the capitalized values of properties which yield valuable uses and which have markets of their own.

[5] Mitchell, *Business Cycles*, p. 27. F. C. Mills likewise has made extensive and illuminating studies of the price system. His emphasis has been primarily on patterns of structure and patterns of change within the price system rather than on administratively introduced innovations, which are the major theme of this book. Both Mills and Mitchell, however, make it clear that they recognize the existence and the importance of dynamic factors injected into the price system by the business executive even when their own studies happen to be directed to the examination of stereotyped situations or stereotyping influences. See, for example, Mills, *Prices in Recession and Recovery* (1936), pp. 456 ff.

in which prices would be made for such kinds and quantities of goods as would be produced if economic men "let the old cat die," applied no new recurring pushes, but let previous disturbances and motivating forces fully work themselves out and come to rest. In such a closed system, it is true, measurable and predictable forces would determine the whole pattern of prices. Permanent relationships would become established between prices in the cross-section pattern, and the only time changes by which this pattern would be complicated would be the result of the vagaries of taste or of such natural forces as seasonal change, climatic catastrophes, fortuitous discoveries, or marked demographic growth, decline, or shift.

Admitting the foundational importance of all this, it is hardly adequate as a picture or model of the price-making process which is the core of our present economic system. At least, if one is to expound the process of the real world in terms of a price system, he must place his emphasis strongly on the word "organic" used by Mitchell to describe these relationships. Furthermore, the idea of organism must be used not in the mere sense of vegetable life with its unconscious responses, nor even of brute life with its behavioristic responses to nervous stimuli, but in terms of the human organism—conscious, rational, and capable of evaluating ends and conceiving and executing long-run, intricate, indirect, and sustained programs of conduct.

It is important that we know as much as possible about the underlying character of the great economic forces that operate on both the supply and the demand side of price-making markets. It is no less important that we understand the mechanisms, of ever-changing design and in various stages of disrepair, through which these forces do their work, namely, market institutions. But, after all, attention must ultimately focus on the rationality of the human agent who directs particular kinds of material to this price-making machine to receive the impress of the great natural forces that operate through it.

This, for purposes of economic analysis, means that attention focuses upon the role of the business executive as price policy maker.[6] Every now and then, the idea occurs to someone that if we would just let the technicians alone, their zeal for their craft would give us better things as fast as the mind of man could devise them and in quantity as great as resources and labor would permit. But it must be remembered that inventors and engineers are incorrigible enthusiasts. Each thinks his scheme is the best and most important in the world, and that it should be brought to full fruition with little regard to costs or the claims of other means of human satisfaction. Ways must be found of selecting from alternative lines of production not all of which can be exploited simultaneously and without stint, of conserving effort and of allocating it to those uses which, on the estimate of the consumer rather than the producer, are most to be desired. Even if we did away with capitalism, this function would have to be performed by commissars or by bureaucratic planners, and they would simply change the form of the problem of administering scarce resources to desirable ends rather than escape the need. In America we are still trying to work out this problem through

[6] Both businessmen and economists have taken some exception to my use of the term "price policy," proposing "business policy" as an alternative. But all policies within a business, however much they can be departmentalized, stem from or must be co-ordinated with the company's price policy. I continue to use the phrase, therefore, as a means of keeping attention focused on price as the key to business strategy. The point of view is elaborated in more detail in App. A.

prices arrived at in markets, to some extent through small-scale individual bargaining in which adjustment comes about automatically, but to a large extent, also, through collective bargaining and large-unit administration of prices, investment, and technique.

We observed in Chapter I and again in Chapters II and III that under conditions of individual competitive enterprise, production is unrestrained, the door wide open to the entrance of technical improvement and equally open to the passing on of any benefits of such technological improvement to consumers in the form of lower prices and larger quantities of goods and services. There is automatic adjustment to that level and structure of prices which will clear the market of this increasing flow of product. Under conditions of modern industrial organization, this naturalistic process gives way to one in which a mere handful of executives acquire a delegated responsibility to control the entrance of new techniques and the administration of the labor force. In so doing it takes on responsibility for the way in which the benefits of this increasing productivity are translated into economic well-being for various individuals or groups in the form of property and labor incomes and the prices of goods and services through which these money incomes are translated into real income.

Business executives as the responsible chauffeurs, pilots, or machine tenders of the industrial price system need a high degree of professional competence as technicians of price relations. In interposing their influence to effect adjustment of these relations, they exert either a helpful or a harmful influence on the working of the economic system. They put oil or sand, as the case may be, in the bearings of the business machine. Over the whole period that the present scheme of business organization and operation has been developing, the total gains to the public have been enormous.[7] But it is indisputable that business executives did not find ways of continuing such gains after 1929 nor of agreeing with government agencies on how to resume prosperous operation. These confusions give urgency to the quest for understanding of the basic principles under which a price-organized society must operate.

While the variety of price relations and price-influencing actions is infinitely complex and swiftly changing, the broad issues may usefully be focused upon three strategic areas or types of managerial action. The first to be considered is the relation of prices of products to the size and capital value of the plant by which they are produced. This leads to consideration of the relation of prices to wages, and that in turn to prices in relation both to costs and to purchasing power. These three types of adjustment are the means through which productivity is determined and distributed among capitalists, workers, and consumers.

Looked at historically, private capitalism has, as to price relationships and practices, been primarily concerned with the values of productive properties and with ownership incomes. Capitalist producers have shown a strong tendency to use whatever position of control they might have to charge prices that would maximize the rate of profit on capital. This would cause capital itself to grow larger and larger as more new resources are discovered and new capital-using methods are developed.

The practical wisdom of rapid accumulation of capital was clear in the early days of capitalistic development,

[7] Attempts to show in quantitative terms the distribution of these gains to the several beneficiaries are beset with enormous statistical difficulties. (See Mills, *Prices in Recession and Recovery*, Chap. 9, and Spurgeon Bell, *Productivity, Wages, and National Income* (1940).)

when plant was grossly inadequate to the application of new machine-using techniques. It was appropriate also to a period of rapid population growth such as characterized the United States and other relatively young countries during the nineteenth century. A high rate of capital return and rapid expansion of capital at such a period are necessary if new natural resources are to be made accessible and new machine techniques to be at all rapidly exploited. But if the same routine of accumulation is continued after this initial building up of plant has been accomplished and in the face of stable or declining population, then price practices designed to continue an equally stimulative return to capital leads either to the amassing of idle capital or the accumulation of idle or partly utilized plant. This in the long run defeats even the intention to maximize capital return.

Nor can it be argued that the piling up of personal incomes of that part of the population in whose hands capital ownership tends to concentrate under high-profit types of business policy adjusts itself suitably through the higher spending of the favored class. The possibilities of actual consumption of goods and services are physically limited (to say nothing of the psychological limitation upon the derivation of satisfaction from lavish consumption). Hence the processes of actual use as a means of clearing the market are retarded; mere personal ownership is no adequate substitute for actual consumption. While prices may be measurably maintained on this basis, it is only at the expense of limitation of further productive volume. This in turn is accompanied by retention of less efficient methods of production or the shrinkage of employment, or a combination of both these depressants of economic enterprise. If capitalistic control were to apply generally such a philosophy of price-making, the economy would tend not toward progress but toward stagnation on a low level of production.

But the "capital first" philosophy of price-making has always found other parties to the economic process aggressive in demanding a broader distribution of the benefits of improving techniques and organization. The principal influence here has been the demand of labor for a larger share in increasing productivity. Labor has been unwilling to accept the theory that, because increases in productivity were accompaniments of new and ever more complex capital plant, all the increase should be ascribed to the specific productivity of the capital partner. There might have been endless metaphysical theorizing about the nature of productivity, but labor turned to organization as a means of increasing its power to participate in the process of pricing labor.

From the side of the businessman, wage adjustment constitutes our second "strategic area of managerial action." While labor has struggled for higher wages as a sharing in advanced productivity, practical businessmen have gradually come to perceive reciprocal relationships between labor income and the cash market for their product. American manufacturers frequently accepted and occasionally even initiated wage scales for unskilled or semi-skilled workers definitely designed to bring the amount of consumer purchasing power into line with the volume of goods which industry was capable of turning out. Understanding on the part of corporation executives and labor union executives of the interrelated adjustments of prices, of labor use, and of capital use can do much to lubricate the price system. Gains from changes in cost relationship which are introduced as business enterprise explores and exploits new techniques of production will then be quickly and effectively disseminated (voluntarily by the ownership interest or in response to labor pressure). This would go far toward attaining "dynamic equilibrium" for the whole system— an economy that keeps good balance between its working parts at the same time that it is making progress, in fact as a condition of such progress.[8]

There are, however, certain features of wage adjustment (particularly by collective bargaining) which preclude its being used in conjunction with profit adjustment to attain the closest approximation to harmony possible within the price system. The use of collective bargaining as a principal means of formulating the wage structure means that certain crafts, types of work, or broad classes of labor will be paid uniformly wherever they may chance to be employed. Technical improvements, with their accompanying gains in productivity, occur, however, at specific spots in the industrial system. If wages at these points are not advanced, workers do not share in the gain to which they are a partner. But if their rates cannot be advanced except there be similar advance in the rates of workers at other places, where such increase of productivity has not occurred, the task of adjusting the price structure (as between skilled crafts, clerical employees, routine factory labor, shop and store employees, farmers, and other groups) as a means of distributing efficiency gains presents insuperable difficulties. This brings us to the third major aspect of the businessman's technique of adjusting price relations.

The road by which the most general diffusion of the gains of technological progress can best be effected is

[8] If militant unionism, possibly backed by government support, forces over-distribution of gains to labor, resultant readjustments in the price system will tend, through enhanced labor cost, to check declines in commodity prices or even force them higher. This aspect of the pricing problem is dealt with in Chap. 9.

through the lowering of prices of goods and services as they are sold to the great body of primary and secondary consumers. Since the wage and salary worker's ultimate concern is with real income, that is, with the consumer satisfaction he can command rather than with money wages, the whole struggle over the wage *level*—if only labor and management could realize it—is flanked if technological gains are passed fully into price reductions. Then the vast problem of wage adjustment is simplified to considerations of the adjustment of the price *structure* of labor to the differential productivity and scarcity of particular classes of workers.

There is a further reason why the lowering of commodity or service prices in step with reductions in their costs of production constitutes the technically correct device for adjustment of the price system. If efficiency gains go to consumers in the form of lower prices, demand is expanded for the very products in which greater output from a given input is being brought about. Where the securing of economies is contingent on greater volume of output, it is of course inevitable that the reduction in cost, or a large part of it, be passed on in the form of lowered prices. That fact, as much as or more than the insight displayed by sellers, explains the extent of price lowering that our market has actually experienced. In other cases, however, the pricing practice lies more fully within the discretion of management. If, in these situations, gains are passed on entirely or largely as increased disbursements to capitalists or to laborers, the enhanced purchasing power appears at entirely different spots in the price system. It therefore fails to exploit the increased efficiency of the new method of production. It may even result in the bidding up of prices of other goods and thereby introduce other distortions of the

THE WAY the business man, under a regime of mass production, will approach the matter of prices is well illustrated by Mr. Ford's policy, which he explains as follows:

My policy is to reduce the price, extend the operations, and improve the article. You will notice that the reduction of price comes first. I have never considered any costs as fixed. Therefore I first reduce the price to a point where I believe more sales will result. Then we go ahead and try to make the price. I do not bother about the costs. The new price forces the costs down. The more usual way is, I believe, to take the costs and then determine the price, and although that method may be scientific in the narrow sense, it is not scientific in the broad sense, because what earthly use is it to know the cost if it tells you that you cannot manufacture at a price at which the article can be sold? But more to the point is the fact that, although one may calculate what a cost is, and of course all of our costs are carefully calculated, no one knows what a cost ought to be. One of the ways of discovering what a cost ought to be is to name a price so low as to force everybody in the plant to the highest point of efficiency. The low price makes everybody dig for profits. I can make more discoveries concerning manufacturing and selling under this forced method than by any method of leisurely investigation.

Of course, this is nothing new under the sun. Most business men are doing this every day—that is, lowering prices as a bait to customers. The fact that lower prices mean more customers is not a discovery of yesterday. But the point I want to make is that heretofore we business men have used this principle mainly as a

Continued on page 132

price structure away from a sound cost-price relation.

To look to reduction of consumer prices as the means of making the attainment of technological gains most fully possible simply means securing under the complex production and price administration characteristic of corporate industrialism adjustments of the price system as good as or better than those that came automatically under the simple business life of individual competition among self-employed producers. It is our contention that unless private industrialized enterprise expresses itself freely by accepting and indeed vigorously stimulating cost-reducing, volume-enlarging, and quality-improving techniques, and unless it passes these benefits on into the consumptive channel promptly and fully, it is not achieving results comparable even to those accomplished by the simple system of *laissez-faire* individual enterprise from which it sprang. At its best, corporate administration of prices effects this adjustment more far-sightedly, neatly, and consistently than naïve supply-and-demand reactions of simple men can. At its worst, it ties the price system up stupidly and mischievously.[9]

Our previous volume, *Industrial Price Policies and Economic Progress*, undertook to analyze the constructive principle of price reduction as practiced by certain "pace-makers" in the industrial world. At the end of that volume "a challenge to free enterprise" was stated

[9] Mills in his *Prices in Recession and Recovery* (pp. 458-59) lays stress on the importance of the number of "points of diffusion, centers from which the effects of changes in industrial productivity [are] diffused throughout the price and distributive system. In a frictionless, fluid economy these effects would be as quickly transmitted from a few points of diffusion as from many, and there would be prompt and immediate adaptation to them. But when frictions are present the number of points for the dissemination of the effects of changes in productivity becomes of prime importance. With many points of diffusion the influence of particular frictions would be lessened, and prompt utilization of released energies, human and other, would be expected. With few points of

method of disposing of goods that have grown obsolete on our shelves or in our warehouses, or as a means of reducing our inventory when we have become overstocked as a result of unscientific buying, or to meet competition, or for other similar reasons. The thing that needs to be said, repeated, and emphasized is that we are entering a period of stress and strain in which we shall, if we want to survive and succeed, be obliged to adopt this principle as a constant rather than an intermittent principle of our business policy. If it were possible to make only one point in this book, I should throw everything else to the winds and devote every page of this volume to a discussion of the contention that the first lien on profits should be reduction of prices. . . . The reduction of prices underlies the social progress of the future . . . the freedom of the masses is dependent upon it. Mass production, into which we shall be increasingly driven by business necessity, will force us to the adoption of this principle.

Edward A. Filene, *The Way Out*, pp. 80-82.

We must remember that mass production is *production for the masses*. It is production motivated by the desire to sell the greatest possible quantities by giving the greatest possible values at the lowest possible cost to the greatest number of people. It is so motivated, however, not because of any sudden outburst of altruism, but because the great stream of human selfishness compels that line of action. Since mass production must have the widest possible market, this complete abandonment to service is imperative.

Filene, *Successful Living in this Machine Age*, p. 11.

as the need to "generalize" over the whole system these constructive practices of the leaders in price-making and related productive management.[10]

There is by no means universal confidence that any such generalization is practically possible. The remainder of the book is devoted to considering this possibility from various angles. Before proceeding to such a concrete problem, however, a word must be said on the relation of our interpretation of free enterprise to the principle of democracy, of which it is a particular expression.

DEMOCRACY AS AN ECONOMIC PRINCIPLE

In our introductory chapter, it was stated that democracy was assumed as one of our objectives not merely on historical or sentimental grounds and not merely as relating to the form of our political state. Beyond this, we asserted a belief that the basic principle of democratic organization of human life carries over into the economic field and there affords a guide to sound structure and efficient operation. It was explained that such a

---

diffusion (as when restricted groups secure the first advantages of higher productivity) only a remote connection would exist between the new purchasing power accruing to particular economic groups and the energy released by advancing productivity, and the obstacles to prompt utilization of these energies would be many. The frictions and impediments characteristic of a modern economy would impede the rapid spread of purchasing power shifted from its original channels."

With the point that prompt and full "utilization of the energies . . . released by advancing productivity" is impeded "when restricted groups secure the first advantages of higher productivity," the writer is in full accord. But there seems an implication that there is no way of approximating the results that would be attained in a frictionless, fluid economy so long as we have the "frictions and impediments characteristic of a money economy." The writer's general argument is to the effect that strategic centers of control *may* be used to accelerate rather than retard diffusion and that as the number of centers of control in a money economy is reduced, it becomes increasingly important that these controls be used for purposes of acceleration rather than retardation.

[10] This price philosophy is epitomized by a well-known business leader in the quotation on pp. 130 and 132.

line of analysis would be further developed at appropriate places throughout this book. By implication rather than directly, that procedure was carried out in the chapter on free enterprise, the discussion of competition, and the comparative interpretation of concepts of profits. We have now arrived at a point where these several threads should be woven into a more specific and comprehensive statement of the philosophy of economic democracy.[11]

It is doubtful whether Americans in general subscribe to any precise or thoroughgoing doctrine of democracy in the economic field, however loud might be their protestations of fealty to political democracy when it is threatened by the vague menace of foreign "isms." Let us begin therefore by a simple definition of our term. Lincoln's superb characterization, "government of the people, by the people, for the people," is focused primarily on the political aspect of democracy. To get a readier economic orientation but still fully within the spirit of Lincoln's phrase, we may define democracy as *organization of a producing society for self-direction through competitively selected specialists, in the common long-run interest of all as consumers.*[12]

To see how such a system must operate in the economic field, two lines of approach are to be traced. The first considers the meaning of democracy as a guide to the organization of production. The second examines democracy as a principle of consumption.

Economic science seeks efficient and provident use of the nation's productive resources. Chief among these is the labor of its people, labor of hand and brain, scientific

[11] The writer has developed these general ideas at greater length in an article, "Democracy as a Principle of Business." See App. B.

[12] It might be stated as "economic organization of the people, by the people, for the people." The machinery of competitive selection assumed in the definition in the text is that of individual and group bargaining.

insight, administrative enterprise, artistic genius. Economic efficiency would dictate that persons should not be relegated to idleness regardless of their having useful and sometimes scarce labor capacities, or to positions of opportunity and control simply because of birth, wealth, or social position. These canons of productive efficiency coincide with the basic principle of democracy that all shall have opportunity according to their capacity. This would not mean that rewards would be equal, but it would mean that they would be arrived at by the democratic process of free bargaining in the market.

This democracy of labor placement and reward has been realized not perfectly but in substantial measure in the United States. It has brought a high degree of productive efficiency in the qualitative sense. But national economic efficiency in the quantitative sense demands constant provision of opportunity for everybody to work according to his talents, training, and industry. Free enterprise in any broad and literal economic interpretation (see Chapter II) means that each individual must be able to work as steadily as he himself desires, not merely that those who work shall be as suitably placed as is possible under the best techniques of personnel management and union practices. The whole idea of "economic democracy" is negatived by widespread and persistently recurring unemployment.

Since the possibility of anything like general self-employment has long since disappeared from our society, responsibility for providing a full measure of work opportunity devolves upon the executives who must decide issues of both scale and direction of business operations. By virtue of their administrative positions, they accept responsibility for the efficient organization of the country's labor force. They must produce a generally acceptable result if private enterprise, whose directive officers they are, is to be permitted to remain in control of the field of business. If this does not prove possible within the limits of their skill and the conditions imposed by union wage policy, or if they do not find ways of innovating new practices or compromises between capitalist policy and labor policy under which it will be possible, it will not be long—in a democracy—before resort will be had to government as a utilizing agency. First, government will be asked to organize in productive work the residue of labor not utilized by private enterprise. Ultimately this might spread until we should find the whole labor force organized in public enterprise.

Turning from the labor to the capital aspect of the problem of efficient organization for economic production, we find the democratic principle equally applicable. The proposition as to capital use is in fact essentially a corollary to that of labor use, since neither can be made productive without the other. If productive property is withheld from labor's use as a means of exacting a predetermined rate of return to certain individuals or to a propertied class, there is reduction in the quantitative efficiency or total productivity of the economy. Economic administration as an aristocracy of wealth conduces to incomplete utilization of the nation's human and material resources. Democracy of economic effort or resource use promotes maximum national efficiency. (See Chapter XI.)

A second approach to democracy as an economic principle may be made from the standpoint of consumptive efficiency rather than productive organization. Under modern industrial conditions, it is the workers' cash earnings that primarily determine market demand and hence production schedules. The amount of employment offered, at existing rates of pay, dictates the general pattern of expenditures for food, clothing, and shelter, constructive outlays for school days of children and the "rainy day" of the aged, and whatever frivolous outlays personal taste may urge or individual frugality permit. Whether the wage earner's spending practices take the form of a meticulously planned "consumer budget" or the most whimsical scattering of purchasing power, the family's standard of living is the end product after wage rates, duration of employment, and consumer prices have largely been set by others. And these in turn are laid down without specific reference to the levels of consumption necessary to maintain the working population in physical efficiency and high morale, and without measuring this efficiency standard over against the potential productive capacity of that same population.

In this practice, our modern industrial and commercial system differs notably from the economic functioning of simpler societies. The ancient tribe or clan, the feudal unit of medieval times, and even the self-sufficing family group of pioneer individual enterprise integrated the consumption and production program into a single coordinated whole. And in this integration it is the consumer's budget rather than a speculative scheme of market promotion that takes the lead in both planning and execution. Such economic welfare as the group can achieve for itself within the limits of its resources, technique, and willingness to work embraces a scheme of group responsibility for the consumption of all its members.

There are, of course, disparities between the consumption of feudal lord and cotter or even among members of the patriarchal family. But there is also an acceptance of responsibility for the maintenance of productive efficiency throughout the group which foreshadows the principles of economic democracy. The young, the sick, and the weak do not have their allotment of subsistence cut down to the limit of their immediate productivity but are maintained on such a standard of subsistence as is calculated to develop youthful powers to the full when maturity shall be attained, to conserve the capacities of the weak, and to restore the working power of the sick or injured. On its most cold-blooded basis, consumption is a means to the end of efficient production—like fertilizing the ground or stoking the engine.

In the early stages of its development, modern industrialism was thoughtless and wasteful in its use and cultivation of human resources—just as it was in its exploitation of natural resources. In more recent years it has, partly through its own insight and partly through outside compulsion, accepted much higher standards of responsibility for the great block of the population attached to organized private enterprise only through a wage contract. Such changes have embraced employers' liability, old-age pensions, and many forms of company welfare work. The general effect of these developments has been to underwrite certain standards of physical, and to some extent intellectual, well-being through the use of company revenues beyond those disbursed in the pay roll. However laudable the purpose and however beneficial the effects of thus approaching economic efficiency from the side of consumption, such attacks attain that goal only at specific spots without assuring all-round or democratic efficiency in terms of consumption standards.

Political democracy has gone a long way farther toward incorporating this principle of economic efficiency through assured consumption into our scheme of modern economic life. Free public education; subsidization of medical, surgical, and dental care for adults as well as children; and extensive provision of parks, playgrounds, and various types of entertainment underwrite a large amount of productive consumption. Primarily, it is the consumption of persons of low purchasing power, but a substantial part of it goes to the comparatively well-to-do. In recent years, there has been much more resort to this consumption approach through the democratic organization of economic life by underwriting minimum standards of nutrition and by widening considerably the responsibility that the public has long exercised with reference to the aged and infirm.

It is not our purpose to discuss these programs in detail here or their possible future trend. Our purpose at the moment is to call attention to those unsatisfied wants that are capable of making market demand for all the goods and services our labor force is capable of producing and thereby employing all present plant capacity —and doubtless much beside.[13] The real question is how much of this consumptive need (in the sense of national efficiency) private enterprise will succeed in converting into commercial demand in the market. Such a result calls for price policies designed to keep prices at the lowest practicable level through capacity operations, the reduction of distributive cost through price appeal rather than high pressure salesmanship (Chapter VIII), and the designing of goods to embody the maximum of useful service in the plain and simple form that puts them within reach of the largest possible proportion of the population. The price structure must be fitted to the income structure in order to facilitate the maximum of productive activity. Business in the aristocratic tradition of ever more

[13] Statistical evidence of this situation was presented in Edwin G. Nourse and Associates, *America's Capacity to Produce* (1934) and Maurice Leven, Harold G. Moulton, and Clark Warburton, *America's Capacity to Consume* (1934), and in other similar studies.

elegant service for the upper classes has limited prospects of growth with the advance of science and skill.[14] Addressed to the democratic goal of full and efficient utilization of resources to the maximum satisfaction of the wants of the masses, it has an enormous area of development before these groups would prefer more leisure (or unemployment) to more goods and services.

CONCLUSION

Let us turn now to bring the discussion of this chapter to a focus on the specific questions which were posed in the introductory section.

Is there inconsistency amongst the fundamental principles involved in a system of private ownership of capital, with individual enterprise free to exercise itself in the pursuit of profit but also bearing the losses both of bad judgment and of bad luck? To this question, we would answer "no." Not only is there no inherent inconsistency in these principles but they make an institutional design of such structural strength and functional efficiency as to be worthy of the respect which it has won as the American way of economic life. When, however, we turn to the question of whether the practice of these principles has been carried out in such a way as to preserve their internal harmonies or to fulfill the requirements which would have to be met to assure truly successful operation of a system so designed, the answer is quite different.

As to the favorable side of the story, the factual record and the statistics of achievement in the United

[14] In many quarters one finds that the hope of both businessmen and economists for recovery from the depression or for economic prosperity after the war is centered on efforts aimed at more goods for the well-to-do and more elaborate goods for this class rather than on ways to organize the labor of the less favorably circumstanced part of the population for the satisfaction of plain but wholesome types of consumption.

States from 1776 to 1929 show an epoch of economic progress which must command admiration. It is clear that a substantial fraction of this prosperity was due to the fact that we were appropriating the long-stored riches of a virgin continent and gaining momentum in scientific methods. But it seems evident also that our practice of private capitalism proved reasonably well suited to the rapid conversion of these natural riches, in combination with our own labor, into a rapidly advancing flow of well-being for our people. There is little to suggest that these institutions habitually restricted prosperity or seriously retarded progress.

But real question has now arisen as to whether the continuation of these practices would assure the maintenance of comparable progress in the future. Modification might be called for because of the fact that surrounding conditions within which the system has to function have changed in significant ways. Or faulty practices of the past or errors of adjustment which did not reveal themselves in the exuberant period of youthful national growth may have been gathering cumulative power to hamper progress so that their revision must be faced in the years of our more mature national life. The tenor of our discussion in the preceding chapters has run distinctly to the conclusion that changes are called for.

We have noted how the progress of industrialization has inevitably resulted in the centralization of private business enterprises in the hands of corporate institutions, many of them very large. The executives of these corporate enterprises constitute a small class of economic administrative agents who accept—indeed seek—the responsibility of directing the private enterprise system. They must, of course, administer this system within the conditioning factors set by economic resources, economic

THE financial and managerial components of our Free Enterprise System must prove, by deeds as well as by words, their full comprehension of their social responsibilities—their deep sense of public service—and their unmatched capacity to positively plan—to put into effect—and, if you will, to police by self-imposed rules, a constitution for industrial and commercial progress acceptable to the majority of our people—people whose economic security and destiny are vitally affected by the decisions of these controlling components of the system. And in the circumstances surrounding us today, who will doubt that this action must be prompt and positive, and of a character which will demonstrate, beyond the chance of successful challenge, that the public-spirited people administering private enterprise inherently and actually excel the people comprising political organizations—no matter how sincere the intentions of the latter may be—as instrumentalities for insuring an ever-increasing measure of economic freedom and security for all of the people—save the indolent—all of the time?

> Charles E. Wilson, Pres. Gen'l Electric Co., address American Institute of Electrical Engineers, January 1941

IF [the Free Enterprise System] fails to meet that challenge squarely and successfully, we shall move toward an era of state capitalism or state socialism—call it what you will—an America far different from the one we have known. . . . The Free Enterprise System must either deliver the goods or be pushed aside . . . for government agencies which will come into being.

> Charles E. Wilson, *The American Magazine*, November 1941

laws, and economic institutions, particularly commercial and financial legislation, labor unions, and labor laws. But even within these limits they have a latitude of managerial discretion which permits them to affect the character of our economy to an important degree.

They may interpret free enterprise in the aristocratic sense of maximum freedom for the strong, clever, or ruthless rather than the democratic sense of maximum assurance that each individual will have opportunity to express his personal enterprise as willingness to work according to his talents, however small. They may administer it in the aristocratic sense of progressive accumulation of ownership control in the hands of a functional group which tends to divert subsequent gains largely to itself. Modern industrialism builds up a class of professional managers—by no means identical with the ownership group—who may seek tenure of office by following unreservedly the dictates of the proprietary group. Or they may adopt policies designed to accelerate activity and maximize efficiency of the whole population. To do so implies that their own remuneration shall be established in an open supply-and-demand market for managerial talent. It implies that capital shall find its return at the level which will just maintain plant in the volume which will be fully utilized and in the quality which will keep step with advancing technological knowledge. Similarly, property values must find their level in conformity with the rate of capitalization and the earnings that result from full-scale use of labor.

In the light of these alternatives, we turn to our second question: Are there discernible possibilities of modification in practice that would assure the efficiency of the system of private profit-seeking capitalism? Our answer is "yes," and we believe the key to such modification is to be found in the adjustment of our complex system of price relations so as to promote rather than retard maximum activity of productive resources and of the satisfaction of consumptive wants, as freely expressed in the market, up to the limit set by such use, both full and efficient. Obviously the enlarged product of full employment is capable (even after improving the subsistence of the working force) of maintaining the store of capital goods and remunerating owners better in the long run than would partial employment.

It is our belief that private enterprise thus organized and operated affords the most efficient scheme for carrying on the economic life of a free people. Opening the gates of production and exchange to assure product and letting valuation adjust itself freely to such activity would promote successful private capitalism. Withholding productive effort as a means of protecting predetermined valuations shrinks the total national dividend from which all must draw their shares, and thus in the end defeats the whole system.[15]

The modifications in practices of private capitalism needed to attain, restore, or maintain successful operations have, of necessity, only been sketched in terms of broad principles or lines of attack. In Part II we shall return to examine several types of practical problems that inevitably arise in any attempt to carry such principles into current practice.

[15] The quotations on p. 142 show how fully one leading industrialist accepts the responsibility of businessmen to demonstrate the economic capacities of capitalistic private enterprise and his apprehension lest the system be shortly superseded if it does not give such a demonstration in convincing terms. Appended to the article from which the second quotation was drawn were cordial endorsements by five prominent business executives and the president of the A. F. of L.

PART II

PROBLEMS

INTRODUCTION

In several preceding chapters we have reviewed some historic changes and some typical divergences in lay and professional ideas of free enterprise, competition, and the profit motive. These were taken as major aspects or ingredients of "the American way" of economic life. In Chapter V the attempt was made to choose mutually harmonious strands from this exposition and weave them into a pattern of individual-and-group enterprise, co-operatively competing in the attainment of technical and organizational efficiency in such ways that total product would be maximized over the years. It was our conclusion that maximum productivity could be attained and maintained most surely if the gains of economic progress inure democratically to the people as consumers.[1] This end is to be effected by consistently following a policy of price making through which gains in productive efficiency are passed on to consumers. Thus distributed, they do most to stimulate and direct the efforts of the current generation and most to discover and develop the productive powers of the rising generation.

In embarking on the discussion of particular problems involved in the general approach to price making thus outlined, it seems desirable to adopt a simple phrase

[1] The chief corollary to this proposition is that the price paid for the use of capital and for the several classes and varieties of personal effort be adjusted as continuously as possible by the verdict of an open competitive market or (if administered) be adjusted in conformity with policies basically identical with those governing the sound pricing of goods. The relation of this corollary to the major proposition will be noted further in Chaps. 9 and 11.

with which to label this kind of price making for handy reference. It must be reasonably expressive and not too open to misinterpretation. For that purpose the phrase "low-price policies" has seemed most suitable.

It is to be hoped that consistent use of this phrase may help to dispel some of the confusion and misapprehension that constantly crept into discussions of our previous study, *Industrial Price Policies and Economic Progress*. In spite of specific warning,[2] some people seemed to identify the idea of a general low-price policy with the already muddy concept of price "flexibility," while others saw it only as more or less episodic acts of "price cutting."

"Low-price policy" is to be differentiated from that interpretation of price flexibility which places emphasis on experimental feeling out of the demand schedule in times of business depression and lowering prices to a point where it is supposed that they will stimulate recovery. It is not a part of our present investigation to consider the shortcomings or limitations of that theory in the situations to which it is applied by so many students.[3] It is sufficient to remind the reader that the focus of our analysis is not that of cycle phenomena or recovery measures but of continuous types of economic

[2] Edwin G. Nourse and Horace B. Drury, *Industrial Price Policies and Economic Progress* (1938), p. 9.

[3] See Gardiner C. Means, *Industrial Prices and Their Relative Inflexibility*, S. Doc. 13 (1935); Don D. Humphrey, "The Nature and Meaning of Rigid Prices, 1890-1933," *Journal of Political Economy*, Vol. 45 (1937), and "Price Reduction as a Stimulus to Sales of Durable Consumers' Goods," *Journal of the American Statistical Association*, Vol. 34 (1939); Jules Backman, "Price Inflexibility and Changes in Production," *American Economic Review*, Vol. 29 (1939); "The Causes of Price Inflexibility," *Quarterly Journal of Economics*, Vol. 54 (1940); "Price Flexibility and Inflexibility," *Contemporary Law Pamphlets*, Series 4, No. 4; Rufus Tucker, "Reasons for Price Rigidity," *American Economic Review*, Vol. 28 (1938); Edward S. Mason, "Price Inflexibility," *The Review of Economic Statistics*, Vol. 20 (1938).

adjustment designed to maintain the operations of a modern private enterprise system on a prevailingly high level of efficiency and hence prosperity. This means the kind of adjustment that makes for stability of full-volume operations rather than instability.[4] Such adjustment provides a regimen of general health, not medicine for a specific disease.

Our argument is to be distinguished also from the view that the "frequency and amplitude" of price fluctuations may be taken as a criterion of the economic soundness of a pricing program. Incessant price changes, mostly small, constitute the mechanism by which market prices are supposed to respond sensitively to every factor of change which comes into a competitive market of small sellers and buyers. Statistical tests of flexibility designed for studying the "behavior" of prices in such markets may be employed to the degree to which "administered" prices show a different pattern. But they are not significant or trustworthy indexes of the soundness of a price structure in the field of large industrial and commercial organization with which we are concerned. Within this field, sound tactical considerations may dictate the use of more or of less frequent, of larger or of smaller revisions in quotations and of more or less rigid adherence to these quotations in one or another situation. We join with those who believe that, in the matter of flexibility, differences in the character of the commodity and differences in market structure and commercial procedures are so influential that attempts to base appraisals of policy on statistical measurement of amplitude and frequency of price changes are more hazardous than enlightening.

[4] In a later chapter on "The Timing of Price Changes," the relation of price policy to cyclical forces will be discussed.

The nature of the manufacturing process for automobiles, prevailing methods of sale and financing, and current beliefs as to consumer psychology dictate a flat price for any given type of car over the whole period between model changes.[5] Such power as automobile manufacturers have to bring price and productive operations into working alignment is used by all of them in substantially the same way. They stabilize prices over a suitable operative period and seek to have prices that they pay for material, labor, and other cost goods stabilized for the same or even longer periods.

In another typical industrial situation we find the price-making executive purposely departing even farther from the flexibility by which prices would be made to conform at all stages to the cost situations under which he is operating. This would be the case of a manufacturer of a variety of electrical or chemical products, who from time to time introduces a new article designed to cater to a new demand or which provides a new way of satisfying an old want. Great expense must be incurred before the first units of the product can be put on the market. The producer does not attempt to sell his first year's output at a unit price which will pay current operating costs, including normal profit, and amortize 15 or 20 or some other per cent of developmental and plant outlays. He is likely instead to offer the product at a price which he expects to maintain over a period of some years and which will attract an initial volume of sales necessary for efficient plant operation and permit the cultivation of a broad field of consumer demand. He may not expect that it will enable him to reach the

---

[5] Adjustment to local conditions, changed general situation within the year, or the business policy of particular distributors is effected by the dealer through manipulation of trade-in values for used cars.

"break-even" point for several years or return satisfactory net profits for an even longer time.

When the day arrives in which expanding volume or improved processes lower the unit costs, and profits have reached a point where a further reduction in price suggests itself, this reduction, instead of being small and cautious, may be a daring slash designed to make a dramatic appeal to new buyers or to secure more liberal consumption by all buyers. Such a reduction may extinguish profits for a period or even entail losses which, it is calculated, will in due time be replaced by profits as the full response of the market to this price appeal is developed and as further economies in production and distribution materialize.

This would be a highly inflexible method of pricing, with prices conceivably changed only once or twice in a period of 5 to 10 years. Prices would be "maintained" —for considerable periods below cost, and at other periods quite substantially above cost. But such a procedure of inflexible pricing would be in full conformity with our criteria of a low-price policy *if* initial prices gave consumers an anticipatory gain from the technological progress being innovated and *if* subsequent price reductions kept in step with market expansion and further technological and organizational improvements.

A settled low-price policy is to be distinguished also from "price cutting" or "cut-price sales," daily or weekly "loss leaders," and similar tactical devices. Price reduction as a means either of attaining capacity operation or such change in method as will lower unit costs is a step designed to be permanent, and taken voluntarily in pursuance of a long-range strategy of economic development. "Price cutting" is often a temporary measure designed to liquidate a perishable stock or to embarrass

or outmaneuver a business rival. It is frequently the
weapon of a price war, and it is expected that "cuts"
will be "restored" as soon as the war (really a battle or
skirmish) is over. Aside from these difficulties, price
cutting is an inadequate term for our use because often
a policy of passing on to consumers the benefits of technological progress may take the form of maintaining a
conventional price while quality is improved or at a
time when prices in general are rising. Or it may mean
a price increase less than proportionate to changes in
quality or general price level.[6]

The phrase "low-price policy" is intended to refer to
the position of a given price in relation to others, not
its short-run variations. It contrasts sharply with the
high-price or "charge-all-the-traffic-will-bear" policy
which is traditionally associated with ideas of monopoly
and only in less degree with any situation in which
prices are "administered" in "imperfectly competitive"
markets. We seek to show by economic analysis that
in fact the traffic will not in the long run bear the load
thus thrown upon it. To use such power to maximize
unit profit and short-run gains prevents maximum utilization of resources, that is, maintained and widespread
prosperity. But the same power may, under another
type of policy, be used to promote full and efficient
utilization of human and natural resources. We could
not, however, use the term "anti-price-maintenance
policy" because the term "price maintenance" implies
keeping prices unchanged for a standardized product,
whereas the essence of low-price policy is frequently
the changing of product or the services which go with

[6] Contrariwise, our criteria of functionally correct pricing would not
be met by merely nominal downward revision in price when the change
in these collateral factors was substantial.

its distribution, while money price remains unchanged.[7]

The price of a given commodity is "low" or "high," in any significant economic sense, only in relation to other parts of the price system. Dollar prices have to be interpreted in terms of the general price level. They have to be interpreted also in terms of total costs. These, in turn, thanks to changes in technique, do not necessarily move in step with unit costs of materials and labor. Hence, there is no inherent contradiction in the idea of lower prices for product at the same time that wages are maintained or even advanced. Similarly, higher taxes are not necessarily a barrier to further lowering of prices; nor would the abolition of taxes be necessary to the complete consummation of low-price policies.

No single phrase can express the full range of characteristics of the kind of price policy necessary to the efficient functioning of a system of capitalistic private enterprise. "Low-price policy" has a functional meaning that has to be discovered in the practical situations to which actual prices are to be fitted.[8] It should not be interpreted to mean—as some suppose—that producers and sellers should start a universal, indiscriminate, and more or less uniform slashing or paring of prices. The lowering of prices as a means of disseminating the gains of technological and organizational progress can take place only when and in proportion as such gains are in fact brought about.

But, besides being alert to the perception, measure-

[7] See Nourse and Drury, *Industrial Price Policies and Economic Progress*, Chap. 3.

[8] For reasons such as these, statistical attempts to determine whether a price is "low" are likely to prove disappointing if not misleading. But a man on the ground can readily tell in what direction an airplane is traveling even when he cannot measure its altitude or speed. The quality of price policies may be clearly perceived even when strict quantification is impossible.

ment, and proper administration of current efficiency gains and besides stimulating their future extension, it is necessary that we should also review past developments and in some cases rectify them. If suitable price adjustments have not been made in the past as new elements of efficiency were introduced, the maladjustment persists as a demand—and opportunity—for subsequent readjustment. In such cases, however, the problem of what will constitute the economically sound adjustment has been complicated by compensations already introduced in the form of wage or salary absorptions or property valuations, some good, some bad, but all of them difficult to change.

With "low-price policy," then, as a shorthand abbreviation for a comprehensive economic philosophy, we shall proceed in the next six chapters to explore certain major problems in its practical application. *Industrial Price Policies and Economic Progress* examined some of the not inconsiderable number of cases in which business executives had formulated and applied low-price policies. It pointed to the benefit which would follow if such practices were generalized over the whole system. From some quarters the reply has come that such generalization is impossible. We propose now to consider certain problems which would be confronted in the attempt to disseminate low-price practices.

CHAPTER VI

AREAS OF APPLICABILITY OF LOW-PRICE POLICIES

By definition, a policy is not something which expresses itself; it has to be formulated and then applied in actual situations. And the attempt to put a policy into practice brings us up against a variety of productive and market situations. In some of them a low-price policy almost suggests itself and is relatively easy to carry into effect. In others, such a policy may be conceived only by those who are most studious or possessed of deepest insight. And, even when its intrinsic merit is perceived, it may in those situations still remain difficult of practical attainment.

The several areas of the economy, likewise, vary widely as to their strategic importance for the initiation and prosecution of price policies. Some are clearly marked for a leadership role; others can do little more than go with the procession. We shall therefore undertake in this chapter to compare the characteristics and the strategic importance of several areas of possible applicability of low-price policy.[1]

PRICE POLICY FOR CONSUMERS' GOODS

Along that frontier of the productive process where sellers of finished goods directly meet the ultimate con-

[1] The analysis presented in this chapter may well be compared with and supplemented by two documents in the TNEC series: Clair Wilcox, *Competition and Monopoly in American Industry* (Monograph No. 21); and Theodore J. Kreps, *Measurement of the Social Performance of Business* (Monograph No. 7).

sumer, we find one of the areas where low-price policies are most likely to flourish. This is a point at which the favorable results that price lowering may have on expansion of the business are promptly and clearly evident. Here, too, pressure to have prices lowered is often both intense and articulate. The great mass of consumers are poor by comparison with the abundance of their longings. The struggle to balance the budget of their wants makes them perennially "price conscious." To be sure, the ancient efforts of the individual buyer to "hammer down" prices through haggling at the store counter or in the market place have largely disappeared with the change in store methods and public manners. But even today the buyer of food and clothing and other personal items has many face-to-face opportunities to say to the merchant or the producer's representative, "Your price is too high; I'll go elsewhere," or perhaps, "I'll go without."

But the seller at retail may pursue a course of price lowering as a matter of voluntary policy, not as a mere yielding to duress. It is enlightening to think of the retail merchant as being in fact the purchasing agent for the housewife and for every other individual who seeks to command as many satisfactions as he can from his all-too-meager pay envelope or salary check. The merchant's professional attainment is to be measured by his ability to find cheaper sources of supply or to devise more economical means of assembling and distribution. A lively realization of this fact has animated the more aggressive efforts of recent years to reorganize retail trade under the leadership of department stores, mail order houses, chain stores, and federated independents. The consumers' co-operative movement is simply an attempt to build up a retail and wholesale system (and perhaps eventually fabricating and even extractive concerns) that will operate more single-mindedly or obediently in the consumer's service.[2]

Where distributors of finished goods grasp this concept of themselves as purchasing agents for the great body of consumers, they have exerted a twofold influence in the direction of lower prices. First, they have sought to eliminate or reduce wastes and inefficiencies (either physical or commercial) in the process of assembling, handling, and passing on goods to the consumer. Second and more important, they have become in a sense professional representatives of the consumer, ranging farther than he possibly could in search of the most economical sources of supply, better equipped than he to discriminate differences in quality in relation to price and the uses to which an article is to be put, and aggressive in using the collective bargaining power of a large clientele to induce price concessions from the producer or to stir him to improvements in manufacturing methods or alterations in design which will make possible larger consumer satisfaction with less outlay.

It may be objected that the pressure for lower prices exerted by the consumer or by his "purchasing agent" is a blind, unreasoning force which does not hesitate to destroy the producer to make a consumers' holiday. It is of course true that buyers always want lower prices, whether they have any reason to believe that rising efficiency or otherwise lowered costs conduce to such a reduction or not. At times these demands become

---

[2] The problem the consumer co-operatives have to face is whether they can command capital and managerial talent necessary for efficiency equal to or greater than that of the agencies already functioning in this field. Most important is the question of allocation of directive control and enforcement of responsibility. And the narrower the existing distributors' margin, the less will be the appeal of such ventures.

articulate, even violent, in the form of a "buyers' strike," particularly during a depression. Such resistance may be justified; or it may be wholly unreasonable. Organized in the more orderly form of a consumers' co-operative, a chain or mail-order distributing system, or a large-scale processor or fabricator seeking lower prices from underlying producer concerns, the process tends to more rational and economically beneficial manifestations.

The continued existence and prosperity for these integrated marketing agencies depend on a widening of the consumer market as well as upon consumer preferences for them as sources of supply.[3] Such expansion of outlets is also a fundamental concern of the producers from whom they buy. Hence, there is essential community of interest. Looked at from this point of view, it is to the advantage of the distributor or manufacturer to keep the supplier in business and in a high state of efficiency.[4] The executives of these larger distributors, if they consider intelligently the way in which their power shall be used in their own long-run interest and that of their clients, must formulate a buying policy which will balance the claims of consumers with those of producers so as to maintain a long-time flow of supplies of desired quality at efficiency prices.[5]

[3] "Almost invariably [the mass distributor] has sought to obtain his profit by selling in greater volume at a lower price. By integrating operations, purchasing in quantity, eliminating costly services, increasing managerial efficiency, cutting operating expenses, and reducing profit margins, he has decreased his prices and increased his sales. His vigorous competition has forced the independent merchant to serve the consumer more efficiently. In the opinion of the Committee on Distribution of the Twentieth Century Fund, it 'has brought widespread improvement of methods and lowering of costs and prices throughout retailing.'" Wilcox, TNEC Monograph No. 21, p. 57.

[4] Compare p. 426 n.

[5] An extremely aggressive attempt to promote low-price distribution is to be found in the "farmer-consumer campaigns" which chain stores have

Loud plaints have been raised against the "bludgeon" of the large-scale buyer who seeks aggressively to get lower prices in his supply market. No doubt the power is sometimes abused,[6] and sometimes used to the unnecessary enrichment of the mass buyer rather than the benefit of his client, the consumer. But likewise this pressure from highly organized and expertly manned

inaugurated as a means of getting full utilization of crops of which there is a local or seasonal glut. Such undertakings have included a national California canned peach sale, "abundant-production" dried fruit sale, springtime egg festival, national "economy" pork sale, "quality crop" canned pea sale, Idaho potato and onion week, and many others. Systematic development of the program began with a joint conference of chain-store executives and agricultural leaders in May 1936. Mr. C. C. Teague, chairman of the National Council of Farm Cooperatives, called the meeting "an economic landmark," and John A. Logan, president of the National Association of Food Chains, later observed that accomplishments of the first five years "suggest to imaginative leaders among producers, distributors, and consumers the great potentialities of carrying the program forward on an even broader front: of developing facts and using them for more efficiency; of conference and the solution of marketing problems—large and small, national and local—on a basis of mutual benefits." Describing the program as "based on the solid foundation of the profit motive," he said: "The question has often been asked 'why are food chains interested in agriculture?' The answer is evident. The reasons may be termed enlightened self-interest and good business practice. . . . Food chains recognize that the nation cannot well prosper without a prosperous agriculture. Agricultural income bears a direct relationship to national income and, as the purchasing power of the nation increases, business of food chain stores—as well as other business enterprise—improves." (National Association of Food Chains, *An Economic Landmark Recorded, A 5-Year Record of Organized Cooperation between Agricultural Producers and Chain Food Stores,* September 1941, p. 3.)

[6] What constitutes good and what becomes bad economic practice is still a matter of dispute even among the experts. Thus, for example, the Federal Trade Commission thought it necessary to abate the zeal of a mail order house in securing low prices for its customers and/or profits for itself. Here the issues depended (aside from the secret character of certain rebate agreements) on whether the differential paid for tires bearing the manufacturer's trade-mark and distributed by independent tire stores and those of private brands of substantially identical quality was harmfully discriminatory or was based on legitimate differences in costs of alternative methods of distribution. This, of course, involves

mass fabricators and distributors has in recent decades brought a striking amount of technological and organizational progress into our economy. It has pressed hard on unprogressive producers of raw and manufactured materials and on superfluous middlemen, notably brokers and jobbers. The ability of the newer schemes of merchandising to establish themselves as innovators in an ancient field has, of course, been based on price appeal (often with some curtailment of service) and has also been predicated upon their achieving expansion in volume through this pricing scheme sufficient to give them advantages of large-scale operating efficiency and bargaining power. Hence the gains achieved must in relatively large proportion be passed on to the consumer. In many cases it is not too much to say that only as benefit goes largely to him can they be achieved at all.

We have been speaking primarily in terms of the merchandising agency. But the manufacturer of final consumer goods is about as likely as is the merchant to be aware of the sensitiveness of demand for such goods. The situations of the two groups are, however, not strictly identical. A given amount of change in price at the factory in many cases has its influence weakened before it reaches the consumer. Thus, for example, a reduction of 10 per cent of the factory price, which might perhaps be 25 per cent of the fabricator's charge (price less raw materials), even if transferred intact to the consumer as a price reduction, would appear there

---

the collateral issue whether the consumer is adequately protected in his discrimination of quality. It involves also the question of possible superiority of the service rendered by the specialized tire store and the willingness of consumers to pay for this added service if the facts are known. See Federal Trade Commission Docket 2116, and compare Lloyd Reynolds, "Competition in the Rubber Tire Industry," *American Economic Review*, Vol. 28 (1938), p. 459.

only as a lesser proportionate reduction (say 4 to 6 per cent), depending on the size of transportation costs and distributive margins. The smaller the proportion of manufacturer's price to consumer's retail prices (the higher the percentage of transportation costs and retailer's margin), the greater the difficulties the manufacturer encounters in making a low-price policy effective.

But beyond such a (partly unavoidable) dilution of the influence of a manufacturer's price reduction, there may be an actual nullification of its stimulating influence. In the preceding section we considered the distributor who is so aggressively interested in expanding volume that he exerts himself toward securing lower factory prices as well as lower costs of distribution. Here we note the other side of the same situation. The distributor who is not concerned about larger volume at lower prices may undertake to appropriate all or part of the manufacturer's price reduction as an addition to his own handling margin. In the event of his success in this effort, a low-price policy by the manufacturer as a means of expanding the market is defeated. Some manufacturers have taken over the distribution of their own products in order to avoid this division of interest or have found ways of seeing that distributors pass price reductions on, possibly reinforced by savings from distributing costs.

More conspicuous, however, has been an influence of the opposite sort. Many manufacturers of consumers' goods have joined with distributors in activities aimed at price maintenance on trade-marked or branded goods. To the examination of this type of impediment to low-price policies, we shall return in Chapter VIII.

Bearing in mind the qualifications just stated, there can be no question as to substantial responsiveness of the market to price changes of many new and exciting forms of consumers' goods, such as the automobile, the radio, amateur movie cameras, and color films. Another kind of potential response is less obvious and slower to be appreciated by manufacturers of staple consumers' goods—for instance, in the food, clothing, and house furnishing groups. This is in part due to the fact that such commodities are regularly bought by the rich in quantities which fully meet their desires with little regard to the prices at which they sell, and the middle classes come so near to full satisfaction that their response would not stretch very much even at lower levels of price. On the other hand, it is a matter of common knowledge, though not apparently of sufficiently active belief, that the very large number of unsatisfied wants among the lower income groups creates here a high degree of expansibility of market demand if substantial reductions in prices of these articles can be brought about.

In the extent to which low-price policies have been found applicable in this general area, wide disparities between different industries are to be noted. Early in the century there was an enormous forward surge in the application of mass production methods to the field of ready-made clothing. Utilities have continued to be added, economies effected, and style features incorporated until this range of goods—from sturdy overalls to smartly tailored wool suits, not to mention hats, shoes, gloves, and galoshes—shows an exploitation of technological possibilities in the interests of middle and low-income groups comparable with what the $800 automobile and the $10 to $30 radio do in theirs. On the other hand, there is general agreement that our economy has not brought housing to any such satisfactory basis of economic organization. Here the trouble seems to lie not merely with the construction industry itself but with many at least of the materials and appliances that go into making a furnished home. If metal, rubber, plastics, and upholstery fabricated into automobiles sold on the same level that they do in bathroom and kitchen fixtures and living-, dining-, and bed-room suites, the automobile would still be a luxury article.

Notable by contrast is the promptness and vigor with which nylon hosiery was dropped from the de luxe area to the broad appeal of the $1.39 counter. Similarly, it is interesting to see how fully the moving picture industry has abandoned the idea of high-priced introductions and premiums for each new innovation. Today technicolor is thrown in as an added value at regular prices, and double features (at least one of them a new picture) may be seen on 42nd Street, New York, for 15 cents up to one o'clock. Thirty-five-cent admissions keep the "neighborhood houses" well filled.

The fact that the field of ultimate consumer goods has shown active manifestation of price lowering as both cause and effect of an expanding market and the realization of rapid technological advance does not mean that this is simply an area where "competition" automatically produces such a result. It would be a mistake to attempt to explain these developments in terms of competitive forces outside the realm of business policy developed by the executives of the large concerns that have pioneered new processes and new schemes of organization. The spontaneous reactions of individual consumers and small shopkeepers were constitutionally incapable of producing such a result. Growth of mass purchasing and mass distributing systems has marked successive steps toward managerial concentration and a greater degree of price administration, but also toward a guiding policy of stimulated progress in technique and organization and larger satisfaction of consumer wants at lower unit prices. To speak thus in recognition of the achievements in this part of the business field is not to deny the patent fact that depression and unemployment have wasted many of the gains so painfully contrived by these business leaders. To that aspect of the problem we shall return at later points of the exposition.

What has already been said has implied an answer to the question whether such application of low-price policies as may be effected in this area have relatively great or slight strategic importance. The implication is that, since this is the frontier where the completed productive process is put to the test of consumer acceptance, remuneration, and market absorption, it must be an area of great strategic significance. We noted also how effects originating here ramify back through the whole structure of the economic system.

Not all points along this frontier, however, are of equal importance to the winning of economic victory or the suffering of economic reverses. A lower price for bread as a result of technological improvements in wheat growing, processing, bakery fabrication, and market distribution would have repercussions on popular diet and on the farmer's use of mill feeds and grain for livestock. But these effects would be dissipated in a series of economic ripples limited in both number and force.

On the other hand, there are types of consumers' goods which so articulate with the psychology of the consumer, with technological requirements and possibilities, and with social habits and institutions that the lowering of prices and expansion of volume (even in the early stages of accomplishment) put in motion far-reaching forces that quicken the pace of economic activity, enlarge employment, and raise the level of living for large numbers of persons. Thus, for example, great popularization of the automobile through relative reduction in its price has had far-flung and almost revolutionary effects on highway construction, metallurgical techniques, suburban growth and the decline of local trading villages, hotel operation, the demand for housing accommodations, and a host of other economic situations and practices. These long chains of influences can best be discussed, however, in conjunction with the strategic considerations raised in connection with the other areas of applicability of low-price policies.

RAW MATERIALS AND EXTRACTIVE PRODUCTS

From that area where manufacturers, processors, and distributors formulate business practices and price policies for goods which are to move directly into the hands of final consumers, we turn now to the opposite pole of the economic world. Here agricultural, mineral, forest, and like materials are first appropriated or cultivated and harvested and turned into the stream of fabrication and commerce.

This area presents sharply contrasting situations for economic analysis. Some of these products leave the original producer's hands in the exact form in which they come to the consumer; some go through elaborate processing, fabrication, and assembling before yielding even finished producers' goods. They may never reach the domestic consumer. Likewise, this area is characterized by small and highly competitive units but also by some of the largest, most highly integrated, and most monopolistic business organizations.

Typical of the articles which move from the extractive producer's hands to the final consumer without processing or fabrication are fresh fruits and vegetables, which may even be packaged for the retail market on the farm where they are grown. In these cases and certain others, such as timber products, fresh fish, and domestic coal, we are, of course, still dealing with consumers' goods and hence with the kinds of problems that have already been examined in the preceding section. But we are approaching them from the opposite point of view. We are no longer asking whether consumers, by organizing in co-operative agencies, can force or facilitate low-price practices in their supply market. Nor are we asking whether distributors or final fabricators can be expected to follow low-price policies and also exert pressure in the direction of more efficient methods and narrower profit margins in the areas from which they derive their raw materials or partly finished products. The question we now ask is: What, from the primary producer's point of view are the advantages or the compensations of low unit prices for their products considered in relation to producers' long-run returns?

In considerable measure, the whole question of price *policy* is irrelevant to this area. In so far as we are dealing with small-scale individual farmers, local sawmills, "wildcat" oil men, "snowbird" soft-coal miners, or "gopher hole" metal miners, this is an area outside the field of administered prices, in which executive policy becomes a significant price-making factor. In parts of the agricultural field, however, there has been a considerable development of producers' co-operative organization as a means of concentrating the selling function for a strategically important volume of product. When such an organization is established, the question of price policy occupies the forefront of discussion, though its corollary, production policy, has not been found amenable to control by these voluntary groups. In the non-agricultural part of the field, there have been regional and national trade associations of timber and lumber producers, coal operators, petroleum producers, fishermen, quarrymen, and the like. Nominally, these associations do not have a price or related production policy—still less any power of enforcing its observance upon members. But the import of educational, statistical, and accounting activities of such associations as well as their legislative efforts has certainly been in the direction of defining a solidarity of interest and an essential harmony of action which take on the color or magnitude of policy formulation.

Broadly speaking, the policy out of which such associations of primary producers grow is that of checking price declines which are regarded as "ruinous" by a substantial percentage of the producing group—with the public in some cases concurring. It is a striking feature of the area of extractive products and raw materials that, since we are dealing with products of nature, we encounter here the most striking of the cases of "natural monopolies," but also the areas of most uncontrollable supply. Now that science is presenting us with more and more keys—even "master" keys—with which to unlock these hidden riches of nature, situations emerge that are characterized by such "surplus" that many of these products have in recent years become the object even of government-supported controls and production restrictions. Public sanction and aid have in different situations been brought to the support of price-maintaining and production-restriction programs for wheat, coffee, cotton, sugar, petroleum, rubber, timber, coal, tin, and others.[7]

[7] The small agricultural co-operatives were largely superseded during the early 1920's by "national" centralized marketing agencies expressing the new "commodity marketing movement." When these agencies found

Sometimes this has been designed to preserve the values of agricultural land, of groves and orchards, of stumpage, or of sub-surface mineral rights—in general, in support of capitalized values or the credit structure erected on them. Sometimes, they have been brought to the support of the small firm or individual proprietor against the stronger and often more efficient large corporation—that is, in support of small enterprise. Sometimes, such support has been invoked in maintenance of numerical employment or the rate of labor remuneration among extractive workers. Both because of these labor and capital considerations and because the situations involve waste or conservation of natural resources, and thus a long-time public interest, both state and federal governments have viewed this area of economic life as one involving questions of public policy. They have become parties to its settlement through the oil proration laws of the Southwest; agricultural prorate legislation in California, state milk marketing acts, and the federal Agricultural Adjustment Administration; and the agencies administering the Bituminous Coal Act of 1937.

In retrospect, it appears that when agricultural cooperative associations or trade associations of other extractive producers have felt any substantial power in their hands to carry out a price policy, they have in-

themselves inadequate to the task of price maintenance or restoration, they resorted to legislative aid in the form of a Federal Farm Board and "Agricultural Stabilization Corporations." When the Farm Board concluded that prices could not be maintained by mere holding operations, however large, resort was again had to legislative aid. An Agricultural Adjustment Administration was set up to curtail production as well as manipulate stocks.

The coffee valorization scheme of Brazil moved to government control with less preliminary experimentation with private controls. The Stevenson plan for stabilizing rubber, on the other hand, relied more on the action of large private interests, though within the support of government approval.

variably sought economic advantage through a high-price rather than a low-price policy. This may be illustrated in the field of fluid milk marketing, where sanitary requirements, transportation arrangements, and distribution methods have been combined to isolate a geographical area and protect both methods and margins which result in high-priced milk to the consumer. The organization has not sought such co-ordinated productive and distributive effort as would combine the maximum amount of remunerative employment for dairymen as a whole with maximum supply of wholesome milk for consumers.[8] Similarly, fruit and vegetable growers have in a majority of cases tried to improve their economic situation through emphasis on fancy grades, special packaging, and intensive advertising. They have discarded as culls a great deal of product which was wholesome but not of maximum "eye appeal," on the theory that any admission of this product to distributive channels would spoil their market. There have been a few instances where orchard run, "jumble" pack, and bulk shipment by truck or railway have exploited lower price policy and volume distribution with good results. But such undertakings have been discouraged even by a substantial amount of the technical advice of agricultural colleges and experiment stations, singing the slogan, "There's always a good market for premium quality product."

In the bituminous coal industry, low prices and high unemployment led to efforts at price maintenance un-

[8] Restrictionist influences here are perhaps more a matter of distributor policy than of producer policy. The producers have, however, acquiesced in and added to price maintenance or enhancement efforts rather than opposing them. Roland W. Bartlett, *The Price of Milk* (1941); John M. Cassels, *A Study of Fluid Milk Prices* (1937); John D. Black, *The Dairy Industry and the AAA* (1935).

der an NRA code. After its breakdown there was demand for some special form of control. Public acceptance
was made easier by the interest in conservation of an
essential resource. The Bituminous Coal Act of 1937
provided for minimum prices at the mines[9] in accordance
with a complicated set of standards. Minimum prices
were to "equal as nearly as may be the weighted average
of the total [operating] costs per net ton" for the given
minimum price area—thus accepting whatever labor
costs may result from the collective wage bargaining
recognized in the act. Capital return was dealt with only
in fixing the margin by which maximum prices might
exceed the minimum. This margin was intended to yield
"in the aggregate . . . a reasonable return above the
weighted average total cost of the district" and "a fair
return on the fair value" of each mine.[10] The interest
of the consuming public was represented through the
Consumers' Counsel, a separate division of the Department of the Interior having powers of investigation and
the right to appear in any proceeding before the Coal Division. It seemed to be more active, and probably more
influential, than most of the consumers' counsels with
which we have had experience. There was no provision
for control of production or allocation of quotas. Consequently producers were free to compete for the market
by increasing their sales effort and through indirect
price cutting by giving added service or better quality.

[9] The Bituminous Coal Division of the Department of the Interior,
under which the act was administered, had no jurisdiction over wholesale
or retail dealers in coal.

[10] L. S. Lyon, Victor Abramson, and Associates, *Government and Economic Life*, Vol. 2 (1940), pp. 972 ff. Maximum prices had not yet
been promulgated when the general price ceiling was announced by
OPA. This new control (and that of the Solid Fuels Administrator) make
it impossible to judge what the effect of the Bituminous Coal Act itself
would have been.

A "consumers' counsel" was also included in the organization of the Agricultural Adjustment Administration. It represented an attempt to reconcile the desire of the consumer for cheap products with the producers' requirement of a remunerative price. Of late, the expanding interest in the improvement of nutritional standards has shown some promise of shifting government activity away from emphasis on unit price and toward an effort to utilize agricultural capacity as fully as possible in increasing the "abundance" of consumer satisfactions without prejudice to producers' incomes and planes of living in the country.

Since marked technological and organizational progress has been made in agriculture and other extractive industries during recent years and still more is clearly possible, this should be regarded by control agencies, either private (co-operative) or governmental, as an area of applicability for low-price policies. Obviously, it is also an area of strategic importance for the application of such policies because these types of products are both raw materials for industries and important determinants of the cost of living for labor. Advances or declines in this area therefore have a strong "leverage" factor throughout the price structure.

This fact has been thrown into high relief in connection with current discussion of wartime "inflation" and means of combating it. Agricultural leaders, however, have shown but little inclination toward policies of price moderation in this situation, and it seems doubtful that they will change their attitude much after the return to peace. Whatever the intention of the interested parties, it must be recognized that low-price policy cannot be carried to any large measure of success in extractive industries unless similar low-price and full production policies are being carried out in manufacturing and distribution.[11]

Metal mining, unlike the production of bituminous coal, petroleum, and agricultural staples, presents many cases in which scarcity of natural resources facilitates monopoly. Nickel, tin, chromium, tungsten, beryllium, bauxite, and even special types of iron ore are localized in occurrence and have very specific areas of non-substitution in industrial use. Many mineral industries require expensive plant and large-scale business organization for economical production and distribution. Finally, these products in general differ from those extractive products which move direct to the consumer. The metals typically pass through many stages of processing, fabricating, and assembling. For instance, there are ores which may have to be milled, concentrated, reduced, smelted—possibly undergoing two or three successive processes—before they are ready even to be rolled, drawn, cast, or alloyed into the first type of construction material for the manufacturer. This basic material may be machined and assembled to make producers' goods which, in turn, are to be used in making other producers' goods that at long

[11] The precise objectives of government agricultural policy remain somewhat obscure. To some extent, there appears to be an intention to make the best of an unsatisfactory situation. Since devices of price maintenance and production restriction have become so strongly entrenched in large and strategic sectors of the economy that it seems impossible to break them down, it is proposed to set up countervailing controls throughout the remainder of the economy and then proceed to administer the whole under a comprehensive regime of "planned economy." As to businessmen's reaction to such a possible line of development, it is interesting to speculate. Will they conclude that under such a system their relative advantage would disappear and that they might indeed be positively disadvantaged? Faced by such an alternative, will they think it better on the whole to give up many of the controls which they have secured for themselves and participate wholeheartedly in an attack on neo-mercantilism and move vigorously toward the restoration of genuinely free private enterprise?

last may contribute to the making of goods for final consumption. Does this succession of price-making situations lend itself to the application of low-price policies?

Historically, the answer seems to be "no."[12] The power to formulate and implement price policies in this area has almost always been exercised through programs of greater or less price maintenance at the expense of restricted output. There are exceptions, like that in steel sheets for automobiles, where the strength of the consumer organizations has been great enough to force a reduction. Aluminum, magnesium, tungsten, beryllium, molybdenum, chromium, and even steel and copper have in varying degrees exemplified the restrictive tendency.

In a large measure there has been in this area a concentration of industrial development in the hands of a comparatively small number of firms who have tended to support prices on a plane which is high relative to the potentialities of technological and organizational improvements. This they have done either through voluntary acceptance of price leadership by the strongest or through the development of a protective solidarity of the trade association type. Our institutions of land ownership and patent right have strengthened the controls on which such monopolistic practices could be built, and the progress of metallurgy has tended to increase the scarcity value of certain of these metals. In other directions, however, it has enlarged the range of possible substitution. Still more useful as a means of sharpening market competition has been the develop-

[12] Donald H. Wallace, *Market Control in the Aluminum Industry* (1937); Wilcox, *Competition and Monopoly in American Industry*, TNEC Monograph No. 21, pp. 79, 95, 123, 133, 148, 222; William Yandell Elliott and others, *International Control in the Non-Ferrous Metals* (1937).

ment of non-metallic substitutes, notably the plastics and lacquers. Timber engineering has even brought in laminated wood trusses and other structural forms as a competitor for structural steel, at least under emergency conditions.[13] But examples in which individual firms or industrial groups in this area have voluntarily sought to put in practice a low-price policy are extremely scarce or difficult of convincing demonstration.

The producer of raw materials for fabricating industries cannot observe directly, study, and seek to exploit the responsiveness of ultimate consumers' wants for his wares as can the manufacturer or distributor of finished products. Often, too, this potential responsiveness may be dissipated by the fact that these products constitute only a small factor in the cost of a fabricated consumer article.[14] Or, as was noted in the preceding section, price reductions by underlying producers may be absorbed by fabricators and distributors, thus nullifying any possible stimulative effect on volume of sales. But the thoughtful businessman in this area can hardly be unaware of the fact that there is such a responsiveness, however much it may be dimmed, obscured, or distorted by the succession of intermediate users through whom that ultimate demand must be translated to him.

And the more aggressive and resourceful executives

[13] See publications of National Lumber Manufacturers' Association and its subsidiary, Timber Engineering Company, Inc.

[14] This argument has frequently been used in reverse by producers' organizations when seeking an advance in prices. They argue that, since their product constitutes so small a factor in the cost of the consumer's finished product, an advance large enough to make the difference between prosperity and disaster for them would not materially affect the consumer or could indeed readily be absorbed by the distributor or processor. The cumulative effect of price advances by all raw material producers, based on such a theory, is obvious.

in these lines from time to time find ways of making contact with this responsive market. Vertical integration is one of the most obvious means to such an end.

On the other hand, pressure for price reduction may come from above. The manufacturer who is seeking to enlarge his sales in a market of limited purchasing power presses back upon the purveyor of raw materials to produce and sell his wares at the lowest price made possible by the most efficient technology and organization that he can devise. In some areas, this pressure from the user upon the producer of primary materials may be sufficiently direct and specific to assure reasonably good price performance on the part of firms in the raw material field. But there are other commodities for which the uses are so diverse, with the given commodity so small an ingredient of rough and partly finished products as well as those completed for consumers' use, that such pressure from the consumer or such evidence of responsiveness in consumer demand is too remote, scattered, and tenuous to have any considerable effect on the basic price-making process.

In sum, this is an important area of applicability for low-price policies though not characterized by extensive or concerted application of such policies in the past. It embraces some of the spots at which small-scale competition operates most actively to keep prices low. But whenever these lines of production permit of large-scale organization and the establishment of economic control, the price administrator finds price maintenance rather than low-price policy "the easy way." Private enterprise has not been very ingenious or very aggressive in the way of price-moderating efforts in this field. And public policy has been (in recent years at least) quite as much concerned to put a floor under spots where competition was severe as it has been to put on ceilings to prevent "undue" enhancement of prices.

Technological developments in these lines of production are sufficiently numerous and significant to give a substantial amount of increased productivity to pass on into the stream of business operations which leads toward the ultimate area of consumer satisfaction. Likewise, these products are of such wide uses and strategic importance in our whole industrial life that benefits conferred at the raw material level would persist and cumulate throughout the whole system. A positive price policy on the part of executives themselves is necessary if we are to expect technological progress to be aggressively promoted and its results adequately reflected in a downward trend of prices. In this regard the raw materials industries present economic characteristics similar to those of producers' goods. Hence we will postpone further elaboration of this point till we have examined that area.

PRICES FOR FABRICATED PRODUCERS' GOODS

Fabricated producers' goods (such as tools, machinery, and factory equipment) embrace an area of administered prices *par excellence*. As an area for the application of price policies, however, it differs widely from the area of fabricated consumers' goods. Its wares are far removed from the markets where finished products pass into the stream of ultimate consumption. Hence, the consequences of price changes are less promptly and vividly to be seen.

The general facts as to the character of fabricated producers' goods are so well known as to require little elaboration. Typical of this group are such products as locomotives, rolling stock, and rails; trucks, hoists, and power shovels; pipe and pipe fittings; machine tools; extruded and fabricated metal forms; boilers, turbines, generators, and motors. These products include many which have distinctive features of design, are protected by patents, or are built to particular specifications that restrict their manufacture to a sort of "custom" basis rather than permitting standardized manufacture for a general market.

As a corollary to the qualities of these products, methods of sale and distribution are also specialized. There is a great deal of direct and individualized selling, with a relative absence of advertising; a great deal of manufacturing on specific order rather than adjustment to a general market flow or sale to competing wholesalers or jobbers. Often the geographical location of plants with reference to market areas, power or raw material resources, or transportation facilities further differentiate these producers and enlarge their power to adopt whatever price and production policy promises to give them maximum return according to whatever interpretation they may give to that term.

This freedom in writing their own price tags is enhanced by the fact that these products make up a group as to which the buyer is less "price conscious" or less able to act in response to the consumer type of price motivation. These products are bought, not for any direct satisfaction that they yield, but purely as necessary adjuncts to the carrying on of a given business. They are items in the broad category referred to as "capital goods." When business is active, such articles will be purchased without *primary* regard to price; when business becomes inactive, they will not be bought freely—however attractive the price. Locomotives, machine tools, and factory power installations are not purchased in larger number just because the price has been somewhat reduced but because the old equipment is worn out or is ill adapted to turning out a new product or employing a new technique. Nor do buyers of such articles often refrain from buying simply because the price seems high or has been advanced. Their decisions are more influenced by the estimated ability of the machine to make substantial economies in production costs, the prospect for a business upswing, and the possibility of financing the purchase (and subsequent production) on favorable terms.

For the most specialized types of such articles, buyers have little or no possibility of turning from one supplier to another because of a difference in price. The time involved in working out elaborate engineering specifications and adapting the operations, equipment, or working forces of a plant to the production of the required goods sometimes reduces the choice of a source of supply to one. The seller's ability to meet requirements exactly and to assure time of delivery curbs such disposition to bargain as the buyer might have. He is in a very different situation from that of the ultimate consumer, who is disbursing a personal income for articles that pass immediately into consumption. Instead, he is making an outlay of capital funds to secure the kind of producers' good which will enable him to operate efficiently at a time when he foresees a productive market for given products. Quality and time of delivery of the machine greatly outrank price as a factor in determining the expectation of profitableness of these operations.

This brief analysis suggests that fabricated producers' goods industries present an area within which low-price policies are peculiarly inapplicable. That is, the market situations do not themselves conduce to the adoption and carrying out of low-price policies. Such a view has been vigorously put forth by spokesmen in this field. We quote from a publication of the machine tool builders:

> The prices of capital goods . . . must always reflect, as nearly as may be possible, the full effect of changes in demand for them. That is to say, prices and costs which are naturally and inevitably increased in periods of increasing demand, must be reduced in periods of diminishing demand. . . . In no other way than through reasonable application of the principle of elastic movement of prices and costs in response to fluctuating demand can the peaks and valleys of demand for new capital goods be levelled out in a capitalistic economy.[15]

Since purchases of capital goods tend to grow during periods of prosperity, when the profit outlook brightens, and to dry up in periods of depression, the policy outlined in this quotation means that prices of such goods should be advanced during prosperous times as rapidly and fully as demand for them increases—essentially a rephrasing of the old principle of "charging all the traffic will bear." While the quotation refers to "elastic movement of prices [to] level out the peaks and valleys of demand for new capital goods," the writer proceeds at once to admit the relatively small degree of flexibility in prices of capital goods and concludes:

> . . . since capital goods must always be sold upon the basis of economic justification for their purchase, this factor [rigidities in cost] is often of such importance as to reduce the expectation of profit on the part of the prospective buyer to the point where the purchase is deferred.[16]

[15] Machinery and Allied Products Institute, *Capital Goods and the American Enterprise System* (1939), p. 37.

[16] The same, p. 38.

But he himself does not really believe that it is deferred to a time of depression when costs are lower, for he says:

For instance, production of locomotives practically stopped in the United States during the depth of the depression. Locomotives, for the most part, are built on order to specifications of the purchaser. They represent the type of capital equipment for which demand can be and frequently is deferred. There is no stock of new locomotives on hand which has to be disposed of at whatever price they will bring. Production follows rather than precedes demand in the capital goods industries. Consequently, volume of production, rather than price, tends to fluctuate in business cycles.[17]

Thus he closes the circle of his argument that capital goods are characteristically bought in a seller's market and should be priced to exploit the strength of the demand to the utmost.

But to say that the producer goods industries constitute an area in which high-price policies are easy or may even be formally advocated by official spokesmen does not mean that low-price policies cannot be carried out in this area or that it is a matter of indifference to the economy whether or not they are in fact introduced. Even though circumstances do not lead or push the price maker toward a low-price policy, are there perhaps broad strategic considerations that may cause the executive of deeper insight into the demands and responses of our economic life to see this as an area which presents opportunities for economic leadership even through a course whose advantages are not immediately obvious?

It would seem self-evident that, if the benefits of new materials and new processes are not made available to producing consumers by appropriate price policies at those remote and underlying places in the price system

[17] The same, p. 39.

where they knock for entry, it will be impossible to have them reflected in the finished goods through whose purchase and use alone the consumer can become the beneficiary of scientific and economic progress. In the first section of this chapter emphasis was placed on the way in which the consumer's desire for and ability to reward the conferring of such gains works back to induce, encourage, stimulate, and even force this kind of pricing upon producers of raw and partly finished materials. In many cases, however, such influence is not of itself adequate, and such a condition is even more pronounced in the field of producers' fabricated goods. If such a dissemination of productivity is to be realized in high production, therefore, it becomes essential that this type of business practice proceed spontaneously from the insight and intention of the responsible executives in the protected areas of policy-making for scarce materials, highly differentiated products, and highly specialized producer organization.

Costs no longer necessitated by the state of the arts or the scarcity of nature's resources, if kept in the price structure at these levels pyramid through the whole structure and load the consumer market till purchasing power equates with only a small volume of goods. On the other hand, economies and new efficiencies introduced here as price reductions infuse the whole exchange system with an expansionary force which expresses itself in volume of employment on the one side and volume of consumer satisfactions on the other.

The issue of how any such general purpose is to be translated into practical business procedures must be left to later chapters in this book—and to such business philosophy, organizational changes, and purposeful procedures as businessmen may themselves evolve during the years ahead. But before leaving the general question of applicability of low-price policies, we need to examine one other aspect of the problem.

PRICE POLICY AND THE AGE OF THE FIRM OR THE INDUSTRY

In considering ease in applying low-price or price-lowering policies, both businessmen and economists are inclined to focus attention also on the stage of business evolution. It is often argued that price reduction occurs easily, almost naturally, in young and expanding industries and will not, indeed cannot, take place elsewhere. This proposition contains an obvious element of truth, but is easily exaggerated. It affords a convenient excuse to price-making executives whose grasp of the character and requirements of the economic system does not dispose them toward low-price policies.

Persons entertaining this view regard low-price policies as a brief phenomenon associated with occasional revolutionary changes such as the introduction of the automobile to popular use. They consider Henry Ford a somewhat artless individual, over-impressed by the significance of his pricing experiments and the results which, under these particular circumstances, flowed from them.[18] Pointing out that after a brief period of rapid price reduction and volume expansion the automobile industry settled down on a plateau of fairly stable prices, they describe it as passing from "price competition" to "product competition."[19] Some go so far as to say that

[18] While Henry Ford and the automobile are popularly associated with the lay exposition and the practical application of low-price theory, Edward A. Filene was a more logical and adequate expositor and applied it to more varied and more refractory situations. See Edward A. Filene, *Successful Living in this Machine Age* (1931), and certain chapters from *Speaking of Change* (1939).

[19] The use of these terms is often confused and confusing. The two processes are not distinct and mutually exclusive. Instead, they are, in all

price lowering and volume expansion are the characteristic conditions of new industries or lines of production and that old industries and established products settle down to stable prices.

In a quite limited and highly literal sense this is all very true. A product expands its market most rapidly during the early days when its purchaser is discovering and exploiting a new economic opportunity. Equally true and obvious is it that people grow more rapidly during infancy than in mature years or old age. But even in normal children there are periods of more rapid and of less rapid growth, and the whole process may be modified though not precisely controlled or standardized by more intelligent or informed direction of feeding, play, sleep, and other relevant conditions.

To say that a policy of price reduction has been the rule in new and expanding industries challenges us both to look at the historic record and to scrutinize the logic

---

except highly standardized articles, interwoven. If a producer keeps the price of an article stable but enlarges it in size, increases its performing power, adds to its durability, beauty, or other utility, this "product competition" is based on price appeal and constitutes price lowering just as truly as does the marking down of the dollar price of an article which remains unchanged in size and character. On the other hand, if a price remains unchanged while the commodity is altered in ways which do not increase its capacity to satisfy the real wants of consumers but which simply give the commodity some individual characteristics which can be used as "sales points" by the distributor, then we have a kind of commodity competition which is really different from and inferior to the price competition we are discussing. The automobile is an excellent example of a product in which, for some years back, prices have shown little or no decrease but where the commodity has been modified very sharply by size, power, and quality changes, many of which have a price significance to practically all buyers that is quite equivalent to that of the models from which this upgrading started. Others, however, are refinements, complications, and even potential causes of breakdown which would be rejected by many buyers if they could be separated from the basic article. This kind of change is definitely the opposite of price competition or low-price policy.

of the statement. The "new" aluminum industry of the nineties certainly did not have either a vigorous policy of price reduction or a rate of expansion which was commensurate with the technological possibilities of the new material. The management of this company was in the hands of men who had no glimmer of such a philosophy of industrial growth but rather conceived of a monopolistic position as presenting an opportunity for making profits through a small volume of sales at a high margin. Nor did the "newness" of the automobile business suggest a policy of price reduction to Olds, Durant, Winston, Stearns, and the majority of pioneers in that industry. When Mr. Ford conceived this novel principle and attempted to put it into practice, he drew down upon his head a full measure of derision and opposition from orthodox industrial and financial executives.

And just as it is over-simple to say that price lowering may normally be expected in new industries, so is it too simple to say that the process necessarily slows up and comes to a standstill as soon as the area of easy conquest has been occupied. Such a view fails to take account of an essential aspect of the modern industrial process. This is the fact that costs are not fixed nor is even the character of the commodity. The desire to lower prices becomes the stimulus for devising lower cost methods so that in a very real sense it may be said that costs are pushed down by voluntarily reduced prices rather than that prices follow declining costs down.

The significant point for us to consider here is not the calendar age of the industry or the corporate age of the firm. Within each industry and within any industrial firm which acquires longevity there is a growth fringe at which change and rejuvenation take place even though the industry as a whole or the firm as a business entity remains nominally the same. The steel industry is in certain senses new, even though crude forms of iron-making go back far in the history of the race. It is probably more correct to think of this industry as neither old nor new but as having acquired a sort of agelessness within which the process of technological and organizational change may and should go on indefinitely. Nor is it fanciful to say that this ageless industry, the United States Steel Corporation may go on "forever." It will get ever farther away from the "fresh paint" corporate newness that it had when it was born out of the amalgamation of the Carnegie Steel Corporation, the American Bridge Company, and others. The products which it produces will continue to change, old plants will be dismantled and new plants built, and policies and prices will continue to be revamped instead of being brought to complete conformity with a rigid set of specifications and costs. This is equally true of Bethlehem, Republic, and National Steel.

In fact, as business becomes institutionalized—and this is the striking aspect of modern industrial development—the making of these very changes which mean better technology, more efficient organization, and lower cost becomes an integral part of the established processes of business. Accomplishing them is an indispensable factor in the continuation of the firm in business and must have its counterpart in ever-new price adjustments.

The point of view that identifies price lowering with new products or industries also reflects an old-fashioned or retrospective view with reference to current administrative procedures in price-making. Under simple factory processes it was largely true that prices for a new product began at a high level and were gradually lowered as the process was perfected, costly mistakes eliminated, short-cuts discovered, and volume production developed. Under modern scientific industrialism, however, a different procedure is introduced. High initial costs of an imperfect process are largely eliminated through careful laboratory preparation and test-plant operation before the product goes on the commercial market. Likewise, decision is made in advance as to the volume of output which will be necessary to launch production on the basis of large-volume, low-unit-cost operation, and the price is made at the start on a level[20] calculated to attract such a volume of buying.

Both nylon yarn and cellophane are excellent illustrations of products of this type, which were launched on a relatively low price to induce large sales but which have subsequently enjoyed successive further reductions as refinement of processes and expansion of the market made such reductions feasible. Obviously, if in the course of time no further progress in either of these directions can be made, the price would level out and further price reduction ultimately cease. But this does not mean that the process of discovering new ways of satisfying the public's desire for durable and beautiful textiles or for strong, attractive, and moisture-resistant packaging materials may not, instead of continuing in a straight line of development over the path of technology, go off at a tangent in some new direction— depending on where the innovating individual or company might come forward.[21]

[20] Quite possibly a price below average cost of current operation and almost certainly below the cost of such operation plus a charge sufficient to recoup the cost of research and development within the first year or possibly several years of commercial operation.

[21] A special case is presented by a "dying" industry. Here it is obvious that price reductions will not stimulate total demand and thus be to the interest of all firms in the business. Similarly, in such an industry it is not likely that invention and technological improvement will be so active as to conduce to price lowering through cost reduction. The remaining

For brevity's sake, we often use "technological progress" as the phrase to describe the general process by which cost (in relation to quality) is reduced. But this phrase is intended to cover not merely scientific and engineering improvements but also organizational changes which make for greater economy and efficiency. These are taking place in old industries as well as new, and in established firms as well as newcomers in the field. The local grocery and butcher shop are among our oldest institutions of retail trade, but the coming of the chain store here has certainly inaugurated a new process of cost and price reduction which there is no reason to suppose will cease after a few initial improvements have been introduced. The essential point is that modern scientific organization and technology both introduce a process of systematic investigation, research, and invention designed to assure continuing review of processes and organization and the adoption of economies—large or small, the stepping up of efficiency, and modification of design and character of products or serv-

customers of the trade are likely to be those who because of necessity or stubbornness will continue to take product more or less regardless of price. It might even seem that this is a situation in which prices should be advanced in order to recoup higher unit cost on a shrinking volume of output. Such a policy, however, tends to accelerate the death of the industry, perhaps to the needless inconvenience of confirmed users of the product and needless prolongation of inefficient and unprofitable operations on the part of many individual firms. As a matter of fact, even a dying industry may present distinctive opportunities for organizational improvement and cost reduction. Shrewd appraisal of the situation will enable the astute manager to curtail research outlay, fruitless advertising expense, and programs of sales promotion which were appropriate to earlier days but which are no longer necessary or productive. A reexamination of depreciation practices in the light of the changed situation may lead to the formulation of a liquidation policy in which lower prices designed to concentrate a dwindling business in the hands of a few firms whose size and distribution enables them to handle the residual task most economically may conserve profits for the few and check losses for the many. Astute business and good sportsmanship should convert the dying industry into a sort of "Last Man Club."

ice whenever and wherever possible. When business comes to be conceived as a profession of increasing efficiency in the supplying of wants rather than as one of maximum short-run acquisitive gain, there is no reason why the process of price lowering should not be continuous. Certainly the expansibility of the market is still an active factor until all members of society are supplied with as full a budget of consumer goods and services as have in their estimate a greater marginal value than the marginal value of leisure time.

The "new" factor in much recent and probably still more in future price reduction and production expansion enterprise will be in bringing more and better goods within reach of the lowest income strata of our population. Price lowering taps new groups of consumers. Many families have an automobile who never had or would have had a horse and buggy. Many a tenement or cabin dweller who has a ten-dollar radio set never bought or would have bought ten dollars' worth of books. Families that never spent $2.00 for a theater ticket regularly pay $5.00 to $20.00 a year for 10- to 35-cent movie admissions. These, of course, are "new" buyers of "new" goods. But industry that will utilize our full productive resources must also price to reach new—that is, more adequate—consumption of old goods among old consumers. This is notably the case with industrially produced food and clothing items and should be true of housing. And there is no reason to suppose that, in spite of the lack of newness in these lines of production or the non-expansibility of the groups to be served, the process of reducing prices in proportion to quality has come to an end or must be given up.

"Gold is where you find it," and that may be in either new or old fields. After the easy gold of rich placers was snatched off, a steady and larger flow of gold continued to come from the hydraulic mining of lean gravels, from deep dredger mining, from crushing quartz and using cyanide instead of mercury. Low-price policies are like the chemical and mechanical processes that get riches from the poorest mineral deposits.

JOINT DEMAND AND CONCERTED ACTION

Thus far, we have been talking about individual goods and services as though each were sold in an independent market or had a practically separate demand. As a matter of fact, most goods and services are grouped in bundles or bought and sold in composite packages. For durable goods, the consumer is constrained to remember that what he can afford "isn't so much the cost as it is the upkeep." His decision to purchase an automobile involves consideration of finance charges, gasoline cost, tire and battery replacement, garage and parking charges. Similarly a cut in electric current prices might evoke little market response if the prices of washing machines, stoves, refrigerators, and farm implements were maintained. A simultaneous reduction of line construction costs, electric equipment prices, and rates for current is the surest way to realize the full potential expansion of demand for each item. The housing field presents an outstanding illustration of the interdependence of price influences and consumer response for a large bundle of goods and services which must be used together or not at all—lumber, cement, steel, brick, plaster, paint, hardware, labor of a whole group of skilled crafts, and unskilled labor. It is useless for the producers of one of these goods to expect an increase (rather than shifting) of sales from a lessening of prices when his commodity makes only one or a few per cent of the cost of the finished house. If all producers made their price moves regardless of immediate and specific market response, costs would be kept moving down. Not seeing a clear signal for such a course they all leave responsibility for action to others, and prices tend to stay up regardless of technological progress.

The fact that for many products the demand is a joint demand greatly increases the difficulties of price policy making. It is not too much to say that it is quite impossible for the individual firm or even the whole producing group or industry to chart and follow by itself a course which will be in any real sense constructive for the economy. In fact, the very attempt to employ methods of precision in arriving at managerial decisions may lead responsible executives to misleading measurements and essentially harmful lines of action. This particular problem will be the subject of the chapter which is to follow. For many—perhaps a majority—of corporations, a price-making program broad enough to be adequate to meet the real economic needs must involve harmoniously conceived and simultaneously executed price policies and production programs involving other, often many other, concerns. This situation presents practical problems for the successful conduct of a system based primarily on private enterprise, which will be the subjects of several later chapters. But, whatever may there be said about the importance and the difficulty of securing harmonious or even concurrent action is not to be construed as lessening the importance to be attached to the policy-making function of the executives of individually large and strategically situated corporations.

Emphasis has been given at several places in this chapter to the importance of particular business areas or branches of industry as spots of superior or even supreme importance for the initiation of economic action or the exercise of economic leadership. The automobile industry would probably be universally accepted as such a leadership industry. Ours is so distinctly an automobile economy that marked failure of the "big three" companies to follow aggressive and well-conceived price and production policies when we reconvert our economy to a peacetime basis would seriously prejudice the nation's economic prospects for years ahead. So too of steel, chemicals, electrical equipment, and others in varying degree.[22]

But this is not to say that the task of disseminating low-price policies throughout the economy devolves entirely upon certain large or strategically placed corporations. They alone can put in motion the initial steps in transmitting certain new efficiencies to the public. But if other concerns thereupon try to appropriate to themselves the gains thus transmitted to them instead of passing them on, enlarged by further gains which they themselves introduce, the process of diffusion is checked and the current of progress choked.

No thoroughgoing and sustained economic progress can be carried out under free enterprise unless communication and transportation industries, farms, mining companies, machine tool builders, assemblers, processors, and merchants all join in the process of translating heightening efficiency into lowered prices. In this sense the areas of applicability of low-price policies are as wide as the field of business, varying in intensity only with differences in the rate of introduction of new factors of efficiency. These in turn are stimulated by a consistent *policy* of price lowering.

[22] Compare Chap. 14, pp. 428 ff.

In conclusion: low-price policy is in some areas easy of application; in some difficult. But even the easy reduction does not make itself, and the hard one may be achieved by dint of sufficient ingenuity and effort.

Low-price policy in certain strategic areas has great leverage or leadership value, but general efficiency for the economy can be obtained only if such practices are carried out comprehensively and consistently in all areas.

We recognize that direct and short-run benefits from price lowering are hardly to be expected by producers whose commodity constitutes but a small item in the finished article or bundle of goods and services in which it is delivered to the ultimate consumer. Later chapters will consider possibilities of developing some spontaneous or concerted program of co-ordinated action among the several enterprises or companies.

It is easy to think of price reduction as a phenomenon connected with the early history of a firm or the introduction of new products. It is much more correct, however, to think of low-price policy as the way in which newness may be continuously injected into even the oldest types of economic service to consumers.

This chapter has kept clear of the conventional criterion of "elasticity of demand" as a guide to price-and-production policy, while examining prior issues. The next chapter directs attention exclusively to the meaning of elasticity of demand and its relation to low-price policies in actual business practice.

CHAPTER VII

APPRAISING THE RESPONSIVENESS OF MARKET DEMAND

Certain generalizations as to the applicability of low-price policy to entire commodities, whole industries, or broad sectors of the economy were suggested in Chapter VI. But the administrative decisions of the individual businessman apply to even more concrete and, in the main, quite restricted situations. In working out problems of practical management, the businessman of the past relied largely on personal experience, intuition, rule-of-thumb, or compromise among the divergent views of departmental executives. More and more, however, corporate executives are turning to "scientific" techniques as aids in the formulation of price and production policies.

Of basic importance among these analytical methods are those that seek to get a correct picture of buyers' demand for the product. The sales manager may approach this problem in terms of "sales quotas." The economist has long talked about the "demand schedule." Today he is more likely to call it the "demand function," and the statistician attempts to measure "the coefficient of the elasticity of demand."

In the present chapter, we shall consider briefly the character and significance of the statistical measures of demand thus being developed and applied to the problems of the business executive. We detect a possible danger that, impressed by the advantages of mechanization in the factory, the businessman may become too optimistic as to the possibilities also of mechanizing judgment in the office. Without disparaging the value of research methods as applied to the problems of practical business, it may be suggested that a statistical laboratory and the formulas which it produces are not quite the counterpart of a physical, chemical, or biological laboratory in an industrial plant, and the machines or methods of control which they turn out.[1]

If analysis of market demand is to become the useful and dependable tool of management, the user must be clear as to what constitutes a significant measurement, what are the limitations of its usefulness, and what are the situations which need to be tested by other means. Whatever the value of statistical measurements as such,

---

[1] It is no part of our present inquiry to undertake technical criticism of the statistical devices in current use for the study of volume and price relations. I am not a statistician and would not presume to suggest that the methodologies in vogue do not give mathematically correct answers to the questions put to them. The designers and manipulators of these techniques from time to time disagree among themselves and are constantly seeking to add new precision or "elegance" to the procedures already current. But our question is one of practical economic significance, not one of abstract technical correctness.

Neither are we here concerned with the adequacy of the data used or available. It is a matter of common knowledge that the material has often been of deplorably low quality. Often, too, it has been given scandalously careless inspection and culling by those who have used it. They may be interested primarily in perfecting devices and methods and thus be quite justified in using such data as are available, at the same time that they recognize and warn other workers of the weakness or non-usability of the results. But, human nature being what it is, there is a tendency to become engrossed in the fine workmanship or the superficial beauty of the product and hence fail to heed the warnings of the makers of such measures or the experimenters with such methods of measurement. Academic, governmental, and commercial workers become so eager to get quantitative answers (even to problems that by their nature do not admit of quantification) that they yield to the temptation to take tentative methods, used experimentally on admittedly dubious data, and stretch and strain them to new uses, to produce still less trustworthy quantitative answers. These become dangerous guides to practical action.

they need to be supplemented by non-statistical methods of broad appraisal of the demand forces which are most important in the functioning of the modern industrial price system.

STATISTICAL MEASUREMENT OF DEMAND

Early economists gave preponderant emphasis to costs as an explanation of price. In time, attention shifted to factors, particularly the physiological and psychological ones, that influence consumers' behavior and thus become important determinants of prices. Alfred Marshall sought to give due weight to factors both of cost and of demand, with market price as the point where these forces strike an equilibrium. It was he who introduced the phrase "elasticity of demand" and he defined it as follows: "The *elasticity of demand* in a market is great or small according as the amount demanded increases much or little for a given fall in price, and diminishes much or little for a given rise in price."[2] He also introduced the usage now conventional among economists and statisticians of calling demand *elastic* if a price change of 1 per cent is associated with a volume change of more than 1 per cent; *inelastic* if the volume change is less than proportionate to the change in price.

Assuming omniscience, it would unquestionably be possible to tabulate for each individual the number of units of each commodity that he would buy at various hypothetical prices. This schedule might be presented graphically as a "demand curve." Such a curve would, of course, be valid only so long as he followed the same pattern of economic behavior—probably only once. That pattern would be subject to change, not merely because

[2] Alfred Marshall, *Principles of Economics* (1890), p. 162.

all the actions of some people and some of the actions of all people are whimsical rather than strictly rational, but also because the consumer would be influenced by educational or propaganda efforts of sellers, or by other changes in his tastes and habits, by modification of his purchasing power or the prices (in conjunction with qualities) of alternative purchases.

The producer or market distributor is interested in these individual demand curves only as they add up to an aggregate demand curve for his product. Both because of the satiability of the individual's want and the limitations of his purchasing power, the curve which would portray aggregate market demand is like the curve of individual demand in that it shows volume of purchases relatively high at low prices and relatively low at high prices. The fact, however, that the market consists of distinguishable groups, with different tastes, habits, and purchasing power, means that a market demand curve may show sharp change in slope at the point where such a consumer group comes into or drops out of the picture. These may amount to such complete breaks that the various groups of consumers would better be regarded as constituting separate markets. To that type of demand situation we shall return later.

The systematic attempt to devise statistical techniques for the measurement of market demand began with Henry L. Moore, who in 1914 published a study, *Economic Cycles: Their Law and Cause*, in which he set forth the "statistical laws of demand" (pp. 66 ff.).[3] The

---

[3] In the same year that Moore's book appeared, R. A. Lehfeldt published an article, "The Elasticity of Demand for Wheat" in the *Economic Journal*, Vol. 24 (1914), p. 212. In 1917, Moore applied his method of multiple correlation more intensively in another small book, *Forecasting the Yield and the Price of Cotton*. Marshall's discussion in the *Principles* implied that he had made some attempts to measure de-

particular problem which Moore set himself was that of ascertaining how much the prices of certain agricultural staples would fluctuate under varying conditions of crop yield. He was undertaking to devise a statistical methodology capable of establishing certain factual relationships which would substantiate a weather theory of business cycles. His methods were elaborated with much diligence and ingenuity by agricultural economists and statisticians,[4] who sought means of predicting the price results which would follow from the release on the market of larger or smaller supplies of staple or reasonably standardized farm products.[5]

Henry Schultz, elaborating methods used by Moore, generalized a technique for measuring demand curves but limited his own applications to the field of agricultural staples. The questions which he set up for inquiry at the beginning of his voluminous book were these: "If the price of a given crop is reduced by 1 per cent, will sales increase by more than 1 per cent, or by less than 1 per cent? Is a large crop worth more or less than a small crop? What, in short, is the elasticity of demand for the

mand statistically, and the French mathematician and economist, Cournot, had derived a mathematical formulation of "the demand function" as early as 1863.

[4] Mordecai Ezekiel, *Methods of Correlation Analysis* (1930), Chap. 22, and E. G. Nourse, "The Meaning of 'Price Policy,'" *Quarterly Journal of Economics*, Vol. 55 (1941), p. 177n.

[5] The ultimate use of such knowledge of market response was to give farmers "scientific" advice as to production and marketing policy— acreage expansion or contraction, rates of breeding and feeding livestock, the timing of marketings, and the distribution of products among markets. These techniques, first employed in the advisory guidance of farm enterprisers through the agricultural extension service, were later implemented by the holding operations of the Federal Farm Board and, to a much greater extent, the production control and market manipulations of the Agricultural Adjustment Administration, the Commodity Credit Corporation, the Agricultural Marketing Administration, and numerous other agencies, coming in time to operate under an "ever-normal granary" philosophy.

crop? What is the shape of the demand curve? Is it essentially fixed, or is it subject to change? With the passage of time, does the curve retain its height, or does it shift upward or downward? If it does shift, at what rate?"[6]

In spite of the widely known fact that volume of sales responds to changes in price differently at different levels of price, computers of demand elasticities ordinarily derive a single coefficient of elasticity for all points within a considerable range, supposed to represent a cross-section of the whole market. Since the price quotations used for such a calculation must cover a period of time, the figures given for the coefficient of elasticity of demand are in fact the results of rather arbitrary mathematical processes that throw together and manipulate data in such ways as are supposed to remove the influences of changing conditions.[7] Thus for example, Schultz states in his conclusions that wheat showed a market elasticity of demand of 0.2 for the years 1921-34; the coefficient for potatoes was 0.3 for 1915-29; and for sugar 0.3-0.4 from 1875 to 1929.[8]

Such a highly conventionalized or averaged expression of demand curves covering the whole range of prices ob-

---

[6] Henry Schultz, *The Theory and Measurement of Demand*, p. 5. As a matter of fact, Schultz did not press his inquiries as to the shape of the demand curve with anything like the thoroughness with which he explored its height and the direction and rate of shifting. This was due in part to the inadequacies of data available to him, but in part also to his range of interests. Other students of elasticities of demand for the less staple agricultural products have gone farther in examining the different elasticities of particular markets or sub-markets and of segments of the demand curve.

[7] The careful reservations which the statisticians may make concerning the validity of their findings are usually hidden away and the reader is liable to get exaggerated ideas about the applicability of the computed coefficients of elasticity.

[8] *The Theory and Measurement of Demand*, pp. 399, 427, 229.

served over a considerable period of time has been found significant and useful for the agricultural policy-maker, since he is concerned as to how the general market will react to a total crop volume.[9] Statistical students of the relation between the volume of total supply and the price level for certain agricultural products over the whole market were dealing with commodities that were practically uniform, like sugar, or highly standardized under official grades dealt in on organized public markets, as for instance cotton and cereals.[10] These products remain the same over a long period of market trading and, under the established methods of dealing in these markets, quoted prices and "sales realization" are practically identical. Finally, consuming habits as to the products are quite firmly established and such commodities are all so low in price as compared with possible substitutes that practically the whole population remains steadily in the buying market for a substantial satisfaction of their wants at any range of price that we have known. Hence the "coefficients of the elasticity of demand" (in most cases much less than 1) which have been derived for these products are clearly significant measurements for the purpose for which they have been devised. They have shown themselves quite trustworthy as aids in predicting the probable course of prices in response to changing conditions of supply.

[9] It is less adequate for the analytical study of a fluid milk market or for fresh fruits and perishable vegetables.

[10] A great deal of work has also been done on potato prices. Although not organized under an exchange system, the potato market is quite sensitively inter-connected and practically limited to one standard grade and "culls" which are fed to livestock on the farm or, to a very limited extent, processed. In the livestock field, market demand for hogs has been carefully studied in conjunction with the formulation of a theory of "hog cycles."

But are the questions raised by these agricultural students of elasticity of demand precisely the same as those confronting the maker of industrial price-and-production policies? And are the methods which satisfied Moore in his formulation of a weather theory of business cycles or which satisfy the writer of an agricultural "outlook report" or the theorist of the "ever-normal granary" capable of giving useful answers or safe guidance to the steel-maker, the automobile executive, and other price-administering businessmen?

ADMINISTERED PRICES AND MARKET DEMAND

Moore applied his method not only to what he called "the representative crops: corn, hay, oats, and potatoes,"[11] but also to pig iron as "representative" of industrial commodities—with amazing results. By resort to simple mechanistic reasoning, he argued that these other commodities must have a "new type of demand curve," which linked larger volume with higher price. His statistical study of pig iron prices yielded such a demand curve, for which the elasticity of demand was $+.527$, that is, an increase of about $\frac{1}{2}$ per cent in volume of sales with each increase of 1 per cent in price.[12]

The great vogue which quantitative methods have

---

[11] Moore, *Economic Cycles: Their Law and Cause*, p. 112.

[12] The same, p. 114. Schultz apparently followed his "master" to the extent of accepting this conclusion. To be sure, he shrewdly limited his own studies to the half dozen agricultural commodities examined by Moore, plus two excellently chosen items—wheat and sugar—and a ridiculous third—buckwheat. But in 1934, he referred to the "problem of the demand for producers' goods or the problem of the positively sloping demand curve" as one of two "unsolved problems in the statistical study of demand." Quoting Moore's findings for pig iron as "showing that the price rises with an increase of the product, and falls with its decrease," he concludes: "It is not for nothing that all statistical economists, with the exception of Professor Moore, have confined their studies of demand to foodstuffs. The problem of the demand for producers' goods calls for a re-examination of accepted theory as well as of the statistical tech-

attained in recent years has led other statistico-economists to use similar methods for deriving alleged coefficiencts of elasticity of demand for a number of industrial products. In order to see how successful such experiments are likely to prove, how trustworthy the results of such computations are, or how useful the coefficients of elasticity of demand for products in this other area, several questions need to be asked and several distinctions drawn.

Theodore Yntema, taking up where Moore left off with pig iron, introduced more realistic principal determining factors and more adequate mathematical methods.[13] Instead of an *increase* of slightly more than ½ per cent in volume of pig iron sales with each per cent *increase* of price, his methods derived for "steel" the conventional type of market demand curve, showing slightly less than ½ per cent *decline* (elasticity approximates −.3 or −.4) in sales resulting from 1 per cent of price *increase*.[14] This result raises two questions, first as

nique by which concrete demand curves are deduced. Let us hope that Professor Moore will throw more light on this problem." Essay contributed to *Methods in Social Science*, Stuart A. Rice, ed., pp. 658-60.

Schultz was still hoping for this further light when he published his own book in 1938. He headed the list of four fields for future research in demand with "Investigations in the demands for non-agricultural commodities" which, he said, "had thus far defied mathematical analysis. It should be the aim of research in this field to derive the statistical demand functions for such representative producers' goods as iron, steel, copper, and coal; and for such groups of representative consumers' goods as food, clothing, and housing." *The Theory and Measurement of Demand*, p. 661.

[13] Broad outlines for dynamic analysis of time series such as are involved in the problems under discussion have been indicated by Max Sasuly in a paper, "Generalized Multiple Correlation Analysis of Economic Statistical Series," in the *Journal of the American Statistical Association*, March 1930 (Suppl.) pp. 146 ff.

[14] U. S. Steel Corporation, *A Statistical Analysis of the Demand for Steel, 1919-1938*, Nov. 1, 1939, p. 2. Yntema's computations yielded four possible answers: +0.12, +0.52, −0.21, −0.88. From these four possible answers, he chooses the latter two on *"a priori"* grounds and

to the validity of the idea of a composite elasticity and second as to the applicability of the elasticity measurement to the price-making problems of the industrial market.

As to the first of these questions, does it make economic sense to talk of a coefficient of elasticity of demand for "steel," based on a composite figure of tonnage and of prices for the many products of the United States Steel Corporation? They include rails, plates, structural shapes, merchant bars, sheets (black and tin plate), cold rolled strip, wire, tubular products, angle bars, tie-plates, axles, wheels, bolts, cement, and even products of which copper is a principal ingredient. It would be evident in advance that the price elasticity of demand for rails, fish plates, spikes, car wheels, axles, and the sheets, plates, and castings used in rolling-stock would show an extremely low price elasticity of demand. On the other hand, we know that there is a substantially higher elasticity in the demand for corrugated roofing, light sheets, strip, and tin plate which go into a variety of uses where they compete rather sharply with lumber, glass, plastics, and various metals. To jumble these products of patently different demand elasticities into a single

---

two additional judgments of what is "probable," followed by a guess that "if the lags of shipments and industrial profits behind bookings were removed," the last two relations "would both give about the same results for the elasticity of demand, yielding a figure of 0.3 to 0.4 [that is, −0.3 to −0.4]. The evidence and argument adduced in the preceding pages of this paper support the conclusion that such a value—or one even lower—for the elasticity of demand for steel is not a statistical happenstance, but a reality." The same, p. 28.

Interrogated in TNEC hearings as to what it meant to say that his coefficient of elasticity of steel demand presented "reality," Yntema replied that the reason was that "it made 'sense,'" that is, the device of statistical measurement does not afford proof but is to be trusted only when and if it substantiates *a priori* reasoning. *Investigation of Concentration of Economic Power*, Hearings before the TNEC, Pt. 26, 76 Cong. 3 sess., p. 13740.

coefficient is to extinguish any light that price analysis in these different situations might shed on the several price-making processes.

A single coefficient of elasticity of demand for wheat, we have seen, gains significance and usefulness from the highly standardized character of the commodity and the highly organized marketing system through which it is sold. Obviously, there is no comparable price-making mechanism even for pig iron or steel billets, and still less for the fabricated products and by-products turned out by a highly integrated steel company. It is to be doubted that the agricultural economists would, in the absence of a general wheat market, ever have undertaken to derive a single coefficient of elasticity of demand for wheat by using a weighted composite volume index and a weighted composite price index for high protein bread flour, low protein pastry flour, alimentary paste, semolina, shorts, bran, mixed mill feeds, and breakfast cereals. In fact, durum wheat is not regarded as wheat at all for such statistical purposes.

Our second question is whether a coefficient of price elasticity of demand even for a single narrowly defined commodity in the industrial field would furnish a safe and useful guide to the price-making executive.[15] The

[15] Yntema emphatically asserts that his studies were not designed to give the U. S. Steel Corporation policy guidance or to suggest a positive answer to the question of whether price should be lowered or raised in any given instance. He says: "[These studies] were not made with any idea of providing the United States Steel Corporation or the steel industry with a formula which could be used as a basis for price policy. As a matter of fact, steel men were well aware of the characteristics of the demand for steel and the behavior of costs long before we began this study. We have merely applied the methods of statistical and economic analysis to the facts and presented our findings to the committee in the simplest way we could. Our objectives in the analysis of demand . . . were to ascertain approximately how the quantity of steel

answer to that question rests primarily on the fact that in most industrial price situations we are dealing with production processes which are under a very considerable degree of control—of scale of operations, of char-

---

sold by the industry responded to changes in price. . . . We have presented these findings to the committee in the hope that they may throw some light on the possibilities, and on the limitations, of increasing steel consumption by reducing price and on the extent to which such price reductions could be borne by a company such as the United States Steel Corporation . . . there was never any suggestion on our part that our analysis reflected or had anything to do with the businessman's criterion of desirable price. . . . I do not think it is possible for the steel industry to have a pricing policy." (*Investigation of Concentration of Economic Power*, Hearings before TNEC, pp. 13651, 13654.)

This seems to mean that Professor Yntema merely brought the statistician's tools of precision (which give answers ranging in value from .12 to .88 and having either plus or minus signs) to show the scientific "reality" of the steel business from 1919 to 1938. This was a purely detached piece of scholarly fact-finding not supposed to color the thought or action of practical businessmen. In spite of these caveats, which presumably accompanied his report when submitted to the Corporation, the latter did make certain applications of the facts. In its published summary of the report, we find the following: "Because of the low elasticity of demand for steel, the increase in volume resulting from a reduction in price is certain to be less than the increase needed to offset the adverse effects of the lower price on profits. Regardless of the volume of operations taken as a starting point, the percentage increases in volume necessary to compensate for various percentage reductions in the average 1938 prices, so that profits or losses would neither be increased or decreased by the price reduction, are [from about ¼ to 1/14 of the amount] required to offset price decrease." *Steel Prices, Volume and Costs—Controlling Limitations on Price Reductions*, an analysis prepared by the U. S. Steel Corporation in connection with hearings before the TNEC, Oct. 30, 1939, p. 4. Does this not mean that Yntema would think the officers of any steel company quite justified in using his findings as the basis of a course of price maintenance—indeed stupid if they did not read the handwriting he had put on the wall? The whole study focused on price "flexibility" and price reduction as a means of stimulating recovery from depression. In the TNEC Hearings (Pt. 26, p. 13588), he gives as two of "the basic questions to which our studies were addressed": "To what extent will the production and sale of steel respond to changes in the price of steel?" and "How far, if at all, is it feasible for the steel industry to achieve additional sales, production, and employment in depression by reduction of prices?"

acter of product, and of price and labor income relations.

This is the situation that Moore encountered in his study of the demand for pig iron. He hailed his result as a new type of demand, which linked larger volume with higher prices and which was, he thought, characteristic of industrial commodities. Economists were quick to point out[16] that what he had was more like a supply curve.[17] Yntema's first two equations yielded him a similar result, that is, coefficients of elasticity of demand of +.12 and +.52. He, however, turned from them as not reasonable since the larger takings at the higher prices did not reflect price elasticity strictly but were strongly influenced by changing business conditions. To take account of other economic forces, he brought two more factors into his equations—industrial profits and consumers' income above the level of necessitous expenditures. With these adjustments, he got coefficients of the orthodox form −.3 and −.4. This means that he was separating price elasticity from income elasticity. We shall speak presently of the usefulness of income elasticity of demand. But first, what of the significance of the coefficient of price elasticity isolated from other conditions? It no doubt has value for certain uses such as determining the effectiveness of tariff duties. But as a practical guide to the price-and-production policy-maker in the United States Steel Corporation or in any other industrial company, it turns his attention away from

[16] P. G. Wright, review of Moore, *Economic Cycles, Quarterly Journal of Economics*, Vol. 29 (1914-15), p. 638; E. J. Working, "What Do Statistical 'Demand Curves' Show?", the same, Vol. 41 (1926-27), p. 212; Harold T. Davis, *The Analysis of Economic Time Series* (1941), p. 137. See also E. W. Gilboy, "Demand Curves in Theory and Practice," *Quarterly Journal of Economics*, Vol. 44 (1929-30).

[17] Unless one says with Wicksteed that there is no such thing as a supply curve.

rather than toward the questions of greatest significance. It is likely to become a new rule-of-thumb less realistic and sound than the rules intuitively arrived at by the purely "practical" business manager. These statistical and theoretical "isolationists" in abstracting a single factor from a complex total situation are not giving the businessman a safe or useful tool of management.

To tell the business administrator what the volume response to price changes *would* be if all other determinants of the buyer's action were withdrawn, gives him an abstraction which has little or no practical meaning for him. If such a numerical gauge is taken as a guide to action in spite of the fact that other determinants of consumer action are present, operating, and also subject to alteration by the policy and action of the businessman, it becomes a force misleading instead of guiding him.

This is particularly true as we move from the more basic materials like pig iron, copper, coal, or lumber to the area of finished consumer goods. These are practically all rather highly differentiated products, selling at administered prices, with a complex variety of passable substitutes generally available. Not merely is the whole market divided into many special markets for nonstandardized products, but also the market for a given kind of product is subdivided into different grades or types of product appealing to different tastes or consumption habits and particularly to different income groups.

A coefficient of composite or average elasticity of demand if computed with a high degree of statistical competence for a single consumer item such as five-passenger sedans, three-piece wool suits, ladies' silk hose, electric washing machines, workmen's overalls, or three-tube radio sets may be found significant and useful for many types of study undertaken by advertising agencies, banks, government bureaus, or social agencies. But it does not have anything like the pertinence to individual company or commodity situations or the flexibility in application which are necessary for analysis of its own operations and policies by an individual firm. Attempting to apply in the field of consumers' finished goods such a coefficient of elasticity of general market demand as Schultz developed for agricultural products or Yntema for steel would be, in G. B. Shaw's phrase, like "hunting butterflies with an elephant gun."

DEMAND ANALYSIS IN THE INDIVIDUAL FIRM

A simple type of quantitative study of these market responses is both practical and useful. It is one merit of the large manufacturing and distributing corporation that it accumulates within its own organization a mass of sales data large enough to be useful for price analysis and more accurate as to quality differences, selling terms and conditions, and net sales realizations than official market reports can possibly be. This makes it feasible for a large company to undertake continuous experimental adjustments in prices of various articles and grades of articles, and to keep a careful check on results in terms of volume of profits and other economically and technologically important results that appear to follow from such changes.

This fact is fairly well recognized by market analysts and even the statistically untrained sales managers of most manufacturing and distributing companies. They do not ordinarily attempt to derive a coefficient of elasticity of demand for a company's entire output—such as "G.E. products," or even demand for all the "household appliances" made by that company. Instead, they undertake to define or identify a particular commodity which presents certain significant problems for price analysis in a specified market whose particular responsiveness is important for purposes of study and policy-making. This may involve breaking down what is conventionally thought of as a single commodity according to price lines, special designs, graded sizes, geographical preferences, and all the multifarious determinants of market responsiveness. These are the essential counterpart of the high differentiation of product and the administrative strategy of price-and-production policy-making—and changing —that are characteristic of our present regime of monopolistic competition. The question which such a policy-maker puts to himself is: How will some particular group of buyers respond to some modification of price-and-quality bait which I can put before it?

Some light for the guidance of policy-making and for its experimental testing may be derived from simple correlation studies of previous sales-and-price relations in the most closely related field. But obviously any study of established or antecedent relationships can shed but a limited amount of light on what may happen in the area of a proposed innovation. This is particularly true if the accepted theory of elasticity measurement is applied, based as it is on idealized, smooth, "infinitesimal" price changes.

The price mechanism of the organized commodity exchange conformed beautifully to that criterion. Wheat prices regularly move by breaks of $\frac{1}{8}$-cent a bushel, say .125 per cent of the unit price, and cotton prices by "points" of 1/100-cent, say .08 per cent of the unit price. Such reactions of centralized trading demand in a continuous market for standardized products have few if any parallels in the experience of the industrial price maker. With a product differentiated rather than standardized,[18] with no centralized transaction center, and with price changes discontinuous, the amounts of such changes must be substantial if they are to operate as a motivating force on buyers' actions.

A timorous nibbling at the price structure of the modern consumers' goods market will not produce results that justify themselves to the practical executive or that admit of significant measurement. The statistical record of such price and volume data, manipulated by the conventional elasticity measurement methods, could confidently be expected to produce a result which on its face would proclaim that there was little or no increase of sales as an accompaniment of price reductions. This methodology is in fact rather popular in certain quarters as a means of bolstering intuitive beliefs that price reduction is inherently bad on the theory that price maintenance and profit maintenance are synonymous.

To the careful market analyst, however, the fact that he finds a particular succession of price reductions un-

[18] Even those industrial products that we know to be quite highly standardized according to technical tests acquire commercial differentiation at the hands of the advertising manager or other sales promoter. Actual areas of consumer preference or habit or convenience of supply are built up for germ-proof oil; "fire chief" Texaco, "blue" Sunoco, and "that good Gulf" gasoline; "milder" Chesterfields, "not-a-cough-in-a-carload" Old Golds, "cool slow-burning Camels" ("I'd walk a mile") and "preferred-2-to-1-by-tobacco-experts" Lucky Strike cigarettes, in the face of mechanical smoker and blindfold tests, octane ratings, and practically standardized refinery processes. The radio makes me feel that there is life and death difference between dentifrices, but when I ask my dentist which is best, he says, "Oh, any of the advertised brands." Pressed as to whether I should stay with my present choice he adds cynically, "It does have a nice flavor. But some people prefer the taste of ————."
Producers' goods are differentiated with more technical precision and to a greater extent than is popularly recognized. (See Chap. 6, pp. 34 ff.) The U. S. Steel Corporation's report points this out as to certain of its products. "The steel industry produces thousands of steel products, most of which are practically made-to-order to the chemical, physical, shape, and dimension specifications of each buyer." *A Statistical Analysis of the Demand for Steel, 1919-1938*, p. 2.

accompanied by satisfactory increases in volume may simply raise the question whether he has not reached the fringe of absorptive power of a particular market. It may set him on a voyage of discovery or on an exploring expedition into a different sales area, to be reached or developed by more drastic price changes accompanied possibly by change in the character of his product. This may result in maintaining or expanding his business through what amounts to development of a new line of enterprise for the concern. A practical case of drastic price change is set forth by the economist of a certain manufacturing company who says:

> In one instance we were able to formulate a unique demand curve for a certain class of floor covering. We found that demand increased as price decreased until we reached the lowest price at which these goods had been offered by ourselves or our competitors. At this point the demand curve seemed to lose its responsiveness to price changes—indicating that, since this product was the one best suited for the use being considered, it would be purchased at the current price in about the same quantity that would be demanded if the price were decreased only moderately. As a consequence, we concluded that a major reduction in price would be necessary to tap enough new demand to make the change worth while. We made a major reduction in price and found that the increased volume did warrant the change.

Markets for specialized consumers' goods do not have the smooth and continuous stretch or contraction which inspired the concept of "elasticity" as applied to the competitive market of economic theory, which is approximated in organized commodity exchange markets. The responsiveness of industrial markets under monopolistic competition shows rather sharply marked breaks from one "shelf" to another, the rather persistent maintenance by one seller of a price-quality-clientele combination while another seller by-passes this position to gain or enlarge his market. To capture the public's interest, to get a response from consumers, he offers the stimulus of a 5 or 10, even a 25 or 50 per cent reduction in price. Sometimes this price change is accompanied by and sometimes is without changes in design, material, or size, which operate as offsets to the change in nominal price to which consumers react.

Time does not permit our entering into the many refinements and intricacies of these price-making techniques. In this connection it is a matter of common knowledge that price changes for finished consumers' goods are often ineffective or adversely effective just because many consumers judge quality by price and fear that a price reduction inevitably means a "cheapening" of the product, or they have a tendency to be ashamed to ask for or be seen using any but a "standard brand." For this reason, it is likely to prove easier for the producer to get the desired volume response from a price reduction if he makes design or package changes (accompanied by advertising claims) which break up any association of the new price with an old product.[19] This, however, raises a question in our next area of consideration commonly referred to by the clumsy phrase "income elasticity of demand."

Even while we have been focusing attention on the so-called "price elasticity of demand," it has been evident that such responsiveness is not fixed, but is relative, changing, and subject to constructive treatment by the businessman. In fact, the market demand with which we are concerned consists of (1) the actual

[19] The seller of producers' goods does not encounter this type of difficulty in the same way because his buyers are professionals rather than amateurs, and he is better able to demonstrate to them the fact that quality has been maintained even when price is substantially reduced. Much of this buying is on engineering specifications or laboratory test.

intensities of want which the public has for different amounts of different economic goods, (2) the objective market bids that result from these subjective wants in view of the purchasing power of the various consumers, and (3) the changes in this consumer behavior which can be brought about by education of consumers and the varied devices of salesmanship. We have pointed out that these three phases of market demand are inextricably blended in a total situation to which the businessman must adjust his action or which, within limits, he can shape to his purpose. Since, of course, it is demand related to or clothed with purchasing power in which the businessman is particularly concerned, we shall turn now to examine in more detail some aspects of the relationship of prices to income.

PRICE RESPONSIVENESS AND PURCHASING POWER

One of the few "laws" that economists have (even tentatively) accepted and labelled with the name of its discoverer or formulator (after the manner of the natural sciences) is "Engel's law" of expenditure. From a study of family budgets he arrived at several generalizations as to the proportions in which the share of income apportioned to major classes of expenditure—food, clothing, housing, and sundries such as education, health, and recreation—differs according to levels of income. Modern studies have pursued this line of inquiry further,[20] not in the belief that mechanistic "laws" of such a kind can be established in economics, but rather to reveal broad though changing patterns of human behavior within the setting of economic institutions and practices,

[20] Leven, Moulton, and Warburton, *America's Capacity to Consume* (1934); National Resources Committee, *Consumer Incomes in the United States: Their Distribution in 1935-36* (1938); National Resources Planning Board; *Family Expenditures in the United States.*

both individual and social, which are subject to more or less control and direction.

In our consideration of price elasticities of demand, we distinguished between the intensive theoretical study (straying off into psychology) of individual demand curves and the extensive statistical study of market demand curves. In much the same manner, the study of income elasticities of demand may be approached deductively in terms of the theory of consumption and what would normally happen to the expenditure pattern of an individual family as its income rises or falls. Or it may be approached through extensive statistical study of market takings, classified according to the income position of the various purchasers. The latter type of study, sensibly conducted, may be of enormous use to producers and sellers of differentiated products, such as characterize the larger part of the market for consumers' finished goods.[21]

Market demand may usefully be thought of as consisting of three zones or bands—a middle area of price and volume relations actually experienced, an area of

[21] Methods of measuring income elasticity of demand are of course not applicable in the same way to markets for producers' goods. It is probable that there are some instances in which a large corporation takes a greater volume either of supplies or of capital goods at a given level of price because of the fact that it is a large and rich company or because it is at the particular time enjoying increased income. This might be a case of forward buying on a rising market. Purchasers' policy might also be influenced by a firm's tax situation. By and large, however, the purchasing policies of industrial buyers are dictated by engineering specifications or the expert judgment of operating executives as to quantities required and the necessary or possible price to be paid than is the case with domestic consumers administering a personal income more or less thriftily and astutely to command as many conveniences and luxuries as possible in addition to what might be called "operative necessities." The corporation administers income toward the objective of profits, not the gratification of a higher standard of living. But, now and then, corporate management behaves like the individual and goes in for luxurious ornate offices, "showplace" factories, and cultural broadcasts whose cost is disproportionate to their advertising value.

potentially higher prices and restricted volume at one side, and an area of potentially lower prices and expanded volume of business and consumer satisfaction, on the other side. It is not correct to think of this lower priced area of the market as one of less ardent consumer desires or less pressing consumer needs, nor the higher priced area as one of more intense consumer satisfactions. The economically significant difference lies rather in the fact of more meager purchasing power in the former and of more ample ability to command goods regardless of their price in the latter. It is a matter of great importance to the "custom" producer to find out how tenaciously his clientele will stay with him in the face of rising prices. But the price behavior of "the carriage trade" and the psychology of "snob appeal" represent the contracting rather than the expanding phase of market elasticity. What the typical corporate executive in an age of mass production wants to know is how rapidly individual takings may be expected to expand or the number of takers be recruited if a lower price is offered. The real job of businessmen as a class is to provide satisfaction of the maximum number of wants through price relationships that promote the most active and efficient use of the labor and property resources of all would-be demanders.

Beside the fact that rich people have relatively inelastic demand schedules for all but super-luxuries, poor people elastic demand schedules for all but stark necessities, stands the fact that there are more poor people than rich even in the American population. This tells us that the market demand curve for most finished consumers' goods will show a sustained type of responsiveness in its lower reaches. Indeed there are practically no possibilities of selling more units of any commodity to the very rich man than are required for replacement, because he already is being supplied with all he can use. Price reduction will not stimulate his buying and, in numerous cases, may even check it. There are only limited possibilities also of selling additional units of necessities and conveniences to the well-to-do for the same reason. Expansion of sales of semi-luxuries, however, may assume important proportions. Within this broad middle bracket, quantitative studies of sales of automobiles, radios, and the like will inform the manufacturer or distributor rather usefully as to the approximate point at which families enter or can be dragged into the two-cars-in-the-garage class or at what point they become susceptible to the lure of extension telephones or of having a radio in the kitchen and bedroom as well as the living room, getting a portable radio, or having an automobile set installed.[22]

When we come to the truly low-income groups, there are enormous possibilities of market expansion by addition of more units of such things as these consumers already buy, as well as new purchases of things which they have thus far had to go without. There are a great many people yet to be supplied with their first unit of many conveniences and simple luxuries or even to secure as much food or clothing as their own sense of need or the "home economists' " criteria prescribe.

Obviously, if such needs are to be met, it must be through the adjustment of either the wage structure, the price structure, or both. To the wage question we shall

---

[22] In their study of automobile demand Roos and von Szeliski used the very illuminating separation of "supernumerary income" from total income. Supernumerary income is defined (*Dynamics of Automobile Demand*, p. 41) as that part of total income which is still available for expenditure after necessitous expenditures have been met. The base above which this income significant for the study of automobile demand is measured is $800 for a family of four (adjusted for changes in cost of living from the 1926 figure). These authors decided further that the most useful index of car price is that of the three low-priced automobiles, Chevrolet, Plymouth, and Ford.

give some attention in the next chapter. What is important here is that producers may seek profits either through
the turning out of more luxurious types of goods, even
mass production goods, or through the utmost simplification or reduction of costs in order that essential services
may be rendered to persons whose incomes still are
severely restricted. The methods of quantitative study
of the responsiveness of this market must, as was said in
our parallel discussion of price elasticities, be conducted
on a short-run, "spot," and experimental basis largely
within the range of current data supplied by large companies or trade associations. Income elasticity studies
which are designed to yield a measure of the general
public's capacity to consume multi-priced "food,"
"clothing," and "shelter," or even such lesser categories
as meats, entertainment, medical care, are too generalized
to be of much practical significance to the individual
business manager.

In order that "income elasticity of demand" studies
should be of maximum use to the business policy-maker,
two conditions would have to be met. First, we should
need much fuller pictures than we now have as to the
actual apportionment of individual and family expenditures among various goods and services, identified as to
their specific prices by size and quality. General studies
undertaken by national statistical agencies can give only
clues that, after careful analysis by the particular producer, may set for him certain specific questions for spot
studies of his own. These will show the distribution of
his different price-and-quality products among consumers in different income classes. Kept up over a period
of time, such studies should show what response attends
efforts to reach a particular income group by each specific
quality and price adjustment to its taste and buying
power. Second, all that can be learned about the relation

between income differences and purchasing behavior needs to be subjected to searching analysis and constructive interpretation by the policy-making executive.

Quite clearly, he needs to consider the question how he can adapt himself to the income structure by which he is confronted or to changes which may come into that structure from forces outside his control. If incomes chance to be rising, knowledge of the volume of past purchases in each successive income class gives the producer advance information as to how much he may expand his business at old prices with a general rise in incomes or how much he may raise prices and keep his old volume. If, however, incomes are declining, correlation studies of volume and price by income groups show him how he will have to lower prices by economy or redesigning of product if he is to hold the business he now has.

But income studies may shed light not merely on how to adapt price policy to income situations. They also show how to get volume at a given price level by seeing that the necessary income finds its way into the hands of the purchasers needed to make the market. This aspect of the matter involves very large issues of economic theory and business practice. An approach to them will be set forth in the closing section of this chapter and they will be examined in some detail in the next chapter.

JOINT DEMAND AND MARKET RESPONSE

Thus far we have been speaking of price and volume relationships as though they could be dealt with for each commodity in isolation. As a matter of fact, any adequate understanding of actual market response rests on the idea of price interrelationships. Those who are interested in the narrower concept of demand "elasticity" and in mathematical means of measuring it are not unaware that prices are interrelated. Still they are content to go on seeking in the main to isolate a given price relation from its complex environment and to reduce it to quantitative terms in a denatured or abstracted environment. This procedure is useful for certain purposes, provided the economist or statistician knows and remembers what his mathematical answers mean.

But prices are a manifestation of the life activities of men, and the price system itself takes on much of the character of a living process. Only a very inadequate or even distorted view of this process can be secured by the isolation and laboratory examination of its several parts.[23] The thing loses some of its essential qualities under such treatment just as does an animal organ when it is dissected out of the living body and sectioned, stained, pickled or otherwise prepared for mechanical or chemical examination. Such techniques yield certain kinds of useful knowledge but they never tell the full story.

Mathematical economists have sought to classify the simplest relations between prices as "competing," where one commodity is a substitute for another, and as "completing" where the two must be used in conjunction with each other. Statisticians have experimented in extending measurements of price elasticity of demand to such cases of joint use. Schultz, for example, attempted statistical measurement of the mutually competing demand for lamb and beef and of the complementary demand for coffee and sugar, and of tea and sugar. The enormous difficulty of this task is immediately suggested by the fact that the use of sugar in tea or even in coffee makes up so small a part of the market demand for sugar. This difficulty is all the greater because the elasticity of de-

---

[23] This is in the field of economics essentially the same view as that advanced for physiology and psychology by Alexis Carrel in *Man, the Unknown*.

mand for sugared tea is certainly very different (in the United States) from the demand elasticity for sugared coffee—with pie, ice cream, domestic and industrial uses of sugar all showing their characteristic intensities of joint demand.

In a somewhat more complex setting, the automobile gives us an admirable illustration of the interdependent character of market responses. In the first place, the automobile employs a wide variety of metal, plastic, textile, glass, rubber, paint, and "composition" products in its make-up. Automobile manufacturers thus become joint demanders—having both completing and competing demand—with other industrial and final users of all these types of commodities. In the second place, the automobile is in one sense not a finished consumers' good but simply the major item in the final consumers' good, transportation. Its market will respond to price changes in gasoline, oil, tires, garage rent, service and repair costs, and others. There would be no conclusiveness to a study of the public's reaction to prices of automobiles except on certain assumptions or facts as to prices for gasoline, tires, and batteries, and a given supply of garages, service stations, hard-surfaced roads, hotels, country clubs, road houses, and summer and winter resorts —all with their own distinctive price relations.

So greatly does this limit the possibility of making any valid measure of market response computed for a single price in such a bundle of consumer expenditures that the automobile industry's own study of automobile demand observes: "Annual operating and other maintenance costs are three or four times as large as the cost of replacing scrapped cars with new cars, and therefore should influence the maximum ownership level more than the new car prices."[24]

[24] Roos and von Szeliski, *The Dynamics of Automobile Demand*, p. 69.

Roos and von Szeliski bring the complementary factors of automobile upkeep into their calculations. Having estimated a coefficient of price elasticity, running from about 2.5 to 3.5 in the decade 1929-1938, they proceed to lower these elasticities by the amount of price responsiveness that is to be ascribed to reduction in costs of car operation, thus concluding "that 1.5 may be accepted as the elasticity of passenger car sales with respect to price" (of the three leading low-priced cars).[25] Such a procedure takes account of the fact that the demand for automobiles had shown such responsiveness as it had, in part because of the accompanying decline in prices of goods and services needed for car operation. But to take this lower coefficient of elasticity as the guide to action for the automobile maker is to ignore further possible declines in operating costs. What it is important for the manufacturer of automobiles to know is how much further response in car sales could be secured if any or all of these operating costs could be lowered in any given combination with car costs. Similarly, each seller of goods and services that enter into the costs of car operation wants to know how much his market will be helped by lowered car prices as well as lower prices for tires, gas, or whatever.

An important reason why the statistical measurement of price-volume relations for industrial raw materials and partly finished goods does not yield coefficients of price elasticity of demand significant for the guidance of management is because the same product becomes an ingredient of great numbers of finished consumer products each of which has a distinctive market demand, but in many of which the given material plays only a minor, perhaps even an insignificant role. The United States Steel Corporation study recognizes this fact formally

[25] The same, pp. 92, 94.

(but fails to give it proper weight in its conclusions). The report says:

> In the case of low-priced automobiles, the cost of steel is about 10 per cent of the delivered price. This percentage would be lower for a more expensive automobile. For a representative list of canned food products, the cost of tin plate per can varied from 3.4 to 13.9 per cent of the retail price of such food products. The cost of steel consumed by the railroads is estimated to average only about 5 per cent of the value of transportation services furnished by them. In the construction industry, steel costs range from 4 per cent of the total cost of a frame house to as much as 30 per cent of the total cost of a steel bridge. For a modern automatic packaging machine, the steel cost component was found to be less than 2 per cent of the selling price. Extreme examples may be cited showing a very high or a very low ratio of the cost of steel to the price of the finished product, but 10 per cent appears to be a reasonably typical proportion. On this basis, a 10 per cent reduction in the price of steel would correspond to a 1 per cent reduction in the price of the finished product made from steel.[26]

Unless some statistical means can be found for measuring simultaneously and in their interrelations the reciprocal responsiveness of all the markets in which the various goods and services are presented in all sorts of bundles for consumer acceptance or rejection, the attempt to measure specific elasticities of demand abstracted from the influence of changes in other commodities will inevitably present to the producer of each separate commodity apparent proof of the futility of any price reduction. Indeed, it not merely points to the folly of anyone lowering prices but, by inference, points to the wisdom of everybody raising prices.

Reference was made in Chapter VI to the interrelation of demand for various materials and types of labor in the housing industry. This is such that a separate coefficient of elasticity of demand for builders' hardware

[26] *Investigation of Concentration of Economic Power*, Hearings before TNEC, p. 13592.

or shingles or mill-work is deprived of any practical meaning except as a warning not to lower prices while the prices of all other housing materials are maintained. The housing market could not possibly respond to a price change for any single item except on the condition that simultaneous changes of significant magnitude took place in all or most of the other items of the tied group. Thus the vital problem of the responsiveness of the market for the individual article produced by the industrial firm is that of the response of general markets and general business to price relations or price adjustments which pervade the whole price system.

This emphasizes the extremely limited range of usefulness of statistical studies of demand "elasticities" within the area of industrialized production and sale of specialized and jointly used economic goods. It suggests that business management, instead of hoping for calculating-machine answers as to market behavior, must master broader, more intimate, flexible, and resourceful techniques for the appraisal of the conditions of responsiveness to which it must adjust its productive operations.[27]

MARKET RESPONSIVENESS AND THE PRICE SYSTEM

Let us begin our concluding section by reviewing briefly the steps thus far taken in this chapter.

If statistical measures of market demand are to have any considerable credibility or usefulness, they must be

---

[27] Frederick C. Mills has approached the statistical study of prices on a much broader basis than that of "elasticity of demand." He has devised various measurements of the "behavior" of prices both individually and in combination. He conceives of basic price relationships as "net-works or constellations" and is concerned to identify both "patterns of behavior" and "patterns of change." Mills' *Behavior of Prices* centers on the pattern-making influence of basic economic forces and was designed to shed light on the problem of business cycles rather than furnishing guidance to the industrial price policy maker.

derived from the data of a free competitive market for a staple product of widespread and continuous consumption. It is only under such conditions that we get a sufficiently wide range of price observations under flexible supply conditions and that we are dealing with a sufficiently stabilized type of demand. Even so, these generalized expressions of price elasticity of demand are applicable only to broad national or industry-wide policy-making, such as tariff proposals, domestic excise measures, or United States Department of Agriculture production programs before the Agricultural Adjustment Administration introduced any substantial controls.

Such coefficients of elasticity of demand are most trustworthy when applied to situations which lie well within the range of actual recent experience as to volume of supply and associated price. They become extremely dubious if the question being asked is how much would consumers buy if we had a supply substantially greater or substantially less than any that was previously known, or how much would consumers absorb if the cost were changed materially from any past price.

The predictive value of statistical measures of elasticity of demand is greatly reduced when methods developed in the agricultural market are applied to industrial situations in which large-scale producers have employed their control over production to limit price movement to a narrow range, adjusting the flow of supplies to this relatively rigid price structure.

Such generalized and statistically conventionalized measurements become not only untrustworthy but positively misleading if applied to the particularized problems confronted by the producer of differentiated products—producers' and, still more, consumers' finished goods. Such a producer is constantly trying to detach himself ever more sharply from the general demand for a stabilized kind of want satisfaction and to create a special response to what he can offer. This is the imponderable but constructive factor that private enterprise contributes to business—costs lowered through efficiency, character and quality of product adjusted more closely to buyers' desires and purchasing power, and the goods thus differentiated merchandised skillfully to draw out the full responsiveness of carefully delimited and developed markets of individual concerns.

Studies of the elasticity of demand in relation to income differences are more useful to the industrial policymaker; they center on changes in volume at a given price in different income groups or with change in income of a given group.

We pass now from summarization of the separate points already made to commentary on the broader conclusions to which these steps in the analysis lead. To measure the complex, subtle, but widely ramifying aspects of demand and its responsiveness to productive enterprise in his particular business, the industrial executive must in the main look to types of analysis and effort which are both less pretentious and more pretentious than the statistical derivation of mathematical coefficients of price and income elasticity of general market demand.

As to the less pretentious devices for the guidance of price-and-production policy, there should be intensive study of experimental price reduction, design change, and promotion of new areas of consumption, with results constantly checked by simple arithmetical study of the accompanying volume and profit changes.

Such procedure lies within the established practice of all progressive business management. These spontaneous efforts of private enterprise to innovate better and more economical business service and to secure the necessary volume response primarily through price appeal should be continued and intensified. The responsiveness of the market should not be prejudged as incapable of taking an enlarged volume of product simply because statistical studies based on other premises show a low coefficient of elasticity of general demand. But these simple experimental procedures for testing short-run reactions are not alone an adequate means of deriving a price policy or procedure.

Here we pass to the consideration of guides to policy-making, which were referred to above as "more pretentious" than statistical measurement of market demand. We have called this aspect of business management "appraising the responsiveness of market demand" rather than "measuring the elasticity of demand." Economic "responsiveness" is a very complex and roundabout process involving wide and long repercussions, not a simple and complete cause-and-effect relation between a moment's price and a moment's profit.

To "appraise" reciprocal responses of this complex price system involves much more than the mathematical manipulation, however refined, of a somewhat conventionalized body of market statistics. The problem must be approached by a functional analysis of the process out of which purchasing power springs or within which it is created and of how the individual firm can best take advantage of these flows at the same time that its activities contribute most to maintaining the sources of the flow and directing its course most effectively.

Formal "measures" can be applied only to certain rather narrow relations. The total process must be appraised by looser but more aggressive methods embracing inventive or imaginative elements, half intuitive judgments based on experience and reflection, and a willingness to take "calculated risks."[28]

If the current system of "administered prices" under private enterprise is to function smoothly and successfully, there must be somewhere in the organization persons who are capable of discerning what constitutes mutually consistent adjustment of prices of cost goods to prices of sales goods, prices of labor to prices of consumers' wares. They must be capable too of taking those lines of action which are necessary to bring such working adjustments about. Price-making executives in the leading firms in strategic industries cannot make policies merely on the basis of taking the level of national income as they find it, both as to total amount and distribution. They cannot in the long run adjust their company operations to a flow of national income which maintains itself from some outside spring. The source of national income lies in business employment itself, and business management must so organize the operations of the price system that income is to be found at the proper places to take off the total product—or, stated from the other side, that goods are produced and priced within the limits of existing incomes.

A major phase of this problem of mutual adjustment of labor income and market prices to each other will be examined in the next chapter.

[28] To say this is not to show lack of faith in "scientific" methods of business guidance. "Science is measurement" says the seal of a contemporary statistical institute. But either science is more than measurement or the price-making art or the art of business management transcends the limits of quantitative science.

CHAPTER VIII

DISTRIBUTION COSTS—WASTING AT THE BUNGHOLE

A rejoinder made by many businessmen whenever recommendations for a low-price policy are advanced is this: "How can consumer prices be lowered when distribution charges are being pushed up all the time?" This response "passes the buck" from one major class of businessmen—the manufacturers—to another great class—the distributors. It brings into our discussion a phase of the pricing problem which was touched on briefly in Chapter VI but which will now be taken up for more detailed examination.

In considering the areas of applicability of low-price policy, we recognized that a given manufacturer (including producers of semi-finished and raw materials) might apply himself with the utmost skill and diligence to lowering production costs and might pass on all these savings as reductions in the price of his product and still not confer a proportionate benefit on the consumer or inject a proportionate stimulus into the market. At that point in our analysis we distinguished three typical situations:

1. Efficiency gains translated into lowered prices of fabricated products may be absorbed by the distributor as added profit or higher costs of operation and thus confer no benefit on the consumer.

2. Such savings in production costs may be passed on by the manufacturer to the distributor and be passed on by him to the consumer in the full absolute amount but, being a smaller percentage

of the retail price, have a less than proportionate effect in stimulating sales. If so, the reward to the enterpriser who introduced the lower-cost method of production would be lost or lessened. This, in turn, would remove or weaken the stimulus to further steps in cost saving.

3. Savings made by the manufacturer, being matched by new efficiencies introduced by the distributor and both passed on in the form of lower consumer prices, will have their full effect in attracting business to both the distributor and the manufacturer, who thus team up in joint effort toward enlarging their own enterprises through the introduction of productive innovations and the conversion of these efficiency gains into the largest amount of consumer satisfaction.

In effect, the manufacturer who says it is useless for him to follow a low-price policy because of high distribution costs maintains that the last of these three situations does not in fact exist but rather that the first two are universal or even that the first is dominant in his particular sector. We shall begin our examination of this problem therefore by endeavoring to see a little more clearly what are the facts.

THE BLURRED FACTUAL PICTURE

For several decades past, there have been recurrent and indeed more or less chronic complaints against the high cost of distribution and assertions that it absorbs a larger and larger percentage of the consumer's dollar. In a certain overall sense, this is unquestionably true. The percentage of the working population that is classified by the Census or the Bureau of Labor Statistics as engaged in distribution at successive dates has increased considerably. Likewise, imposing arrays of price statistics can be marshalled from many lines of business to show that the farmer, the miner, the original processor, or even the final fabricator of manufactured goods each gets a smaller percentage of the money paid by the consumer at the retail counter than was once the case.

These figures, like much of what is offered as statistical "proof," need to be interpreted with a high degree of discrimination. What is classed as distribution is by no means clearly separated from functions performed by concerns or individuals classed as engaged in production.[1] Activities once performed in the home or the shop are now organized on a commercial basis and what is nominally distribution of physical goods often comes to mean the rendering of additional and sometimes quite unrelated services. Some producers perform functions that in other cases are performed by distributors, and some distributors include in their business services that are in fact part of production. As a result of these ambiguities and realignments, our examination of distribution charges will have to be analytical and

[1] In certain significant ways, the very economies and efficiencies which have been introduced by, and which are credited to, production agencies add to the task of distribution and thus lessen the possibility of cost reduction by these agencies. Thus, for example, the shoe manufacturer economizes in manufacturing costs by standardizing his product for mass production. But it is important to retain the advantages of long wear, good appearance, and comfort which are associated with individually fitted goods. Hence the retail merchant must carry a full line of lasts and sizes, must employ well-trained clerks, and the latter must take sufficient time to make a careful measure or estimate of the requirements of the customer's foot and locate in the large stock the particular shoe which will meet these requirements. The clerk may perhaps have to spend added time and exert further skill in reconciling the customer to some adjustment of his preferences as to style, color, or material to the requirements of a proper fit. Similarly the typical large ready-made clothing store operates a rather sizeable tailor shop or dressmaking establishment. In a custom-made product, the analogous functions of measuring, try-on, and alteration are classed as production rather than distribution costs.

qualitative, not quantitative (statistical or accounting) in character.

At the outset, we must distinguish the several aspects of what is frequently lumped under a single figure as "distribution charges." First, there are the costs of physical handling, financing, credit and collection, and routine selection and fitting of goods. Second is the more active phase of selling, involving discovery of prospects, creation of demand, and effecting the actual sale ("name on the dotted line" or "cash on the barrel head"). Third, we should distinguish a class of expenses frequently incurred by distributors or manufacturers which bears no relation to the physical and financial process of marketing and which is related to the task of salesmanship only in the indirect and general sense of creating or maintaining the prestige of the company or which in fact constitutes a redistribution of the company's earnings to the general public as a sort of profit-sharing or as a beneficent gesture.

These three types of distribution charges will be discussed separately at later points in the chapter. But before passing on, we should make one general observation as to what the quantitative studies which have thus far been made of distribution charges seem to indicate. In spite of the difficulties of definition, classification, and accounting, there is general consensus that these charges do constitute a larger factor in consumer price today than in the past. Stated in another way, more of our business effort goes into distribution in proportion to that which goes into actual production. In the attempt to get a comprehensive picture of the situation and trend, the Twentieth Century Fund put as its first approximation the statement that the census of 1870 showed only about one-quarter of the population engaged in distributive and service callings and three-fourths in direct production, whereas by 1930 the proportion approached 50-50.[2]

Along with general consensus on the fact that distributive activities have come to absorb an increased proportion of our business effort or that the producer or fabricator of physical goods gets a decreased and perhaps decreasing percentage of the consumer's dollar, there is a high measure of agreement on one other argument running through at least a majority of the very numerous studies of market distribution. This is to the effect that the wide distributive margins are not accompanied by disproportionately high profits for these agencies. Weight of evidence seems clearly to be that if such charges are to be reduced, it must be primarily through elimination

---

[2] *Does Distribution Cost Too Much?* (1939), p. 9. Limiting his classification to more strictly defined marketing functions, N. H. Engle shows an increase from one-seventh to one-third of the "gainful workers of the nation."

"The rising trend of distribution costs which was concomitant with the Industrial Revolution was inevitable. In the simple village economy which preceded the growth of the factory system, the few purchases of consumers were made without appreciable marketing costs. With the exception of the limited number of items then in general commerce, the exchange of merchandise was effected by direct contact between the buyer and the maker. After the factory system was established, the growth of large-scale, specialized units producing a tremendous variety of merchandise necessarily was accompanied by increasing costs of bringing about exchange. In addition to such essential marketing costs as those for transportation, warehousing, and credit, it was necessary also to incur the costs of bringing buyers and sellers together in the market. Sellers had to be informed of buyers' wants, and buyers had to be informed of merchandise available, if exchange was to take place. The costs of the selling process, i.e., providing the information and persuasion needed to effect exchange, became larger as the industrial organization became more complex. But sellers have incurred selling and distribution costs greater than the minimum which may be deemed necessary to effect exchange. They have resorted to competition in advertising, personal selling, and other non-price forms of competition, all of which involve cost." Neil H. Borden, *The Economic Effects of Advertising*, (1942), p. 852.

of some of the "services," real or imaginary, now
rendered in exchange for these charges or through an
improvement in the operative techniques by which given
services are performed. Such a view orients the problem
in terms of the basic issues of business enterprise,
efficiency, and technological and organizational gains,
which constitute the major theme of this book.

THE SWELLING RANKS OF SALESMEN

Before proceeding to a more detailed examination
of the possibilities of eliminating or reducing inefficiency
or waste in the distributive process, a word needs to be
said about occupational distribution of the working population. The very idea of technological efficiency suggests
that in a progressive economy more and more people
are released from the basic task of producing subsistence
and thus left free to follow lines often referred to as the
cultural callings. We would normally expect in an advanced civilization to find the ranks of education, research, medical care, and the arts growing in proportion
to the numbers in extractive and fabricating industries.[3]
There is, however, another aspect of the dispersion of the
working population which claims our attention briefly.

At the same time that modern industry, by stepping
up its efficiency, frees an increasing percentage of the
population from the processes of material production to
expand the life of the spirit, there is also a tendency for
the intensive development of corporate industry to dis-

---

[3] This classification of course is not clean-cut in view of the increasing
tendency of industry to provide medical care for its employees, to
conduct research in pure as well as applied science, to maintain its own
studios of design, and its own psychological laboratories for labor
placement and training. Thus, census and other statistical enumerations
will count some doctors, scientists, artists, and writers as employed in
manufacturing. To a lesser extent, such specialists may be included in
the ranks of transportation or trade.

card a good many workers. It may fail to provide them with wage-employment opportunities in its highly selective activities when it disrupts the opportunity for self-employment. Such occupational stragglers not swept along in the march of industrial progress tend to provide employment for themselves in those callings where "ease of entry" is greatest. Broadly speaking, the best alternatives of this group appear to be two in number— farming and small merchandising.

We shall not pause to elaborate on the character of agriculture as a "residual calling." Subsistence farming furnishes a sort of economic backwater measurably distinct from the more intensive areas of high-efficiency commercial farming. In a similar way, members of the non-farm population who do not find their talents fitting them into industrial wage employment, who are unwilling to accept its disciplines, who are displaced by the technological changes or by cyclical contraction of employment opportunities are inclined to turn to the starting of a tiny shop on a shoe-string, to selling some kind of goods on commission, or to resort to outright peddling. "They may turn to house-to-house canvassing or operating a roadside stand or a gasoline station or— at their most abject stages—to passing out advertising cards or carrying a sandwich board."[4]

All such swelling of the ranks of those classified as engaged in distribution magnifies the proportion which this branch of business bears to extractive and manufacturing industry. It produces an unfavorable showing in any general statistical presentation of the costs of marketing. It adds to or enlarges a fringe of business enterprises conducted by persons typically of limited experience or low efficiency, of scanty and poor equip-

[4] Twentieth Century Fund, *Does Distribution Cost Too Much?* p. 21.

ment, and who handle an uneconomically small volume of business. Whether the result is seen as inadequate remuneration to these who are distributors by force of circumstances (rather than by choice or aptitude) or as inordinately high distribution costs depends on the kind of pecuniary calculation or theoretical analysis which is applied. At its worst it constitutes a hard core of casual employment, distress self-employment, or even purely nominal occupation.[5]

But does a tendency for those who are classified as distributors in statistical enumerations to grow in numbers entail resistance to the progress of technical and economic efficiency in distribution as such? And can the "producer" pass responsibility for defeat of his efforts at price lowering to the "distributor" on the grounds that the residual character or ease of entry into the business of merchandising makes distribution costs high? And even if this be so, who or what is to be held responsible for the plethora of recruits to the ranks of distribution?

Our answers to the last of these questions must be deferred to later sections of the chapter and indeed in some part to subsequent chapters. As to the first question, it is easy to see situations in which the "scab" competition of amateur and economically desperate small shopkeepers, peddlers, and solicitors tends to reduce the volume of business of established distributors, disrupt

[5] It defies complete elimination since there must always be a bottom layer to the economic organization of even the most efficient society. However, the persistence of a large class of supernumerary distributors—and still more its growth—constitutes a challenge to the efficiency with which our industrial society as a whole is organized. It is simply a milder form of the faulty utilization of resources which is to be found in the economies of backward countries. Witness the bazaars of the Near East, the "three peanut vendor" of China, so vividly portrayed in Alice Tisdale Hobart's, *Oil for the Lamps of China.*

their efforts toward large-scale and highly equipped efficiency, and preclude the attainment of lowest unit costs of distribution. But this is a relatively minor factor in the whole problem of distribution costs and the possibility of their reduction. Of much greater significance is the issue as to whether business enterprise in the middle and upper strata of the distributive industry has shown aggressive and intelligent leadership toward better technique and organization designed to lower costs and toward price policies and schedules of service charges which will most fully convert operative achievements into economic gains for the nation.

BELATED IMPROVEMENT OF DISTRIBUTION TECHNIQUES

The typical manufacturer whose plaint was voiced in our opening paragraph charges in essence that his brother businessman, the distributor, has been less diligent and skillful than the producer in introducing technological improvements into the distribution part of the nation's business and in using gains thus created to stimulate the market for the manufacturer's product. This view has been accepted by numerous students of distribution problems. Notably, the study of distribution costs made by the Twentieth Century Fund said:

For decades the inventive genius of American business has been chiefly dedicated to the lowering of production costs through mechanization and scientific management and to the elimination of inefficiencies in making goods. The results have astonished the world. It is equally true that the same inventive genius has hardly begun to be applied to the reduction of distribution costs.[6]

It is, of course, difficult—in any precise sense impossible—to get trustworthy indexes of the relative

Does Distribution Cost Too Much?, pp. 3-4.

increase of efficiency and technological progress introduced into these two major branches of our business life
and of the comparative times of introduction or rates
of progress. There would probably be general agreement that more effort was concentrated and more success
achieved in the field of production than in distribution
during the latter decades of the 19th century and the
first decade of the 20th. At about 1908 or 1910, however, the sharp focusing of public attention on the
problem of the high cost of living stimulated efforts
toward technological and organizational progress in the
marketing field.[7] Today it is by no means clear that,
measured by the relative possibilities in the two fields,
achievements have been any less creditable in recent years
in the field of distribution than in production activities.

Particularly since the First World War there has
been a vigorous growth and overhauling of old distributive agencies and methods. Mail-order houses have
developed store selling in towns and villages and large
department stores in some cities, correlating these
activities with their older mail distribution. Chain stores
have consolidated the small shops with which they
began into fewer and larger stores and super-markets
strategically located with reference to flows of auto-

[7] The Harvard Graduate School of Business Administration through
its Bureau of Business Research, was a pioneer in the professional study
of marketing problems. This bureau began its field studies and laboratory
analyses of marketing costs and practices in the summer of 1911, since
when it has continued intensive work and numerous publications in this
field. Its godfather A. W. Shaw, a businessman of Chicago, practically
initiated the now voluminous literature of marketing with a small book,
Some Problems of Market Distribution, in 1912, followed by P. T.
Cherington's *Elements of Marketing* in 1920, and F. E. Clark's
Principles of Marketing in 1922. In 1924, the Domestic Commerce
Division was established in the United States Department of Commerce,
and in 1929, the first national Census of Distribution was taken. Today,
there are scores of marketing conferences, marketing associations, and
marketing magazines.

mobile traffic and availability of parking facilities. Independent operators have been forced by this competition to improve their facilities and methods and to enter "voluntary chains" for buying and operating economies.

Warehousing equipment and practices have been improved, truck delivery service expedited and bettered (for example through refrigerated transport); more of the work of packaging put on a factory basis; meat cutting carried back to the packing plant to be done with band-saws and other mechanical equipment by experts; inventory controls improved; means of ascertaining consumer preference made more scientific; weighing, computing, and accounting processes mechanized; and the buying of supplies concentrated and simplified.[8]

In the case of some large chains, mail-order houses, and department stores, the distributor has taken over the whole output of various factories on a contract basis or actually purchased or built factories of his own, thus eliminating all intermediary marketing charges and securing better control over design, materials, and quality. For example, the Great Atlantic and Pacific Tea Company in 1930 operated 35 bakeries, 13 dairy product plants, 9 general food factories, 7 coffee roasting plants, and 6 salmon canneries.[9]

The effort to economize in the distribution process has proceeded also from the other end. Some manufacturers have discerned in traditional types of distribution wastes and duplications which have stood in the way of their making satisfactory profits or reducing prices as much as they might in the interest of stimulating their trade.

[8] See P. D. Conover, "Labor Saving Devices in Marketing," *Journal of Marketing*, Vol. 4 (1939), p. 150.
[9] Federal Trade Commission Report on Chain Stores, *Cooperative Grocery Chains*, S. Doc. 12, 72 Cong., 1 sess., Chap. 10; *Chain Store Manufacturing*, S. Doc. 13, 73 Cong., 1 sess.

Such an attempt to reduce intermediary distribution costs has been a factor in the vertical integration of many industrial concerns. It has also led to the addition of wholesale or even retail facilities to companies which started as manufacturers but which have felt that the costs of distribution or quality of service rendered by existing distributing agencies interfered with the satisfactory development of their market.

It is not our purpose here to attempt a definitive appraisal of any particular phase of these efforts or of the practices which have been developed in any particular concern or industry. It seems clear, however, that business enterprise has during the last quarter century or so become active in its search for cheaper and more efficient distribution methods not less than for the improvement of production processes.[10] Whether or not this means that the gap by which this business area was supposed to be lagging behind the efficiency gains being made in the factory or production sector has been closed, it would be impossible to say and to support the assertion with convincing quantitative evidence.

Careful and candid consideration of the matter even reveals that in spots at least it is clearly the distributor who has set the pace of efficiency.[11] In *Industrial Price Policies and Economic Progress* (pp. 54, 84, 108) and in this book (p. 156) attention has been called to the fact

[10] Compare Theodore N. Beckman, "Criteria of Marketing Efficiency," *The Annals*, Vol. 209 (1940), p. 133.

[11] Since this chapter appeared in pamphlet form, a prominent business executive has made available an interesting statement of such a broad concept of the distributor's role and responsibility:

"Sears, Roebuck and Co. has attempted to do in the distribution field what Ford and many other manufacturers, large and small, have done in the production field. Many people talk about economies in distribution as meaning economies in the running of a store—self-service vs. salespeople—non-delivery of goods—low rent locations, etc. We think in entirely different terms. We recognize that distribution begins when

that distributive agencies have sometimes shown a capacity to become leaders in technological change not less than in the price policies by which such changes can be geared most effectively to the efficient functioning of the whole economy.

It is clear, however, that any serious effort to make as much progress as can be made in reducing the costs or raising the efficiency of distributive methods involves the elimination or curtailment of certain individuals,

---

an article leaves the machine, passes inspection, and is packaged, ready for shipment. It makes no difference whether many operations from there on are carried forward by that same manufacturer or by other agencies. . . .

"A gallon of paint which took 24 minutes to make now takes $2\frac{1}{2}$ hours to get sold to the consumer—6 times as much for distribution as for production. Other items take 3 to 10 times. Our manufacturing friends have done a grand job. From the middle of 1923 until the middle of 1940, there has been a steady decline in per unit labor costs, so that on the average, unit costs by 1940 were a full one-third—$33\frac{1}{3}$ per cent—less than in 1923. By 1940 average hourly wages in manufacturing had risen 40 per cent over 1923—40 per cent higher wages; $33\frac{1}{3}$ per cent lower costs. A real tribute to industrial management. The machine has made this possible. . . . But if it is desirable to invent a machine to turn out some wanted article with fewer man hours of labor involved, isn't it even more desirable to attack this extremely costly distribution side as well?

"Yet . . . it is here that constructive efforts are discouraged and even opposed by many in political as well as business circles. . . . There is no sense in encouraging the shoe manufacturer to find ways to make a shoe in one hour and 15 minutes, or one hour even, and then turn around and say that the $6\frac{1}{2}$ hours of distribution cost must not be touched; that it is not in the social interest to find some way to reduce that to $5\frac{1}{2}$ or $4\frac{1}{2}$ hours of time, and to that extent bring that article within the buying reach of millions of people who might not be able to purchase it otherwise. . . . No manufacturer has discharged his responsibility to the public until the lowered costs which machines give him are in turn given the public in the price of its finished goods, regardless of the successive manufacturing or distributing processes which follow. . . . The wastes of traditional distribution must be minimized so that the people get the full benefits in lower prices and better goods which private enterprise promises them. Here is the test of our system. It has worked pretty well so far but not nearly so well as it should." Address by T. V. Houser, vice president, Sears, Roebuck and Co., *Post-War Merchandise Planning*, Boston, Mass., Jan. 8, 1943.

companies, or types of distributive agency. It is a matter of common knowledge also that attempts to streamline distribution have brought a storm of protest from vested interests in the field. The charge has been brought that this is an undertaking on the part of big business to squeeze out the little fellow, and progressive taxes on chain stores and other protective measures have been secured from legislatures to check the process.[12] At the same time the Federal Trade Commission and the Department of Justice have scrutinized with care both the structure and the practices of large-scale marketing agencies to make sure that any powers which go with size should not be abused.[13]

The volume and character of protective legislation passed in recent years makes it appear that vested interests have secured a degree of protection through legislative and administrative channels which, on the whole, has slowed down the rate of progress toward distributive efficiency which would have come about under conditions

[12] See John H. Cover, "Legislative Barriers to Marketing Progress," *The Annals*, Vol. 209 (1940), p. 176; E. T. Grether, *Price Control under Fair Trade Legislation* (1939); L. S. Lyon, M. W. Watkins, and Victor Abramson, *Government and Economic Life*, Vol. 1, Chaps. 10, 11.

[13] Under N.R.A. and under A.A.A. marketing agreements, numerous struggles arose between interests desiring to effect economies and those who wished to preserve supernumerary jobs in the marketing system or continue the payment of charges for functions which perhaps had once been essential but had become purely nominal. This, for example, was true of certain traditional brokerage charges where the actual service was no longer necessary; nor in fact did the functionary even go through the motions. Notorious also have been the attempts to protect the position of wholesalers and jobbers after more direct methods of dealing had made the position obsolete.

The war, with its shortage of manpower and pressure for direct and economical methods is a powerful influence in many lines of industry toward current simplification and economy in distributive business. Whether these efficiencies induced by war pressures will be continued after the war or whether more cumbersome and higher costs will be restored remains to be seen.

of free competition. One student of current marketing laws observes: "If legislation is to be substituted for competition, then price will lose its significance, channels of distribution will become ossified, marketing procedures static, and enterprise paralyzed."[14]

This brings us to the point of at least tentative conclusion as to the second phase of our inquiry. First we accepted the widely supported findings of many marketing studies to the effect that the existing level of distributive margins is not associated with inordinate profits to marketing agencies. Here we conclude that the weight of evidence is that private enterprise has in recent decades been moving toward raising the efficiency of physical distribution with a vigor comparable to that to be found in the productive process. But at the same time we qualify whatever encouraging conclusions are to be drawn from this view by noting the tendency, somewhat pronounced in recent years, for traditional distributive agencies and for small-scale operators to invoke legislative aid to protect themselves from elimination or shrinkage which they suffer under unrestrained competition toward the reduction of marketing costs.[15] This brings us to a consideration of the third phase of the problem—or the area in which the trend is not toward efficiency and lowered costs but toward inefficiency and wasteful methods.

[14] John H. Cover, cited in footnote 12.

[15] In discussing the possibilities of cost-reducing improvements in methods of physical distribution we have not dealt with the issue of labor costs (including those coming indirectly as transportation charges). Nor have we mentioned the fact that various kinds of shiftable taxes constitute an item of increasing importance in distributive margins. Labor costs as a factor in both production and distribution charges will be discussed in the next chapter, where also we explain our reasons for omitting tax discussion from this book.

THE HIGH COST OF PERSUASION

In our preceding section, we have given the distributive industry credit for considerable vigor and ingenuity in attacking the costs of physical handling of goods and the related technical processes of marketing. But when it comes to the selling function and to pricing policies, which make up the other part of the distributive process, the situation is much less satisfactory. What has come to be known as "high pressure salesmanship" is an outstanding feature of much of the distributive industry and of the marketing philosophy and selling activities which are retained or have been taken over by manufacturers or other producing concerns.

Here we need to bear in mind the observations made in our opening section to the effect that producing and distributing functions overlap or are intimately intermingled so that, in a very large proportion of cases, it is not possible for the manufacturer to say: "I introduce the economies and produce the cost situations which are favorable to price lowering, but someone else—the distributor—nullifies these savings, dissipates or reverses these favorable conditions." In the nature of the case, the manufacturer himself normally acts as his own primary distributor—that is, wholesaler. As has already been noted, he frequently goes farther than this and may handle distribution clear through to the retail consumer. But even where he does not himself actually conduct the operations, his control of price schedules, commissions, discounts, advertising allowances, free deals, and other promotional devices makes him in most cases an active partner in marketing. Whereas the distributor as such must bear major responsibility for the inefficiencies and wastes in the physical process of marketing, it seems at least probable that the manufacturer himself must bear major responsibility for the undue burden of selling efforts and selling costs.

The selling process may be analyzed under various terms, such as consumer appeal, creation of market demand, market stimulation, sales promotion, and demand manipulation. To a very limited extent, these activities are designed to quicken the appetite or acquisitive desire of consumers to the point where they will work harder in order to enlarge their incomes so that they may purchase the offered goods. To a somewhat larger extent probably, the purpose is to cause people to spend freely such income as they have rather than hoard or invest it. But by all odds the major emphasis in selling effort is on channeling as large a flow as possible from the general income stream toward the purchase of a particular kind of product from a particular merchant or producer-distributor within a given time period. This effort, therefore, must be directed toward creating some distinctive and appealing differentiation in each kind of manufactured article or in the person or agency through which it is offered to the public. Differentiation may include anything and everything from the color of material used in the product to the last detail of the retail package, from the location and architecture of the store in which it is sold to the manner and the manicure of the girl who sells it.

In all this, it is evident that there are characteristic differences between what private business enterprise has been accomplishing in the field of physical production and what it has developed in the field of market distribution. In manufacturing, the basic trend has been toward simplification, standardization, and mass production. In contrast with this mechanical, impersonal, or even depersonalizing influence, merchandising has a strong tendency toward the individual appeal, the differentiated product, the personalization of manufacturer and distributor as well as purchaser. The play of behavior patterns—either making or breaking "consumer habits" and the manipulation of individual psychologies—claims attention and pyramids expense.

At the present stage in our business evolution, we seem to have reached something of an impasse between mass production and individual consumption. In a very real sense gains in productivity so ingeniously and industriously "saved at the spigot," are blindly or improvidently "wasted at the bunghole." Such a result, however, is not universal, nor are clever means of attempting to avoid this difficulty altogether lacking. The "self-service" principle introduced by chain groceries and apparently still spreading with considerable vigor, recognizes the fact not merely that a considerable amount of salesmanship was being wasted under conventional methods but that some of it was actually detrimental. It appears that within limits the consumer will "sell himself" better and in larger quantities as well as more cheaply if allowed to browse through the store or even the stockrooms, subjecting himself to the lure of everything that catches his eye rather than telling the clerk what his "needs" are and letting the latter determine—and thereby circumscribe—his range of choice . This procedure, of course, presupposes that goods are standardized as to quality and are suitably packaged.

Such reform, however sound its basic principle, can hardly be expected to attain the dimensions of a major saving in total distribution costs. It limits somewhat the function of the sales person, but it does nothing basic toward limiting the effort of rival sellers or rival producers toward persuading the general public of the desirability of their merchandise or of its superiority to that being offered by others.

This brings us to the knotty problem of sales promotion devices in general. These include (1) elaborate packaging and store display; (2) personal service to the purchaser, either advice in selection or physical aid in installation and subsequent maintenance, and (3) advertising—informative, stimulative, and manipulative. Many volumes have been written to present—or distort—the facts as to these activities and to analyze their economic consequences and possibilities of improvement. The commentary which seems appropriate for our present purpose may be made very brief.

Each of these types of activity and its accompanying burden of expense shows a solid substratum of genuine utility and economic justification. Each shows also distinct possibilities and a clear history of exaggeration or abuse.

In its mere physical aspects of preventing loss or deterioration of the product, careful packaging economically performed is economy, not waste. But deluxe packaging is one of the prevalent and expensive types of stimulating consumers to buy a product and to direct their patronage toward a particular producer or merchandiser. There is no control inherent in the system of free enterprise which would keep expenditures for packaging within reasonable bounds or prevent this form of competition for patronage of the individual concern from running to destructive excesses. Much the same may be said with reference to store display.

Technical service to the prospect and purchaser likewise starts on very solid ground. It is not to be expected that consumers can all be good judges of their own requirements or be fully informed as to all the possible alternative means of gratifying their desires. A legitimate service is rendered, and one which reduces economic waste, if trained selling personnel makes a skilled and honest appraisal of the kind of product which will best meet the prospective consumer's actual needs, of estimating the most economical quantity or size of unit to be purchased, and of drawing engineering or artistic specifications for its application or use. It is equally important to accompany the sold product with such advice or aid in its installation and maintenance as will assure economical performance for the consumer and protect the reputation of the merchant and manufacturer. But it is quite obvious that the ordinary process of competition between individual firms may cause these useful services to degenerate into the recommendation of poorer or less suitable product, overselling the prospect on quantity, or maintaining an unduly large staff of service men to make unnecessary calls on the company's clientele.[16]

Advertising in part performs the function of display of product for "eye appeal" and the advisory, informative, or educational function already discussed under "personal service." We assume that everyone admits the importance in a technically progressive society of carrying on extensive and continuous publicity cam-

---

[16] "Up to a point the addition of such services does undoubtedly give the buyer an economic utility and thus adds to the product which should be credited to the group rendering the service. Nevertheless it is obvious that the process of giving the potential purchaser educational service as to the technical or artistic merits of goods, figuring with him as to the economies to be made by purchasing particular pieces of equipment, driving him about on inspection trips, consuming his time with demonstrations, plying him with personal visits or perpetually interrupting his work with telephone calls, congesting his mail with circulars and littering his desk with blotters and calendars may come to the point where the alleged "service" of a high-pressure system of salesmanship may actually result in dis-service to buyers as a whole." Edwin G. Nourse and Associates, *America's Capacity to Produce* (1934), p. 390.

paigns for informing the public as to the availability of new products and expounding, even arguing, the desirability of such products. We assume also that everyone will grant the legitimacy of a certain amount of "good will" advertising, such for instance as explaining a company's labor policy, its health and safety activities, its support of general research beyond its own technical needs, or any other information which would cause the public to feel that a given company is the kind of business institution which they wish to patronize. But in all these activities, it is also possible to go beyond reasonable and useful education and cultivation of solidly founded good will and to indulge in appeals to ignorance or prejudice and resort to vulgar and futile "puffing" of every company against its rivals without rendering the public any service or gaining any additional patronage for the commodity as a whole, any sizable or useful shift amongst the several companies. Meanwhile cost is substantially increased, and the possibility of reduction in the price of actual goods to the consumer is by so much lessened.

Producer and distributor groups are fully aware of this outstanding item among the "wastes of competition." From time to time they attempt to combat it by pooling their promotion expense in support of the activities of a promotional "institute" and the advertising of the commodity as a whole rather than individual brands. At best such an arrangement constitutes a sort of commercial truce, which is likely to be broken whenever any individual concern conceives that it could capture a larger proportion of the trade for its own product. Institutional or product advertising, however, wherever it can be inaugurated and maintained, has the economic merit of making it more possible to measure the elasticity of demand for the commodity as a whole and to adjust promotional activities accordingly rather than having this limiting factor overlooked in the scramble of individual producers or distributors each to maintain his own individual place in the market.

In spite, however, of this or other attempts to effect specific economies in the arts of commercial promotion, the high cost of persuasion remains the great leak in the distribution practices and policies of modern industry and trade. Too much of the effort, ingenuity, and originality is devoted to trying to persuade people to buy more goods than they can pay for at prices enhanced by the cost of that very persuasion. It means selling them brands and packages instead of contents; radio programs[17] instead of food, clothes, and house furnishings. It has the effect of keeping one foot on the brake while the other presses the accelerator.

[17] If we are to have a discriminating view of what is actually taking place here, we must recognize that advertising outlays support a program of radio entertainment and education which the public receives free of charge, and they go a considerable way toward defraying the costs of producing newspapers and magazines which the public buys at "popular" prices. If these advertising appropriations were eliminated and the prices of the respective commodities reduced by the same amount, we should either have to forego the radio programs or pay a support fee on each receiving set. We would have fewer, smaller, or lower quality newspapers and magazines or would pay more for them. No doubt some people would think this a good exchange; some undoubtedly would find it a real hardship.

Some of the expenditures which have come to be classed under advertising as a matter of fact have no relation to sale of the specific product and very little relation to maintenance of the "good will" of the given company. It is reported that in the midst of the recent depression, one of the directors of a California oil company challenged its president to show why they continued to sponsor a broadcast of symphonic music. To his protest that "You don't sell gas and oil that way," the president replied chidingly that that constituted the company's "contribution to the cultural life of California." Whether this contribution was paid for by stockholders in lowered dividends or by drivers of trucks and jalopies in higher mileage costs, would be a matter difficult of statistical determination. But it is evident that it introduces a

REACHING CONSUMERS THE HARD WAY

Glancing back to the protest of Manufacturer X with which this chapter opened, it may appear that the present writer shows a disposition to put it in the category of "the pot calling the kettle black."[18] The weight of evidence in serious studies of the marketing problem suggests that distributors as such are not today conspicuously less alert or less able in their discovery and application of new methods and better organization in their industry except to the extent that the greater prevalence of small concerns perhaps makes it possible for small-scale inefficiency to entrench itself behind the ramparts of trade association organization or legislative protection.

Our interpretation of the evidence also leads us to the conclusion that it is not in the physical handling of the goods but in promotion activities and price policies that the deficiencies which have been charged to the distributive industry are to be found, and that responsibility for these shortcomings must be shared

---

schizophrenic complex into the functioning of an industrial company. It is at least arguable that it is sounder economic policy to have each product or service subjected to the test of market reaction rather than to have earnings distributed or charges imposed so that a corporate executive may subsidize the distribution of a product which he happens to like to a consuming group of very different make-up from that which bears the cost.

[18] In certain theoretical analyses of the pricing problem support is to be found for the producer's claim that he cannot get the full benefit of the elasticity of consumer demand for his product because of the rigid cost elements in distribution charges. In so far as such fixed charges are the results of freight rate structures frozen by the Interstate Commerce Commission or of wage structures virtually frozen by various labor laws and labor boards, there is undoubtedly such a barrier to or drag upon the efforts of distributors to match any lowering of margins effected by manufacturers. In this chapter, however, we have been concerned with reductions which might be made in factors of cost which lie within the range of managerial choice or skill of the distributor as organizer and policy maker. The labor cost factor, which applies to manufacturers, transportation agencies, and distributors alike will be considered in the succeeding chapter.

by the producers and distributors rather than shouldered off on the latter.

Indeed, if an invidious distinction is to be drawn between producer and distributor in the matter of low-price or high-price policy and practice, it seems reasonable to rate the large-scale distributor as a more consistent exponent of price competition than the typical large-scale producer. In the nature of the case the distributor is interested in volume of total sales rather than in the fortunes of a particular brand. He will push the line which meets least consumer resistance, that is, the product of the manufacturer who has made a saving and is willing to share it with consumers. When price maintenance on manufacturers' "advertised brands" puts too much sand in the distributive machine, the aggressive large-scale distributor turns to "private brands" as a means of lubricating sales, while still catering to the public's liking for a distinctive name and package. To some extent he even pushes unbranded articles.[19] In our judgment the key to inefficient practice here lies in in-

[19] "Among the strongest forces in the economy serving as a corrective against excessive brand advertising are the large-scale distributors, who in recent decades have become increasingly active in establishing their own brands in various product fields and in offering them on a price basis. These include many, though not all, of the chains, mail-order houses, voluntary chains, and supermarkets, and a lesser proportion of department stores. Through an integration of marketing functions they often have been able when selling under their own brands to attain economies in overall marketing costs not attained when the manufacturer carries out the advertising and promotional functions. Many of the chains, though not the department stores generally, have greatly reduced their competition in offering services to consumers. In instances in which they have followed this policy, they have generally made their bid for business on a price basis. In addition, because of their size they have had strong bargaining power, which has often enabled them to buy merchandise at favorable prices, which, in turn, they have passed on, in part at least, to consumers. They have established their own brands first in those fields in which they have been able to get volume of sales readily

sistence, chiefly on the part of the manufacturer, on the maintenance of selling prices and the resort to high-pressure methods of salesmanship as the means of securing volume. This tends to expand promotional costs, thereby offsetting savings introduced in production expense, and gives a color of justification for the maintenance of high consumer prices.

The situation may well be likened to that in Aesop's well-known fable of the traveler's cloak. The North Wind and the Sun entered into a wager as to which could first get the cloak off. The more the wind tugged at the cloak, the more violent its assault, the less could the traveler dispense with it, the more tightly did he clutch it to him. Then came the sun, smiling upon the traveler, warming his blood, relaxing his resistance until, of his own volition, he laid his cloak aside.

There is something between the ludicrous and the cynical in the attempt to justify to-day's heavy promotional expense, the cost of "high pressure selling," as a necessary cost of getting goods sold—of "creating demand"—in a world hungry for conveniences and luxuries even in the case of those who can, without much worry about prices, meet the cost of necessities.[20]

---

and without undue promotional costs. Many of them have been desirous, however, of extending their brands into fields strongly dominated by manufacturers' brands. . . . Thus they have become an increasingly strong force to limit competition in advertising and non-price forms in all the fields in which they have entered with their own brands." Neil H. Borden, *The Economic Effects of Advertising* (1942), pp. 876-77.

[20] The consumers' co-operative movement has made an attack on this problem from the buyers' end, in despair that it would be adequately dealt with from the producer end. The economic philosophy of consumer co-operation is in essence: "Our wants are already awakened. We know both the quantities and the qualities of goods we desire, and we want them physically distributed to us with the minimum of service cost. To have this done, we must organize and conduct the business our-

The warming sun of lower prices is a more effective approach than the stormy methods of "aggressive"— and cost-increasing—salesmanship.

Seeking reasons for the present situation as to marketing charges and both producers' and distributors' price practices, it seems that it is in part due to blindness, slothfulness, or lack of imagination on the part of policy makers. To a considerable extent, however, it is due to the fact that courses of action which seem sound or necessary for an entire industry or for the economy as a whole may be impossible or highly difficult of adoption and execution by the individual company. This problem will be returned to later, but particularly in Chapters XIII and XIV.

---

selves." In the case of highly standardized farm supplies such as fertilizers, mill feeds, and seeds, where farmers can take car-door delivery in bulk or where only very simple store service is called for, notable economies have been effected and very prosperous and stable agencies established. Such are the Grange League Federation Exchange in New York and Pennsylvania, the Eastern States Exchange in New England, and others in the Mid-West and South. An estimated total of $375,000,000 worth of goods was handled by farmers' buyers cooperatives in 1940. (See Joseph G. Knapp, "The Rise of Co-operative Purchasing," *American Co-operation: 1941*, p. 555.) Some success has also been attained in handling shelf groceries, staple clothing, and standardized household supplies through both rural and city stores. But the further one goes toward style goods and other differentiated products the greater do the hazards of co-operative enterprise become. With the financial and personnel barriers to entry into these lines of business and the degree of efficiency and price competition now attained by chain stores, mail order houses and the like, and the temperament of our people being what it is, it does not seem likely that co-operative distribution will attain more than "yard stick" proportions.

CHAPTER IX
WAGES AS COST AND AS MARKET

Chapter VIII took off from a question put by "Manufacturer X," who doubted that efforts he might make toward price lowering could be fully effective in view of the fact that distribution charges were being raised or at least not being lowered in step with reductions in manufacturing margins. As the chapter proceeded, we were brought to consideration of certain rigid factors in distribution charges, such as transportation and labor costs. Since a major source of rigidity in transportation and handling charges runs back in turn to the cost of labor, it seems appropriate now to raise the whole question of wages as a factor in prices, whether it be wages paid by the transportation or power utility, by the distributor, by the mining company, or by the manufacturer.

While manufacturers and other producers are prone to pass the blame for high prices on to the marketing agencies, spokesmen for all branches of business are disposed to blame labor. They find in wage rates and labor union practices an ever-present bar to price lowering. "How," says Employer Y, "can we be expected to lower prices when wages are being pushed up all the time?"[1]

In considering this question, we must examine not merely the way in which employers define the issue and the ways in which they attempt to settle it. Workers

[1] Generally this remark takes the form, "when wages *and taxes* are being pushed up." With reference to the tax phases of the matter, see p. 282 n.

also have their own ways of looking at the problem and their own tactics for dealing with it. Union officials, as has been noted incidentally in earlier chapters, are important price-making executives in the labor market and their economic philosophies and strategies must be given careful consideration by the economist and the businessman. After Employer Y has pointed to high and rising wages as a bar to price lowering, Union Official Z may be heard to say: "We are not greatly concerned with whether manufacturers and distributors succeed in knocking a few cents off the price of tooth paste or a few dollars off the price of an electric refrigerator. What we propose to do is to see that wage rates are put up to a level where we can afford to buy goods on the market without haggling over their price."

While the economic philosophy and business practice of corporate executives and labor union officials are in many ways intertwined, we shall in this chapter try in general to examine first the employer approach to wage-and-price policy and then relate to it the wage-and-price policies of organized labor. But first a few pages of general background.

WE LOOK AT THE RECORD

To the question, "How can you expect prices to be lowered when wages are being pushed up?" one simple and rather impressive answer suggests itself. It is because prices have over long periods in the past gone down while wages were going up that we believe such conditions can be repeated in the future. The chart on page 255 shows a considerable reduction in wholesale prices from the opening of the nineteenth century to the Civil War, during which period there was a slow but steady *increase* in weekly wages. Between the Civil War and the World War the index of wholesale prices moved down rather rapidly until the end of the depression in 1896, while at the same time weekly wages, after a brief decline, resumed their advance at a rate as great as or

TRENDS OF WHOLESALE PRICES AND OF
MONEY WAGES, 1802-1915[a]

(Three-Year Moving Averages, 1926 = 100)

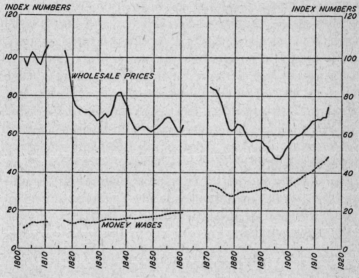

[a] For data, see App. C.

greater than that of the pre-Civil War period. After the depression of the nineties, the increase in weekly wages went on at an even faster rate, and the index of wholesale prices reversed its trend and rose sharply from 1896 to 1914. Inasmuch as the length of the work week was reduced very materially during the late nineteenth and early twentieth centuries,[2] the wage rate or cost of

[2] This reduction in working hours was most pronounced during the latter part of the period, and still more under influences of the First

an hour of labor to the employer rose even more than is indicated by the chart. The fact that commodity prices were advancing rather than being lowered during this later period suggests that increased labor costs may have been a factor in the rise of commodity prices. Even so, the purchasing power of a week's wages was 17 per cent higher in 1914 than in 1900 and 61 per cent higher than in 1880.[3]

The chart on page 257 gives us a somewhat clearer picture of the tendencies since 1900. Instead of a general index of wholesale prices, which includes prices of farm products, we have for this period an index of prices of manufactured goods. Instead of weekly earnings we have hourly rates of wages. Thus we are able to focus attention more sharply on our specific question, namely whether prices of industrial products have been lowered at the same time that wage rates have been increasing.

In contrast to the nearly parallel rise of wages and prices from the turn of the century to the First World War, we here see wages rising considerably from even the new high level of 1921-22 to the peak of 1929, while prices were lowered in about the same proportion. The table from which the chart was prepared shows

---

World War and the National Recovery Administration. "From 1890 to 1937, a period during which records of hours of work have tended to become more complete and, on the whole, more reliable, the average length of the work week of factory employees in the United States declined from 60 to probably 42 hours, or 18 a week; of labor in the building trades from 55 to 39, or 16 a week; of steam railroad employees from 60 to 48, or 12 a week; and of anthracite and bituminous coal miners from 60 to 35, or 25 hours a week." Leo Wolman, "Hours of Work in American Industry," *National Bureau of Economic Research Bulletin 71*, Nov. 27, 1938, p. 1.

[3] The index of purchasing power of industrial wages rose from 42.2 in 1880 to 58.1 in 1900 and 68.0 in 1914, measured as a ratio of wages to wholesale prices. See table, App. C.

hourly earnings of workers in manufacturing rising from an index of 87.0 in 1919 to 134.3[4] in 1941, while the price index for manufactured products during the same period declined from 130.6 to 89.1 after being down

TRENDS OF WHOLESALE PRICES AND OF
HOURLY EARNINGS, 1901-40[a]

(Three-Year Moving Averages, 1926 = 100)

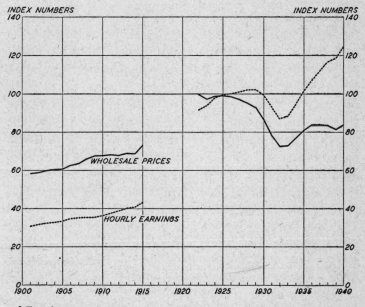

[a] For data, see App. C.

to 70.3 in 1932. From the bottom of the depression in 1932 to 1941 wage rates were pushed up 60.6 per cent, while wholesale prices of manufactured products rose only 26.3 per cent.

The events portrayed by these data have been too

[4] From 47.7 cents to 73.6 cents in manufacturing. Some comment on rates of advance for different lines of work will be made later.

much disturbed by depression influences and by institutional changes, and their real trend has not been sufficiently clarified in the perspective of time to permit any very considerable generalization. However, it seems clear that manufacturers still found it possible during the prevailingly prosperous period from the end of the First World War to the beginning of the depression in 1930 to reduce prices substantially and rather steadily, at the same time that wage rates were being raised from an index of 87.0 in 1919 to 103.3 in 1929. The significance of the somewhat similar relative movements to be observed in the period 1932-41 requires special consideration at a later point.

Individual manufacturers have not been slow to point with pride to the fact that they have, for their particular products, been making substantial price concessions to the public at the same time that they have been meeting the high wage demands of labor. For example, data supplied us by one company and presented in *Industrial Price Policies and Economic Progress* (p. 294) showed that the prices of that company's products were reduced 25 per cent between 1926 and 1937 and that during this time hourly wages of the company's employees rose 50 per cent and total profits of the company 68 per cent (78 per cent in 1936 and 88 per cent in 1935). Data furnished us by another leading industrial company covering one of its outstanding products showed a reduction in selling price between 1928 and 1937 of about two-thirds, while the cost of an hour's labor rose 36 per cent, net cost per pound declined nearly 60 per cent, and total net profits rose 294 per cent. The phenomenal reduction in prices of automobiles while wages of automobile labor were being substantially advanced is a matter of common knowledge, and similar, even though less striking, illustrations are to be found in many other lines of manufacture.

It may of course be objected that these illustrations are all taken from "new" industries, novel products, and rapidly expanding lines of business. It is sometimes argued that such conditions are not typical of industry as a whole and are only temporary in character. To this objection, we must respond, as we did in Chapter VI (p. 185), that new techniques and new business organization, though of course not universal or uniform, *are* typical of American business, are not temporary influences in our economic life, but are the very essence of increasing industrial efficiency which is supposed to be the fine flower of free enterprise. It is with these successive areas of expansion, of finding ways of bringing new satisfactions to the consumer by better utilization of our natural resources and our labor force that this book is concerned. It is upon them that business enterprise is, as we believe, primarily focused.

BUSINESS ENTERPRISE AND EFFICIENCY GAINS

Stated in its simplest terms, business enterprise is persistently seeking out and, in spite of local defeats, meeting overall success in finding more efficient and hence more economical ways of producing goods for the satisfaction of consumers. With the foundations we have laid in natural science and with the growth of our systematic knowledge of engineering applications of these principles, there seems every reason for confidence in the continued and presumably accelerating rate of technological advance in the future.

Thus our first (partial) answer to the question put by Employer Y at the beginning of this chapter emerges in the following terms: "It is possible, as contemporary experience and the historic record show, for industry as a whole to make a general reduction in consumers' prices at the same time that there is a general advance in the wages of workers. Business enterprise has been effecting such great improvements in productive efficiency that benefits could be passed on in both directions at once."

But the mere fact that certain general trends were to be observed over a considerable period of time does not mean that all manufacturers contributed to this favorable result in the same degree. Nor does it mean that any particular manufacturer could raise wages to the amount forced by competition or union pressure and still be able to reduce the prices of his product. Probably there were a great many individual cases of price and wage setting during the period considered which were not perfect or indeed satisfactory adjustments to the situations in which they were made. In fact, the charts suggest to us that possibly even broad patterns of wage and price relations which showed a good deal of stability during the nineteenth century may have been broken up or superseded by new trends in the twentieth century. This forces us to face the question whether in recent wage and price adjustments employers and unions have been following economic policies and practices which have been soundly conceived or which, if projected into the future, would promote prosperity for the employer and a high level of consumption for the worker.

Our hypothetical Employer Y must work out as best he can a great many practical problems of wage and price adjustment to his individual situation. So must all the other individual employers.[5] Such decisions, however,

[5] Sometimes, even the most intelligent answer that can be made will not enable the given employer to escape commercial failure and elimina-

cannot be soundly arrived at, even for the small business, except in the light of some understanding of how these actions are dependent on and contribute to the broader currents of influence that flow through the business world. For the very large corporation in a strategic economic position and for the labor union, most of whose decisions apply not to single plants or corporations but to crafts or industrial groups over wide geographical areas, it is all the more important that price-making executives study their individual actions as part of a widely interrelated system of prices.

To these broad and complicated questions both the businessman and the worker must ultimately make precise answers in terms of cents in the wage rate, dollars in the pay envelope, and "plain figures" on the commodity price tag. Naturally they would like to be supplied with a simple rule or exact formula under which corporate management or the labor union could work out such answers from day to day. But it must be evident that the situations involved are too complex and too rapidly changing to permit the giving of quantitative answers in advance or even the working out for a single specified commodity of an "example" that would be valid and significant.

It does not, however, follow that we must throw up our hands at this point and say that all that can be done is "muddle through" and hope for the best. It is possible and useful in a very practical sense to pursue our analysis of the question of wage advances versus price

---

tion—or reorganization. At the same time, realistic adjustment to the new conditions by the better situated or more astute managers may enable them to stay in business, perhaps with undiminished or even enhanced profits, and yet be sowing seeds of later disaster for their companies, their industry, or the entire economy. Some of these possibilities will be examined later in the chapter.

reductions somewhat further on the qualitative level even when we cannot compute quantitative solutions to the individual firm's problems. This means seeking clearer insight into the operative principles involved by seeing what happens, in terms both of immediate results and of remote consequences, when wage rates are advanced, and similarly what train of influence is set in motion by lowering prices in conjunction with a change of technique or of operative organization designed to enhance productive efficiency. Only through practical understanding of the nature of these relationships within a comprehensive price system can we bring the parts into working harmony and attain the full and efficient use of our economic resources. We must learn how to avoid, in each situation, "too lean a mixture" or "too rich a mixture" if we are to get proper economic carburetion.[6]

We could, of course, conclude our answer to Employer Y at this point by a brief endorsement of the implication of his question. We might say: "Of course

[6] Such a figure of speech can, of course, only be suggestive, not precise. When one is dealing with the relatively simple and exact relations of a physical mechanism or a chemical reaction, he finds the sequence of cause and effect immediate and demonstrable. If one sets the carburetor of an automobile for too rich or too lean a mixture, the characteristic results of smoke, sputtering, and loss of power promptly ensue, with complete stoppage of the engine if the maladjustment is more than slight or temporary. Other parts of a machine do not adapt themselves to maladjustment in a given part, but uncompromisingly proclaim and resist it.

It is a peculiarity of the price system, however, that, although it is completely interconnected, these connections are of elastic, adaptive, compensating, pliant character. Results partially worked out suggest new lines of action to the human (purposeful) observers and participants and thus we have a continuous flowing process whose trends may be discerned and their intensity to some extent measured by the initiated but which does not have some single and permanent "correct" set of mutual adjustments to which all parts must be brought and held. It can, however, through skill, be guided toward goals of high performance. Likewise it can, through ignorance and brute force, be kept operating at low levels of efficiency.

you cannot lower prices of goods if labor is using the power of collective bargaining to seize all the gains of advancing productive efficiency as fast as—or faster than —they are put or can be put into the productive process." But this, like our other partial though more optimistic answer on pages 259-60, would cover only a single type of situation and still leave unexplored the basic questions of how the price of labor is related to other parts of the price system.

These price and productivity relationships are not simple mechanical connections of the plus-and-minus variety. They are complicated functions of an organic price system. We need therefore to consider, first from the side of the employer executive and then from the side of the labor union executive, the reasons that lead to current types of pricing effort and the consequences that follow the attainment of given types of price setting.[7] In the next section we focus attention on how the wage policy or practice of the employer helps or hinders him in attaining prosperity for his company and how this is related to the most productive adjustment of our whole economy.

THE EMPLOYER'S TWO-FOLD QUEST

It has been customary to think of the capitalist employer as engaged simply in the quest for profits. In fact, however, the attempt to make profits resolves itself into

---

[7] The reader should perhaps be warned at this point that our analysis will not proceed upon the assumption or with the types of reasoning characteristic of "wages fund" doctrines of distribution or "quantity theories" of money. We are not even concerned here primarily to discover the ultimate limitations beyond which an economic aberration cannot be pushed before corrective forces will assert themselves. Rather are we concerned with the area of discretionary choice that lies between these controlling limits, to see how best we may avoid blind and harmful excesses.

a quest for lower production costs on the one side and for a more satisfactory market on the other.

In the early days of the Industrial Revolution, the capitalist employer was much inclined to use his power as owner of plant and dispenser of jobs to hold wages down or push them lower as a means of widening his profit margin. Hours of work were long and rates of pay so meager that at times the laborer had to send his women and children into the mines and factories to supplement his own wages. Capital being very scarce in proportion to the pressing demands for new machines, owner-entrepreneurs were in a position to enforce a first claim on all the gain from a new technique. Through monopoly of jobs they might even exact a share so large as sometimes to put the masses in a worse position as consumers than they had been before.

But the very harshness of such conditions became an important factor in their removal. Long hours, low wages, use of women's and children's labor held the productivity of the working population down to a point so low that it became apparent that the technical demands of factory efficiency itself called for a change. The more enlightened employers saw, and the more short-sighted were taught by practical experience, the unwisdom of trying to monopolize efficiency gains for the profit account. But a succession of "Factory Acts" was needed to establish a higher plane of competitive practice against the "chiseling" of stupid and unscrupulous individuals. Gradually the "economy of shorter hours" was generally accepted, along with the strictly operative value of safety precautions, sanitary and even pleasant working quarters, and social activities for employees and their families. Eventually also wages were raised, voluntarily or with some urging, by employers who saw or could be shown the "economy of high wages."

Since the latter part of the nineteenth century the quest for profits has moved toward improvements in productive efficiency instead of exploitation of the workers. More and better machinery has been introduced. The working process has been better organized, with more compact and convenient lay-out, more accurate timing, more careful selection and handling of personnel—in a word "scientific management." All this means labor saving. As a result, the same amount of labor will produce more and better goods; or the same flow of goods can be produced with less labor. If labor continues under these conditions of enhanced efficiency to be employed as fully as before,[8] it is possible to raise wage rates in proportion to the amount of net savings[9] effected and not at the same time raise the unit price of the product. Or the price of the product may be lowered in proportion to the gain in efficiency without lowering the wage rate.

This brings us to the capitalist employer's second quest —that for a better market. As soon as the progressive industrialist succeeds in his first quest—for greater efficiency or lower unit costs—he must start on his second. He must seek a larger market in which to sell his expanding product. In so far as his business operations are farseeing and fully rational, the two goals will in fact be pursued jointly. Otherwise the enlarged productive capacity of the industry will be only partially utilized and high "overhead" will offset low operative cost. The enlarged labor capacity will be only partially utilized and "technological unemployment" will give rise to the dole or other

[8] Whether it does or not will be considered in a later section.

[9] Net because some of the direct labor saved must go into the production and upkeep of machinery and some of the wages saved must go to pay interest on additional capital.

forms of "relief." The industrial system cannot pursue the logic of its own development to the limit of automatic machinery, minute division of labor, and synchronized line assembly except as the infinitely varied products of this highly organized system of mass production move promptly away from the end of the assembly line through a system of mass marketing into active consumption. Mass production for elite consumption is a contradiction in terms. The capitalist employers who assume the responsibility of introducing technological improvements must also accept responsibility for disbursing purchasing power in such a way that industrial life shall be as well adjusted in its distributive phase as in its productive phase.

We shall consider presently whether employees have assisted employers in discovering and applying sound principles in this field or whether they are, as Employer Y's question (p. 253) implies, preventing management from pursuing the economically correct course. But, turning again to the historical record, it is apparent that some manufacturers did extend their interpretation of the "economy of high wages" to include that other sort of economy which expresses itself in adequate purchasing power in the market. Henry Ford early came to the conclusion that even cheap automobiles could not be sold (in numbers needed for low-cost technique) in a society in which working men earned only two or three dollars a day. As early as 1914, he took the revolutionary step of adopting a 5-dollar a day minimum for his factory labor (then getting an average of $2.40)[10] and raised it shortly to a 6-dollar minimum. The results not only appeared to

[10] Henry Ford and Samuel Crowther, *Today and Tomorrow* (1926), p. 157. The wage advance was accompanied by efforts to improve the general scale of living of the recipients, especially the newer immigrants. In fact certain standards of cleanliness and comfort in the worker's home were required for one to qualify for the higher wage. Henry Ford and Samuel Crowther, *My Life and Work* (1923), p. 128.

satisfy him, but to impress other automobile companies so much that similar raises were made by them and the practice spread to other lines of industry. Payment of high wages came to be regarded as an important factor in the industrial prosperity of the twenties and became the object of study even by industrial delegations from abroad.[11]

Undoubtedly the fact that practically every workman whose pay was raised by automobile and other manufacturers had an ambition to possess an automobile (even a Ford) led to a favorable sales response to his action.[12] But, owing to the diversity of consumer expenditures and

[11] Cf. National Bureau of Economic Research, *Recent Economic Changes* (1929), pp. 1-6.

[12] Mr. Ford himself talked about the relation of high wages both to productivity and to purchasing power. Two passages will illustrate this: "I believe in the first place that, all other considerations aside, our own sales depend in a measure upon the wages we pay. If we can distribute high wages, then that money is going to be spent and it will serve to make storekeepers and distributors and manufacturers and workers in other lines more prosperous, and their prosperity will be reflected in our sales. Country-wide high wages spell country-wide prosperity, provided, however, the higher wages are paid for higher production." Ford and Crowther, *My Life and Work*, pp. 124-25.

"It is bad financial policy to reduce wages because it also reduces buying power. If one believes that leadership brings responsibility, then a part of that responsibility is in seeing that those whom one leads shall have an adequate opportunity to earn a living. Finance concerns not merely the profit or solvency of a company; it also comprehends the amount of money that the company turns back to the community through wages. There is no charity in proper wages. It is simply that no company can be said to be stable which is not so well managed that it can afford a man an opportunity to do a great deal of work and therefore to earn a good wage. On the cost sheet, wages are mere figures; out in the world, wages are bread boxes and coal bins, babies' cradles and children's education—family comforts and contentment." The same, p. 163.

Edward A. Filene was a vigorous exponent of Ford's views, together with his own observations "from a shopkeeper's tower." He said: "In the future a really big business success on the basis of mass production and mass distribution will be impossible except as it makes for both high wages and low prices. . . . Low wages and high prices manifestly cut down that widespread and sustained buying power of the masses without which mass production sooner or later defeats itself. In other words, the business man of the future must produce prosperous customers as well as saleable

the specialization of industrial concerns, it must be laid down as a general proposition that only as the movement to enlarge the money wage income of the masses is participated in by employers rather generally can the individual concern count on this favorable sales response in its own particular market.

It is, of course, very easy to see that a general scaling up of money incomes would not in and of itself be a means of bringing about business prosperity (except as it might have a stimulative effect through the brightening of businessmen's anticipations—that is, creating an inflationary rather than an deflationary psychology). On

---

goods. He cannot think of his business as an adventure in getting money from masses of people who, in one way or another for which he had no responsibility, have got money from someone else. His whole business policy must look forward to creating great buying power among the masses. Otherwise mass production cannot succeed. The business man of the future must fill the pockets of the workers and the consumers before he can fill his pockets. . . . You cannot have high buying power in the public and low wages in the factory, office, and shop. But the business man who is driven to make high wages a part of his policy, will be driven to every possible effort to make his employees worth the high wages he pays them." *The Way Out*, pp. 162, 167.

It is clear that Mr. Ford regarded the raising of wages in the lower brackets as only one element in a sound industrial strategy. He saw that there were practical limits to the extent to which the prices of even the plainest automobile could be reduced in the general price situation, over which he could of course exercise little influence. He might and did do something toward lowering iron and steel prices and toward resisting the high price policies of the aluminum monopoly. So too in the field of glassmaking, paint, and textile supply. But, having carried his economic attack as far as he could on the price front, his generalship turned to a flank attack on the income side.

If all producers had been lowering prices as aggressively as he, enough purchasing power might have been released to make a satisfactorily expanding automobile market without wage advances. But since this was not the case, he started a movement on the lower grades of industrial incomes which he no doubt hoped would, by the force of competition in the labor market, spread to other manufacturers. He also regarded the general level of farm income as too low to permit the adequate participation of farmers as buyers of industrial products. Hence he lent his support to efforts to bolster the industrial market for agricultural products.

the other hand, the scaling up of wages but not salaries, or the levelling up of the lower parts of the wage structure while the wages of skilled crafts are unchanged might have a considerable beneficial effect. The process by which such results come about will be examined in some detail later in the chapter.

It could be imagined or employers might claim that if they had been let alone these wage and price questions would have been worked out in a sound and satisfactory way. Would not capitalist owners, owner-managers, and salaried professional managers of corporate industries discover for themselves what they could afford to pay for labor, how much they would need to retain as profits on capital, what it was strategically desirable to do in the matter of prices in view of what they would discover as to the price elasticity of demand and the income elasticity of demand for their products? These adjustments, it might be claimed, would be made with such reasoned understanding and such operative skill that the whole labor force would be kept at work, that just the right amount of productivity would be applied to the provision and improvement of plant, and purchasing power disbursed to the various participants in just the right amount to enable them to take the whole end-product of consumers' goods promptly off the market.

In practice, however, there have been frequently recurring situations in which plant capacity has been expanded substantially beyond the capacity of the consumer market to absorb its output (at the prices set) out of the purchasing power disbursed—predominantly as workers' incomes. At the same time, employees have been so generally dissatisfied with the results voluntarily attained by management that they have organized to exact a share in the industrial product more in conformity with their own ideas. Such organizations have become a major factor in the functioning of our price system. The essence of the employer's plaint with which this chapter was introduced is that the policies and practices followed by organized labor in setting their prices, that is, wage rates, interfere with or prevent the following of a low-price policy by manufacturers, distributors, and other employers. We must, therefore, look at our problem also from the standpoint of those who make or influence administered prices in the labor market.

UNION OFFICIALS AS PRICE-MAKING EXECUTIVES

At the opening of the previous section we noted an extreme interpretation of capitalism which would allocate all productivity gains to the owner and/or controller of invested funds. At the opposite pole, there has been a school of thought that credits labor with being the only truly productive factor and thus the legitimate claimant to all productivity gains. While such an ideology has frequently found expression in labor ranks, the organized labor movement has been essentially opportunistic rather than theoretical. It has been quite ready to take its gains where it found them—or could force them. It has not been concerned to prove the existence of productivity gains or to measure the amount of these gains as a basis for wage adjustment.

Leaders of the union movement asserted that such wage increases as were voluntarily made by employers who expressed belief in the "economy of high wages" were simply the astute means by which management enlarged its profits at a still more rapid rate and kept in its own hands the lion's share of the gains of technological progress. Union officials sought, therefore, to take advantage of whatever labor scarcity could be discovered in particular skills or in particular localities and to create additional labor market scarcities through apprenticeship rules or other limitations on entry to the trade. Not content to await the slow process by which labor-saving efficiency might, under the administration of employers, express itself in higher real wages (more money to spend or more goods for the same money), they sought to expedite and enlarge their harvest by insistent demands for wage increases backed up by frequent resort to force as the means of attaining them.

In some cases, such forcing of higher wage rates no doubt promotes productive efficiency by making it necessary for the employer to economize in his production method. While we are accustomed to think of efficiency as being introduced into our economic system spontaneously by the enterprise and the profit search of the employer, a not inconsiderable part of the efficiencies of better equipment and improved organization which have been introduced over the years have been induced by the necessity of meeting high wage demands made by the workers.[13] A manufacturer enjoying a wide or even comfortable margin of profit might be quite disposed to let well enough alone, avoid the hazards of a new technique, the financial strain of furnishing new equipment, the mental strain of operative reorganization. Workers, however, seeing or suspecting these comfortable profits and wishing to share in the profitableness of a situation to which they conceive themselves as having been in

[13] This, to recall the analysis of the nature of economic enterprise sketched in Chap. 2, would mean that the personal enterprise of the individual worker, apparently extinguished by the concentration of certain enterprise functions in the officials of large corporations, resurges and finds a new means of expressing itself through the group enterprise of the union. Both the dangers and the constructive possibilities of this development will be noted as the chapter proceeds.

some measure a party, make new wage demands upon their employer. If their strength is sufficient to win their demand or even to exact a compromise, the employer is bestirred to find a new means of saving labor which will offset its increased cost.

Even the fact that labor unions, in this pressure for wage advances, have made little or no discrimination between the capacities of different employers to pay higher wages has not been wholly bad in its economic effects. By "putting the heat" on all employers to attain higher levels of efficiency as a means of improving the economic position of these workers' groups, organized labor has become a factor in the selective process as to management. Those concerns that could meet the higher demands most fully would be able to survive and even expand. Those that were unwilling to bestir themselves to more efficient performance or unable to attain it would tend to be weeded out. If the necessity of paying higher wages forces some employers out of business, this would mean the elimination of the high-cost, low-efficiency producer and the diversion of this volume of business to other firms better located or better managed.[14]

But the wage struggle of the unions has also been marked by policies and practices that have reduced efficiency. For often the workers have demanded that some efficiency device should not be used because it might

[14] Likewise, the force of wage-raising efforts has been somewhat mitigated in its incidence on different employers by reason of the fact that the one who has a large profit margin to draw on will presumably be the one who will yield such gains most readily, whereas the one with a narrow margin will by this fact be stiffened in his resistance and at times at least be able to make to union representatives a sufficient showing of inability to pay so that he will not be forced to the wall. The more universal union agreements become and the greater their insistence on flat wage contracts, the less effective becomes this ability of the individual to defend himself.

displace workers or that it be used only with the old "full crew" or at least with some supernumerary workers kept on the payroll. Through "jurisdictional" claims they have forced an employer to hire specialized work-· ers for tasks which do not require craft skills, such as an electrician to turn on a light switch or a union band to "stand by" while a recorded or transcribed program is being played. Or they may limit the amount of work a wage earner is permitted to do in a given time. It is obvious that these methods retard low-price policies by reducing the amount of gain there is to be passed on even though they give the particular group a short-run gain in the form of dollars to spend.

It is quite possible to push the militant or "strong-arm" type of collective bargaining to a point where, instead of merely eliminating the submarginal employer, it produces results harmful to the industry, to the whole economy, and hence in the long run to labor itself. If wages are forced up beyond the point where the increase can be paid from profits without impairing the solvency of the company or its ability to finance further technological improvements, the wage increase must be reflected in an increase in the price of the product. This, in all but exceptional cases, must mean decline in the volume of sales and the amount of employment. Even if the demand is so inelastic that sales do not decrease nor employment shrink, the gain which appears in workers' pay envelopes is all too soon dissipated in the increased cost of living which follows commodity price advances. In the short turn and in a given case, the particular commodity price advance may, of course, not boomerang back upon the same persons who force the wage advance. But any general practice of wage raising forced through in the absence of (or in excess of) efficiency gains will be borne in large part by the supposed beneficiaries. In the end, the workers will be disbursing more money but not enjoying a higher scale of living.

If the efforts of labor unions come to be directed toward raising wage rates in situations where the higher pay is not accompanied by enlarged output, the net result is nothing but price inflation. Such an outcome does not mean merely that the workers fail to gain from the nominal increase in earnings. They lose directly the money they have put into the support of the agency that conducts this bootless kind of wage boosting. Beyond this, the inflation of prices that results increases the difficulty of selling goods to other classes of purchasers whose pay has not been raised and complicates the problem of business management. In presenting the charts earlier in the chapter, we suggested that wage advances during recent decades might perhaps be of this price-boosting character. Looking particularly at the chart on page 257 one finds the wage rate since 1923 rising more or falling less than commodity prices. This situation looks favorable on the surface. But it tells only a partial story, which to be complete requires the addition of data for volume of employment. Even so, wage rates advanced so fast in the late thirties as to raise the question whether price-boosting consequences could be avoided unless scale of operations were substantially increased.

While organized labor has, as was said above, not been much inclined to theorize about its policies or programs, a look at the historical record shows that its general attitude has favored taking its gains from technological progress in the form of higher wage rates rather than as lower prices. Such a line of action is easily explained. Labor has been able to exert positive powers of wage setting through its control over indispensable or strategic blocks of labor, enforcing this control through strikes, restriction of entry to the trade, and contract or statutory limitation of the work day or week. Workers' ability to influence the course of prices, on the other hand, is limited at best to what seems to them the indirect and uncertain power of the "buyers' strike" or the consumer co-operative movement. This has meant, however, that organized labor's efforts toward enlarging its own complement of consumer goods have very often taken the form of actions which tended to reduce the total output of industry.

The results of such a course of action are rather evident. A small group within an economy can improve its relative position by enforcing a scarcity price against the mass of population. But the whole labor class cannot use its control of output to push up its money wages regardless of change or lack of change in productivity and still hope to enjoy more ample real wages. It is only through enlargement of the stream of total product that labor as a whole can permanently gain. We shall turn therefore to consideration of the relations between employee wage rates, prices of goods, and the volume of employment.

LABOR SAVING AND LABOR WASTING

We have said (p. 259) that the efficiency gains through which economic society propels itself forward along the road of material progress resolve themselves in the last analysis into techniques of labor saving. But if the labor thus saved is not applied to additional production[15] then we are no better off—possibly worse off, since

[15] Or desired and constructively used leisure. In the sense of giving the worker time for other desired activity, recreation and whatever improves his physical and intellectual being are of course themselves economic gains to him.

the laborer when not employed deteriorates. Labor saving thus degenerates into labor wasting. We need therefore to examine the steps by which improving efficiency may be translated into high real incomes and the missteps by which these potentialities may be lost.

Three general channels for the distribution of the gains resulting from improved productive efficiency are to be noted—profit expansion, wage raising, and price lowering. We will take three simplified illustrations of these methods of distribution and trace through in brief outline the several steps of economic consequence which may be expected to follow when one or another of these methods is adopted. We shall try in each case to see whether the higher level of operative efficiency attained is combined with a high ratio of utilization of our labor and plant resources, thus attaining the highest practicable level of total production.

Let us begin by assuming that the capitalist, by installing labor-saving machinery, reduces the work required directly in producing a year's output of consumers' goods by one million hours. This at 50 cents an hour, gives him an added gross profit of $500,000. Let us then suppose that for the machinery repair and the rebuilding necessary to keep his equipment operating at its new level of efficiency, one-fifth of the gross saving or $100,000 annually is required. Out of the remaining net profit of $400,000, the capitalist, we will assume, spends $200,000 for additional consumers' goods for himself and invests the remaining $200,000 in buildings and more machines to increase the efficiency of the future. By thus administering the profits which came into his hands, spending them completely and immediately (or as quickly as he had paid the funds out in wages before the labor-saving change was introduced), the capitalist would promptly re-employ as much labor as had been displaced.[16] Since prices and wages are unchanged, the scale of living of workers would neither be depressed nor raised. The scale of living of capitalists would be improved, and further potential improvement for someone would be accumulated within the system.

It is apparent that one cycle of such a distributive process could be carried through quite successfully. But could an endless series of such settlements be carried through and the economic system still be maintained in smooth operation, with consumption expanding by the amount of the technical improvement?

It is evident that the $200,000 going into larger or more powerful plant and equipment could not be currently counted as economic gain—that is, realized material well-being. That part of the nominal gain from labor saving would maintain employment but not enlarge total consumption until such time as the new plant poured a product of additional goods into the market and those goods could be taken out of the market by buyers and put to actual consumer use. Since, in the case here set up, no wages have been raised and no more current employment created, the sources of such a consumer market would have to be found among those whose income had been increased by the retention of profits from the preceding increase of efficiency and those who draw incomes from the new plant. It thus becomes a question of the capacities of these two groups to consume as compared with the technical efficiency of new capital goods.

Such a proportion between new investment and added consumption by profit receivers as is suggested

---

[16] Assuming that the new goods require the same relative amount of labor in their production or that both are, in the last analysis, all labor.

in our illustration would, for successful indefinite continuance, require either a low productivity of new capital goods or quite fabulous capacities of consumption on the part of the group who receive profits.[17] Unless there is a prompt market absorption of the added product created by the new capital goods, inducement to further investment of profits is weakened and a still higher percentage would have to be returned to circulation via consumption or would accumulate as hoarded funds.

How successful an all-to-profits disposal of the gains from labor-saving efficiency would be as a means of meeting our problem depends very definitely on how widely capital ownership is diffused. If ownership of the whole industrial plant were represented by corporate stock, and this were held by all the workers in industry in proportion to their several wage and salary positions, distributing efficiency gains entirely to capital would be a virtual wage raise and lead to active consumption.[18] But under existing distribution of capital, turning all efficiency gains into the form of profits would put them into the hands of so small a class of consumers that profitable utilization of the new plant and equipment purchasable with this fund would not be physically possible. Suits, shoes, and hats in the closet, fleets of automobiles standing idle much of the time, and town houses,

[17] Obviously, under the conditions experienced in industrial America, technological advance has been so rapid as much to outrun the capacity of the capitalist class to utilize the whole gain. The sharing of these gains with consumers either as higher money wages or as lower prices of consumer goods, has itself sustained and accelerated the rate of technological progress. Attempt to monopolize gains for a small class in the population by restricting expansion of the market, weakens the motive to develop more productive means of supplying that market.

[18] There would, however, be an inevitable lag in disbursement due to the fact that wage payments go out weekly or monthly, whereas dividends go out quarterly or at longer intervals. In practice, however, purchase may be made in anticipation of the receipt of dividend checks.

country houses, summer cottages, and winter cabins standing largely untenanted are not the equivalent of goods promptly worn out and calling for replacement by persons of modest means, always below their potential level of active consumption.

Thus, though we found, when we limited our analysis to one turnover under this type of distribution, that it might conceivably provide full employment of the displaced workers during that period, the attempt to extend this method indefinitely ends with a clear picture of congested consumption, hoarded savings, and more or less unutilized plant capacity, all three of these situations resulting in unemployment or wasted labor, offsetting to a greater or less degree the labor nominally saved.

We turn therefore to our second case and consider wage-rate advances as a means of distributing the gains of economic progress. Again assuming technological or organizational improvements which save a million hours of labor worth $500,000 and necessary charges of $100,000 on the capital that produced the labor saving, we suppose that all the remaining $400,000 goes as wage increases to workers who are still retained on the operating force. Since there is no change in prices, these workers will be able to satisfy their old wants at their accustomed prices. How will this group (larger than the capitalistic group and more hungry as consumers) administer the fund derived from efficiency gains which now has come into their hands? Presumably they will have on the average a lower ratio of saving than have profit-receivers on the average, but certainly some part of their gains will go to new investment or enlargement of the capital fund. There would seem to be rather less danger of such over-saving as would result in idle funds or such over-investing as would result in unutilized plant capacity, under a distribution of efficiency gains to labor as wages than under a distribution of such gains to capital as profits.

But the most that this group can do by way of sustaining employment is to enlarge their individual consumption and offer some funds for investment, the total limited, however, to what was already being disbursed in the market. Since prices are not lowered, there is no tendency to expand the market for the product these people turn out and hence to employ additional labor.[19] Wage raising as such creates no jobs for the displaced workers.

What then of the workers whose millions of hours of labor have been "saved." Will all this labor power be wasted? We may fairly assume that these workers are possessed of some initiative, which they will exert toward finding or creating new jobs for themselves. The savings of those whose wages were raised might furnish them some capital with which to equip themselves, or there may have been inactive funds or unutilized plant or enterprise looking for a new promotional opportunity to start a new business. Such happy circumstances may combine to save this group from unemployment, but whatever employment and added product are thereby brought about cannot be put down to the credit of the wage-raising method. They are extraneous as to their origin and unpredictable in amount.

Besides this general defect of the wage-raising method as a means of passing on the gains of technological progress, several particular shortcomings in its operation need

---

[19] Since these increased wages originated in efficiency gains, they did not cause an increase in commodity prices. With prices unchanged, the increased-wage group would presumably be freer spenders, but this would be offset by the reduced expenditures of the displaced workers unless or until they were again fully employed.

to be considered. What may perhaps seem almost too obvious to mention is the fact that the wage raising we have here been dealing with is not quite the kind of wage raising with which we are familiar in current industrial relations. The wage raises discussed in our illustrative case were explicitly defined as those made possible by and limited to the amount of efficiency gains actually made in given industries. But the whole system of union organization and collective wage bargaining tends toward flat wage rates for a given craft or type of labor nationally or over all plants in a relatively wide area. Even if the initial demand for and granting of a wage increase is based on and commensurate with an actual gain of efficiency at a particular point, generalization of this increase to cover all other situations means that at many points the producer's cost will be increased and his selling price advanced.[20] This will normally cut down sales in those markets and thus exert an influence toward unemployment.

Labor unions have often argued that any and every wage increase is good because it "creates purchasing power." This involves a fundamental fallacy. As we have shown at various stages of the preceding argument, it is increasing productivity due to enhanced efficiency that creates potential gains in purchasing power, but this force has to be released in the market through proper adjustment of the income-to-price relationship if it is to create real additional purchasing power. While we have argued that such an efficiency gain may be effectively realized through raising wages of workers who are actually employed in the more efficient productive process, using this situation as an excuse for raising wages where efficiency has not been increased disrupts other parts of

[20] This point has already been alluded to on p. 128.

the business world and tends toward unemployment rather than employment. If wage raises are forced simply by union-created labor scarcity, by sympathetic or general strike, or by pressure-group legislation or intimidation of administrative boards, the least harmful results take the form of price inflation, and the most harmful results appear as market demoralization and unemployment. It is only if such indiscriminate wage increases should happen to coincide with industrial efficiency changes and the reciprocal responses of the consumer market that these wage raises are compatible with economic progress.[21]

[21] The smaller the proportion of the labor group that is embraced in the union or the fewer the kinds of workers so organized, the less is their power to limit employment. If the union sets its wages too high, it will tend to shift employment to non-union workers and to promote mechanization or changes in labor management that lessen reliance on these strongly organized trades. But the nearer labor organization comes to embracing all the workers of the craft or the industry or eventually the whole labor force, the more impossible it becomes for labor to escape the results of any serious mistakes it may make in judging what is a workable wage rate. Thus if all labor were effectively organized and insisted on a general wage raise of, say, 15 per cent, it seems clear that the result would be mere price inflation and consequent trade demoralization or checking of operations and immediate unemployment.

While recent broadening of the labor movement from craft to industrial types of organization and the supplementing of private organization by public support of collective bargaining activities and legislative underwriting of wages tends to bring wage disbursements in areas of deficient purchasing power, it threatens, if no means can be found for levelling down the rate of payment to those who have previously succeeded in pushing their rates higher than their differential productivity justified, to bring the whole wage level to an inflationary and/or widespread-unemployment situation.

In this connection it is worth remembering that we have a large and increasing body of government employees—policemen, firemen, "white wings," court-house retainers, state and federal bureau staffs—who have and use political means of securing blanket wage raises, often combined with insistence on the employment of supernumerary "workers." The cost-raising effects of this influence are to be seen in our tax bills.

It was suggested on p. 253, that the businessman customarily mentions tax increase along with wage increases as an insurmountable bar to price lowering. In the original outline and the early drafts of this study, a chapter on "The Tax Burden and Business Policy" was included.

Less evident perhaps is the fact that wage advances tend to be generalized not alone throughout a particular trade or employment. By the force of mere imitation, through competition, or through resort to cost-of-living arguments, it tends to spread to many other lines of work. Thus, if re-employment is found for all these displaced workers, some and perhaps all of them must now be paid an enhanced wage scale. To that extent the $400,000 of payroll made available to the economy through the labor saving improvement will not employ as many workers as were displaced, and some of the labor saved in the first instance would still run to waste after the adjustment of higher income to re-employment had been completed.

This brings us to an examination of the results which flow from use of the third channel of distribution, namely lower consumer prices. Of $500,000 saved from the former labor requirement, we will as before say that $100,000 is paid by the employer as capital costs of the new labor-saving equipment, wages remain the same, and $400,000 gets into the hands of consumers in the form of lower prices for the goods which they have been accustomed to buy. In the first place, the change operates at once and with initial force to expand the market demand for these particular goods. To the extent that this demand is elastic, there will be a market for a larger output of these same goods and thus an immediate re-

---

The tax question, however, is so complex and at present so deeply involved with issues of war financing and inflation control that it has seemed better to drop that chapter. This decision was influenced further by the fact that the Brookings Institution is planning one or more books and pamphlets which will deal more comprehensively with the tax issue. Many readers will no doubt readily see how the same lines of approach which have been used in this chapter could profitably be used to examine taxes as factors in operative cost and in determining the purchasing power of the market.

employment of some part of the workers who had been threatened with displacement. Let us say that $50,000 goes for this purpose and creates a proportionate amount of re-employment. The remaining $350,000 in the hands of consumers of these goods as a result of the reduced prices would be available either for saving or for spending on other types of consumption goods.

Now if the labor saving is effected in the production of necessitous goods of practically universal consumption, it seems clear that the gains from lower prices will be promptly spent. The great masses of lower income receivers are always denying themselves full satisfaction as to the things they do buy and are going without other things of only little less pressing desire. The cents or dollars left in their hands by the lowering of prices of accustomed goods thus go quickly and fully into other consumer expenditures and create a demand for enlarged employment in those industries. As we go up the income scale, we find consumers less pressed for necessities but still eager to enlarge their budget of conveniences and erstwhile luxuries, so that the rate of expenditure remains high until the small numbers in the top brackets are reached.

It may be laid down as a general principle that the more widely the gains of labor saving are distributed and the larger the number of spenders to whose administration it is exposed, the more promptly will it be spent and turned back into the channel of labor employment. It would seem too that the small sums left to consumers (even the relatively affluent) as a result of price reductions are more likely to move promptly into consumer expenditures than are the more sizable sums that come on periodic dates as enlarged salary and dividend payments. The latter are likely to be set aside for a

time at least while alternative means of profitable investment are being carefully convassed and even left unin-
vested for a long period if prospects are not bright.

We conclude therefore that putting labor-saving
gains into price reduction is the surest and most complete
way of providing for the re-employment that is necessary to prevent labor-saving from becoming labor-
wasting.

THE MUTUAL INTERESTS OF EMPLOYER AND EMPLOYEE

At the opening of this chapter, we were confronted
by a more or less representative employer, who argued
that price lowering is made impossible by ever-recurring
advances in wage rates. We were confronted also by the
all too typical labor union executive who conceives that
he is serving the interests of factory hands and office
workers, of school teachers, musicians, and government
employees if he forces wage rates up whenever he can
get enough internal strength in his organization or external support from government so that he can exact
such a settlement.[22]

In attempting to find the highest common denominator between these two kinds of lay economic reasoning,
we have set forth five general propositions:

1. The nature and purpose of free business enterprise

[22] The expression "all too typical" is used advisedly. But the comments
of this chapter on short-sighted or blindly militant policies of labor unions
do not imply that better-informed or better-directed adjustment efforts
are entirely lacking. Sumner Slichter gives detailed evidence in *Union
Policies and Industrial Management* (1941) of cases in which unions
have co-operated with company executives in carrying out programs of
efficiency improvement or have even taken the lead in inaugurating such
undertakings and showing employers how such improvements could be
effected. For exposition of the more constructive types of union policy from
the point of view of union officials themselves, see Clinton S. Golden and
Harold J. Ruttenberg, *The Dynamics of Industrial Democracy*, (1942).

is to discover and put in operation more efficient means of production so that a given amount of labor may produce a larger volume of material satisfactions.

2. The fruits of such increased productivity may be taken in the form either of higher cash incomes or of lower commodity prices.

3. The economic insight with which prices (including wages) are set determines in large measure how fully business enterprise shall express itself in the form of technical improvement of our productive operations and at the same time secure or permit full utilization of the labor capacity of our people.

4. Probably the greatest danger in current practices of capitalistic management and organized labor is that, in making administrative adjustment of prices for large industrial output and of contract wage rates for large groups of employees, both management and labor have depended too much on the exercise of power rather than on careful reasoning from objective facts to probable economic consequences. They have not sought or attained sufficient flexibility nor have they manifested enough concern for simultaneous adjustment of mutually dependent prices in a delicately interrelated price system.

5. In the preceding section, we have undertaken to show that price lowering is the economically-to-be-preferred method by which the several agencies of industrial management may attempt to stimulate the fullest flow of new efficiencies into the productive process and the conversion of this high *productivity* through full employment into high *production* or maximum real wages for the total working population.

But, as has already been said (p. 261), these general conclusions of our analysis cannot be reduced to simple economic "laws" for the business manager's guidance or translated into precise formulas for application by the union official. This is where business-executive and labor-union leadership plays what we regard as its most important role. We believe that sound managerial decisions can be taken only in the light of such broad considerations of the operation of the economic process as have here been outlined, and that these decisions must be essentially joint determinations of price and wage issues participated in by both parties. Furthermore, if such decisions are to make for more productive and more stable price and income adjustments, they must be made initially not by force and in the darkness or twilight of partially disclosed facts, but by reasoned negotiation on the basis of frank disclosure of pertinent information. Since even then there is ample opportunity for doctors to disagree, the process of price-and-wage setting should include continuous experimentation, expert study of results, and careful readjustment at suitable intervals.

Executives of the individual corporation are characteristically striving to make a profit for their own company without concern for, or even at the expense of, other companies. They have not been accustomed to consider very intensively either the repercussions of their short-term actions on the remoter future of the industry or their responsibility for underwriting high real wages for the working masses as a means of assuring a stable and prosperous future for their own companies. Sometimes they have been short-sighted in turning too readily to the introduction of "labor-saving" machinery without considering adequately whether they could in fact pay the wage rate demanded or what would be the ultimate effects of trying to "save" this labor outlay.

Labor union officials, on their part, have not given enough consideration to the economic requirements of capital formation and to the need of profit incentives if remunerative jobs are to be permanently provided for them and their children and if better and cheaper goods are to be put on the market for them to buy. They have not even been deeply concerned to maintain and enlarge the work opportunities and the purchasing power of labor as a class. They have been much more concerned to enlarge the pay envelopes of favorably situated groups regardless of what happened to other workers or to write higher hourly rates into the wage contract regardless of what effect this might have on opportunities for employment. They have been all too faithful to the counsel promulgated by Samuel Gompers: Whenever you have to accept defeat in your negotiations with employers, accept it in the form of unemployment, not in the form of reduced wage rates.[23]

After all is said that can be said in support of the specific claims of the individual corporation and for those of the particular labor group, it must be recognized that at bottom the most important interests of all capitalists, all managers, all workers, and all consumers are mutual. Capital and management cannot be profitably

[23] This counsel was even urged on the farmers by Mr. Gompers and it exerted a powerful influence on this great class of self-employed workers also to follow the lead of organized labor in seeking economic well-being through curtailment of production. "At the National Agriculture Conference in Washington in January 1922, Gompers described the methods used by organized labor. He explained to the farmers that he had advised laborers to take all their punishment in unemployment rather than in wage reduction. He then pointed his finger at the assembled farmers and said, 'Go thou and do likewise.' . . . The Federal Farm Board, established in 1929, was the first actual response by government to this demand of the farmers. . . . The Farm Board was replaced by the Agricultural Adjustment Administration which . . . carried forward the major market-control practices of the Farm Board and adopted the principle of limitation of production which had been urged by the Farm Board as necessary to market stabilization." Henry C. Taylor, "The Farmer in the Groupistic Regime," *The Journal of Land & Public Utility Economics*, Vol. 16 (1940), p. 257.

employed except with the co-operation of workers and with workers disbursing an adequate purchasing power in the market. Neither can labor be given full opportunity to exert itself toward the satisfaction of its consumer wants under conditions of high efficiency unless the appropriate amount (with ever-improving quality) of plant and equipment is made available.

We should not permit ourselves to be brought to the economic impasse in which those in both the wage and the capitalist class would be working so blindly to improve their relative positions as to produce a "donkey race" of production restriction. Broader policies for the administration of our economic resources must somehow be devised by individual executives and group officials if private business enterprise is not to be superseded by government direction and even government operation.

The conditions necessary, the criteria for judging them, and the means of attaining them will be discussed further in later chapters. It is evident there is no possible way, in a world of large corporations and national unions, by which an economically correct administration of either labor prices or commodity prices can be had except as the process of wage and rate setting takes account of and gauges as scientifically as possible the interaction between each such price and its neighbors in the price system. This means collective bargaining must not be an attempt to win a point by the mere weight of numbers or strategic position. It must become an attempt to co-ordinate the resources within the administration of local and central executives so as to promote the maximum productivity of industry as a whole.

CHAPTER X
THE TIMING OF PRICE CHANGES

Throughout this book and the preceding volumes on price policy and the distribution of income in its relation to economic progress, we have tried to keep clear of the phenomena and the theory of the business cycle. Attention has been steadily focused on economic progress as a long-time trend, not upon the ups and downs of business booms and depressions. We started out to explore the possibility of "attaining a permanent high standard of material well-being."[1] We scouted the idea that "our economic society is working in excess of its normal capacity in periods of prosperity [after which] our economic body must have prolonged resting periods of low activity. . . . The problem becomes not one of checking the exuberance of boom times but of maintaining and indeed increasing even that rate of productive operation."[2] What we call "low-price policy" was dissociated from current doctrines of "price flexibility" often put forth as a "remedy for depression."[3]

This distinction between "fundamental forces which operate continuously" and "the disturbances of the so-called business cycle" was again noted in the opening chapter of this volume (page 21 n) and in the introduction to Part II (page 151). The reader was warned in advance not to expect a discussion of cycle analysis and recovery measures, but that his attention would be

---

[1] *America's Capacity to Produce* (Foreword), p. 2; *America's Capacity to Consume*, p. 126.

[2] *Income and Economic Progress*, p. 9.

[3] *Industrial Price Policies and Economic Progress*, p. 9.

directed toward "continuous types of economic adjustment designed to maintain the operations of a modern
private enterprise system on a prevailingly high level of
efficiency and hence prosperity."

But even while we emphasized this distinction, it was
recognized that the present book would not be logically
complete without extending "the argument of the previous volumes in this series so as to include certain
time considerations of a relatively short duration." It is
obvious that every decision about price policy must be
taken in one phase or another of some kind of business
cycle. These decisions must be made when businessmen
are suffering from bad times or apprehensive of worse,
when they are enjoying good or anticipating better
times.

We therefore at this point ask four questions: (1)
Should businessmen definitely follow a rule of timing
their decisions to raise, maintain, or lower prices according to the phases of the business cycle, its course being
regarded as independent of price policies? (2) Should
they think of price lowering merely as a means to engender business recovery? (3) Should they move prices
up as fast and far as possible during prosperity periods?
(4) Is there any condition of business activity which is
particularly appropriate for translating technological
improvements into price reduction?

This matter is very often approached in terms of
"price flexibility." But if that phrase is to be used, we
need to distinguish three general concepts of flexibility.
The first can well be described as price sensitivity to
short-run changes on either the demand or the supply
side. The second identifies price flexibility with a general
policy of cutting and recutting prices in times of depression until recovery spontaneously ensues. The third

usage relates to the dependability with which price reductions can be counted upon to follow cost-reducing improvements in productive technique.[4]

The first of these concepts we shall dismiss from consideration here since such flexibility, whatever its merits and weaknesses, is an attribute of exchange markets for highly standardized commodities and of auction and small higgling markets for perishable or personalized wares. It is not pertinent to the area of administered prices for differentiated industrial products, which constitute the subject matter of this book (though, of course, the price-making executive might make his price reductions in frequent small changes or in less frequent moves of greater magnitude).

The third concept of flexibility is a part, but by no means the whole, of the doctrine of low-price policy which is the central theme of our investigation. We shall attempt in the latter part of this chapter and in the one which follows to show what that relationship is.

But before that we need to examine the second concept of flexibility. We shall consider whether favorable opportunities for the making of price reductions based on technological improvement are to be found in depression periods, and whether the sort of price cutting that is resorted to in the hope of stimulating trade and industrial recovery is an application of or is unrelated to the low-price policy which we are advocating.

PRICE CUTTING AS A DEPRESSION CURE

It is often argued by both businessmen and economists that a "flexible" price policy should be followed when business recession comes so as to clear markets and re-

---

[4] In the economic theorist's terms, whether, when costs are reduced, the pattern of administered prices conforms to the "behavior" of prices under (perfect) competition.

store prosperity. If at such a time price cutting could be applied judiciously to specific prices which were out of line with the general cost structure and other prices be held stable while these adjustments were being effected, sounder market relationships would be restored and recovery might be to some extent facilitated. But if all prices slip or are indiscriminately pushed down as the given producers are confronted by a less active demand, no real adjustment process is involved but simply a general and self-accelerating price deflation.

Practical experience testifies that price cutting to move goods that have become congested in a market which has passed the crest of a boom is almost sure to reduce sales and lead to the progressive contraction of demand rather than its revival. Buyers argue that when price cutting has begun it will probably go on through several steps. They therefore withhold orders, waiting to see whether they cannot buy at yet lower prices. Manufacturers and merchants become apprehensive too as to how large supplies they will need if slackening in the tempo of business is perchance foreshadowed by these initial price cuts. Their hesitation necessitates or induces further cuts by sellers, and these in turn lead to further contraction of sales and the cumulative phenomena of business depression.

The price flexibility argument grows out of the classic theories of automatic adjustment of prices in a competitive market in response to the law of supply and demand. We have pointed out in a previous chapter[5] that this kind of spontaneous adjustment does not, in the absence of *perfect* competition, promote business stability, even in an environment of small-scale operating units, but excessive swings toward high prices and low, hectic busi-

[5] See p. 58.

ness and business paralysis. While we can see how it is that agriculture and a few comparably situated industries are able to live through such disorderly conditions, this does not suggest that the quite different procedure of lowering prices at the same time that production is kept under control would have substantial remedial effects in an area of administered prices.

The vicissitudes of the so-called business cycle (perhaps better the industrial cycle) relate very largely to postponable expenditures and durable goods—both consumers' and producers'. It is the expansion in sales of these goods which is most marked in periods of business prosperity, and it is in these industries that decline in sales is greatest in periods of depression. People buy automobiles when they have jobs and particularly when they get salary raises or feel the relative security of a period of business prosperity. They forego owning a car or postpone the time of replacement when jobs are scarce, hours short, work irregular, and a general sense of insecurity develops. At such times they withdraw from the market for automobiles, radios, and washing machines; they do not build houses, nor do they rent more or better space from those who would build houses or apartments for hire. Their decisions in these matters are swayed but little by reductions in the prices at which such goods are offered, a great deal more by their desire to husband their reserves.

Much the same may be said about the builders of factories, enlargers of plants, purchasers of new factory equipment or of transportation facilities. A few large companies which have a relatively stable market and liquid reserves may take advantage of lower construction or machinery costs, available in periods of business depression. But by far the larger part of industrial buying of durable goods is activated by the presence or prospect of a brisk consumer market for the products or services turned out. The savings in unit cost of product ultimately contributed by the new machine will not be affected very strongly by cuts of 10 or even 20 per cent in the price of the equipment (except very short-lived kinds) that might be replaced during a depression.

On the other hand, experience indicates depression price cutting grows by what it feeds on. An "epidemic of price cutting" develops into a vicious sequence of declining confidence, impaired credit, forced liquidation, unemployment, loss of purchasing power, and so on indefinitely. Such a process does not, in our interrelated industrial and financial world, engender early recovery. Indeed, the question may be raised whether it does not lead to needlessly long prostration before recovery forces are able to reassert themselves.

The most prevalent argument for price and wage cutting in time of depression is that if employers can get wages and material costs down to a point where they think a profit margin between production costs and prices is assured, they will have the managerial confidence needed to open their factories, expand the amount of employment, and increase their purchases of raw materials, thus initiating a recovery movement which will spread and cumulate.[6]

Naturally, a depression-engendered fall in prices of raw materials and supplies lowers the costs of producing

---

[6] Labor, on its part, is pretty sure to resist the lowering of its rates as a means of assuring the employer profits in the hope of starting recovery. Workers will argue that the lowering of their purchasing power impairs the market and retards still further the revival of business rather than promoting it. Employers are not willing or able to commit themselves to take on enough additional labor at the lower rates so that there will be a net strengthening of the consumer market thus enabling producers to sell the increased volume of goods on which any such recovery must depend. And laborers do not have sufficient assurance that wage rates lowered for recovery purposes will be restored when prosperity returns.

fabricated wares. But since prices of finished products as well as cost goods melt away at such a time (many of them at an even more rapid rate), there is no strong or general tendency for profit margins per unit of product to show significant improvement. In fact, it is not until volume of sales enlarges substantially that the company's earning situation will improve enough to be itself a stimulative factor. If the manufacturer or distributor fails to follow along with reductions in his prices which fully reflect declines (if any), in cost of materials and labor, it is evident that he would be contributing to the depth and duration of the depression. But this is a merely negative case for recession price-cutting.

Price cuts (even to the extent of incurring temporary losses), which get bulky inventories off the market, will have a quickening effect on the business of particular firms or even industries and lead to a market psychology more favorable to the initiation of new business. But such price cutting in late stages of a recession is a mere tactical maneuver, suggestive of the smart general who counts certain personnel and equipment as "expendable" in a local foray designed to create a more favorable general situation. It certainly does not follow that, within the area of administered prices, the business manager should think of price lowering as something to be resorted to only when forced to it by conditions of business recession or that, so used, he could get from it its distinctive benefits.

Summarizing this analysis in terms of the question with which we started, we should therefore conclude that emergency practices of price cutting in time of general business distress have limited effectiveness and in some situations adverse effects. They do not reflect a reasoned policy of passing on the gains of technological progress to consumers and are therefore largely unrelated to low-price policy as a basic principle of price making.

SHOULD PRICES BE PUSHED UP IN GOOD TIMES?

The practice of price cutting in times of depression that we have just been discussing seems to reflect a general "charge-what-the-traffic-will-bear" philosophy of pricing rather than any more sophisticated pattern of business administration. We would expect the holder of such a view likewise to *advance* prices at a time of easy sales as far as he could without unduly curtailing volume of sales. We would expect him to accumulate all the profits possible at such a time regardless of the effect that this course, if followed generally, would have on the total business situation. We would expect him to retain these company profits in a war chest to fortify him in cutting prices even below cost in a subsequent period of business depression when volume of sales fell off.

The price-making executive who makes no distinction between the practices natural to sellers in a small-scale competitive market and those appropriate to a regime of administered prices would say: "Of course, a shrewd businessman who sees the appetite for his product sharpened or the purchasing power of potential buyers expanded will move up his unit price so as to take full advantage of these favorable conditions and thus enhance his profits to the greatest extent possible."[7] But,

---

[7] Such a view, of course, implies that the given business, however large, is not a significant factor in determining the continuation of prosperity or the advent of depression. It regards industrial price administrators as passive factors in the price-making process just like the atomistic market competitor, for whom no course other than adaptation to an external market situation is available. Nor does it contemplate the possibility that, though the individual actions of no single company, even the most gigantic, could be determinative of the general business situation, a concerted policy or consistent philosophy of business leadership entertained by a relatively small number of executives of large and strategical-

even though the manager, by such means, seeks and attains a maximum short-run profit position for the business month by month or day by day as the business upswing continues, we are moved to consider what economic consequences are likely to ensue.

If a high-price and maximum-profits policy is followed during a period of sharp upswing, the results do not appear merely in the form of larger productive capacity and ampler flows of consumer goods. Manifestations include also the unproductive and ultimately harmful phenomena of runaway stock markets and land booms, in which the bidding up of property values absorbs some of the inflationary pressure but leads to subsequent "headaches" and disruptions of business. Even where the excessive profits of such a period go into new corporate promotions, the erection of new industrial plants, or the extension of other physical facilities, the amount of this expansion is not set by capacity shortage, but by the ease with which stock or other property can at such a time be unloaded on the public. Many such properties will have to be reorganized, devalued, or dismantled, or will stand idle after the boom psychology has subsided.

If industrial price makers (including trade-union officials) jointly and severally wash their hands of any responsibility for the course of general business, healthy prosperity gives way to a mere price inflation. In the subsequent downswing, even the excess profits that were impounded in a depression reserve not only will prove

---

ly placed concerns might determine the general business atmosphere and establish a trend of action which would be followed by smaller executives to such an extent as strongly to influence or effectively determine whether business as a whole would go actively forward or would be involved in a general retreat. This broad issue will be examined in some detail in later chapters.

to be needed but also they will then be dissipated in merely struggling to preserve the life of the company—bringing neither recovery nor a higher level of productivity. In the end, such management—or lack of it—will result in averaging high profits and subsequent losses to show only moderate or meager returns over a span of years that embraces a complete cycle[8] and in which productive capacities were fully used only at the peak and may have averaged only 70 or 80 per cent utilization over the entire period. This means a loss to consumers as a whole and particularly to those whose consumption is strictly governed by their ability to find employment, without a compensating gain to managers and capitalists. If the latter ride the easy tide of high prices and high profits in the belief that they are "saving for a rainy day," they wake up eventually to find that they themselves have helped to bring on a rainy spell.

The relationship between prices in the upswing of the business cycle and the wage problem needs also to be considered. Boom prices tend to furnish excuse for workers to agitate for pay increases, both on the ground that cost of living has advanced and on the ground that these high prices connote high profits, out of which employers can afford to make wage advances. At the same time, the employer finds himself in a weak position to resist advances which he may think are not justified by the long-run earning position of the business. Since union wage rates are notoriously inflexible against any decline, employers who follow a price policy which leads to temporary high profits invite trouble for themselves

[8] Taxes undoubtedly have a bearing on these phenomena, but just how they will affect price policy is uncertain. Will steeply progressive tax rates on corporate profits moderate the price policies of executives in boom times? Or will the fact that only part of the profits of such a period remain with the companies tend to cause them to crowd harder than ever to increase these short-run profits?

in dealing with their wage problem during subsequent periods when only meager profits can be obtained and even losses may be incurred.

Hence it is much sounder long-run policy to refrain from charging all the traffic will bear in boom times and to adjust prices downward as either improved efficiency or expansion in volume lowers unit costs. To follow the easy road to large short-run profits, which can be extracted from a market infected with boom psychology, is to mistake the shadow of price inflation for the substance of productivity gains. Larger company incomes derived from such a source carry danger rather than benefit. Real prosperity is spelled by more goods for the same money, not by more money for the same goods.

THE NORMAL TIME FOR DIGESTING EFFICIENCY GAINS

The policy of making price reductions rather than advances during the upswing of the business cycle rests on positive as well as negative grounds. We have pointed to some dangers of not following such a course. We want now to consider the economic benefit which ensues when it is followed. The point to be made in this section is that a consistent low-price policy operates as a countervailing force to stabilize business when the impact of technological progress tends to unsettle it.

We examined in Chapter IX one major effect which technological change exerts toward the unsettling of business, namely the displacement of workers. The characteristic economic form which technological improvement takes is labor saving, and its primary manifestation is found in the discharge of workers who are no longer needed under the new technique. If no compensating adjustment is made, labor saving becomes labor wasting and no economic gain is realized.

Throughout this book the analysis has been based on the phenomenon of rising productive efficiencies, introduced through the exercise of business enterprise. For the industrial world to make maximum progress, it must provide both the incentives and the facilities for discovering or devising the techniques of these new efficiencies and must at the same time secure full utilization of the labor force and other resources. More skillful use of particular units (qualitative efficiency) must be joined with maximum production (quantitative efficiency). (See p. 118.) This latter objective can be attained only by enlarging the general market demand for goods by an amount sufficient to reabsorb displaced workers (though possibly with some shortening of hours, since leisure is one of the forms in which we desire to take our economic gains).[9] And as an enterprise economy functions, this expansion of sales and re-employment of labor can be most promptly and most satisfactorily effected by lowering prices in proportion to the net labor saving. The problem is really solved only when prices are so adjusted that full-scale production can be absorbed out of currently earned incomes.[10]

Another major aspect of the unsettling effect which technological changes have on the course of business is that they frequently involve the installation of plant capacities in excess of the current absorptive power of the market. Full practical capacity must be used if potential cost reduction is to be realized and the invest-

---

[9] Thus the formula for economic progress may be written: shorter hours of more effective labor rendered by more highly developed people using more and better equipment to produce a volume of goods so large and varied that more leisure time must be available for its consumption.

[10] In a prosperous period, producers are prone to evade this downward adjustment of prices by the extension of consumer credit even to semi-durable goods, often on lax terms.

ment is fully to justify itself. But to move this larger product there must be larger incomes in the hands of the consuming masses if the price is to remain the same, or lower prices for the goods if the general income level remains the same. Industrial executives need to be on guard lest they follow a pricing rule which will stand in the way of effective exploitation of the new process.

Most employers appeal to some sort of investment principle in adopting technological improvements. One may say that he will not put capital into such a machine (or method) unless it will pay for itself in two years, in five years, or in some other specified period. There appears to be a widespread philosophy, as to the lighter types of equipment, that such investments should amortize themselves within about three years.* If such a policy is followed, it is likely to mean that the price of the product is held up during that period to take large profit margins where the employer feels that any resulting unemployment will not have unfavorable repercussions on his own market or on the general business situation during that period of time.[11]

[11] In Chap. 6, p. 186, we discussed the somewhat longer range investment-and-price policies followed by some large corporations having broad vision and ample capital or credit resources. Particularly in the case of a novel product, for which a practically new market demand must be built up, such a company may not merely adopt a long (10-15 year) amortization period but also facilitate early development of a mass market by pricing below cost for a year or even longer.

* Since this chapter appeared in pamphlet form, the writer has become acquainted with Ruth P. Mack's interesting and suggestive volume, *The Flow of Business Funds and Purchasing Power.* On the basis of interviews with a considerable number of business executives, she reported: "All of the companies with whom the question was discussed made replacements only when the capital seemed likely to be returned in six or eight years or less; the most usual requirement was for return of investment in three years or less, and a one-year interval was not unusual. The longer intervals were more likely to be tolerated for heavy equipment. In some industries, such as textile, baking, and packing, technological change seemed to provide relatively few changes

What is significant for our present analysis is that the manager should then be sure to reconsider his price policy at the end of the amortization period. Since the capital ventured in the improvement of technique has then been repaid, there is certainly no longer any occasion for his capital charge to include anything for depreciation or to be based on an interest rate above the safe-lending rate, since all uncertainty as to the outcome of the venture has been removed.[12] Furthermore, the argument that the rate of profits needs to be kept up to a level which will "attract new venture capital" has no force—unless it be in reverse. That is to say, the maintenance of a profit rate which will attract new capital to the given line of business simply means attracting competitors into the field to split his market and make it more difficult to exploit fully the economies of full-capacity operation. Hence it behooves the introducer of new and better methods to lower his prices so promptly and steadily that such over-expansion will not be invited.

Technological improvements are introduced into our

---

that would return capital in less than three or four years so that firms that believed in modern equipment would frequently have to accept a 20 or 15 per cent return on the investment. A good many of the companies required a higher rate of return in poor years than in good ones in spite of the fact that frequently this percentage return was calculated at current volume." (pp. 255-56.)

Mrs. Mack also cites the earlier study in *Recent Economic Changes* (p. 139) to the effect that of 200 respondents to a questionnaire, 43.6 per cent replied that they would not purchase new equipment unless profits promised to repay the investment within two years; 64.1 per cent only if repaid in three years, 76.9 per cent if paid out in four years, and 100 per cent if paid in five years or less.

[12] It may be objected that in the practical use of cost accounting as a guide to business policy no such specific adjustment of the capital charge for individual machines or pieces of equipment is made. But it is just the easy reliance on generalized rates of capital charge and similar types of "standard" costing which keeps many businessmen from recognizing and measuring efficiency gains, as they become available for price reduction.

productive system in a continuous though not uniform stream. In time the price structure must adjust itself to these reductions in the cost structure. Disparities between the two may, however, be protected and carried along by individual managements, multiplying the vulnerable spots in the price structure until the whole thing is subjected to drastic destructive revision under the unfavorable conditions of a period of general business recession. At such times, as we have already pointed out, the possibilities of getting favorable market response to belated price adjustments are most unfavorable. Good management would take this price adjustment in stride. Sound price policy would exert itself not to postpone but to expedite the price lowering which would maintain activity and assimilate into the price structure the reduced cost made possible by the new technique.

The older theory, that prices inevitably rose as the tempo of business activity was stepped up, was based on the assumption that labor is always fully employed (as it would be under self-employed individual enterprise) and that suppliers of raw materials had constantly to contend with shortages or high extraction costs. Now that science has provided so many ways of finding cheaper substitute materials and of lowering extraction and transportation costs or even of developing synthetic products from practically inexhaustible sources of supply, the upward tendency of the supply-cost curve has been changed to constant cost or even a downward tendency. Similarly, under conditions of chronic unemployment or under-employment, running from perhaps a tenth to a quarter of the labor supply, there is no such natural scarcity as would characteristically force labor cost up whenever business approaches full scale. At such times there are possibilities of substituting lower-priced labor or labor-saving methods. On the other hand, artificial or arbitrary advances in wage rates through union control of the labor supply tend to operate as a factor in advancing the labor cost whenever the quickening of business seems to the union strategists to afford a favorable opportunity for marking up the price of their factor of production. Both a better understanding on the part of labor as to the often illusory nature of gains in money wage rates, and greater wisdom on the part of industrialists in raising real wages by means of price reductions, are needed to check this inflationary tendency.

Price lowering during prosperous times is not only dictated and facilitated by the producer's cost situation. A prosperous period likewise furnishes a consumer atmosphere favorable to such a course. It is technically desirable to adjust prices promptly and fully to improvements in method and organization as these cost reductions become available in normally active and prosperous business times because they are then introduced in an atmosphere of business confidence. Instead of being made uncertain by a price concession and inclined to wait and see whether, by waiting, one may be able to get a still lower price, industrial buyers are at such a time ready to buy supplies or equipment because of the active market for their own product. The consumer too has then a general sense of security, maximum readiness to improve his scale of living and to disburse his purchasing power freely to this end (without impairing any pre-existing program of savings he might have—perhaps even expanding that program a little).

Furthermore, a continuous stream of price reductions during recovery or stable periods of business exerts a sobering influence against the possibilities of boom. At the same time, reductions made under such circumstances do not bring about an epidemic of price slashing as in a period of recession. If a prosperity period gets out of hand and runs into boom conditions or progressive price inflation, production costs must inevitably increase. But if this pathological phase of the cycle is avoided, the progress of ordinary business prosperity is marked by declining costs rather than increasing costs. It thus becomes a time not only when prices *should* be lowered but when it is relatively easy and natural for the economically sophisticated price-making executive to follow such a course. It is in fact *the* time for translating efficiency gains into economic progress measured in consumer satisfactions.

To summarize: sound price lowering is functionally related to decline in technical costs, on the one hand, and responsiveness of sales to price reductions, on the other. Hence, cyclical trends of general business do not furnish a proper guide to the price programs of individual companies. Each must adjust its practice to its own peculiar circumstances. Price-making executives of basic industries should not take extreme cyclical swings for granted as something to be exploited by opportunistic policies. A constructive philosophy of price administration aims at moderation of these disturbances, better sustained production, and more uniform profits. The proper time for applying low-price policy is whenever cost reductions appear or can be brought about. The passing on of such gains should not be "too little and too late"—reserved for periods of recession or panic. Neither should the practice of low-price policy be laid aside when prosperity comes. If efficiency gains are passed on to the consumer market as fast as they can be developed, they nurture and expand consumer demand instead of blighting it; they hold the profit rate to a conservative level that rewards capital but does not encourage over-capitalization of assets, speculative operations, boom, and collapse. As we have remarked before (page 149), low-price policy is in the nature of preventive care, not emergency medicine or surgery.

With these general findings in mind, let us turn to examine briefly their practical application to a particular situation in our recent past. We shall then consider what light they shed on the possibilities of boom, collapse, or carefully and wisely contrived prosperity in the years following the present war.

PRICE POLICY AND THE RECESSION OF 1920

The First World War left us with a high price level, liberal purchasing power in the hands of the people, and a general desire to forget the restraints of the war period and return to peace and prosperity as fast as possible. Throughout 1919 and much of 1920, a short-run postwar boom, such as has followed many another conflict, swept the country.[13] This boom was rooted in the shortages of consumer goods and was greatly accentuated by extensive speculation in inventories. The operation of the forces of demand and supply, unaccompanied by any restraining influence in the form of conservative price policies on the part of industrial leaders, resulted in a rise in prices much more rapid than that of the war period itself. From April 1919 to April 1920 the price index of textile products rose from 114 to 195. Likewise in a period of about a year, the metals and metal products index rose from 124 to 157, building ma-

---

[13] See Harold G. Moulton and Karl Schlotterbeck, *Collapse or Boom at the End of the War?* (1942).

terials from 98 to 168, household furnishings from 96 to 150, and fuel and lighting from 99 to 210. Hides and leather increased in a period of five months from 138 to 209. (See table below.)

INDEX NUMBERS OF WHOLESALE PRICES BY GROUPS
OF COMMODITIES AND BY MONTHS[a]
(1926 = 100)

Year and Month	Hides and Leather Products	Textile Products	Fuel and Lighting	Metals and Metal Products	Building Materials	House- furnish- ing Goods
1919						
January	135.1	127.2	108.5	135.5	101.3	98.8
February	136.3	119.0	103.2	132.3	100.2	96.8
March	137.7	114.2	101.3	128.8	99.1	96.0
April	141.7	113.7	100.6	123.9	97.7	96.7
May	152.5	119.8	99.3	123.5	100.1	97.7
June	172.1	130.5	99.8	124.5	108.7	103.8
July	192.4	140.1	100.8	127.5	118.7	106.0
August	209.3	144.2	103.3	134.7	128.7	109.0
September	207.5	145.2	105.1	134.1	130.2	110.9
October	203.8	148.9	107.7	134.7	130.3	113.6
November	201.8	156.6	106.7	136.0	131.9	119.9
December	199.0	164.5	115.3	137.0	140.8	125.0
1920						
January	200.9	187.0	117.8	140.5	155.0	133.9
February	203.4	193.9	121.8	147.8	165.2	137.3
March	197.4	192.5	131.1	152.8	167.6	138.7
April	197.0	194.6	149.1	156.0	168.3	139.0
May	193.2	188.3	159.8	155.5	164.4	143.3
June	175.7	180.6	177.4	153.9	154.8	143.3
July	170.3	169.0	198.5	154.5	151.5	149.8
August	160.7	160.8	209.9	157.3	150.0	149.7
September	153.7	144.8	201.1	156.6	144.8	148.0
October	145.8	132.2	190.1	146.7	136.7	145.7
November	132.4	121.5	163.9	140.4	124.1	139.4
December	125.6	113.6	144.2	133.7	118.3	133.5

[a] Compiled from monthly bulletins of the Bureau of Labor Statistics.

This episode furnishes an example of industrial price policy—or lack of policy—operating at its worst. These increases in prices were not made necessary by corresponding advances in costs. The prices of raw materials and wage rates, the two primary elements in manufacturing costs, had risen considerably less than had the prices of finished products. In consequence, financial profits were very large. We say *financial* profits because most of the gain shown on the books was the result of advancing prices rather than increased volume. They were in the nature of speculative mark-ups and were not the rewards of productive effort. In the main, they were short-lived.

As to the effects which this price boosting had on the course of business, rapidly rising costs of living naturally stimulated demands for compensating increases in wage rates. Acute industrial unrest developed. There was an epidemic of strikes, and an extremely low level of per man output. Many laboring groups were severely pinched because of the failure of wages to keep pace with advancing prices, and the fixed income and salaried classes also suffered acutely from the high cost of living. Volume of sales was restricted because of the steadily worsening ratio of prices to buying power in the form of wages and salaries.

The situation came to a head in May 1920, when the so-called "buyers' strike" forced horizontal reductions in retail prices by leading mercantile establishments. This was quickly followed by extensive cancellations of orders and by curtailments of production schedules, which in turn resulted in a general collapse of prices. The all-commodity price index declined from 167 in May 1920 to 93 in June 1921. The paper gains of the boom period were wiped out by the losses of the ensuing debacle.

As business later progressed through its real recovery period, its prosperity was not on a foundation of advancing prices but of prices that were stable or even declining. The general price level, which stood at 138.6 in 1919 and 154.6 in 1920 was 96.7 in 1928, as it had been also in 1922. During the intervening years, it had ranged from 95.4 to 103.5. Even the decline from war levels, however, did not adequately reflect the low-unit costs of production which were being realized under current techniques and current rates of activity. High rates of corporate profit added fuel to the flames of the stock market boom and other speculative developments which led up to the collapse of 1929.

PRICE POLICY ISSUES AFTER THE PRESENT WAR

In concluding our consideration of the timing aspect of price policy, we come to the question of war's end and a time that will provide a searching test of what we as a people have learned about the basic problems of price management. We raise specifically the question whether, or in what way, the low-price policy discussed in this book is applicable to the postwar situation.[14]

There is widespread agreement that (possibly after an initial period of hesitation), the early postwar years are quite likely to take on the character of a business boom. Even the period of initial hesitation may be less noticeable than it has been after previous wars owing to gradual demobilization and unusually active forward planning, both private and governmental. General purchasing power will be high not merely as a result of active employment opportunities but because of the phenomenally high accumulation of savings which has occurred during the war period. "Mustering-out pay"

[14] The course of prices and business activity in 1936-37 does not encourage one to think that great progress in dealing with these problems had been made in the fifteen years since the 1920-31 recession. To the writer's mind the failure of business managers and labor executives to nurse a budding recovery along to high production volume by means of low prices was at least a significant contributing factor in the "disappointing recovery" from the depression of the thirties. The situation, however, was so complex that a separate detailed monograph would be necessary to support or refute such a hypothesis.

for soldiers (perhaps bonuses later) will add a further special class of involuntary savings. Furthermore, the re-appearance of installment selling will add some billions of dollars of immediate purchasing power based on future incomes. Sellers of consumers' goods in this period will not be confronted with the basic and ultimately ines-capable problem of balancing their output against the current spendable income of the population. At the same time, owing to the delays incident to reconversion opera-tions, it will be some months, even a year or two, before the various reservoirs are filled and a full market flow of finished goods can be attained. This is precisely the kind of situation in which it will be easy for businessmen to initiate a general and cumulative upward movement of price.

Old and new agencies of businessmen all over the country are planning for a period of high business activity after the war. This will undoubtedly fortify us against the possible onset of depression due to the lack of specific planning to guide reconversion activities or to the presence of great uncertainty as to which way the cat is going to jump. But with this hesitation overcome, there is a no less serious danger that confidence itself, without sound understanding of the forces involved and the proper methods for their control, may lead to a short spurt of hectic activity followed by a collapse as severe as that of the thirties, perhaps even more devastating.

In spite of the fact that most individuals and groups give at least lip service to the idea that price inflation is bad, there will probably be strong pressure at the end of the war to get rid of the restraints of such price con-trols as we have had. And even if price control in some form is retained, the tendency will be to restrict controls to a limited number of standard and basic products. It seems unlikely that they can be extended and made effective on the wide variety of consumers' goods whose production will be expanded after the war. Nor is there any assurance that price control will be tolerated for any long period. The faster and more fully controls are removed and the private price maker "put on his own," the greater will be his responsibility for conditions that ensue.

If the abnormally high volume of available purchasing power is mopped up during three or four years of easy postwar boom, producers will thereafter have to face the problem of adjustment of prices on a lower level comparable with spendable incomes currently produced or else adjust production downward to the volume that could be sold at the prices established during the boom years. Since curtailment of production would mean discharge of many employees, current purchasing power would be further impaired, and the cumulative phenomenon of recession would be under way. The other horn of the dilemma, however, would be almost equally uninviting. During the period in which higher prices for finished goods could readily be extracted from the market, comparable prices for machines, semi-finished goods, raw materials and labor would have become established and be difficult to adjust downward promptly as an accompaniment of general price lowering in the field of consumer goods.

It must be clear, therefore, that the part of wisdom for businessmen who want to see postwar business put on a sustained level of high activity and reasonable profit-making opportunities is to exert every effort to keep prices after the war at the lowest level possible through the greatest realization of efficiency or fullest expression of technological possibilities in low prices.

Labor also has a part in meeting these postwar responsibilities. The wisdom of wage-making executives will be challenged not less than that of manufacturing and mercantile administrators. The union officials, by exploiting war pressures to push wage rates up wherever and as far as they can and by insisting on maintaining emergency rates when we are trying to get back on a peace basis, may create maladjustments that prevent effective operation at various points in the system and may throw the whole into confusion.

No doubt, labor boards will experience difficulty in any attempts they may make to get wage rates lowered after the war, however clear it may be that a particular rate is out of line with other wages, with particular prices, or with the general price structure. It will be no less difficult for employers, however sincere their motives and astute their economic analysis, to persuade their workers to revise their scales of payment downward. And union officials, whose hold on membership has traditionally been based on advances in rates more than any other thing, will be little disposed to go before their members urging the constructive value of a low-price policy for labor, however limited or temporary the area to which it might be applied.[15] But these years will pro-

[15] But this does not mean that no way of meeting the situation can be devised. For example, one way in which a constructive approach toward postwar adjustment could be introduced might be in the form of contingent rates, based on volume of employment. Since the need of facilitating high rates of employment is so crucial a factor in the adjustment problem after the war, this approach should make maximum appeal to both employers and employees. Such a program would seem to have particular applicability to the building industry, where wage rates have been notoriously high and the number of days worked per year notoriously low. If the employer who provides 300 days' employment in a year could get his labor for $1.25 per hour while the one who provides only 200 days of work would have to pay $1.60, there would be a strong incentive for employers to operate on a full-work basis. Declining labor costs would facilitate lower prices of houses as output

vide a crucial test of the ability of organized labor to follow policies which will promote labor's own long-run interest because they permit and facilitate the operation of private business, or policies which will make the operation of such a system impossible and thus invite the coming of statism.

It is impossible for anyone to say in advance how the output of the actual capacity we shall have after the close of the war, using the techniques that war production has demonstrated, would equate with the purchasing power realized from full employment at then existing rates of wages. To attain sound adjustment, management must in its own interest be alert to hold prices down to a point where full product can continuously be taken off the market by the current purchasing power.[16] If the product is not absorbed by the market, there will be no possibility of going on turning it out, employment will not be kept up to full scale, plant will not be used to capacity, and we shall be back on the level of unsatisfactory performance which spells depression.

Finally, the timing of such price adjustments is important. To be fully effective, action must be taken decisively in advance of the period of operation or even of the equipping of plant and determination of the scale of production. If the price is set tentatively at a level so high as to be profitable with the volume of sales 20 or 30 or even some greater percentage below the war

---

increased, while annual income of workers would also be increased. Expansion of the market for building materials and stabilization of employment in this basic industry would exert a pervasive stimulating effect that would be felt in many other lines.

[16] This point will be developed further in Chap. 11, together with reasons for the writer's "optimistic" view as to technological progress and the economies arising from full-scale operation.

level or postwar full-scale rate, then that is the volume of sales and employment and use of invested capital which will be realized. If price makers think they can ignore or defer the period of adjustment of their prices to an efficiency cost basis while they garner in the accumulated "easy money," they will have made the task of real adjustment more difficult if not, in any full sense, impossible.

The general argument of this chapter may be briefly summarized under four heads. (1) Price changes should not be made in conformity with phases of the cycle on any merely mechanical rule. (2) Reductions undertaken by a producer in time of depression as a desperate expedient to induce recovery are not an exemplification of low-price policy in the sense used in this book and its predecessor. (3) Prices should not move up to exploit all the traffic will bear in the short run of boom times. (4) It is when business is active and there is no particular pressure on the seller to lower prices that he should systematically and aggressively translate efficiencies into price reductions, pushing this policy the more vigorously if the market shows signs of speculative exuberance and boom tendencies.

To these general conclusions may be added two more which relate specifically to the postwar situation: (5) Shortly after the end of the present war the public will have both deferred consumer needs and hungers and accumulated savings which will make it easy to continue prices on the war level or start a price boom. (6) This possibility must be foregone and low-price policy as the means of securing and maintaining high volume of output must be recognized and put into practice by producers promptly and fully if we are to effect a satisfactory conversion from war activity to peacetime prosperity.

With these conclusions on our general point of attack, we turn in the next chapter to consider the criteria through which such a policy can be put into practice.

CHAPTER XI

BASIC CRITERIA OF PRICE POLICY[1]

It has not been possible to carry our discussion this far without referring frequently to criteria of price policy. But these have been merely incidental comments in connection with other topics such as competition, the profit motive, democracy, responsiveness of the market, wage policy, and the timing of price changes. We shall now gather together these scattered suggestions about criteria and undertake a more systematic statement of the standards, or the tests of probable result, by which businessmen formulate their rules or acquire their practices of pricing or by which they might judge the wisdom or feasibility of new as against traditional policies. This statement will have special application to the kind of industrial society that is to emerge after the war or the manner in which businessmen will approach the problem of the return of business to peacetime operation.

BUSINESS CENTERED ON "MAKING MONEY"

Common sense and every-day experience teach us that business is conducted for the purpose of making money. A given businessman may be strongly animated by the enthusiasm of the inventor or an almost mission-

---

[1] The reader should bear in mind that price policy does not mean something separate from other phases of business policy, such as technological policy, organizational policy, employment policy, wage policy, investment policy, marketing policy, that are inextricably intertwined in the business executive's total strategy of operation. But business management deals with the price aspects of these operational problems, and any penetrating and adequate analysis of business policy must therefore take price relationships as its key line of attack.

ary zeal to get some new form of want-satisfying goods into the hands of the largest possible number of consumers. But, as has already been observed (see p. 52), as a general rule "men do not go into business 'for their health,' but to get ahead, to make gains." To say, however, that money-making is the goal of business immediately raises three rather troublesome—and interrelated—questions: (1) How much money? (2) By what means? (3) Money (profits or gains) for whom?

The short answer ordinarily given to the first of these questions is "as much as possible." While the minimum condition necessary if a firm is to stay in business is that its revenues must exceed its expenses, real success is measured, in the business world, by the size of that excess. A major purpose of this chapter is to examine the factors that determine how much is in fact possible. Emphasis is put on the conditions of long-run success.

The short answer given to the second question by actual business practice appears to be "by skill and by bargaining strength." Business concerns may make money (1) by increasing the efficiency of the technical processes which they employ (including physical layout and personnel organization); (2) by acquiring at the lowest possible prices the materials and equipment which will yield the necessary services in the business; and (3) by selecting the time and place of marketing and by gauging the quantity of product to be placed on the several markets in such ways as to take advantage of the strongest spontaneous demand and existing purchasing power or by stimulating or redirecting effective demand where this can be done at costs less than the added net revenue. Of these three means of increasing the earning power of a company, the first may be classified entirely as technological skill, the second and third as commercial skill mixed with varying degrees of trading pressure. Business profits made by the use of skill raise the efficiency of the individual firm and thus total productivity; business profits made by exerting trading strength or market control are at the expense of other firms or of consumers to whom the given firm sells or workers whom it employs.

The short answer to the third question is generally "profits for the owners." To "make money for the company" is practically synonymous with paying dividends to the owners or enlarging the value of their assets. This concept is less simple in fact than it appears in words and it is subtly intertwined (as shown by the last sentence in the preceding paragraph) with the idea of means by which profits are to be made.[2] Hence, the analysis contained in this chapter will be closely related to issues of how the economic interests of owners, workers, and the public are interrelated and may be jointly served.

Many practical businessmen themselves qualify the objective of making as much money "as possible" by adding "decently," or with "due regard to the rights and welfare of others." These terms, however, are vague

[2] At first glance it might appear that any use of technological or commercial skill means that businessmen are promoting the best allocation of scarce resources to productive use and thus moving toward the very goals that the economist would set up. The use of bargaining strength, on the other hand, has customarily been classed as "monopoly" and its harmful effect taken for granted. The real issue, however, is not what degree of control or trading strength a given firm has but whether this strength is employed to enhance production by the way it administers the firm's money relations with its suppliers, its employees, and its customers. If the distribution process is not properly adjusted we may have highly skillful techniques but low total use of resources, material and human. This has been described in a previous chapter (5, page 118) as the difference between qualitative efficiency and quantitative efficiency or full production. Business men cannot be said to have been true economizers if their making of company profits is accompanied by low utilization of plant and large amounts of unemployment.

and unreliable when practical application is to be considered. They are somewhat difficult to validate to the executive who says, "business is business." At the same time they reflect a recognition on the part of the typical business executive that he has a measure of power or control, within which he can exercise discretion and pursue a policy. But they do not suggest that these executives have any confidence that economic principles can be brought to bear effectively in the guidance of that directive control.

The economist as such is not concerned with sentimental or ethical considerations which may enter into the selection of a managerial policy. If he "sticks to his [professional] last," he too must say, "business is business." But he is concerned to discover objective criteria for charting the course of business in an environment of administered prices (and wages), continuous technological change, fickle demand, and other kinds of business uncertainty so that in fact it may be quite steadily directed toward maximum returns for each individual enterprise and for business as a whole. Though sometimes conflicting in the short run, company profits and general prosperity of the economy must be reconciled in the long run. In this chapter, therefore, we shall examine such criteria of business policy as would best aid the practical business executive in navigating his corporate craft amid the winds and tides of natural economic forces.

THE TRADITIONAL CRITERION—MAXIMUM PROFITS "FOR THE OWNERS"

In an earlier chapter we noted that "no particular problem as to the meaning of profits or the operation of the profit motive arises so long as business is conducted on the basis of individual enterprise"[3] or pre-capitalism.

[3] P. 82.

The individual was self-employed or, more accurately, business was organized on the basis of the family's unpaid labor. The pure case would be that in which the only capital employed consisted of such productive goods as were accumulated from the labor of the family in rearing livestock and fashioning simple devices and appliances or in which such equipment was secured in trade for some of the family's produce.

There was, under such circumstances, no separate capital account or distinguishable income-to-capital. Nor was there any possibility of increasing gains to anyone by withholding productive labor or the use of such equipment. On the contrary, the more labor input, the more subsistence for the workers. Effort would be diverted from consumption goods to the making of machines or other labor aids when that course promised more than proportionate returns in the future, and these would, without undue hesitation, be reabsorbed into the stream of consumption whenever that seemed expedient in view of a changed situation or scale of relative values. The essential point of the relationship was that labor use was paramount, and capital existed only for the purpose of making that labor more productive.

At the opposite pole, under any fully developed communist or other autarchic system the problem is disposed of in a somewhat similar way. The provident state would take the place of the self-employed workers or the individual heads of families. It would take responsibility for putting the whole labor force to work and for allocating workers' efforts to the production of consumers' goods and the provision of capital equipment in suitable proportions. A capital account might or might not be kept. But there would be relative indifference to the fate of particular capital goods or the maintenance of high earnings to individual bits of the capital fund. This

would be in contrast to the considerable indifference that
private capitalism manifests as to the income position of
the individual laborer in general or as to the utilization
of the whole labor force at high efficiency.[4]

Between these two extremes, with their reliance respectively on automatic and on authoritarian price making, private capitalism relies largely on administered
price making by professional managers to adjust consumer prices, contract wages, profit margins, wage and
salary bonuses, and profit-sharing distributions. We expect these adjustments to be such as to attain a high
level of performance for the economy, that is, high real
incomes for its several participants, based upon full
utilization as well as proper allocation of resources.

The professional manager is not, to any considerable
extent, risking his own capital as does the owner proprietor under small-scale types of capitalist operation. Both
his professional prestige and his financial emoluments,
however, depend primarily on his success in protecting
the capital of his company and so managing it that it
will yield profits. In this role it is customary to think
of the manager as trustee for capital. But this trustee-
ship cannot be adequately discharged if the manager
entertains a narrow view of his objective or follows
merely defensive tactics for its accomplishment. In the
last analysis, managers are, under private capitalism,
trustees for the economy. Their real objective is to
cause the individual company to function with the highest degree of economic efficiency as an interrelated part
of the total business process. How, then, is the individual manager going to discharge his primary trustee-

---

[4] That an autarchic economic organization also has its own distinctive
problems and dangers is obvious, but they are no part of our present
analysis.

ship—maximum profits for owners of the individual firm—by promoting the larger objective—maximum production from full and efficient use of the nation's resources?

In approaching this problem we need to consider the administrator's policy and action from two points of view. The first concerns the need of *having* profit, or the consequences of giving profits a larger or smaller proportionate place in distributing the harvest from economic efforts. The second concerns the managerial practices by which profits are won or at least sought.

A distinctive feature of our capitalistic system is that the earnings of the business are credited on the books to the capitalist owners, to be held there as an addition to the value of their proprietary interest or to be disbursed to them as dividends. It may at first thought seem absurd to suggest that managers in looking at the rate of profits earned in a given year should ever entertain the thought that such profits are too high. They may argue that, since capital furnishes jobs and makes labor more efficient, it is of the first importance to the country as well as to the owners to have profits so high as to get maximum accumulation of capital within the various companies or to stimulate the highest possible saving and investment from the public. This, however, overlooks the fact that the reason for accumulation is not a direct and absolute demand for capital as such but is contingent and relative to the productive use that will or can be made of it.

If all the profits derived from a year's operations are kept in the company and immediately devoted to expansion of plant and operations, they keep the spiral of production, distribution, consumption, new production, new distribution, and new consumption, moving at full tide during that year. This is likewise true if some or even all the year's profits are distributed to shareholders and by them promptly disbursed in consumptive expenditures or committed to active investments which result in expansion of productive operations in some other line. But the total of such productive expenditures must in the process of time bear a definite functional relationship to the flow of product which comes from the new capital goods and the rate at which that product is being actually consumed. This, in turn, depends on the amount of purchasing power which is disbursed as interest, dividends, wages, and salaries, and the division that these income receivers make between consumption and saving.[5]

The market is the "payoff." Unless the rate of market absorption is kept up to a level which will take the full product of the new plant at prices above cost of production, justification for that rate of accretion of capital through the maintenance of such a level of profits disappears. Everyone would agree, no doubt, that it is desirable for the productiveness of the economy that we keep enlarging our supply of aids to labor at as rapid a rate as those implements will be actually used in pro-

[5] If all capital were owned by workers in the same ratios that individual wages and salaries bear to each other, it would be a matter of indifference whether business revenues went to higher profits or to higher (percentage) labor incomes. If capital ownership were equal per capita, higher profits (fully distributed) would be the equivalent of consumer gains. In either case, however, there would still be the question whether the effect that a high-profits policy would have in raising the general price level might not be bad.

But, in view of the existing concentration of capital ownership, recipients of dividends may save a larger proportion of this part of their income than can be actively used as capital goods, and even their personal expenditures may constitute a sluggish type of consumption as compared with that of lower-income groups.

duction.[6] But to pile up capital goods or funds in excess of such use means that capital ceases to provide employment or increase productivity and becomes a cause of unemployment. "Capitalism the creator"[7] is distorted into capitalism the waster.

It is easy enough to see that if all the product of current operations went to current consumption, we would not only be arresting our further economic progress but even destroying a vital source of our present

[6] This is of course an oversimplified statement because capital goods may be used with widely varying degrees of intensiveness and the degree of intensiveness which is to be regarded as economically justifiable as the criterion for its creation or preservation will vary according to a large number of price relationships. The "fullness of use" criterion therefore will have to be determined on the merits of each case. Recent experience with unemployment suggests that any possible danger of lowered "qualitative efficiency" which might be incurred by setting profit sights too low would be considerably less than the great losses in "quantitative efficiency" with which we are all too familiar as a result of setting profit sights too high. Saving is not something which is a good in itself but rather a necessary evil, since it means that the fruits of labor cannot be currently enjoyed. Society, like the individual, wants to save as little as is necessary to the maintenance of a given state of real income. The almost fabulous outpouring of capital, both private and public, in the creation of additional plant in connection with the war effort suggests that capital shortage will be much less of a threat to national prosperity after the war than possible labor disuse.

[7] In a book under this title, Carl Snyder has put forth in stark simplicity the favorable aspects of the case for maximum capital formation without concern for the consumptive process with which it must be correlated.

Such an economic philosophy (or religion of wealth) reduces capital goods and capital funds to the role of "sacred cows," worshipfully tended by a people suffering from deficiencies of both meat and milk. A release from this Brahman psychology among our stupid cousins overseas would not result in the disappearance of the bovine population but in its growth in numbers, in service, and in public esteem. Nor would release from a Brahman economic psychology among our not too perspicacious selves lead to the death or decay of capital but to its propagation on more scientific principles, with a larger steady flow of current product and substantial enjoyment from the incidental liquidation of such units as, brought into being in the normal technique of operation, proved to be "surplus" from the point of view of its most economical continuance.

efficiency—improvidently "eating our seed corn." It must be equally evident that if all of current product went to create capital to be used in future enhancement of productive efficiency, we should all starve while waiting for that glorious day. The art of business management consists in finding the best practical balance between today's consumptive satisfactions and provision of the means by which we can have a little more to enjoy tomorrow.

It might be conceded by the businessman that such a view as to the distributive process is true in general terms. But he still might ask how he could apply the lesson in his own operations. The first answer to this question would relate to the manager's policy and practice under more than ordinarily favorable conditions: (a) in periods of high prosperity, (b) when a product has an exceptionally favorable market response, or (c) when striking savings in production cost have been made through technological or organizational improvement.

The first of these cases has been discussed in Chapter X, where we pointed to "good times" as the situation in which it was most easy and most beneficial for business to translate high efficiency into low prices rather than seeking ever higher immediate profits. The second and in part the third case were dealt with in Chapter IV (page 108), where it was observed that the attempt to freeze high initial profits into the price structure checks orderly progress of an industrial system rather than causing it to continue to function on a prosperous basis. The third case was considered further in Chapter IX under the head of labor-saving improvements. If the effort of management is exerted toward absorbing this labor saving into higher and higher current profits rather than passing it on in the form of more goods and maintained employment, again the consequences run not toward stabilizing prosperity, but toward chronic technological unemployment.

All these situations call for recognition on the part of management that profits may at a given time be too high for the continued healthy functioning of the system. The willingness to interpret the profit motive as meaning the creation of new sources of profit through the exercise of new enterprise rather than exacting a perpetual toll for past contributions makes for the "contrived, scientific, functional" profits (see p. 107) which are the real objective of professional management.

But the businessman's quest for profits and use of a profit criterion as a guide to operative policy is not limited to those easy days when, by grasping for the maximum "take" which can be secured, he creates future difficulties for himself and for the business community. The other side of the story concerns the attempt to keep profits as high as possible in ordinary times. Here we face no question of getting profits maximized to an unhealthy degree but rather the effort to prevent profits from falling below a level which he considers desirable or necessary to operation. This carries us from the first question raised on page 323—the problem of how high the businessman may with safety or wisdom set his profit objective—to the second question raised there, namely the means by which he attempts to effectuate that goal or to defend his position at some lower point which he regards as essential to hold.

Profit seeking through production control. To a greater or less degree in their various situations, business managers have power to adjust their scales of production to a profit objective, even to support profits or check their decline by means of management practices that lead to restriction of production. In this regard, the nature of profits in an advanced system of industrial capitalism differs considerably from profits in the simple system of individual competition upon which a great deal of our thinking is based. There, everyone is exercising his individual enterprise to choose among and shift between alternatives in a situation in which even the last man may be self-employed. Profit is the spot premium he gets for making a shrewd choice—or for sheer luck. But under conditions of administered price making, where the professional manager makes lump decisions for the commitment of capital to productive operations or for the withholding of such commitment, the profit position of capital as a claimant to returns may quite definitely be made better during the year or other operating period by restricting production even though this means leaving some of the owner's capital unemployed.

The manager will set his price schedule and his scale of operations simultaneously for a year or other operative period. These decisions will be made with certain profit objectives in mind. If he does not believe that at full volume he can attain as good a profit during the period he is planning for as he would with less of his own product going on the market, he will hold down operations to the volume which he estimates will best maintain a profit or at least protect him against too great a loss. This he may do even though it means non-utilization of some part of his plant and discharge of some of his employees. Of course this criterion of profit on invested capital is a somewhat variable one, not absolute. But the figures of the accounting department, the counsel of his bankers, the principles of depreciation that he has adopted, and the reserves that he feels he must accumulate for future contingencies all constitute an apparatus of managerial decisions that puts a profit criterion above full utilization of resources as a standard of business action over larger or smaller areas of industry at all but the most favorable times.[8]

If this power of the industrial manager to administer a price-and-production program is to be used to the real advantage of the capital owners of his company, he must keep always in mind the distinction between profit *margin* per unit of product, *rate* of profit on invested capital for the year or other accounting period; and *total* profits or aggregate long-run earnings which the owners of this capital can derive from its operations over as long a period of time as they think it wise or proper to take into account.

Even if one had complete control over the source from which goods of a given type are produced, he could not afford to charge the highest price that could be exacted for a single unit or a small number of units.

[8] A very orthodox statement of business thinking has been supplied by a prominent executive, then president of the Iron and Steel Institute:

"You must charge a price, under any given condition, which covers all of your costs—including the cost of carrying unused capacity—and returns a reasonable profit. If you fail to charge such a price, you must give something away. And in business, if you continue to give something away for very long, you eventually give the business away. No one is justified in asking business to do this. . . . Management has not been profit-minded. Instead, it has attempted to conduct business on a basis of losing as little as possible. It has resorted to dodges and stratagems . . . such as deliberate acceptance of unprofitable business in the hope that the increased volume will cut overhead costs enough to make it possible to break even or escape with a small loss while holding an old customer or getting a new one. It has justified acceptance of business at a loss on the theory that this unprofitable business would pay in the long run by helping to maintain plant, equipment and personnel. No such attempts to rationalize acceptance of business at a loss can be right. Losing business remains losing business. It produces a loss in the first instance and, human nature being what it is, when one producer gives an unwarranted price, competitors meet competition. The result is that the concession sets a new industry-wide price still farther below the level of profits and even of costs. . . . Management, which after all is hired by the stockholders to make profits, has failed in its principal duty." Ernest T. Weir, "Profits and Patriotism," address before the American Institute of Steel Construction, New York, Oct. 17, 1939.

He would maximize his profits not by exacting the widest margin per unit but by accepting such margin over cost as would sustain a flow of sales that would give him the best rate of profit year after year.

In passing from the idea of *margin* of profit-per-unit of sales to that of *rate* of profit-per-unit-of-capital employed, we bring the time factor to the forefront of consideration. The rate of profit is commonly stated in terms of a year (occasionally a quarter). But, except in very casual business operations, management must do its thinking and shape its policies, not with reference to a single year but to a considerably longer period of anticipated operations.[9] This would suggest such price and production policies as will maintain as high as possible a level or average of return over a period of years. The greatest *total profit* will result from the best rate (or range) of profits that can *be maintained*.

It may seem axiomatic that the hard-headed businessman will not try to maximize the rate of return in a single year at the expense of subsequent years. But in practice it appears that businessmen often follow courses of action which imply either a very short time perspective, inadequate understanding of how long-run profits are to be achieved, or inability to reconcile individual action with the needs of an over-all process.

To yield the largest ultimate profits for the various individual companies, the nation's business must be kept in as active and efficient operation as is possible— that is, maximum sustained production of the economy. To attain this end, the total capital equipment must be

[9] We have already suggested (Chap. 4, p. 105) that the corporate form of business now prevalent tends to encourage business administrators to consider the long future of the company rather than the making of an immediate "killing."

put at the disposal of the total labor force. Putting the employment criterion in a purely incidental place—if not actually rejecting it—leads to the eventual restriction of profit-making opportunities for capital. Hence maintenance of the most profitable market for capitalist employers as a whole must depend upon the fullest and steadiest possible use of the productive power of labor, and full employment becomes a logical criterion of business policy making, collateral to that of maximum profits or necessary to the winning of maximum profits in the long run.

We shall now turn, therefore, to ask whether it would be possible to "get the lead in the other hand" by putting full employment as the first consideration of business policy, with confidence that profits would, under such conditions, be best sustained and could be brought to their long-run maximum.

A NEW CRITERION OF POLICY—FULL EMPLOYMENT

To set up "full employment"[10] as a standard to be held immediately in view at once suggests the objection that this is a criterion appropriate for the economy as a whole, not for the individual firm or its executives. But we should not be too hasty in assuming that full

---

[10] Full employment is a loose phrase which may be defined either functionally or quantitatively. Earlier in this book it has at several places been referred to functionally as meaning giving all potential workers opportunity of employment up to the point at which they value leisure more highly than further goods or services that could be purchased with their wages. Quantitatively, there seems to be pretty general agreement that an industrial country is not likely to be able to apply more than 95 per cent of its nominal labor force even under the most favorable circumstances. This would mean a "float" of some 3 million or more in this country, not working even when we had so-called full employment.

The point is also made that mere employment is not enough, as is attested by the deplorable conditions of China or other primitive

employment cannot become a practical guide to the price-and-production policies and action of the individual firm.[11]

Private capitalism, as we have known it, has already advanced from a condition of no responsibility for maintaining the quality of the labor supply or for seeing that it is productively used to a point where it accepts considerable responsibility for the workers specifically attached to a given firm or (to some extent) to an industry. But until recently almost everyone has been disposed to feel that, if a criterion of full employment were to be applied, it would have to be by the economy as a whole, that is by government under a scheme of comprehensive economic planning. Such a criterion has been regarded as purely irrelevant for the individual firm. It has not appeared practically possible for these firms

---

countries. What is meant here is, of course, employment with machine equipment up to present efficiency standards and progressively rising. The idea is sometimes advanced that such equipment cannot be provided for the whole population or that idleness of some is offset by the higher specific efficiency of those employed. Fears as to a shortage of capital seem premature in situations in which plant is partially idle or funds inactive. And when both plant and funds have been activated by recruiting the full labor force, any deficiency of plant may be made up by the assignment of a proper proportion of that force to the production of capital goods rather than consumers' goods.

[11] At many places in this book reference has been made to the fact that the official of organized labor has become so important a factor in the determination of price relations as to complicate if not defeat the program that the professional manager might draft in accordance with the general policy and economic philosophy here outlined. Thus far, labor has not been able, nor has it really desired, to take responsibility for the operation of the system. But in so far as it becomes cognizant of the results of its own exercise of power it would have to adopt this same criterion of full employment as superior to its customary exacting of the highest rate that can be secured by the exercise of its control of supply. At the same time it would have to assume the responsibility of making provision for capital sufficient to maintain its supply (including expansion and the research facilities on which progressive technique is based) and afford it incentive for active use.

to set up individual employment quotas or to accept or assume responsibility for any particular labor force as did the family head under simple schemes of economic organization or as government does in Fascist countries or would do under a planned economy in the United States.

But today, practical businessmen are themselves informing the public that they do accept such a criterion of operation and that they propose to put it into effect at the close of the war. Most clear-cut in such declarations are the General Electric Company and the Aluminum Company of America.[12] Pronouncements by these two companies are set forth on pages 334, 336, and 338. Such declarations, however, even if sound in principle, have yet to be carried into practice. Have these companies perfected a procedure for achieving the objectives set, for applying the criterion announced?

ALCOA says, in general terms, that this means "mixing engineering with imagination." This might well mean combining technological skill with economic in-

[12] To this general effect also, the American Rolling Mill Co. expresses itself in a display advertisement in the *Saturday Evening Post* of Apr. 10, 1943. The major part of the text of that advertisement reads as follows: "Will [your boy] come home [from the war] to a normal life—a useful job? That is a question none of us can ignore. Even now, while all the production of the nation is bent upon victory, farsighted men in American industry are planning ahead. There must be no letdown after this war. Industry is preparing now to convert quickly for the manufacture of peacetime products to give jobs to the millions of men now fighting and the other millions of war workers.

"This war has *telescoped* time in improving materials and methods. Here at ARMCO, for instance, our laboratories and mills are developing sheet steels with extraordinary new properties and constantly improving the older ones. After the war, manufacturers will have many new steels for making lighter, stronger, and more attractive products.

"Every time you buy a War Bond you are helping to speed the day when our boys come home. You will have the savings to buy some of the new and better things you will need, and this will help provide jobs that our boys can do with enthusiasm and skill."

AMERICANS LOOK AHEAD.... They see that jobs for all are the first essential to a peaceful peace. ... The number of men you can keep on your pay roll; and the number of new ones you can add to your payroll, when this thing is over, is the real measure of how good a peace we have won.... There are millions of new jobs to be made when this war is over. They are your responsibility and ours.

As we see it, the only thing that will keep men employed then is a large dose of *Imagineering* right now.... We coined the word to describe the audacious imagination, plus action, which is needed to outwit the future. ... The word pins down the thought that it is the individual executive, daring to let his imagination soar, and then engineering it down to earth—it is you doing just that to your business, who will win the peace for yourself, and for America. ... It's a kind of flame lighting America to its future. Alcoa Aluminum is one fuel to make the flame burn brightly.

Start with the bald facts that what America must have when this is over is a low price structure, new things to make and use, new services to render, new ways to make and do old things. Match the new low prices of aluminum, the new techniques, the new alloys and the old fundamentals of light weight and all the rest, against what you yourself face, and what America needs, and you have found the groove to let your Imagineering run in.

Two can run better than one in that groove. We have the old-fashioned idea that if we can help you look at your work audaciously in terms of the product we make, that teamwork will help us both employ more men at a time when America is going to need employment.

Advertisements of Aluminum Company of America, January-April 1942.

sights into the way in which money relationships have to be adjusted if business is to operate at full volume. It might mean having the imagination to see how the peacetime use of aluminum could be expanded to the fantastic proportions of wartime and still preserve the solvency of the company. To such an interpretation of ALCOA's phrases we shall return presently.

Meanwhile, we must examine the somewhat more specific outline of criteria and methods that has been proposed by G.E. Mr. Wilson former president of the company, who first outlined the policy (See App. F.), is an outstanding "production man," and Vice President Prince to whom its execution was specifically delegated is a distinguished engineer (past president of the American Institute of Electrical Engineers). Hence it is not strange that one plank of their platform should call for engineering determinations of the technical specifications of the products which are to make up the volume of output necessary to discharge their responsibility for continuing their wartime labor force in peacetime employment. But besides committing themselves to showing the technological imagination necessary to make this system work, G.E. gives a pencil sketch, even if somewhat shadowy, of the economic mechanism by which they expect to see the policy carried to successful execution. The salient features of the G.E. analysis may be set forth in a single paragraph.

Starting from an assumption of purchasing power sufficient to maintain 110 billion dollars of production,[13]

[13] In the light of subsequent events, Mr. Prince revised this figure upward. Addressing the National Retail Dry Goods Association recently, he "estimated that two years after the war 57,000,000 people would produce, on a forty-hour-week basis, a total output with a value of $135,000,000,000." (*New York Times*, Jan. 15, 1943, p. 30.) In view of uncertainty about the future price level or the course of inflation, no dollar figure can have any significance. What is really meant is simply a full-operation national income.

AT THIS TIME, when our future economic security is at stake, we must call upon all of our vision and imagination—upon all of our resources—upon all of our ingenuity—and, above all, upon the same deep sense of service that now motivates us . . . in providing the materials for our physical security—to the end that all employables will be kept employed—and that the preponderant majority will find employment on the payrolls of the private enterprise system.

Charles E. Wilson, address, American Institute of Electrical Engineers, Jan. 29, 1941.

IF, WHEN THE END COMES, we have made no plans for the postwar period, we may lose all the fruits of victory. We must, therefore, be prepared to take advantage of our victory when it comes and begin to think now about the future. . . .

There are good reasons for expecting an era of full employment after the war. Extensive plans are being made for the government by members of the National Resources Planning Board—plans for public works projects which they propose to throw into the pot if unemployment begins to appear. Therefore the question is not whether or not we shall have full employment but what *kind* of employment we shall have.

We shall start with the assumption that there will be full employment which will yield 110 billions of dollars' worth of production, and then we shall see what the electrical manufacturing component of that total amounts to. We estimate that some 3 billion, 849 million dollars, more or less, will cover the electrical manufacturers' component but that part of that component will represent items that the General Electric Company does not happen to make. Then we will get down to the things of which the parent General Electric Company does produce a part. If we have esti-

Continued on page 338

CRITERIA OF PRICE POLICY

they define the commercial side of their task merely as keeping in touch with the trend of consumer demand so as to know with reasonable accuracy the types of expenditure among which the public will apportion that amount of spending money. Then the company plans to allocate the proper amount of the productive resources under its administration to the lines of manufacture thus nominated. As to the fundamental economic process by which this flow of purchasing power is to be continuously forthcoming, in the first part of this statement faith is pinned to the mere fact that "extensive plans are being made for the government by members of the National Resources Planning Board . . . for public works projects to throw into the pot if unemployment begins to appear."

With the engineering and commercial plank in this platform we are in complete accord. If private business is to operate successfully in the future, one of the two major functions that the professional management of those private enterprises must perform is that of selecting the types of goods to be offered in the consumer market, simplifying and perfecting the technological (including artistic) character of these goods or devising new ones, and keeping closely in touch with the behavior of the public in apportioning its purchasing power among these different goods and responding to such "consumer appeal" as private enterprisers succeed in embodying in their products. There is every reason for the American public to have confidence that the engineering staffs of G.E., ALCOA, or almost any other of our well-established industrial corporations will give highly skillful, soundly progressive, richly "imaginative" treatment to these problems. Detailed blueprints of such developments are accumulating in their research

mates of the national market for those things and if we know also the percentage of the business which we can normally count on getting, we can construct a budget of probable business in the different departments of the General Electric Company. Then, when we match that business against our capacity and our personnel, we shall obtain a figure which represents the number of workers we shall need after the war. And the point is that some of the people now employed will be left over.

However, some of those people will not wish to continue with General Electric. . . . But there will be some people in that group who were unemployed before, or maybe some of them will be youngsters just out of school, and they are the ones we shall wish to keep employed—the ones we shall have to keep employed if the country as a whole is to enjoy full employment. If we do not find work for them and if other companies in the same position do not find work for their excess personnel, unemployment will become a problem again. That means that the country will not reach the 110-billion-dollar output figure and that, in turn, the electrical component will be smaller than we have estimated and our share smaller. Then we shall find ourselves with an even larger group of excess employees. Thus the best thing to do is just to assume that we must find jobs for all the people left on our hands. We owe it both to them and to the country to do our best to provide for them. . . .

If we were to be alone, the whole thing would fall of its own weight. I am very confident, however, that this same kind of thinking is going on in many industries all over the country. I know of a good many specific cases; also . . . certain areas in which industrial managements are thinking about the problem as it affects entire communities.

David C. Prince, address, American Management Association, Mar. 4, 1942.

files. They use some of their advertising space every now and again to give the public a peep into those files and to whet consumer appetites for the postwar market.

But the second major function of management is to perfect a scheme of disbursements that will bring the cost structure, the price structure, and the income structure of the economy into continuous working balance. The prospect that businessmen will see how to do this after the war seems much less reassuring than that technical and operative problems will be well met.

Certainly the economic plank in the General Electric platform is at best ambiguous as to this phase of the problem. It starts out by saying: "We will count on Uncle Sam to maintain purchasing power. This is not our concern." There is no intimation that the General Electric Company, the Aluminum Company of America, General Motors, du Pont, U. S. Steel, and the rest would themselves need to assume or accept responsibility for disbursing the purchasing power necessary to take off the market the whole product turned out by a fully employed people.

Recent experience, however, would suggest that to many businessmen any government promise of employment opportunities to all through public spending constitutes a threat of national insolvency, inflation, confiscatory taxation, and everything that makes private business impossible. If this psychology should prevail after the war, every step that government might take in accepting or asserting responsibility for the productive operation of the economic system would cause private enterprise and private capital to withdraw in uncertainty and fear by one or two steps or even ten steps.

To others, even among businessmen, such a government underwriting of employment is seen as a guarantee of sustained markets which makes business commitments safe. It is apparently in this camp that the General Electric Company aligns itself. Actual responsibility for the supplying of employment is put up to the individual company near the close of the statement (page 338).

If we do not find work for [all our wartime employees who want to stay with us after the war] and if other companies in the same position do not find work for their excess personnel . . . the country will not reach the 110 billion dollar output figure and . . . our share will be smaller than we have estimated. Then we shall find ourselves with an even larger group of excess employees. *Thus the best thing to do is just to assume that we must find jobs for all the people left on our hands.*

This proposal (italicized by us, not the company spokesman) is followed a little later by an admission that such an assumption of responsibility for creating private employment would be futile if any individual company undertook it alone. But that admission is in turn followed by an expression of great confidence "that this same kind of thinking is going on in many industries all over the country . . . areas in which industrial managements are thinking about the problem as it affects entire communities."

So far, so good. If all other employers were to meet the postwar situation with confidence and act with their best managerial skill to allocate men and plant to the supplying of a full-employment budget of consumer wants, the tide of national economic life would set strongly toward reconversion to peacetime operation on a scale of activity equal to the war peak and doubtless better than 1928-29. This would not completely solve the problem, but it would deal with one factor indispensable to its solution. An initial psychological reaction of self-confidence would promote a situation in which private enterprise could move more freely into active investment, and credit would be extended through customary financing agencies so freely that there would be a minimum possibility of plant remaining idle for lack of working capital or of workers failing to find private employment.

Self-sustaining private business. But, then, why bring government promises and government spending into the argument? If each employers' "assuming that he must find jobs for all the people left on his hands" is capable of turning the trick of full employment, why confuse some and alarm others by raising the issue of dependence on government at all?

The more self-reliant position appears to be the keynote of the thinking of the leaders in the nationally active Committee for Economic Development. Through this body the movement "to promote company-by-company planning for postwar opportunities ... jobs and the production in private enterprise which can create jobs"[14] may now be regarded as organized and systematized on a national scale. The Committee has set up a Field Development Division with twelve regional and about 100 district boards. These boards undertake to stimulate and assist small as well as large companies in deciding on types of products to turn out after the war, scale of operations for each, markets available and best means of developing them, and other operative problems of the reconversion period.

The general objectives and methods of work of the Field Development Division are explained by the committee chairman as follows:

Forty-nine million people will be looking to industry, commerce, agriculture and the professions for jobs. . . . To be cer-

[14] *C. E. D. News*, May 1943, p. 1.

tain we not only have jobs enough but also that they are the right kind of jobs, we must increase substantially our gross output of goods and services. Some economists estimate that to provide civilian employment for forty-nine million people after the war, America would have to raise its gross output 30 per cent over the record-breaking peacetime year of 1940; others say 50 per cent. . . . I have the highest confidence in the ability of individual businessmen to plan for the future of their own businesses. In my opinion the initiative and resourcefulness of the individual enterprisers in this country constitute one of our greatest national resources. The problem is properly to develop this great resource, to stimulate hard thinking on the part of these entrepreneurs. . . . We urge that the local C.E.D. committees collaborate and work through existing community organizations. We particularly recommend that, wherever feasible, they be staffed by executives of the local Chamber of Commerce.[15]

In carrying out this program, the Committee for Economic Development draws upon the factual and analytical work of government agencies[16] as well as the technical and managerial staffs of all the many companies who are being interested in the movement. To this it adds a research advisory committee and staff of its own.

Thus far there has been little to indicate the more fundamental economic philosophy of the movement. That is yet to emerge from further study of the problem by staff, advisers, and participants. As to the work of the Research Division, made up of university economists, the chairman of the committee says:

The Research Division is concerned with the creation of an environment in the postwar period favorable to the expansion

[15] Paul G. Hoffman, address before the Wartime Conference of the National Association of Life Underwriters, Pittsburgh, Pa., Sept. 16, 1943.
[16] The Committee emphasizes the point that it is an entirely independent non-governmental agency, formulating its own policies and program, recruiting its own personnel, and supplying its own working funds.

of enterprise. Our trustees are convinced that all policies of government, of business, and of labor that interfere with expanding employment should be changed. If we are to succeed in our efforts to attain in the postwar period a satisfactory level of productive employment we must genuinely accept the possibility of our achieving an economy of plenty. That involves an abrupt about face on the part of all of us. As we examine policies of government, business, labor, and agriculture we find that many of them spring from fears inherent in an economy of scarcity. Monopolistic practices in that area of our economy where competition should prevail result from fears that there won't be enough customers for our goods. Labor's support of featherbedding rules, in opposition to incentive payment, has its roots in a conception that there are not enough jobs to go around. All restrictive measures in the field of agriculture spring from the fear of production in excess of demand. As far as government policies are concerned, they are a mere reflection of all these fears.[17]

Meanwhile, other voices of business leadership are to be heard. Eric Johnston, president of the Chamber of Commerce of the United States, addressing its annual convention on April 27, 1943, expounded an interpretation of "the new capitalism" of "enlightened self interest [which] demands that the well-being of the whole American people be made the sole and final criterion of action" (see pages 344, 346). As to how that over-all criterion is to be translated into a rule of action

[17] Further light on the Committee's approach is shed by a speech delivered by William Benton, vice chairman of the Committee, before the Producers' Council, Inc. and the American Institute of Architects in Cincinnati on May 26, 1943. Commenting on the vast possibilities of the construction industry in the years after the war, he observed: "Practices in the [construction] industry force and keep prices up. They do not bring them down. Every form of so-called monopolistic practice seems to come to full flower in the political, labor, and business standards which prevail in your industry. . . . Many feel that every business practice which impedes employment and production must be fought. How else can business honestly go to labor or to government and say— 'Give us conditions under which we can operate'?"

. . . THE GREAT MISTAKE that many organizations have made in the past has been to plan solely for themselves. . . . A program of principles and of action which may seem perfect from the vantage point of labor or management or agriculture or government —is useless unless it can stand the test of scrutiny from all other points of view. . . .

I believe that enlightened self-interest, whether in the behavior of an individual or a nation, is the most reliable basis for action. . . . But we have learned from tragic experience that the machine will go dead unless full allowances are made for competing and conflicting self-interests. We have learned that we cannot have a healthy farm or factory, or a healthy business or trade-union, unless the country as a whole is in a vigorous and healthy condition. . . .

Whatever immediate advantages any element in the population may grab, must be paid for a hundredfold ultimately in imbalance and chaos. Intelligent self-interest demands that the well-being of the whole American people be made the sole and final criterion of action. . . . America adheres resolutely to its faith in the individual and its preference for high striving and full-blooded adventure. . . .

In the field of economy, democracy has taken the form of a free capitalist society. . . . Far from being played out, free economy in our country is only getting into full stride. . . .

We have mastered the art of mass production. It now remains for us to master the art of mass distribution, so that the products of our magnificent industrial machine may be ever more widely spread among all our people. This is no longer a pious wish.

Continued on page 346

for the individual executive he suggests "low profits on a great turnover." Clearly this would shift the criterion of profit-seeking management away from high margin per unit of product. Would it identify it with high rate of profit on invested capital? Or with best total profits in the long run resulting from more moderate rates currently? We infer that he means the latter.[18]

---

[18] The annual work program of the Chamber of Commerce of the U.S.A. approved by the Board on June 18, 1943, set up three major objectives: (1) winning the war; (2) preparing for victory; (3) long range. No mention is made under any of these heads of the issue of employment or the possible reappearance of unemployment, the means of assuring adequate postwar markets, or the problem of price relations. "As a long-range matter, the Chamber should deal boldly with issues involved in the attainment of free competitive economy, and with the preservation of representative democracy. To do so may mean fighting to maintain the status quo; it may also mean working for readjustments that will enable business to meet new conditions and new demands." The two items of the nine-point "action program" adopted by the Board which touch the problem we are discussing are as follows: "(1) Formulate a constructive program for effective price controls, without subsidies, and with minimum disruption of established business usages; (2) Formulate policies and work for Congressional action to provide now for the orderly removal of unnecessary controls in the interest of a stable transition period."

The Chamber has also set up a Committee on Economic Policy and employed an economist of professional standing to direct its work. Among his activities is included a series of pamphlets on "Postwar Readjustments."

The National Association of Manufacturers has made a somewhat fuller pronouncement in the form of a 47-page pamphlet, *Jobs—Freedom —Opportunity* under date of Mar. 1, 1943. Under "Domestic Requirements for Prosperity," it bespeaks "in the postwar period . . . as there has been in the past, strong competition between business firms, small and large, producing new products and improvements of former products, to supply more and better goods for the public. . . . The volume of business, of new investment, of physical production, and hence of employment, is dependent upon relationships between prices of goods and services which promote exchange of maximum quantities. . . . A condition of balanced price relationships conducive to a high volume of exchange of goods and services is characterized by low prices; that is, prices low in relation to existing incomes.

"There is great danger that, following this war, efforts will be made arbitrarily to maintain price relationships existing at the war's end, instead of facilitating the adjustments that may be essential to the attainment of an equilibrium that will enable the various groups engaged in

It is a concrete necessity. We are geared for unprecedented output of the essentials of life as well as the refinements of living. . . . To absorb that tremendous output, business and labor and agriculture must cooperate to maintain full employment, high wages, and maximum purchasing power. . . .

Only the wilfully blind can fail to see that the old-style capitalism of a primitive freebooting period is gone forever. The capitalism of complete laissez-faire, which thrived on low wages and maximum profits for minimum turnover, which rejected collective bargaining and fought against justified public regulation of the competitive process, is a thing of the past. Those who would turn back the clock of history in this respect are as unrealistic in their way as the addle-brained paper planners of our economic salvation.

American economy . . . today . . . is gearing itself for low profits on a great turnover. The fair distribution of the products and the wealth flowing from the industrial process cannot be left wholly to chance, but must be made one of the essential objectives of industrial planning. American economy cannot reject responsibility for the employment and well-being of the men and women who take a part in it: those who supply the raw materials, those who do the manual labor, those who do the brain work, those who manage enterprise. It must accept this responsibility as an intrinsic part of its function.

The new capitalism, as I prefer to call it, is shedding the last traces of its nostalgic memory of unbridled individualism.

Eric A. Johnston, address, Chamber of Commerce of the United States, Apr. 27, 1943.

It may be that a good practical strategy is being followed by the Chamber of Commerce, the Committee for Economic Development, and others in placing their emphasis so exclusively on expanding the particular enterpriser's own line of production, which runs with his natural predilections, and on furnishing jobs to all who want to work, which businessmen are coming to feel strongly as a patriotic obligation and as a prerequisite to the survival of private enterprise. It might be argued that, once the flood of full production comes upon the market, active competition to move this product into consumption will effect the correct and necessary price adjustment.

Such an argument, however, is not convincing. If the reconversion to private peacetime operations is to be made smoothly, swiftly, and effectively, it is necessary that the responsible executives of business shall understand the process of economic adjustment whose execution lies in their hands. It is impracticable to re-price houses, automobiles, electric refrigerators, or even lesser branded goods, as perishables are priced over the counter from day to day. Under administered price making, the executive must see the whole process of cost-incurring production and revenue-yielding sale through to the end and make a price in advance which will work on a continuous basis. They must take the necessary steps voluntarily, planfully, and in advance, rather than having unforeseen situations suddenly thrust upon them for such hastily improvised action as may then suggest itself or for such blind defensive reactions as might then emerge. If businessmen convert to full-

---

productive activities to buy each other's products with their own. Such efforts to maintain current price relationships would tend to crystallize maladjustments and distortions, restrict the markets for goods on which costs have been increased, and cause unemployment."

scale production on the tacit assumption that goods are to be moved on current or higher price levels, and later find that that volume cannot be moved at that level, is there not danger of chaotic market conditions and mounting inventories, which become the signal for protective and perhaps panicky shutdowns of plant?

Hence we insist that the criterion of full employment does not, on the plane of mere engineering and commercial planning on which it is currently being promoted, furnish an adequate criterion of management either to supersede or to supplement the traditional criterion of "maximum profits for the owners." *Pricing for full sale* must be an inseparable part of planning for *full-scale production.*

THE OPERATIVE CRITERION—ASSIMILATED TECHNOLOGICAL GAINS

Full employment on a peacetime basis of private business calls for the understanding and generalized application of price policies which harmonize full production with current sale of product on an enduring basis of balanced adjustment between necessary cost and mass purchasing power. As a criterion of managerial action this means that the capitalist manager must ask himself not merely the traditional question, "Will this pricing program yield me the greatest profit?" He must amplify this question to say "greatest profit in the long run." Thus to lengthen his perspective implies that he also broaden his concept of the nature of sustained profits to the point where he realizes that long-run profits for every business demand employment opportunities for the whole labor force. It is a great gain, to be sure, if he asks the question, "Will my price policies promote full employment?" But he will still not have the most basic criterion of action that lies within the scope of his own company control unless he asks himself the final question, "Does this scheme of pricing, with its corollary scale of operations pass on to consumers the net gain[19] from technological improvement?" This is the ultimate test of sound pricing in an industrial system in which managers do not have prices made for them by a fully competitive market but themselves determine the pitch and intensity of competition and the scale of activity.

This fundamental operative criterion,[20] expounded in earlier portions of the book, may be restated in a single paragraph to show how our individual firm criterion of passing on technological gains embodies or implements our general criterion of full employment.

When an increase in efficiency (technological progress) takes place, more goods can be produced with the same labor or the same goods can be produced with less labor. If the price elasticity of demand is so high that the market will absorb the expanded product of the same labor force using the new techniques, at a price reduction equivalent to the cost saving, no problem develops. If, however, price elasticity is not great enough to retain all the workers in the given line of production, this is a price indication that such a scale of operations would constitute a poor allocation of resources. But if the price is lowered by the full amount of the net efficiency gain

[19] After providing for the cost of these improvements and providing for further progress.

[20] We refer to this as the "operative criterion" because it is the technical and managerial operators of the individual business who know most surely when technological improvements are introduced or are available for introduction and can judge most accurately as to how fully these techniques are being translated into more goods or being allowed to reduce employment. In this section, we shall consider how in the particular circumstances of the postwar period these responsible executives of individual companies might promote the ends of business success by seeing that technological gains are fully and promptly assimilated into the stream of economic life.

(including possible savings in selling cost) the additional purchasing power thus left in the hands of consumers constitutes a demand for a like amount of labor to produce other consumer (or, through the more roundabout savings channel, producer) goods. Thus starting from a full employment position, a general application of low-price policy would effect the fullest possible safeguard against technological unemployment. Starting from a position of underemployment, the revision of the price structure to conform to this principle would promote progressive re-employment up to fullscale use of available labor. This general doctrine applied to the specific situation of the early postwar years we offer as complementary to the production planning program of the Committee for Economic Development and as giving an operative criterion to businessmen who are ready to subscribe to the vague and general objectives stated by spokesmen for the United States Chamber of Commerce (pp. 344-46) and the National Association of Manufacturers (p. 345 n.).

In order to see how such a criterion would operate in the postwar period, we may well contrast it with two other approaches to price making. In the preceding chapter we pointed to the prospect of an early postwar period of only gradually restored supplies of finished goods in the face of large spending power in the hands of consumers who have experienced some years of wartime deprivation. We argued that in this situation it would be easy for businessmen to follow a course of charging what the traffic will bear, thus riding the wave of a short-time boom to inevitable disaster.

Now let us suppose that business managers are aware of this danger and seek to follow a course of conservative pricing based on their individual company situations as to cost. There will doubtless be a strong tendency after the war for price-making executives to begin by setting down the figures for prewar costs and then stepping these figures up by the amount by which tax burdens have been added and wage rates have been increased. Such cost estimates may be still further stepped up by writing in a higher figure for tools and materials, based on an assumption that these prices after the war will likewise be adversely affected by increases in costs due to higher wages and taxes. Those manufacturers who use raw materials produced on the farm may assume that the strength of the agrarian interest has grown so great that these prices will be supported by government measures at wartime levels or even be still further advanced.

While, naturally, businessmen must always give careful consideration to their cost situations, the mere routine procedure for calculating costs and making prices which has been sketched above would be most inadequate for meeting postwar needs and opportunities. By following this simple and easy course, the business executive would be directly contributing to a cumulative process of general price advance, with each higher price becoming a cost enhancement for someone else and each company or group using the full force of its organizational or political strength to protect itself by out-racing the tide of advancing prices.[21] Such a process might pro-

[21] Talking as we do here in terms of the businessman does not mean that we are forgetting the effects also of labor and farm policies. The writer's studies in the field of agricultural economics convince him that (whatever the justification for the early defensive organization of farmers in the twenties and early thirties), the time has come for them to consider the ultimate effect on the economy of efforts to enhance farm prices further or even to hold war levels in every particular instance. As for labor, it has been argued in Chap. 9 that the power of organized labor to force advances in money wages may readily pass the point where real wages are improved in the process and may result in workers getting merely the illusory gains of price inflation or the roundabout losses that come from

duce the illusion of prosperity as long as wartime savings are being disbursed and consumer credits being extended. But it does nothing toward facing the issue of stabilizing high-volume and high-efficiency production.

The decade of the thirties gave us a striking demonstration of the difficulty, if not impossibility, under prevailing canons of "safe" business management of getting from a condition of widespread unemployment to one of high-level activity on a self-sustaining basis. With all the costs and losses that the war has entailed, it has at least restored business to full momentum (and some excess). It becomes a matter of paramount importance, therefore, that this momentum shall not be allowed to drop below a full peacetime level but that the price adjustments made in the first months and years of reconversion to peace activities be such as will stabilize a healthy relationship between the new technological situations, unit costs under high-volume operation, full-consumption prices, and continuously free-running markets.

Over against the evident fact that postwar costs are in many ways higher than prewar, price makers must give full weight to the technological progress, realized or potential, that has come from the intensive activities of the war period and assess at proper value the economies of full-scale operation as against the partial utilization characteristic of the thirties. Obviously, the situation will differ widely between industry and industry and from one company to another. In some places, advances will have been sharp either because of a marked advance in labor or materials cost or because of a pressing demand

---

disruption of business and falling production. But this book is directed primarily to issues of industrial and mercantile policy and of the economic philosophy with which the business manager must guide his own course in dealing with the issues of postwar (and permanent) adjustment.

situation, whereas in others the advance will, for opposite reasons, have been slight, or there may even have been a decline. But the basic principle is clear. If we are to maintain the economic momentum restored by the war, each producer must give frank and courageous consideration to the actual cost situation which can be achieved by the highest efficiency which current techniques permit under conditions of full-scale operation.[22]

In considering whether or by how much wage and tax increases[23] can or must be absorbed in the schedule of prices inaugurated after the war, business managers must consider not merely changes in technical or organizational efficiency which have taken place during the war period or been made available for introduction into peacetime operations. They must also consider defects of adjustment that existed before the war—not just in the late thirties, but back to the First World War.

The whole series of studies to which this book belongs have argued that even in the twenties the potentialities of advancing technique through free enterprise had not been fully utilized to give us capacity operation in

---

[22] The reader should bear in mind that low-price policy sincerely and effectively applied in a given situation may not be inconsistent with an actually higher dollar-and-cents price. There may be such a general upsurge of prices that the given producer is obliged to pay so much more for all his cost goods and services that his own selling price must be absolutely higher. But if he has not simply floated with the tide but has exerted every effort toward effecting economies, and has reflected these economies proportionately in his prices, he is following a low-price policy and doing his part to maintain economically sound price relationships. And if such a course is followed by all producers, the general price level will be kept on a sound and stable basis.

[23] A good deal of confusion results from thinking of business taxes in general as an addition to production costs. Much of the additional tax "burden" has been in the nature of highly progressive rates on corporate income or the taxing away of "excess" profits. Such taxes do not in fact constitute a cost of production which needs to be written into the price formula.

response to low prices. The persistence of considerable unutilized plant capacity[24] in the presence of large unsatisfied wants[25] and a wide margin of unemployment[26] connoted a faulty adjustment of the price structure to the volume of purchasing power currently disbursed to the mass of consumers.[27] This situation became even worse during the thirties. Amid the frictions and uncertainties introduced into the processes of industrial management by the various recovery efforts of government at home and the further complications of international economic developments, volume of industrial output remained so low that prices had little chance to reflect—or even achieve—the cost reduction that would ensue from full use of the best techniques becoming available through research and discovery.[28] They had to remain merely latent or potential until brought to full realization through the opportunity of full-scale operation.

One of the greatest difficulties of the modern industrial period has been the inability of many business managers really to grasp the fact of how productive their own technologies and organizations would be if given a chance to operate at full capacity. "They don't know

[24] *America's Capacity to Produce*, pp. 421 ff.
[25] *America's Capacity to Consume*, pp. 126 ff.
[26] *America's Capacity to Produce*, Chap. 19 and Chap. 9 of this book.
[27] *Income and Economic Progress*, pp. 157 ff.
[28] For example, the National Recovery Administration was exploited by the various business groups as primarily a price maintenance device. Most of the code authorities became restrictionist trade associations.

As to the decade of the thirties, we believe that for businessmen to have introduced every price reduction that could be made possible through increasing efficiency would have supplemented and been much more consistent with the Administration's efforts to increase employment and restore activity than were its own price-boosting devices such as N.R.A., A.A.A., and managed currency. Such price reduction efforts would have gained in effectiveness as recovery proceeded, and at such time should have been consistently continued rather than being abated on the ground that returning prosperity was making it possible for the traffic to bear a higher rate.

their own strength" nor realize the flood of product there would be to distribute to the mass of consumers if they really "let themselves go" in the unrestrained use of the nation's natural resources, manpower, and managerial ability. Now the war, with its mixture of inducements and necessities, has brought our industrial plant to a full or even super scale of operation such as all the tinkering of the thirties was unable to do. At this full scale of activity it is clear that higher operational efficiency has been achieved and unit costs lowered to a striking extent. And, as always, active and indeed high-pressure operation has served as a fresh stimulus to improvements in technique and organization. Hence we have in the production picture of 1943 a realization of technological gains which expresses both the interrelated factors of capacity operation and accelerated improvement of scientific, engineering, and organizational techniques.

Men close to the facts of the war effort have had their eyes opened to feats of production that beggar the belief of those who have lived in the twilight of industrial effort that we had from 1930 to 1940. Besides improvement in technical processes, workers have had the barnacles of depression scraped off and new workers have been expertly selected, trained in the latest practices, and organized under novel short-cut processes.[29] Here is a tremendous total of technological progress whose practical reality has been demonstrated in the

[29] On the other hand, it is obvious that resort to untrained and, in many cases, inferior labor when we have to scrape the bottom of the manpower barrel lowers man-hour efficiency. Likewise, wartime productivity is substantially lowered by the number of experts who have to spend much of their time in training novices and because of the slow and bungling work and defective product of new or shifting workers during the training period. There is also progressive fatigue due to long hours maintained over a considerable period of time. To my mind all this suggests that the man-hour productivity of the labor force which would be available for high-volume peacetime employment under normal working hours

"pilot plant" of all-out war.[30] Demonstrated, but not in any full sense realized, for much of this war product has been shipped abroad as promptly as it could be moved from the production line. We have never seen it accumulated or distributed in our own country. It has, moreover, been thrown at once into the destructive operations of war, where current consumption and wear and tear make it melt away at a rate much faster than it would under conditions of peacetime enjoyment and care. Furthermore, some indeterminate but substantial part of this product has been impounded in greater stockpiles against contingencies which cannot be measured in advance. The real question now is whether we are going to realize these technological gains in the future under the conditions of full-scale peace operation or let them go to waste through our failure to parallel the technological skills with similar skills in conducting our economic processes.

As was pointed out in Chapter V, they cannot be achieved as a net addition to profits. They cannot be made to bear full fruit except as part of a complete process in which a major share of the net gains accrue

---

would, because of higher physical capacity, better training, and greater versatility or adaptability, average better after the war than that of workers of the late thirties.

[30] Since the appearance of this chapter and Chap. 10 in pamphlet form, revised production indexes of the Federal Reserve Board indicate that ways have been found of measuring more adequately the trend of production over the last three or four years. These revised indexes strongly support the view that substantial gains of productivity or technical efficiency have continued somewhat steadily over the period. Starting from an index of 100 for physical volume of production in manufacturing during 1935-39, the Board's figures show a rise to 268 by November 1943. Converting this to a 1939 base gives us a production index of 246. Now, using the B.L.S. figures for total number of employees and hours worked in manufacturing, we get an index (1939 base) of 206 for man-hours in manufacturing industry in November 1943. The margin between 206 and 246 seems to point clearly to substantial wartime gains in operative efficiency. It is interesting to note in this connection that the rate by which production was outstripping man-hours seems to be at least as great in the latest months reported as during the two or three years preceding.

as higher real incomes to the workers of all grades or as a higher general standard of living to the masses.

In the nature of the case, advance proof cannot be given as to the relationship of cost, price, volume, and technique which can be established in the first or the third, the fifth or the tenth year after the close of hostilities. But we believe that the potentiality of our technical productivity in these future years is beyond anything with which we have had previous experience and that the conversion of that potentiality into reality presents two alternatives. Either (a) incomes must be high enough to buy at present or prewar prices many more goods than consumers have previously enjoyed, or, preferably, (b) prices must be so much lower that more goods and services—a higher scale of living—than they have ever enjoyed can be purchased with incomes of the masses at the accustomed levels. If the increased productivity is not translated into widely distributed purchasing power, this potentiality will not be realized in practice and the prospects that resumption of business under private enterprise will be effected on a basis of full-scale national production will not be bright.

In this connection, it must be evident that the wage-making policies and activities of union leaders will be not less significant than the price-making activities of corporate executives. The attempt to effect substantial and widespread advances in wage rates at the close of the war would prejudge from their side the possibility of getting under existing rates as high a standard of real wages as will be produced under even these favorable conditions of productivity. It would make increasingly difficult for business managers the task of ascertaining just what technological gains have been made and what is the lowest price on which the product of full activity at this level of technological efficiency can be continuously produced and distributed.

But it is equally prejudicial to the attaining of industrial peace and stability if business managers at this juncture create the expectation of substantially higher prices after the war. The part of sanity and economic statesmanship demands restraint on both prices and wages until a determined effort can be made to ascertain and demonstrate the mutual adjustment between prices and wages which would be basically compatible with sustained full-scale operation.

Such an economic stabilization could, of course, in due time be worked out on any one of several different price levels.[31] But if, after the war, the pattern of that adjustment becomes a militant struggle to get a more advantageous ratio of prices to wages and of wages to prices, we shall invite a spiral of inflationary changes which not merely do not promote a stable adjustment but are certain to invite work stoppages and discouragement of capital investment and plant utilization. Employers must face the logic of their own system that the goal of free enterprise is full activity and advancing efficiency, and that this inevitably entails rising real wages. Workers on their part must manifest more willingness to accept their gains in the form of a better filled market basket rather than a bigger pay envelope, and let the flower of technological progress unfold rather than trying to force it into premature blooming. Only through mutual forbearance and scientific practices in administering the institutions of a price society can we bring about stabilized progress.

---

[31] A relatively high price level would ease the load of a large national debt but would impede export sales and invite import competition. It would also bear heavily on the great middle class of fixed income receivers. To find the level that would best harmonize the interests of our major economic groups and aid adjustment of domestic and international relations would be extremely difficult even if the underlying economic principles were fully grasped.

PART III
PROSPECTS

INTRODUCTION

In Part I we outlined low-price policy as the key to long-run success in the functioning of a system of private capitalism based on competition, free enterprise, and the profit motive.

In Part II, we undertook to sketch certain major considerations as to the practical applicability of low-price policy to the several areas of business and to consider a few of the outstanding problems of application by which the business executive is confronted. This was brought down to the concrete situation by which we are likely to be confronted after the war. We concluded that if we are to shift back from military and political direction of economic activity and are to recover the freedom of individual choice and of private group action whose preservation has been a great motive behind our war sacrifices, low-price policy, though evaded in much current discussion, will be indispensable.

Even those who accept this interpretation of private enterprise in a modern industrial environment may in many instances find themselves dubious as to the practical possibility that private business could make the necessary changes in practice after the war. Such persons might say: "We agree that the requirements for successful operation of a system of private enterprise are substantially as you have outlined them. But no matter how fully businessmen understand these principles and are willing, even anxious, to conform to them, it is not possible for the individual businessman or company to put such policies into operation."

The conflict between management of the individual firm and the functioning of the economy has been touched upon at various points in the preceding chapters. It is the purpose of Part III, however, to consider actual prospects somewhat more fully from two lines of approach:

1. Can the individual businessman perhaps go further than has generally been supposed in attaining the welfare of the economy through farsighted and confident administration of his own affairs? What are the administrative aids on which he can rely in following such a course?

2. Are there certain voluntary and self-governing types of business association through which the policies and programs of individual companies can be synchronized and co-ordinated so as to assure a more successful operation of the economy without foregoing the advantages of free enterprise?

While the role of government is clearly complementary to the question of private business policy and the administration of the individual firm, it cannot be explored within the limits of the present book. It must be regarded as a residual issue whose dimensions and appropriate method of treatment can be determined only after we have pushed as far as possible the line of attack embraced under low-price policy for the individual firm.

CHAPTER XII
SCIENTIFIC AIDS TO POLICY MAKING

Businessmen differ widely as to the scope, definiteness, time span, and rigidity or flexibility of their policies. Some of them are disposed to pooh-pooh the very idea that a practical businessman can afford to fool around with such "theoretical" notions. But to insist that one keep himself free of the trammels of any planful thought and rely entirely on quick and perhaps inconsistent improvisations is itself a policy. Many leaders of great enterprises fully recognize their role of responsible economic leadership and seek to equip themselves to discharge it competently by availing themselves of all the aids that modern science provides. This is one manifestation of what has been referred to on previous pages as "professional" management.

On its technological side, business has, largely within the last generation or two, moved steadily and pretty completely from the plane of trade secrets and personal hunches to the plane of scientific guidance and engineering control. The top executive of a large company would not think of deciding on a new line of product or a new method of production without having careful investigations made by chemists, metallurgists, engineers or designers of high competence. He would expect them to visualize for him all the alternatives, with their relative prospects of advantage, of technical difficulty, and of cost.

A similar development took place in the legal and financial field as corporation law grew in complexity and as corporation finance grew in magnitude. The top executive of a corporation would not today attempt to shape his organization or enter into important contracts without consulting his legal counsel. In undertaking business expansion or the reshaping of his company's financial structure he turns for guidance to his banker. On its economic side, a somewhat similar transition in management practices has begun. It is, however, more recent in its origin, less vigorous and more uncertain in its development. The operative responsibilities of a single industrial or trading corporation today sometimes cover tens or hundreds of millions (occasionally billions) of dollars of assets and thousands or tens of thousands (occasionally hundreds of thousands) of workers' careers. As these responsibilities devolve upon the hierarchy of business executives,[1] they are constrained to remove their action so far as possible from the realm of personal intuition, knacks of leadership, or "received" tradition and place it so far as possible on the solid foundation of systematic study, objective formulation of the issues involved, and scientific exploration of progressively more complete and more accurate means of answering the questions by which they are constantly faced.

This marks not merely potential opportunity but also a potential danger in the corporate form of business and in professional management. It is the belief of the writer that our knowledge of economic principles and our tools for investigation of situations in which they must be applied are such that the individual businessman may, by use of these aids, go far toward stabilizing the economy on a high level of productivity. It is our belief also that much of what passes for scientific aid today actually

---

[1] For detailed examination of the way in which administrative authority is distributed and organized in the large corporation, see R. A. Gordon, *Business Leadership in the Large Corporation* (in press).

operates to the eventual harm of the economy—and hence of the businessman. Being used to enhance the safety or at least the sense of safety of the salaried official entrusted with great responsibilities, these devices of control may be used to impair the spirit of enterprise which was an unquestioned virtue of the small owner-manager regime and which remains an indispensable of economic progress.

In order to see how scientific aids may make policy of the individual firm an adequate means to successful functioning of the economy and to see also the possibility of their abuse, we must look at several types of such aid, considering their origin, outlook, and apparent results.

MARKET ANALYSIS AND DEMAND MANIPULATION

Pioneers in the development of systematic investigation of the problems of business administration were the market analysts. Even without benefit of formal training in the methods of science, the more thoughtful and original of sales managers began many years ago to examine the sources of demand for their companies' products, causes of change in this demand, and ways of adapting product or sales methods to the character of consumer preferences or purchasing power. They sought to discover and gauge unexploited markets, to learn how to intensify demand where it exists or create it where it does not.

As more and more attention has been devoted to this field, workers have turned to refined statistical methods of sampling and measurement, so far as actual performance of past or current markets is concerned, and to psychological analysis to discover why people act as they do or how they might be influenced to act differently. They have sought to relate sales response not only to

THIRTY PER CENT of American manufacturers of consumer goods employ customer research in some form. . . . General Motors' first customer surveys were launched back in 1922. . . . [We] make 20 to 30 surveys . . . a year—contacting over 2,000,000 motorists, owners of all makes of cars, in all price classes and . . . all sections of the country. . . . The motorist is invited to "rate" the degree of importance that he attaches to dependability, economy, safety, ease of control, performance, appearance, speed, "pick-up" etc. Considerable caution must be exercised in interpreting such data into terms of engineering design. . . . The development of any one characteristic or quality to an extreme degree is usually attended by sacrifices in some other direction. . . . A blind acquiescence to the expressed tastes and desires of the consumer, as applied to a highly technical product such as the motor car, might lead to violation of sound engineering, to constructional difficulties, or to increases in cost *outweighing the advantages to be gained.*

The purpose of customer research is to make contributions to the merchandising function paralleling the contributions that the physicists, the chemists and the metallurgists have made to engineering design and manufacturing processes. . . . In its broader sense *merchandising* comprehends not only the sales and advertising procedures, but the very nature and character of the merchandise that is to be offered for sale, as well as the services that help to keep it sold. . . . Efficiencies and economies in the sales and advertising procedures are as much in the interest of the consumer as greater efficiencies in engineering design and physical production. It is as legitimate and as respectable to correct a wrong impression and promote intelligent understanding in the mind of the public as it is to improve design.

Is It Scientific? General Motors Customer Research Pamphlet No. 90.

the character of goods offered but to the manner of offering them and to the income positions of consumers in different groups or at different times. They have drawn upon the concepts, materials, and methods of the "business cycle theorists" and cycle analysts, and have conceived or identified sub-cycles in their own industries or firms.

The purposes and the results of these studies have varied widely. They may conveniently be grouped into undertakings that are *adaptive* and those that are *manipulative*. The adaptive type of market analysis includes efforts to learn the character and intensity of consumer wants in all parts of the market and the changes that are associated with increases or decreases of employment or of wage rates, the trends of fashion, and the impact of new discoveries and educational drives. They are designed to aid the business executive to get a more accurate picture of what his market is so that he may adapt his operations and his prices to these conditions external to his firm.

In so far as these studies reveal what the various classes of consumers actually desire and compare their value judgments with the relative costs of satisfying consumer wants in different ways, they render real service toward getting the nation's resources directed to their most productive uses. An excellent illustration of this kind of managerial approach by the General Motors Corporation is furnished in the quotation on page 366. Carefully drawn questionnaires sent out by the company invited consumers to consider what they really wanted and why. The company at the same time explained the nature of sacrifices in money, safety, or durability which would have to be made if certain supposed needs or mere whims were to be satisfied. This is an interpretation of the principle of the free market quite in contrast to the old Ford dictum: "The public can have any color it wants so long as it's black"—or any engine so long as it was a four-cylinder model using transmission bands.

Another type of "scientific" market study is that which seeks to forecast the trend of cyclical developments. By gauging the strength and probable duration of boom psychology and expansionist tendencies a company might scientifically determine how much the traffic would bear and might estimate the profits it would be necessary to accumulate in a reserve to tide itself over the ensuing depression. On the decline it might use similar methods to defer its purchase of materials or equipment while prices were allowed to fall to the lowest possible level before the company "gets in on the ground floor." By assuming that the market is an independent variable and not a function of the activities of all business firms, each company might seek to adapt its operations with scientific skill to adventitious economic fluctuations—which are inevitably accentuated by such a philosophy of management.

But market analysis has had a manipulative as well as an adaptive phase. Market manipulation may be good, bad, or indifferent in its purpose and effect. At its lowest level, it may be concerned merely in learning the prejudices of the public or the points at which buyers are susceptible to given sales methods simply for the purpose of causing them to choose higher-cost or less serviceable products or to buy more than they want, need, or can afford. Methods of thus manipulating market demand may be indubitably scientific—diabolically so—and may produce gains to the individual firm, at least in the short run, and yet produce no net gain to the economy. In fact they may entail a quite needless and unproductive burden of "scientific" warfare between firms with none of the benefits which are supposed to come from price competition or profit-seeking enterprise.

In its middle reaches, market analysis, though using the methods of science to accomplish its objectives, cannot be said to be *per se* either harmful or beneficial in its effects. It simply finds ways of diverting consumer demand from one means of satisfaction or one supplier of this means to another intrinsically equal and no more and no less costly. If these methods of market study and direction are more costly than those needed for the mere process of distributing goods with the greatest efficiency and understanding on the part of both consumers and producers, there will of course be some net burden on the economy as a whole.

But there is a third aspect of market study and manipulation in which scientific methods may be used to a truly creative purpose, thus forwarding the ends of economic progress. This is where market analyses are directed to getting a fuller and more correct picture of market demand for the purpose of guiding consumers more accurately toward the cheapest sources of satisfaction, educating them to a truer understanding of the fundamental nature of their wants and the relative merits of various means through which they can be met.

The General Motors Company's "consumers' research" outlined on page 366 partakes of this creative character since it is not designed merely to adapt the company's manufacturing program to the public want "as is." It seeks to canvass alternatives of quality and cost with potential buyers so that they may eventually get more for their money and the producer make his outlays most effectively. But such types of market analysis, to realize their full potentialities, must go on from technical aspects of the problem to take full cognizance of all the pecuniary relationships involved. The market analyst should seek to use scientific methods to discover for the top executive better answers to his ultimate questions. How much could be sold if the company's goods and services were to be offered at this, that, or the other level of price? How would volume of sales be affected if a different structure of prices were arranged? Could sales be increased by changing qualities, design, or method of distribution so that the "bundle of utilities" delivered to final purchasers would be fitted better not only to their several desires but also to their different purchasing powers?[2]

Good as these methods are, they do not exhaust the possibilities of market analysis as a guide to price policy. The full creative possibilities of this approach are realized only when market research carries through to an over-all economic analysis. Adequately imaginative exploratory techniques must not be limited by assumptions that other things remain equal when the executive of a large corporation changes his prices. This change is related to changes in technique and in unit cost of production, to distribution processes and "sales resistance," to degree of utilization of plant, volume of employment and workers' purchasing power, rate of return on capital, the confidence of financiers, and the behavior of savers. As was pointed out in Chapter VII, statistical studies of elasticity of demand, widely accepted as the scientific means of guiding the price administrator, fail to cover these wider aspects of the market's responsiveness to price changes. They peer through a knot-hole to get a very restricted view of a process which must be seen in its entirety to be correctly interpreted. The very

[2] *Industrial Price Policies and Economic Progress*, Chap. 3.

precision of the mathematically derived coefficient of elasticity of demand is likely to lull the price policy maker into thinking that he "has the answer" whereas in fact he has at best but one clue to the solution of his problem.[3]

In Chapter IX we called attention to the fact that any adequate analysis of his market requires that the executive consider not merely the way in which he draws purchasing power out of it as payment for his product but also the process by which he and other executives are determining the flow of purchasing power into the market through wages, dividends, bonuses and profit sharing, accumulation of reserves, investment inside or outside the company. If market analysis is to be a truly scientific aid to policy determination, it must carry through to purchasing power analysis which relates the practices of the given company to the process of pecuniary distribution as a whole. In the long run the price maker cannot afford to accept these relationships as none of his concern. Still less can he afford to study the market merely for the purpose of scalping a profit by practices that make those basic relations worse.

Means by which market research may be combined

---

[3] Commenting on Chapter 7, the (statistically trained) economist of one of our largest industrial companies said: "What the businessman wants and needs to know with respect to price policy is what will the effect be of changing prices now, not what prices and related matters have been some time in the past or will be some time in the future. The appraisal of the effect of a contemplated change in one factor assumes, of course, 'other things equal' (unchanged) which is the *net* regression as distinguished from a *gross* regression concept."

It is probably true that that is what the businessman *wants* to know and what the statistician has been inclined to furnish him. But what he *needs* to know is the long-run impact of present price action, his outlook being illuminated as far as possible by discernible or reasonably inferable relations in the past. Other things do not remain equal when General Electric, du Pont, U. S. Steel, Bethlehem, Goodyear, ALCOA, *et al.* take their decisions in V-year, V+1-year, V+2-year, and later.

with other methods of scientific analysis to attain this broader view of managerial policy will be discussed in a later section of this chapter.

COST ACCOUNTING AND SUPPLY CONTROL

Historically the other major avenue of scientific aid to management has led from the side of cost accounting.

As simple business bookkeeping grew up into corporate financial accounting, it faced increasingly difficult problems in valuation of property—particularly intangibles, in choosing appropriate "cut-off" periods, and in grouping or segregating the several accounts. But it still was concerned merely to produce a factual record at the end of a year or quarter. These general accounting figures give the business policy maker a broad general picture of the result of operations as a whole but practically nothing to guide him in the conceiving and executing of price and related management policies focused on particular products or lines of production.

When, however, accounting pushes out into the wild and troubled ocean of analytical cost accounting, it becomes a powerful tool of management, with all the responsibilities and opportunities that go with such a role. A good deal of economic significance, therefore, attaches to the question of how the cost accountant conceives his function and with what preconceptions and outlook he tackles his task.[4] The picture of costs which the accountant or, better, the cost analyst gives the top executives goes far toward determining what the latter will think is "profitable"—what he can "afford" to do.

---

[4] The writer has developed this point more fully in a paper delivered before the National Association of Cost Accountants, June 27, 1939. See *Yearbook* of the Association, 1939, p. 8. See also John B. Canning, *Economics of Accountancy*; William A. Paton, *Recent and Prospective Developments in Accounting Theory*.

It is highly important that any one in charge of the preparation of these materials consider carefully both the derivation and the implications of every figure he uses.

Cost accounts are simply estimates which are arrived at by making some purposeful working up of figures selected from the available physical and financial records. Both the selection of data and their subsequent manipulation reflect some postulates or theories as to a delicate and complicated economic process. Cost figures will have no guidance value to price-making executives unless they show the basis of valuations, where the boundary line has been drawn between overhead and operating charges, how the ingredients of overhead have been selected and distributed—whether as a flat rate or according to some formula of differentiation.

Often the accountant's objective is to develop "standard" rates or "normal" charges. Such conventionalized figures have great usefulness when they are taken as yardsticks for judging operative results under one set of circumstances as compared with those at another period in a firm's life or between separate operating units of the same company or between affiliated or independent companies. They may be used by a trade association as a means of helping members to detect leaks and improve organization, choice of products, or operating methods. But when a cost formula is used as a justification for "freezing" margins or maintaining prices regardless of different outlays or producing situations, it becomes a barrier to economic progress and a brake on business enterprise.[5]

The ascribing of like costs to unlike productive situations is a practice fraught with extreme danger to ag-

---

[5] While this chapter was in preparation, a letter received from a business acquaintance included a comment which bears on this point: "One

gressive or even sound management. No discriminating type of price schedule and no flexible adjustment of prices to meet new opportunities can be worked out unless alternatives are fully explored. The cost accountant will be but a blind leader of the blind if "standard" rates and "normal" charges are the only ones brought to the executive's desk or the only ones to which the executive gives attention.

The cost accountant's role may be conceived either as that of preventing a loss from being incurred in each instance or period taken by itself or as showing how operations may be maintained or expanded on a remunerative basis for an indefinitely extended future. It is of course incumbent on the cost accountant to present figures that show the executive as true a picture as possible of all actual costs, indirect as well as direct. Only so can management be protected against avoidable operating losses. But if the major concern in cost accounting is to include every possible item that may be imputed and to make the estimates so ample as to meet any possible contingency of loss, the practical effect of the cost accountant's work may be to influence the top executives toward a highly restrictive scale of production.

If business is refused because cost estimates are inflated by unreal charges or if the cost analyst fails to show adequately the possibilities of cost reduction under

---

of the problems this manufacturer ran up against was that the retail dealers, by using figures prepared by a prominent university school of business, showed that the dealers' cost of distribution is 29 per cent, that the cost of wholesale distribution is from 12 to 13 per cent. This manufacturer pointed out that the fallacy with respect to these distribution costs is that they combined the figures of well-functioning establishments and poorly-functioning establishments. The cost of 29 per cent for retailers and 12 or 13 per cent for wholesalers is not really the cost of doing business efficiently, but is in actuality the cost of doing business of the average."

fuller capacity operation or the cost influences of other conceivable changes in operating conditions, then the competitive process is interfered with and unnecessary idleness for both men and plant is likely to result.[6]

But there is no inherent necessity that the cost accountant's or cost analyst's work should lead to policies of price maintenance and production restriction. He may develop figures which give not only a discriminating analytical picture of the cost situation actually realized in the past but also project new syntheses of cost factors into alternative patterns of production and price policy. If he makes penetrating analysis of the relation of all sorts of cost elements and valuation procedures to varying conditions of operation, style changes which cause seasonal peaks, unit costs in relation to number of styles and adaptation to individual specifications, alternative ways of conceiving of overhead and providing for its allocation, and a thousand and one others, then his work

---

[6] Here our discussion of costing practices ties back to the analysis of Chap. 11. While in economic theory profit is a residual share in distribution, current practices in charging overhead, in providing reserves, and in valuation of property often amount to writing a stipulated profit over periods of idleness as well as activity into the cost sheets which determine the scale of operation. This results in restrictive control of supplies out of step with the producing capacity of our techniques and resources.

It is common to calculate costs (as a basis of price) on the supposition that plant will be used substantially below capacity, say 70 or 80 per cent. Instead of costs being recalculated and prices moved down when and if a closer approach to capacity operation is attained, profits mount rapidly after the "break-even" point has been passed and often rise almost fantastically as full capacity is approached. It is contended that no other costing and pricing procedure is "safe." In fact, however, the safety of *this* procedure is only nominal. Writing the burden of unutilized plant capacity into the cost sheets and maintaining prices so computed means that any approach to full utilization of resources will induce boom-time excesses followed by recession, which, in the absence of some new and powerful but extraneous stimulus, tends to become chronic in the form of business stagnation. This dilemma of capitalism lies at the crux of the problem of individual firm action and co-ordinated action by many firms. It will be considered further in both Chaps. 13 and 14.

becomes truly illuminating. He then serves as a useful explorer of the territory which must be traversed by the executive in his role of price maker, investor, and employer. Only such an approach to business policy is consistent with an *enterprise* system of private capitalism.

If these constructive ends are to be achieved, the accountant needs to become more of an economic analyst, understanding the nature of the organic process whose price and profit relationship he is supposed to reduce to a transcript in which the administrative head of the business may clearly see major cause-and-result relationship. Or he needs to be more closely allied with economists who take this broader view. Prospects of developing such scientific teamwork are examined later in this chapter.

THE SCIENTIFIC MANAGEMENT MOVEMENT

A third attempt to apply scientific methods to managerial problems has stemmed from engineering roots but has branched into economic developments of no little importance. This was the "scientific management" movement which arose some three decades ago under the leadership of Frederick Taylor and Harrington Emerson. It started with meticulous time and motion studies, analysis of plant layout, engineering determination of machine speeds and tool setting. But, once the "scientific manager" had satisfied himself as to the physiological and mechanical conditions of machine productivity, he sought to devise a scheme of "incentive payment" that would bring factory performance as close as possible to maximum productivity with minimum labor cost. Success in this direction would, so far as these factors were concerned, produce a maximum rate of profits from operations.

While this development of management techniques

was focused primarily on physical output, its concern in reducing labor input or increasing volume of product made for lower unit costs and thus facilitated price reduction at the same time that incentive pay for more output tended to increase the purchasing power of those who came within the operation of the method. The fact, however, that the introduction of these methods characteristically raised the labor stint and sometimes reduced piece rates of payment and resulted in at least short-run displacement of workers caused organized labor to oppose the movement or accept only certain of its features cautiously and grudgingly.

In its initial engineering aspects, it is evident that "scientific management" has a particularistic outlook, as have market analysis and cost accounting analysis, rather than a comprehensive approach to the interrelated problem of how a firm functions as a member in an economy. While the purposes animating demand studies and cost accounting have been prone to be adaptive in character, and resulting action has often tended to restrict production, the outlook of advancement-of-management studies has characteristically been that of innovating more economic use of resources to the end of enlarging product. It has never focused on enlargement of profit through restriction of supply.

It is evident, however, that the scientific management approach does not carry its own logic to completion unless it includes a policy of pricing product which (together with current practice as to investment of profits and utilization of plant) keeps up the level of total spendings when new efficiencies are introduced—that is, converts operational savings promptly into enlarged consumer satisfactions or/and into further improvement of technique. These broader economic applications of

THE FUNCTION of management has vastly changed during the past fifty years. Recently we have been surveying this change and have been calling it a "Managerial Revolution." No revolution, seemingly, was intended. . . . We had simply come upon a time when the lawful owners could not operate their lawful "ownings" and only scientifically trained managers could. . . . As managers, we do not decide by vote as to whether a particular chemical combination or process, for instance, is right or wrong. We do not even tell each other how we "feel" about it. We are not even concerned as to whether or not it is in accordance with *any* tradition. If we do not know the answer to any specific problem, it is our job to find it, regardless of how it may clash with preconceived ideas. . . .

It was not the intention of the industrial manager, perhaps, to interfere with the business policies of the company for which he worked. He may not have considered it his business whether the employers were generous or greedy in their labor relations. But it was his business to discover the natural laws governing machine production, and to obey those laws, quite as much as it was his business to keep from violating the laws of chemistry and physics. And it just happened to be a law, inherent in the nature of mass production, that the machinery could not be kept in operation unless the masses were being served, and their standard of living increased, as new discoveries and more scientific management increased the productivity of the machine. . . .

I propose, therefore, that our Society give some real study, as soon as programs can be arranged, to a considerable list of problems which may have seemed heretofore to be beyond the scope of industrial management.

Percy S. Brown, "Looking Forward," *Advanced Management*, Jan.-Mar. 1943.

the earlier engineering findings have been suggested from time to time by leaders in scientific management, and more persons of economic training and experience have allied themselves with the movement. Many economists could benefit from the realism of the "scientific manager's" approach, whereas the engineering outlook of the latter needs to be enlarged and corrected by all that the professional economist has learned about the organic relationships of the living economy.

Such an integrated concept of the managerial function was implicit in all the writings of Frederick Taylor, father of the formal literature of the movement,[7] and is glimpsed anew in a recent address of the president of the Society for the Advancement of Management quoted on page 378. But if such a development as Mr. Brown proposes is to take place, it will be much more than "scientific management" as now understood. It will have to represent the broadest possible synthesis of market demand analyses, cost analyses, engineering efficiency analyses. The prospects of such a consummation are being increased as the several functional lines of approach here and there develop individuals who get a glimpse of this over-all task of administering the business units of a productive society. The possibility of co-ordinating them under the conditions of private management will be considered in the closing section of this chapter.

THE ENLARGING CONCEPT OF PUBLIC RELATIONS

Still another avenue of approach to the comprehensive understanding and team organization of business

[7] Indeed, such an idea apparently long antedated Taylor. The scientific management movement is reputed to have begun with a paper, "The Engineer as Economist," read before the American Society of Mechanical Engineers in 1886. See article on "Scientific Management" in *Encyclopedia of the Social Sciences*, Vol. 13, pp. 603-08.

has recently been opened up under the name of "public relations." This is a field which has shown notable growth in recent years and rapidly developing aspirations for the attainment of professional status. Public relations departments have been set up in many business corporations, a national Council of Public Relations has been organized, books and serial publications have begun to appear, and in numerous cases top executives even of some of the largest companies have been chosen on the basis of their qualifications as "public relations specialists."

As in the case of each of the "scientific approach" groups already discussed, the public relations specialist may conceive his task and attempt to execute it on either of two planes: trade routine or professional invention; short-run coup or long-run productivity; narrowly acquisitive or broadly constructive—commercially adaptive or socially creative—effort. Public relations may center attention on individual and group psychology as the scientific means of doing a better job of "buttering up" the public or lulling it into a state of personal indifference and political inaction regardless of how well or how badly business managers are discharging the task of directing our economic life. Such were the journalistic, advertising, and oratorical origins of the movement when it was known as "publicity."

Today, however, it manifests increasing concern in analytic methods, notably "attitude studies," which have been developing as a means of determining just what is the source, the intensity, and the character of the dissatisfactions (of the public, consumers, investors, and workers) with the performance of the given company. This understanding is sought primarily as a means of discovering how to relieve any misapprehension as to what is actually being done and what it is possible or impossible to do. But major emphasis is coming to be placed on utilizing this scientifically gained understanding of public wants and group frustrations to put the executives on the road toward removing dissatisfaction by having the company do a better job in administering its part of our limited resources toward achieving a larger measure of human satisfaction.

One public relations specialist has expressed this conception of the task as follows:

Public relations work is here presented as the science through which an organization can consciously attempt to fulfill its social responsibilities, . . . analyze the needs and desires of all interested parties, in order to conduct itself more responsively to them, and so secure the public recognition and approval necessary for success . . . publicity has become less important than institutional policies. The understanding and use of psychological, sociological, and economic factors in building institutional success claim more attention. . . . Experience has taught that sound public relations are based upon policies and practices which forestall and make unnecessary the "trouble-shooting" with which so many publicity men deal.[8]

More tersely it has been defined as "doing a good job—and getting credit for it." If doing a good job be interpreted as causing the company to use with discrimination and vigor the best techniques of administration, seeking to make the company's activities promote to the

[8] Rex F. Harlow, *Public Relations in War and Peace*, pp. x, xi, 130. Edmund M. Pitts, a public relations counselor, observes: "You ask yourself how much your customers know of what the real aims of your business are, other than just to make money. You select what clear picture of your firm your buying public should have, that they may feel bound to deal with you because they respect your course. . . . The heaviest of all the public relations work you executives do is the cultivation of fruitful policies and practices. You patiently develop that hybrid quality which serves multiple interests: the interests of company and consumer, of management and fellow-workers, of private enterprise and government."

highest degree the efficient functioning of the economy, then "public relations" defines the top executive's function of policy making in terms that call for the aid of all the social sciences, and particularly economics (with its statistical techniques) and political science.

The comprehensive character of the public relations approach is evident from the fact that it envisages the several "publics" involved as the consuming public, the laboring public, the investing public, and the great voting public. Defining its province to include consumer relations, it overlaps the domain of market research. Bringing labor relations within its purview, it absorbs personnel management with all its psychological aids and the time studies, job setting, and pay adjustment developed by scientific management. Personnel administration involves not merely psychology and engineering specifications but takes us over into the administrative side of political science, and exploration of the problems of governmental relations carries us still farther into the political scientist's realm. The involvement with the problem and techniques of statistics and economics is obvious. But what is to be noted is that all this implies an integrated attack on the problem of business functioning. Unless this broader viewpoint is kept in mind, the separate techniques will not add up to sound economic guidance for the economy.

MECHANIZED JUDGMENT AND THE SPIRIT OF ENTERPRISE

In the three preceding sections contrast has been drawn between adaptive, manipulative, exploitative, and restrictive uses of analytical techniques and those which are or might be made creative, exploratory, and fruitful for the business manager. Useful as has been the introduction of professionally trained cost accountants, market analysts, personnel managers, and other specialists to give top executives guidance in decision making, the development has its dangers. Business should be served but not enslaved by these techniques. Partial mastery of "scientific aids" may result in a blind confidence in the simple self-explanatory character of the answers they give. Too narrow a setting of the problem for quantitative measurement or too short a time reference may lead to results harmful rather than helpful.

The danger is that the more sophisticated techniques of management may be sought not as means of quickening and fructifying enterprise but merely of protecting the manager against making mistakes due to underestimating difficulties. When viewed in this light, the basic purpose to which these methods are directed becomes the preservation of property or the making of short-run profits, not the maintenance of productive activity. Devices of internal analysis, measurement, and forecasting may be looked to, as was observed in Chapter VII, as a means of "mechanizing judgment." They foster a "cost-plus" psychology, present mathematical measures of the *in*elasticity of the market's demand, and raise the spectre of the "mature economy."

Such results did not follow from the earlier recruitment of the natural scientist and the engineer as technological guides to business administration.[9] The out-

[9] The roster of scientific men in industry has run from untutored geniuses like Thomas Edison and the Wright brothers and well-trained engineers like Charles Kettering and William Batt to "pure scientists" of top professional rating like Irving Langmuir and Harvey Fletcher.

The report of the National Resources Committee on *Relation of the Federal Government to Research* (1938) shows 131 men starred in *American Men of Science* who are located in industrial or commercial enterprises. Excluding 22 engaged in private consulting practice, the tabulation shows 109 such distinguished scientists on the payrolls of 72

standing feature of this relationship has been that the business manager has granted the chemist, physicist, or engineer what the scientific spirit must always have— intellectual freedom. He has respected the natural scientist's ability to probe technological realms beyond the reach of his own traditional tools of investigation. He has given the scientific man access to the accumulated records of the company's past operations and the accumulated experience of its officers and workers. He has said in essence: "We want you to seek without reservations

business corporations (or trade associations). The Bell Telephone Laboratories and General Electric Company head the list, with 13 and 12 respectively. The group of 131 starred "men of science" in industrial or commercial employment compares very favorably with the parallel tabulation of 120 such outstanding scientists located in research foundations, 79 of them being in the Carnegie Institution or the Rockefeller Foundation. Fourteen universities have from 33 to 113 starred men each.

There is, for economics or the social sciences as a whole, no badge of distinction similar to the star in *American Men of Science*. The American Statistical Association, with its membership list of some 5,000 names, distinguishes 95 men as "fellows" of the Association. Of this honored group, 20 are attached more or less directly to business—7 are employees or officers of industrial concerns, 4 are with insurance companies, 4 with banks, 3 act as private consultants, 1 is with a trade association, and 1 with the National Industrial Conference Board. Besides these 20 in strictly private business, one other "fellow" is an official and another an employee of the Federal Reserve System.

In general, the demand made by business for persons of distinguished attainments in the social sciences falls upon men of statistical training, though there are a growing number of economists in business positions. In recent years, there has been some tendency by a few large concerns to call upon economists of broad theoretical training to give counsel on problems of business policy or to make monographic studies of particular practices, such as basing-point quotation or more general analyses of the public effects of particular companies' procedures. Professors J. M. Clark and A. D. Gayer of Columbia, Professor Paul Homan of Cornell, and Theodore Yntema of the Cowles Commission have undertaken such assignments. There has, however, sometimes been difficulty about making the results of such studies available in print or otherwise to the public or even to professional students. The necessity of preparing for TNEC hearings spurred some companies to seek economic counsel outside their own staffs and enabled some useful materials to be published.

the truth as to the technical processes with which we deal."

The man of science on his part had for his motto something approximating the title of a movie of some years back—"Nothing Sacred." He has not felt limited by past techniques or practices of the company. He has been challenged to discover the errors or inadequacies of such methods no matter how high in office the one who originated them or how much machinery would. have to be scrapped in the process of changing them. The whole purpose has been to make production better in the future, not to validate past choices. No one has presumed to say to the scientist: You may go as far as expanding knowledge of physics or chemistry takes you *provided* you do not challenge my inherited beliefs or personal prejudices in these fields. You must not expect to upset what I already "know."

The economist who is inducted as a scientific aid to the business manager is, by contrast, in most cases kept on a leading string and fitted with blinders. With few exceptions, if any, he is not given a full and frank record of company action and the reasons which led to it; results of action as shown by the records, with opportunity for challenging and reviewing the reliability of that record and the interpretation made of it by executives; the difficulties encountered by executives in applying prior analyses in the day-to-day exigencies of company operation; and every other issue which will condition the understanding and articulation of scientific principle with practical necessity.

The businessman has not been disposed to consult with the economist about the real objectives of business or employ him to study the wider repercussions of production or trading operations. The American Telephone and Telegraph Company sets scientists to study "the nature of speech" because, being engaged in the transmission of speech, they realize that they must dig down for the most fundamental knowledge about the phenomena on which their industry builds. They pay for discoveries as to whose ultimate practical use they have no certainty whatever. But the typical businessman does not set social scientists to work considering further the basic nature of business. He thinks that is already fully known. And so, such companies as hire economists too often set them (and their statisticians) to doing certain small tricks of measurement, such as estimating how far one can risk that a current "trend" will continue either up or down.

These technicians shrewdly conclude that their record is going to look best if it shows a high number of instances in which they warned the company against impending danger of an unprofitable venture and kept them from "sticking their necks out." Since restrictive policies by many individual firms cumulate eventually in a general business recession, this system is bound to "pay off" and the counsellor of the individual firm cannot be held responsible for a general condition. Rather will he be commended for helping keep his company in a conservative position relative to the total situation. Conceiving his task thus, the so-called economist (really a management technician) contributes to making the businessman a conformist, a defensive fighter, a safety-first entrepreneur.

Such use—or misuse—of "scientific" method tends to bring the businessman back to a mechanistic basis of policy which can hardly be better than the rule-of-thumb practices from which he sought escape by the use of research. Indeed his last estate may be worse than the first. Devices for detecting and appraising the impact of economic forces on the individual firm are not useful merely to warn industrial companies against dangers of over-expansion. It is not their mission to promote individual safety through reduction in speed or cutting off motive power. Instead of counseling discretion as the better part of valor for free enterprise, the real service of such devices is to enhance economic activity by giving the businessman a bolder sense of enterprise through better understanding of the forces with which he deals and of the ways in which they may be controlled and usefully directed.

SEEKING AN INTEGRATED ECONOMIC POLICY

If business is to escape the limitations and avoid the dangers of the several restricted approaches outlined in preceding sections, it must be by developing an adequate generalized frame of reference to which these particularized studies will be oriented and within which their results may be synthesized into comprehensive managerial policy. This would call for the addition of "general economists," even economic "theorists," to the research personnel of large and moderate-sized corporations. Such economists, to be sure, should be theorists of reality, intimately informed as to the operations of their respective companies, using the highly abstract types of theory only in the ancillary sense that "pure" natural science is used in industrial research. These men should be liaison officers between all types of economic and commercial research conducted by the company and the top executive staff by whom company policies are formulated.

Specialists have their place in business management,

as they do in medicine, but we also need the general practitioner, who makes diagnostic studies of the whole man and considers the patient as a functioning individual. It is in this comprehensive and organic sense that economic research must be linked with the high command in a business. In the last analysis, the essential role of the president of a corporation (or occasionally the chairman of the board of directors) is that of co-ordinator of all the activities of its special divisions and integrator of its total policy in the environment in which it has to operate. This means that he must consider the impact of the corporate policy upon other companies and upon the national economy as well as the impact of other corporations and of the whole economy upon his individual firm.

With the growth of governmental controls, the strengthening of union organization, the "consumer movement" and other institutional factors, the growing complexity of technological and organizational patterns, and the growth in size of many corporations, it becomes increasingly important that this top executive be something of a lay economist himself. He should at least be able to grasp fully and challenge sharply the analytical results made available from the agencies of business research within his company or from outside sources—business survey agencies, university schools of business, trade associations, or others. It is desirable also that he have the counsel of economists of the broadest calibre and that he and his economic staff be able to talk the same language with enough facility so that he can define the issues that confront him in his operational responsibilities in such terms that they can be formulated into manageable and significant research projects.[10]

[10] In all this it must be recognized that there are substantial differences between natural science and social science and between the research pro-

Private enterprise has been accused of "planlessness," and it is true that it has been opportunistic and devoid of any deep sense of responsibility for the economy as a whole. The economist's professional concern, by contrast, is primarily focused on the wealth of the nation. It is not strange therefore that persons trained in the study of the economy as a whole have followed the pursuit of that interest in the quarters where they found welcome and the opportunity for work. These havens have been chiefly at the university and the research institutes and, in recent times, the government bureau. From the standpoint of the businessman, such environments lead to "academic," "theoretical," and "starry-eyed" views of the business process and proposals for the conduct of the economy. It may be suggested that

---

cedures to be followed and results to be expected from each. The chemist, the physicist, and the biologist are fortunate in that they deal with materials which are amenable to a high degree of control and which can be measured under the chosen or created conditions of the laboratory, by methods entailing relatively little expense and small risk. Processes derived on the laboratory basis can be gradually expanded through pilot plant and experimental factory operation until successful results can be established over the whole area of the national or international market. When problems have been found to involve issues far beyond the present reach of scientific knowledge, businessmen have been peculiarly patient in waiting for the unfolding of remoter areas of knowledge, encouraged in the meantime by tangible evidence that the scientist has tools by which he can gradually unravel the mysteries of nature. Indeed, merely systematic extensions of knowledge have often been hailed as "miracles" or magic.

The social scientist labors under the handicap of having to work with human materials, whose quality cannot be standardized and whose actions cannot to any considerable extent be controlled or even freely experimented with. Human behavior constitutes a complex mixture of rational and irrational elements which baffle the efforts of anyone who tries to predict results and to a large extent even defy measurement. A large company cannot conduct controlled and limited experiments with price or wage changes or similar economic processes. Large amounts must be staked on a single decision. If results are unsatisfactory, it is not possible to go back and start fresh. But here the businessman has been prone to deride and reject as "theoretical" any proposals or even queries that go beyond or seem to challenge his accustomed patterns of thought.

businessmen have themselves to thank in no small degree if some of those who exercise their inalienable right of free inquiry about the system through which we all get our living prove to be inadequately informed as to the realities of business life. Though many corporations have in recent years begun to take pride in serving up for public consumption somewhat more factual information about the affairs of their companies, they have not subjected themselves to the searching scrutiny which is the first prerequisite to really scientific study. The businessman has never "come clean" in this regard as he does with his physician in the hope that he may be able to improve his physical health.

If economists have become starry-eyed by congregating in large numbers in government bureaus, remote from realistic knowledge of the operative details of actual business; if they sometimes become discouraged as to the likelihood that private business will devote itself energetically and effectively to sustaining the economic activity and enlarging the wealth of the nation; if some of them veer toward the belief that these ends can be more promptly and more surely accomplished through great expansion in the area of public business and governmental operation as well as regulation, the remedy is not far to seek.

Let businessmen themselves provide opportunities for truly scientific study of the economics of their operations as broad and as deep as the research facilities they have established on the technological side. There is no reason why such positions on the pay rolls of industrial, mercantile, and financial companies should not be able to command the highest talents in the new field as they have in the old. Nor is there reason to suppose that the benefits to business would be any less.

Clearly such a development could not take place over-night. In spite of the excellent progress that has been made during the past generation by both undergraduate and graduate schools of business administration and related departments of economics, much would still remain to be done by way of interesting, selecting, and training persons to the high degree of technical competence demanded by the sort of positions here envisaged. Furthermore, it takes time for an appointee, even of the highest talents and best fundamental training, to become acquainted with the distinctive operative characteristics of the given business and to draft the research projects necessary to get sufficient factual basis for even tentative analytical conclusions. It would take still longer for the economist to "grow up" into a broad understanding of the complex functioning of his firm within the industry, and his industry within the economy, and to gain the confidence and co-operation of the numerous operative specialists on whose facts and interpretations he must draw in gaining a really adequate insight into how the economic process works itself out in the life of the company. Ultimate success would require whole-souled desire on the part of economists to develop an empirical science of economic administration and a desire equally strong on the part of the top executives to avail themselves of the best of scientific aid in their administrative attack.

A final caution needs to be sounded. The head and members of such an economic research staff as we have sketched should be entirely free of administrative responsibilities and should in fact not be expected or even permitted to make specific recommendations as to the company's actual moves. Their role should be limited to analysis of issues, defining of alternatives, and qualitative and, so far as possible, quantitative judgments as to the result or train of consequences that will be set in motion by a given action. The responsibility for deciding what course it is expedient to take, in the light of this or other information, is and must remain the distinctive province of the executive officers of the company.

CONCLUSION

We have surveyed some of the considerations which will determine the ultimate answer to the question set as the issue of this chapter: What are the prospects that our economic system, through the independent and spontaneous action of individual managers, could be turned from the business practices of the past, with their emphasis on short-run profits even at the expense of production restriction and underemployment, to one of high and sustained activity through low-price policy? The answer appears to be that such a result would be entirely possible. But it would require frank and unreserved extension of modern scientific methods of approach to the economic problems involved, comparable to those already introduced in the technical phases of business.

It is the executive group of the individual company that sees most intimately in all their operational relationships the productive situations into which enterprise may introduce efficiency gains. If these executives apply themselves sincerely to the task, they are in a position to devise the most effective means of translating these gains into a commercially workable price structure.[11] In the exploration of these possibilities and in the ap-

[11] Actual price making partakes of the nature of an art, however solidly its foundations may be laid in scientific analysis. For a studious businessman's portrayal of practical price-making problems in the multi-product firm, see E. Stewart Freeman, *The Industrial "Family" of Prices*, App. D.

praisal of the results of action taken, many techniques of statistical and economic analysis are useful, but they may also be abused if conceived too narrowly or employed in isolation. They must be synthesized into a comprehensive system of policy determination in which the top executive acts as co-ordinator of the several functional divisions (production, sales, personnel, prices, and so forth) within the company but as co-ordinator also of the policies and actions of the company within its respective industry and as an integral part of the whole economy. This requires a long time perspective.

To see good prospects of success along such lines of managerial policy we must assume that many managers would be working on this same principle of business administration, looking to a reasonable share in the benefits derived from promotion of maximum production rather than exploiting a strong position (that is, relative scarcity) for their particular product. In the closing chapter some further consideration will be given to the attainability of such a state of business practice. But first, we should consider whether the progress of the individual company toward such a state might be facilitated by affiliation in voluntary associations of businessmen or companies.

CHAPTER XIII
COULD SOUND POLICY BE FACILITATED BY PRIVATE ASSOCIATIONS?

The preceding chapter emphasized the need for the individual business concern to employ scientific methods of studying its own peculiar situation if a low-price policy is to be effectively carried out. Successful use of these methods would require widespread understanding of the meaning of low-price policy and acceptance of it by large numbers of business executives as an essential means of promoting sustained general productivity and hence business prosperity. But, even assuming that such an outlook on policy can eventually be brought about or that it is even now in process of emerging, there is a further difficulty to be met. This difficulty grows out of the fear which grips some firms all the time and all firms some of the time that any effort on their part to put such a policy into practice individually would be fraught with disaster to themselves.

Hence the question to be considered in the present chapter: Can the prospect of general adoption of low-price policy be improved through any practicable form of voluntary association among individual firms? In approaching this question, we must first inquire why it is that private enterprisers feel that they cannot embark on low-price practices independently and what sort of group support they would require or what mutual assurances might be exchanged among business managers.

WHAT ASSURANCE DOES THE BUSINESS EXECUTIVE NEED?

It might seem at first glance that the producer who had made a technological improvement which he wished

394

to exploit by enlarging his market through lowering his price would strongly hope that other businessmen would *not* follow a similar policy but would be sticklers for price maintenance. Such a course on their part would presumably enable him to take business away from them and thus profit from the price reduction even if there were not enough elasticity in the market demand to enlarge total sales to any great extent.

Such a conclusion is true enough within one particular and quite restricted set of assumptions. The first of these assumptions is that the product is one which has a highly independent market, that is, one whose demand is essentially unrelated to the consumption of other products. The second assumption is that the attitude as to the price policy of others applies to such others as are producing articles directly competitive with the given seller's product. There is a minor assumption, also, that the article is one for which there is already a well-established market and relatively low elasticity of demand. Under these conditions there can be little doubt that the typical businessman will be quite content, if other sellers of his product do not follow a low-price policy.

But this case covers only a limited phase of the industrial price-making process. We need to consider several other types of situation. First let us take the product that is somewhat novel in character or whose consumption has previously been limited largely to that part of the population which has relatively high incomes. The enterprising producer who has introduced low-cost methods of production in such a situation may discover that the whole market for the product will be more rapidly developed, and he may benefit from this quickening of interest and activity, if other producers also follow a low-price policy. Getting beyond the more or less instinctive fear that there is only so much business to be done and that a rival's gain is his loss, the businessman may see benefits in price lowering even by competitors in his own line of business.

The classic example of such a situation is furnished by Henry Ford, whom one might be prone to think of as having made his great success from a "lone wolf" policy and as probably desirous that other automobiles should remain high-priced. Even if Mr. Ford's first impulse ran in that direction, it seems clear that, on later thought, he realized that he could not hope to make all the cars that would be wanted below a $1000 price.[1] He may have more or less clearly sensed the fact that even within the competitive area of the automobile industry itself it was a help to his business to have other producers stimulating as well as in part supplying the demand for fast, comfortable, and cheap personal transportation. This would be true also of electric washing machines and refrigerators, cameras, radios, and similar products.

But the fact that a given producer can pursue a low-price policy only—or most safely and effectively—when such policies are being followed also by others relates primarily to *complementary* rather than *competitive* prod-

---

[1] This raises the collateral issue of how fully a single producer will in any given case be able to draw all the benefits of an expanding line of production to himself. As a practical matter, it often proves true that he may not have either the funds, the managerial talent, or the disposition to carry through such a massive expansion. He may only be in a position to accept a proportionate share of the growth of a somewhat generally enlarging industry. Furthermore, there are many instances in which the business code more or less definitely prescribes that any major firm should maintain "its position in the trade." If it aggressively takes business from rivals, its action is branded "cut-throat competition" and private reprisals or attack in the courts may be set in motion. Hence it may be to even the leader's advantage to persuade the rest of the industry to join in a general low-price policy. Various such possible advantages will be discussed as we proceed.

ucts. In Chapters VI, VII, and VIII, we pointed out
that the producer of a raw material, partly finished product, or product of joint use could get the full market response to his price reductions only in case the gains he
undertook to pass on were not absorbed by other companies—fabricators or distributors—but instead were
complemented by any savings in cost that could be introduced at these other points. An outstanding illustration
is that of the sellers of building materials. No one of
them can individually hope to reap the benefits of price
reduction unless the total of all reductions that can be
effected is fully reflected in the cost of finished housing
units offered to the ultimate consumer. The same point
is well demonstrated by carrying our automobile illustration one step farther.

The full benefits of Ford's low-price policy for cars
could be reaped only as his friend Harvey Firestone also
became a pacemaker in the field of lower-priced tires,
and as the independent oil companies forced competitively lower prices into a market formerly dominated by
the high-price outlook of the Standard Oil monopoly.
Getting more power and comfort into low-priced cars
and extending the low-price policy to the higher-
powered and more luxurious models stimulated the practice of long-distance driving, urged the road-building
program forward, and thus activated enterprise in the
fuller employment of the population and the provision
of more incomes capable of buying some kind of car—
new or second hand. But the number of miles of highway that can be financed in turn depends significantly
on whether or not a low-price policy is being followed
as to cement, steel rods, and construction machinery.

In a broader and more fundamental sense, all final
consumers' goods need to be regarded as joint products

in the making up of a budget or scale of living for the general public. The producers of movies, radios, and automobiles would not be able to expand these industries through price lowering as a result of their efficiency increases if producers of clothing, housing, or food were pushing up prices to pocket for themselves the money which the introduction of new efficiency in the production of necessities should leave as a larger residue of family income for amusement, education, or travel.

As was pointed out in Chapter XI, the lag in this process of assimilating efficiency gains into higher living standards produces the modern phenomenon of technological unemployment or stagnation in our post-pioneer (not "mature") economy. The maintenance of a self-sustained system of private business, without dependence on government subsidy or financial supplementation, requires pricing for full-scale operation. To attain this end, the individual manager must not only have confidence internally as to his company that he has a sound criterion of operation. He needs external confidence also that a major proportion of other business concerns are ordering their affairs by the same criterion.

Answering the question with which we started, the assurance that the executive of the individual firm needs or craves is the evidence that a satisfactory level of private employment will be maintained by the totality of individual companies through sound price-and-production policies. Knowledge that all other firms were releasing needed purchasing power into the general consumer market, instead of trying to impound an excess share of the product under their own control, would reduce the sense of business uncertainty which in the analysis of both businessmen and economists constitutes not only the occasion but also the economic justification for large profit margins.

We turn, therefore, to consider the character of the organizations in which businessmen now associate themselves and certain proposals for more positive types of agencies.

POLICY-MAKING ASSOCIATIONS THAT BUSINESSMEN HAVE ALREADY TRIED

As one looks at the run of business associations that have been experimented with in the past, one is struck by the fact that, by and large, these have been alliances in abatement of competition, for price maintenance, and for limitation of production. Such was the "trust" agreement of the late nineteenth century. Such is the cartel, more in vogue in Europe than in the United States. Such was the avowed purpose of a founder of the modern trade association movement,[2] though the same form of organization has subsequently been used in many instances for more constructive purposes and might, conceivably, be used as the organization through which to carry out the scientific application of low-price policy on a grand scale. We therefore pause to consider the nature of the trade association and the NRA in which it was briefly sponsored by the government as a generalized agency for formulating and executing business policy.

In contrast to the trust and cartel, that rely on market domination and monopoly control as the means of exacting high profits, the trade association uses, to a considerable extent, the more subtle "scientific" approaches discussed in the preceding chapter. The trade association might be described as the little man's research department. For a modest prorated charge, the

[2] Arthur Jerome Eddy in *The New Competition* proposed "associations of competing manufacturers and dealers to lessen competition and advance prices" on the ground that, in the industrial race, "the runners are not competing one against the other, but each is running against himself—the winner running faster than necessary, the loser making a hopeless contest." pp. 14, 81.

small concern without resources sufficient to maintain elaborate market analysis or cost accounting departments may, subject to such restrictions as are set by antitrust regulations, get statistics as to inelasticity of demand, saturation of the market, standard costs, safe reserves, and imminence of a business downturn. The same philosophy which would cause the executive of a large company to support costly "research" to keep his own company in a conservative position with reference to these managerial hazards, makes him willing to see that such facilities are available to smaller, possibly lighter-running or more aggressive concerns. By seeing that they are coached in the ways of "safe" management and at the same time reminding such concerns that they can hardly afford to engage in price competition with large and strongly established companies, they build up a discipline of price maintenance supported by production control. By protecting high-cost producers, the low-cost firms have for themselves a wider margin of profit and feel that they are doing as well as they would if they took over the business of the marginal companies by lowering their profit margin.

The understandings that businessmen seek and are willing to give under such trade association arrangements are in fact designed to secure restraint of really competitive enterprise. Under guise of preventing "cut-throat" competition, the trade association that follows such policies is weakening or eliminating the stimulus to economic progress that comes from competition.[3]

---

[3] This restrictive view has been frankly expressed by a trade association official: "Education should start by destroying the illusion that greater profits can be obtained from an increase in volume secured by price cutting. When this illusion has been destroyed the root of the price cutting evil will be eliminated. We can do much to effect this education through cooperation, through coming together and honestly discussing

The "code authorities" established under the guidance of the NRA shed a great deal of light on the behavior of businessmen when drawn together in an overhead organization. In this instance, they sought or at least accepted group association at a time when depression was acute and in the hope that the united action would supply a means of economic recovery and subsequent business stabilization. The early drafters of the plan sought stimulation of production, the maintenance of mass purchasing power, and the quickening of enterprise. But by the time codes were drawn up and machinery for enforcing them was established, the whole effort was suffused with controls of operating hours or new equipment, schemes of price maintenance, and a tendency to brand any real competition as "chiseling."

It is not within the province of this study to attempt analysis of the good and bad points of the NRA. But that episode is commonly cited as evidence that businessmen are not to be expected voluntarily to join and loyally to support a private association of rival companies unless such agency is primarily designed to make their competitive situation easier or to promise some nearby benefit, not some remote improvement or stabilization of the general business situation out of which in varying degrees they would gain in the long run.

The NRA in its regulation of trade practices modified but little the plane of competition already established by common

our problems. Around a conference table, in trade association meetings, this education is possible and without circumscribing the rights of individuals unduly. . . . Trade associations must adopt programs of activities which are obviously for the advancement of their members if they are to win the support of those members. Their activities must be largely selfish. Only incidentally can they afford to be socially minded and offer cooperation with the government." Charles F. Abbott, Executive Director, American Institute of Steel Construction in *The Swope Plan*, J. George Frederick, ed. (1931), pp. 116, 118.

and statute law and Federal Trade Commission pronouncements . . . there is much in the record which, instead of making
competition fair, has tended to lessen competition . . . made
extensive reallocations of power as between individual initiative
and industrial groups . . . extended to important industries, and
in a grave degree, power over determination of the nature,
forms, and area of specialization. . . .

So far as inducing recovery is concerned—interpreting recovery to mean increased production, increased consumption,
increased employment, and increased real wages—it must also
be concluded that the trade practice provisions of codes have
been a hindrance rather than a stimulus . . . so large a part of
the provisions put into effect were restrictive rather than promo-
tive in character that it may be concluded that they more than
offset what gains may have been contributed by temporary confidence. . . .

Although in many cases individuals and groups were not
opposed to [increased wages, reduced hours, and other modifications of conditions of employment] and were even favorable
to them on general humane grounds or because they may have
believed that they would be conducive to recovery, they were
for the most part provisions which they were willing to grant
"voluntarily" only in exchange for an increased control over
prices, production, and other matters which they regarded as desirable. . . . To price rigidities attributable to [freezing of the
wage structure] have been added as well those resulting from
the permission granted to business associations to "stabilize"
prices through concerted action designed to eliminate "cut-
throat" competition. The two factors have combined to increase
resistance to price realignments which are essential to the expansion of productive output.[4]

Even though the NRA suffered an early demise, it
had the effect of strengthening many existing trade asso-

[4] Leverett S. Lyon, Myron W. Watkins, and Victor Abramson, *The
National Recovery Administration* (1935), pp. 744-45, 746-47, 876.
See also Charles Frederick Roos, *NRA Economic Planning* (1937),
Chaps. 9-12 and Arthur Robert Burns, *The Decline of Competition*
(1936), Chap. 10.
For comment on NRA by a businessman who believes in an aggressive

ciations and had led to the formation of a large number of new ones. Thus the federation of individual firms into co-operative overhead agencies for the performance of certain functions remains as a potentially important institution for the shaping of business policy over whole industries. There is no inherent reason why the trade association should not be the high strategy board for its industry, promoting the most constructive policies for facilitating the entry of new efficiencies into the business and of translating these efficiencies into maximum production and maximum consumer satisfaction. Under such an interpretation the trade association or industrial "institute" would become a co-ordinating agency above the top executives of separate companies, large and small. On its upper margin it would seek to use the best devices of economic analysis to fit the industry into a program for maximum efficiency of the economy.

If this end were to be achieved, utmost frankness in analyzing all cost and demand conditions throughout the industry would have to be pursued in the interest of truth seeking, rather than the immediate promotion of the interests of one firm or of the industry at the ultimate cost of business as a whole. These high ideals have been avowed by some leaders in the trade association movement as is indicated by the statement of one secretary:

The guidance and the impetus through which cooperation among competitors through trade association may make the maximum contribution to economic progress . . . is to be found, not by the lawyer, but by the economist. . . . I know of scores of . . . associations in American industries and trades whose

---

interpretation of free enterprise, see quotation from Paul G. Hoffman, pp. 72-74.

activities have been beneficial to buyer and seller, producer and consumer alike, which also have been involved in no litigation and hence had no notoriety, whose constructive activities indicate that the reins of control of American business policy are more and more being assumed by a forward-looking leadership, which, by cooperation between the producer, distributor, and consumer, is seeking in good faith to give to the public the benefits of competition and to the industries and trades themselves the benefits of cooperation. This promise for the future will be realized through trade associations, not so much by keeping their eye upon the Sherman anti-trust law and the Federal Trade Commission Act, but by a consideration in good faith of public interests and the public welfare, and by a determination to share fairly with the public the benefits of lawful cooperation.[5]

Conceivably also such a move toward getting a broad view of economic policy might be strengthened by the erection of a super-industrial federation of trade associations on a high professional plane. The formation in 1920 of a body known as the American Trade Association Executives[6] suggests the possibility of some clearing of policy objectives and criteria on so broad a scale that it conceivably might become influential, even if not determinative, for the economy as a whole.[7]

As in most business groups, opinion in the American Trade Association Executives has divided somewhat sharply between those who wish to see it develop as a

[5] Wilson Compton, The American Economic Review (Suppl.), March 1926, pp. 227, 229, 231.

[6] "The objectives of [the society] include, among other educational activities, studies of the functions, management and operation of trade associations and the dissemination of material designed to increase the usefulness of such associations and to improve their contributions to the public welfare." American Trade Association Executives, Trade Association Executives and Public Relations (1941).

[7] The possible usefulness also of national associations of market analysts, cost accountants, scientific management specialists, and public relations men should not be overlooked in thinking of available means of promoting the consideration of managerial policies on a basis wider than the firm or the industry.

power device[8] and those who see its really constructive possibilities as an agency for enunciating objectives of maximum total productivity and for devising practicable means for helping industry groups and individual firms promote their own success through setting their activities most skillfully into such an overall economic program. The latter group recently found expression through the Association's Committee on Public Relations, which drafted a lengthy report embodying a platform whose major features include the following:

To help trade associations, as representatives of individual business concerns, develop the public service leadership which they should develop in view of the group leadership which they have developed in other phases of business.

To facilitate the improvement of business policies and their execution. . .

To stimulate adequate research by associations in the belief that the securing of many kinds of facts now unknown constitutes a vital approach to the public service question.

To suggest the economic and social significance of business policies, decisions, methods, activities and objectives.

To stimulate the thinking of association executives concerning sound applications of the public service approach to their associations.

To suggest the location of some public relations railroad crossings in the business world so that association executives can "Stop! Look! Listen!" to the advantage of the public and of their industries.[9]

It would be premature at the present time and presumptuous for any student to go farther than to point

[8] Since it is a professional association and not an operative agency in even the restricted sense of the trade associations themselves, there would seem to be little danger of its becoming a "peak" control agency of the fascistic pattern so strongly developed in certain countries abroad and so much to be feared at home. See Robert A. Brady, *Business as a System of Power*, for a rather lurid presentation of this menace.

[9] *Trade Association Executives and Public Relations*, p. 6.

to the existence of such voluntary associations and to
note that they have possibilities as yet undetermined
of putting policy making for the individual company
on the broad plane of optimum operating conditions for
the economy. The still prevailing use of the supra-
company association for purposes of restriction while at
the same time such associations are beginning to be
glimpsed as a possible device for constructive supplementation of individual company management suggests
our second question: Do more inclusive types of business
association, not limited to service work for particular
industries, offer greater or at least additional possibilities
for the generalization of low-price policy?

GENERAL BUSINESS ASSOCIATIONS AND THE CLIMATE OF OPINION

The trade association is essentially an operational
agency. It participates in managerial functions in that its
professional employees gather and process statistical data
or other "educational" matter more or less directly designed to influence the action of the member companies.
In some cases the associations counsel members quite
specifically as to their operative programs. But there are
also more general business associations such as the Chamber of Commerce of the United States, with its state and
local chambers, and the National Association of Manufacturers, with its considerable staff and varied program
of activities. The latter is the older, having been formed
in 1895, and has been on the whole the more closely
integrated body, seeking to rally individual business
concerns, but particularly the larger manufacturers, in
support of specific legislative proposals and more general
public policies.

Whether it be said that members follow leadership

that emanates from the headquarters of the National Association of Manufacturers or that the association is merely responsive to the view of the members, it undoubtedly does wield an important influence. It performs some services of a legal, statistical, or analytical character for its members not essentially different from those of the specialized trade associations. But in the main it is designed to influence the "climate of opinion" about business both among businessmen and on the part of the general public.

This influence has been widely regarded as supporting the view that the country is the businessman's "oyster" rather than conceiving business as an agency for producing the maximum wealth of the nation. Over quite a span of years it was preoccupied with strengthening the system of high-tariff protection[10] and resisting all forms of labor organization. It would have seemed utterly fantastic during that time to think of this organization as coming out in support of the idea that manage-

---

[10] These attitudes seem not to have been characteristic of the founding fathers of the Association. A. G. Taylor in his study of *Labor Policies of the National Association of Manufacturers* (University of Illinois, Studies in the Social Sciences, March 1927) speaks of it as having been "organized to promote export trade in manufactured goods from the United States, to foster commercial education, with no defined labor policy." In its first and third annual conventions, the Association passed resolutions in favor of tariff reciprocity, particularly with South American countries. In the convention of 1898 the association's president expressed gratification over provisions of the tariff law of 1897 facilitating bi-lateral concessions as well as formal reciprocity treaties, adding: "We cannot expect to get concessions which will prove of worth to us, however, unless we are willing to give something in return and a reciprocity in which there is a disposition to give little and to take much it would seem would find scant favor with other governments. We must display a willingness to go at least half way if hope is entertained of our coming to any practical result." On the attitude toward labor, Dr. Taylor says (pp. 13-14): "In the recorded utterances of these early leaders there is to be found hardly a note of hostility toward organized labor. Such a policy of opposition did not appear until 1902 [when] . . . the Association launched an anti-union program."

ment has a responsibility for maintaining the level of employment or of featuring on its annual programs such forward-looking addresses as those delivered by Alfred P. Sloan, Jr., in 1941[11] and Henry J. Kaiser in 1943[12]—telling his fellow businessmen that "our people have rejected the tyranny of wealth." Without painting

[11] "American business management will be directly challenged by the postwar era. That challenge must be aggressively met. There will be a demand for a more complete utilization of the nation's economic resources. The abundance of the early 'forties' in contrast to the shortage of the 'thirties' constitutes a political demand that no administration will ignore. We of industry must assume a militant attitude. We must take the initiative in both planning and action for the postwar period. . . . The great test: Shall we be able to construct a self-sustaining economy—a MUST for real confidence and a great forward movement of business? The dominating forces on the positive side concern the ability of private enterprise to expand employment not only in the production of entirely new industrial products, but likewise by making available existing products at lower prices through increased efficiency in production and distribution. This to expand the real purchasing power."

[12] "The freedom to produce encompasses all of the freedoms. . . . American industrial leadership has its challenge. It can surrender to the social politicians who have little to offer save an ultimate bankruptcy, or it can win the greatest battle of its history by giving America the opportunity to work, and in due time by extending that opportunity through our facilities, through our products, through our finance, into the far corners of the earth. . . . Never before in the lifetime of any man in this room has there been such a challenge to responsible leadership. We are now summoned either to show the way to a decent standard of living and self-respect for our people, or to surrender, perhaps for the last time, to the compulsions and directions of the dictator state. [Let no] one of us cherish in his heart the illusion that he can recapture any of the special privileges or the unwarranted advantages of the past, or that he can once again build a power known as a 'vested interest.' . . .

"The time has now come for American industry to take the leadership and actually put a plan into action. The plain truth is that we dare not wait for any protracted period of national or international contention as to what plan is the best, or as to the methods and procedures for putting one into operation. . . . If industry could now show our people that there needs to be no postwar depression; that on the contrary there can be America's greatest economic and social opportunity, there would be at once a magnificent response. . . . In the heart of every citizen who knows the sense of independence, born of earning and saving, there is the deep desire to believe in our leadership. Shall we risk the loss of any of this trust by our unwillingness to venture boldly now in their behalf?"

the N.A.M. of today as the torchbearer of liberalism, it must be evident to any open-minded student of its role in the national life that the emphasis has shifted substantially away from older and narrower concepts and toward promotion of general economic welfare as a means of business success.[13] This very substantial change in the spirit and economic outlook of the organization suggests that it might not be out of the range of possibilities that it would at some time adopt an aggressive educational and promotional role on behalf of a policy of unrestricted economic activity and orderly and consistent price lowering.

Much the same may be said with reference to the Chamber of Commerce. Everyone remembers the pride this organization took in the early twenties in the fact that its headquarters building in Washington was constructed entirely by non-union labor. Over against this we may now place the enthusiasm with which members re-elected Mr. Eric Johnston as their president in the spring of 1943 after he had for a year been a tireless and brilliant exponent of responsible and progressive business leadership.[14] The potential economic influence of the Chamber is enlarged by the fact that it covers all lines of business rather than being limited to manufacturing, and maintains active contact with the small factory town and distributive center as well as the industrial metropolis.

[13] For example, in a little booklet, *Jobs, Freedom, Opportunity* published in March 1943, the Postwar Committee of the National Association of Manufacturers states: "Prosperity can be attained only if every section of the country, every part of our economic and social organization, and all of us as individuals work together and each expects in return only that share in such prosperity which is commensurate with his contribution. Policies should be designed to benefit the whole population, not just one section or group." (p. 29.)

[14] An excerpt from Mr. Johnston's presidential address quoted on pp. 344-46 gives a fairly clear idea of his outlook on current business problems.

It is not within the province of this book to write eulogies of the broader-minded businessmen who have in recent years liberalized the attitudes of the two great general business associations. Nor is it our purpose to emphasize deficiencies still remaining in their programs. The point for our present inquiry is simply this: Do these bodies go as far by way of assuring the individual business firm a climate of business opinion truly expressive of free enterprise—that is, one of full-scale activity and bona fide competition—as it is possible to go in the present state of business opinion? A corollary question is: Have these agencies today caught up with the march of business thought to the point that they represent as constructive an economic leadership as could win voluntary compliance from their members? Or, if free enterprise is to take back the operative management of our economy after the war, will it need, and could it devise, a somewhat more specific and more aggressive type of overhead policy making today for the whole broad field of business?

This question at once calls to mind the Committee for Economic Development already discussed in Chapter XI. Several features of this undertaking are significant in connection with our present query. C.E.D. is definitely a combined effort (but not a combination) in promotion of full-scale business activity. Its method of approach is the opposite of the business monopoly or the corporate state. It seeks to quicken a sense both of responsibility for, and individual company initiative in, getting maximum utilization of the nation's labor force and thereby such productive profit as a fully employed people would require for high and advancing efficiency. It sets up a grass-roots movement of individual firms, each striving to put itself in the way of making its maximum contribution to the sustaining of business activity by expanding as much as possible the market for articles in whose production it has the greatest technical competence and interest. It is a light-running organization based on the volunteer efforts of individual companies, particularly "small business," all over the country. It is likewise a thoroughly democratic system of contagious free enterprise based on comparing notes on the infinitely varied ways in which each enterprise may expand itself and thus contribute to a healthy environment of general activity and full utilization of resources.

We have already expressed our apprehension at the relatively small amount of emphasis given to the cost side of the picture and to the importance of developing price policy in step with and in workable relation to plans as to volume and choice of products. The Committee's engineering and commercial approach, with its stimulus to high physical volume, would create a situation which might raise the curtain on a drama of revivified competition quite heroic in its proportions. But we feel some doubts as to the wisdom of conducting so aggressive a program of physical operation without more explicit considerations of its price implications. Even so it must be clear that the work of C.E.D. is a striking example of a new type of nation-wide business movement designed to get a positive program among businessmen which would create a climate of opinion and an atmosphere of action definitely conducive to the unleashing of business enterprise. It would operate definitely against the creation or maintenance of any attitude of restriction of production or of waiting to see what everybody else will do before making individual plans.

Another proposal contemplates more permanent existence, a more fully rounded operating plan, and machinery of compliance rather than mere exhortation to voluntary action. This plan, like the enlarged scientific management program discussed in the preceding chapter, also emerges from the camp of the engineers[15] but is by no means limited to a program of physical production. Instead, it views our exchange society as essentially an integrated mechanism whose working parts must be scientifically adjusted one to another if it is to operate smoothly and efficiently. Cost-price and purchasing-power relations thus become the major concern. In order to establish a continuous system of testing and readjusting these relationships, the author of the plan proposes a National or Market Building Association, its membership to be voluntary but to carry a pledge of compliance with a scheme of industrial self-government based on an industrial code substantially as follows.

1. Objective. Continued full capacity production of wanted goods and services.

2. A uniform base wage scale.

3. A uniform price-making policy. All prices to be based on costs at full capacity production with mark-ups as uniform as possible. . . .

4. The margin of allowed prices above full capacity costs to be gradually lowered until 96 per cent to 98 per cent of all potential workers are working efficiently.

5. Uniform accounting methods.

6. Honesty in advertising.

7. Strict rules governing deferred payment selling. . . .

8. Goods produced under this code to be so advertised and labeled.

9. No penalty of any kind to be attached to selling at prices lower than those authorized by the Association. Free enterprise demands free markets.[16]

[15] Its author, John E. Webster, was formerly General Works Engineer of the Westinghouse Electric and Manufacturing Company.

[16] John E. Webster, "Free Enterprise Must Save Itself," *Advanced Management*, July-September 1942, p. 120. For a fuller excerpt from the plan, see App. E.

Businessmen to whose attention this plan has been called are quick to raise their hands in horror at the prospect of the curtailment of freedom that would be involved in such a plan. It would, they say, set up a self-imposed bureaucracy hardly less hampering than the external bureaucracy of a government price control. How much this objection is in fact a rationalization of their unwillingness to be bound by the principles of such a general welfare association at times when they might think they saw opportunities of short-run company profits by breaking away from this group discipline, it is impossible to say. To the writer, it appears that any real compliance machinery would threaten to prove too cumbersome and probably too inflexible to produce the results desired. The voice of experience teaches that it is impossible in times of strain to prevent wholesale desertions from minimum price associations, and there is little reason to suppose that there would be less general defection from price maximum associations.[17] But even

[17] After this chapter was in proof, so orthodox and accepted an agency as Dun & Bradstreet, Inc. has come out in favor of "the establishment of a single integrated policy-making organization within private business, comprising and representing all private business on a representative democratic basis. . . . Business management must cope with the possibility of another depression by the application of preventives, and an integrated policy-making organization representing all business would seem to be the logical medium through which to co-operate and to guide the energy and the potentialities of our business world to this dominant economic end. . . . We need a Permanent Council of Representatives of Free Business Enterprise that will be organized and supported by small business, big business, manufacturers, wholesalers, retailers, banking, insurance, transportation, and public utilities, to solve vital business problems within business, not for the sake of business, but for what the solution of these vital problems will mean to the future happiness, welfare, and prosperity of every man, woman, and child in this great country— *our* United States." Roy A. Foulke, *Financial Implications of the Peace*.

Is this, perchance, the shadowy outline of an incipient American Fascism? Or is it a practical suggestion for the minimum amount of overhead organization that would be necessary to make the following of low-price policy under private enterprise broadly practical? I confess I do not know. But it is an innate fear of the potentialities of overhead

so, as an inventor's model for illustrating the principles upon which a system of free enterprise and free exchange basically operates, the plan seems worthy of the businessman's contemplation.

THE ANTITRUST ISSUE IN A NEW ASPECT

No doubt one reason why any general business association would be hesitant about taking positive steps to implement a comprehensive production or price policy, even if such a course had strong acceptance among members, would be fear of running afoul of the antitrust laws. Conceivably this is a reason also why the Committee for Economic Development should so studiously refrain from any mention of the price issue.

In the case of the proposed National Market Building Association with its machinery for securing compliance, it could hardly be questioned that it would be a combination among business concerns to control or influence prices and related conditions of operation. The same would be true if any trade association took steps to activate a low-price policy in a particular industry or if a federation of such associations undertook to start a more general movement in this direction. This raises the nice question whether such a situation would be accepted by the Department of Justice, the Federal Trade Commission, and the Supreme Court as a combination in *promotion of trade*. Obviously there would be a novel state of facts for the court to consider if all the records submitted to the trade association officials or the headquarters of the Market Building Association were open to scrutiny and if the avowed purpose and the demon-

business organizations, particularly if delegated disciplinary power over members, that causes me to place my emphasis so strongly on the understanding and voluntary action of the individual firm, with business associations designed merely for investigatory, consultative, and discussion functions.

strated effect were to expand output and lower prices. It might indeed be easier for the Court to reconcile such a situation with the public policy enunciated in the antitrust laws than it has been in the past to discriminate "reasonable restraints of trade."

In conclusion, then, we may say that the voluntary association of individual firms is to be viewed at most as a supplementary device in the effectuation of low-price policy. If the executives of the individual firm had full understanding of the economic importance and long-run benefit of such a policy, an overhead association would be largely superfluous. If they had no real understanding of this logic of private business and no consequent purpose to follow it, a mere association set-up would be largely futile.

On the reasonable middle-of-the-road assumption that the mass of businessmen have some realization of the fundamental economic forces with which they are dealing and yet not full mastery of the principles under which they may be successfully directed, the association should be a valuable adjunct to individual management. In the case of small firms not in a position to support a research department adequate to gather the needed factual information or to command the professional specialists to interpret it and adapt its generalized truths to particular developments of technique, popular attitude, or political leadership, the group facilities of an association are almost necessary to a high type of professional management. Even for the largest individual companies, there would be advantages to be derived from making the reasons for their policy decisions known to the smaller members of the economy and of learning the situations and viewpoints of these smaller units in perfecting the strategy and tactics of all.

This may be put in terms familiar to the American

way of life by regarding business as team play. Each man wants to have understanding and support from the team as a functioning unit as well as perfecting his own moves with the play as a whole. He expects to subordinate his own personal glory in the choice of each next play as new situations develop. In all this he must accept coaching but also depend on himself for delivering the fullest effort and displaying the greatest resourcefulness. He even subordinates his own appetites to the discipline of a somewhat abstemious life.

The real purpose of a voluntary association would be to provide a means of declaring principles of democratic business, studying their application to special situations, creating a climate of opinion in support of these principles, and giving publicity to at least major or persistent infractions of these principles. Being a power device, any association is subject to abuse unless it is ready to put both its principles and the practices of its members honestly on the record. Since the members of a trade association are dealing in directly competing products, whereas the membership of a general business association such as the Chamber of Commerce includes producers of complementary products in the broadest sense, it would appear to be much easier for the latter to eschew price maintenance and restrictionist ideas or policies and to promote efforts in support of active business and maximum production, even when the evident corollary was lower prices and moderate though sustained profits.

CHAPTER XIV

COMPANY MANAGEMENT AND ECONOMIC SOLIDARITY

In drawing to a close this study of price making in a democracy, we shall need to have a summary view of the material already presented. This may be outlined under three general heads: first, the position from which we start; second, the goal or objective which we are trying to attain; and third, the means which are proposed for helping a private business system to reach that goal.

In form this review will be presented as a series of brief categorical propositions. In such a skeleton statement it will be easier to check the reasonableness of the several positions and their mutual consistency.

OUTLINE OF THE TREATMENT

The General Setting

Our economic system today is dominated by large corporate and labor aggregations, not by individual proprietorships and unorganized workers.

The flow of business life does not now *adjust itself* merely through the flexible process of continuous small bargains and almost automatic personal decisions. At various administrative centers, it has to *be adjusted* by executives, having varying degrees of control.

Commitments of great volumes of capital and large numbers of workers are made at central points of business administration, by top executives and executive hierarchies, under a time perspective much longer than that of the single transaction.

Price schedules, union wage rates, interest, and returns to borrowed capital are set in advance to cover periods ranging from a season (prices of goods) to a decade or more (bond interest). This system of institutionalized business under professional management proceeds under policies, operative programs, de facto plans which reflect the suppositions of the administrative officials as to how economic processes operate and how the managers can derive greatest benefit for their respective organizations in the course of this operation.

Some of these executives pursue policies that imply mere adaptation to a process which they regard as independent of their action, as the farmer adapts his operations to the weather. Others follow opportunistic patterns of militant action which seek individual company gains without regard to the ultimate effects of their own acts or what the total outcome would be if such patterns of group action were followed generally. Still others are coming to recognize that the economic process itself is conditioned by the acts of its constituent operative units, and they therefore seek to follow courses whose consequences may be expected to be beneficial not only to themselves but to the total business situation.

The organizational features of the economic setting are linked with a technological situation characterized by large accumulations of scientific knowledge and methodology from which a stream of operative improvements are constantly adding to, or are available for adding to, the efficiency of productive labor. How rapidly and how fully these possibilities are attained will depend on whether business executives welcome them and understand the processes by which they may be translated into workable price relations, or whether they fear the consequences of new efficiencies and try to impede their entrance.

Advances in technology make possible the production of better goods, the same quantity of the given goods with less labor, or more goods with the same outlay of labor. Gains may be taken in the form of more and/or better goods. They may be taken also in the form of voluntary leisure. But technological improvements may also be so ineptly dealt with that they result in more or less chronic (not merely transitional) unemployment.

The Goal which Business Must Seek

The commonest formulation of the business goal is: to make as much money as possible for the company or for the owners of the company.

This expression, to be concrete and actionable, has to be given a time dimension. For any but a fly-by-night company it must mean largest sustained flow of earnings for the company.

The economist sets as the goal of business activity the organizing of production and distribution operations in such a way that they will provide the highest total output of the goods and services desired by consumers.

A large and apparently increasing number of individual business leaders and business organizations are today stating their objectives in essentially these same terms. This acceptance may either be direct—as an explicit statement that such must be the goal of business—or indirect—as an argument that the system of free enterprise under private capitalism is good (or best) because it in fact promotes general material well-being. (See pp. 6, 8, 26, 28, 142.) By this criterion they are willing to be judged.

There is substantial compatibility between maximum profits in the long run for capitalist owners and maximum real incomes for the population taken as a whole. Analysis pointing to this conclusion was presented in Chapters IV and XI. Amplification of that position is the major purpose of this closing chapter.

Means by which Business Executives Can Approach the Goal of Sustained Prosperity

Free enterprise by the producer for the market and free choice by the consumer in the market are the surest ways of enabling expanding scientific knowledge to bring about the enlargement of our national real income.

But under modern conditions most individual workers can exercise their choices only among jobs offered on certain terms by employers at wages determined by union-management bargaining. Most individual consumers can exercise their choices only among certain goods (bundles of utilities) whose variety, quality, and price have been strongly influenced by manufacturers and distributors. Thus, executives as co-trustees of these freedoms of choice strongly condition the economic benefits realized or determine how many potential benefits shall be allowed to slip away.

If production costs are reduced by a new technique or improved organization, and *prices* of the product *are maintained*, there will be a reduction in employment if savings retained by the company do not go promptly and fully into expansion, research, or loans to other companies who will spend them in activities that give a proportionate amount of employment. If disbursed by the company as higher wages or dividends, the increased private incomes must, if employment is to be maintained and economic progress realized, be spent by their recipients promptly and fully on added consumer goods, or in active investments—those which result in expanded activity.

If *prices* are *lowered* as a result of reduction in producing costs, there will be some expansion in sales—slight if the demand was practically satiated at the old level of prices, proportionate to or even greater than the reduction in price if the want was largely unsatisfied before. Thus re-employment will be provided—more or less fully—by expansion in the given line of production. Any gap may be fully or partially closed by shift of the consumer's unused spending power (conserved by the price reduction) to other lines of consumer goods or to additional capital goods.

Spending on consumer goods expands most promptly and fully when the gains in the form of higher wages or lower prices go into the hands of low-income groups. It is still active but with a higher proportion of savings when they fall into the hands of the middle income groups. It is most sluggish when administered by the rich, whose wants are already well supplied.

The question as to what proportion of efficiency gains should, at a given time, for the health and progress of the economic system, be deferred (as additions to capital) and what proportion should be cashed in (as current advances in the plane of consumer living) is purely relative to (a) the technical adequacy of existing plant, (b) the ability and willingness of consumers, with their existing pattern of personal incomes to absorb currently the capacity output of available plant, and (c) the ability of this plant and this market absorption to utilize fully the available labor force.

A natural limit to the profitable use of capital goods is set by the need of providing sufficient consumer purchasing power to make a market for the product of additional plant capacity.

Faulty adjustment among commodity prices, wages, and profits, is reflected in the presence of unutilized plant capacity, hoarded funds, or substantial and persistent unemployment.

A policy of transferring efficiency gains into higher scales of living for the masses is sometimes expressed in advances in wages, sometimes in reduction in prices of consumers' goods. The latter process is largely under the control of the management of the producing company. The former is now largely in the hands of union officials whose attempts at wage adjustment are based on fighting strength rather than relative productivity of various types of labor or actual improvements in techniques of production.

There are two important reasons for the superiority of price reduction over wage increases as the means of exploiting efficiency gains. Owing to the wide prevalence of uniform wage rates under modern trade union conditions, wage advances cannot be at all accurately adjusted to efficiency gains. In the second place, it is only when gains are translated into

lower consumer prices that they can operate directly and
fully to expand the outlet for the goods into whose production business enterprise has introduced a new efficiency.
When wage advances won by bargaining pressure are not
consistent with productivity, their beneficial effect for the
worker is largely dissipated in price inflation, assuming volume
of employment to be maintained. In fact, however, wage
advances not matched by productivity gains tend to weaken
the incentive to employment and thus may themselves become a source of unemployment. To the extent that they do
so, labor "prices itself out of its market."

Similarly, if capital will commit itself to new ventures or will
operate freely in old ones only when it can be assured a very
high rate of profit, this will lead to situations in which plant
is unutilized and funds hoarded. Such an interpretation of the
profit motive contributes to restriction of the total long-run
flow of productive effort out of which alone the ultimate
returns of capital must be supplied. Capital, in such a situation
is "pricing itself out of a market."

If anticipated burdens of substantial disuse of capacity are written into cost sheets and are incorporated into price schedules,
full-scale operation will not be attained except during brief
periods when consumers are liquidating past savings or incurring future debts.

The maximum stream of profits that capital as a whole can
secure for itself over the long run will result from utilizing
the whole labor force with plant facilities of the highest
degree of efficiency that can be provided without such a rate
of capital formation as would trench on the volume of consumption which, at each successive stage, corresponds to existing productive capacity.

In the concrete situation of postwar return to private business,
it is important that industrial and financial executives make
sure that the then existing plant shall be directed as fully as
possible to use by all who want to work, and the whole
product priced to sell promptly in the market provided by

that level of employment, rather than mopping up wartime savings through unnecessarily high prices before peacetime production is fully restored, or allowing high profit objectives to impede the attainment of full-scale peacetime output.

The goal of business has been stated on behalf of both economist and businessman in the democratic terms of the greatest total production of goods and services for the people as a whole. Our analysis points to the conclusion that the most efficient means of attaining that goal are also democratic. That is to say, maximum business profit can be attained only through maximum long-run productivity, and this can be attained only through full employment. Full employment can be maintained more readily by passing the net gains of labor-saving improvements on democratically to the mass of consumers rather than concentrating them on a limited class of directors of capital or special groups of labor (overalled or white-collared) which enjoy a monopolistic bargaining position. Individual free enterprise means opportunity for all who want work to support themselves and their dependents rather than freedom of certain individuals to introduce local and temporary restrictions that they can use for their immediate personal gain.

With the general outline of the analysis of the book before us, we now turn to brief comment on the broad meaning of such an interpretation of the requirements for successful operation of private capitalism in an industrial age.

THE PREMISE OF ECONOMIC SOLIDARITY

The whole economic philosophy expounded in preceding pages is based on the premise that there is an underlying solidarity of interest among all parts of an economy and hence among all the participants in its business life. Such solidarity expresses itself as a common concern for maximum production.

This proposition is obviously one which, even though true as a broad and fundamental generalization, is not necessarily governing in each particular instance. But this does not vitiate or even weaken it. The great majority of intelligent people accept and act upon the comparable principle, "Crime doesn't pay," even though almost any one of reasonably wide experience must know or have heard of crimes that paid fairly well or even handsomely. They do not have to be taught that people as a whole cannot get ahead by stealing or by injuring each other's properties or persons, that they must advance themselves as producers rather than as parasites.

I have been amazed, however, to find several very thoughtful persons who read the preliminary drafts of this book challenging even the broad truth of the principle that individual or company isolationism doesn't really pay in business. They seem to think that certain easily discernible exceptions invalidate the principle that business enterprisers would in the long run profit most largely from business practices designed to promote the productivity of the whole economy.

Everyone is aware that there are many personal, group, and short-run advantages that can be secured by actions that lessen rather than enlarge general prosperity. Particular firms in sheltered trades or in peculiar individual circumstances may for all practical purposes seem to lie outside or be able to ignore the principle of economic solidarity. They may pursue their own immediate advantage without regard to the wider repercussions on other companies or individuals or the remoter time effects of any management policy that they may see fit to follow. There can be little doubt that certain concerns whose employees are few in number and whose product is not a major factor of staple manufacturing costs or a significant item in the consumer budget of the masses, might continue to charge prices that would give them inordinately high rates of profit indefinitely without inviting adverse effects at a later time.

But this does not mean that the great body of producers of staple products of standard use or popular consumption could follow a similar policy of high prices regardless of volume, without this course proving ultimately harmful even to themselves. We must not let the exceptions swallow up the rule. As a fundamental principle for businessmen seeking long-run profits for the majority of companies, I see no escape from the proposition that they can make the largest ultimate gains from doing business in a society which is maintained on a high level of activity and low level costs attained through operative efficiency, and that to the maintenance of such a condition the individual company must consciously undertake to make its own particular contribution, its "cut" in the total product being determined on the basis of its productive contribution, measured with as much scientific accuracy as possible.

I know of no method of statistical or theoretical "proof" that could be invoked to verify so elemental a proposition. It seems to me to state the basic logic of a self-administered business system. Hence, I have used it as a premise throughout my analysis.

STRATEGIC LEADERSHIP AND GENERAL COMPETENCE AND MORALE

To say that the successful functioning of a free enterprise capitalistic system demands widespread acceptance of and compliance with an over-all principle of economic solidarity does not mean that the demands upon or the opportunities for positive business leadership are the same for all industries or all company executives. In fact, some readers seem to have gained the impression that the writer interprets low-price policy as something to be effectuated by the largest business concerns, and that its practice would contribute to the further growth of big business and the elimination of small companies. This is by no means the case. He does accept it as an accomplished fact that technological needs and organizational efficiencies require the continuance both of large operating plants in some lines of manufacture and of perhaps even larger financial and managerial organization in certain industrial and mercantile lines. But on the other hand, many types of business activity are not amenable to consolidation, and a healthy industrial system would continue to have large, small, and middle-sized units. They should be peacefully and efficiently articulated under a complex system of local autonomy and central co-ordination, which would be in a continuous state of experimental evolution.[1]

[1] A suggestive and intimately informed exposition of this character of our economic structure is supplied by a prominent executive:

"Sears, Roebuck and Company is obviously representative of mass distribution. . . . Its retail stores, some large and some very small, or its catalogs . . . are what meet the eye, but of themselves these facilities have no more use than a dining room without a kitchen. In the background are some six to seven thousand manufacturers. Out of this number are hundreds of plants whose production is closely geared to the requirements of these stores and catalogs. These factories earn good profits, because their job is a simple production job and there is a minimum of uncertainty, of idle machine time, or of overhead not needed in this relationship. These manufacturers know that the moment an article is ready to come off the assembly line thousands of salesmen will be presenting it on "Main Street" to the public, and before long a catalog presenting this article will be placed in one-third of the rural and suburban homes of the country. Important as it is to have efficient operation of these retail units, moderate investment, and proper planning and co-ordination of effort one with the other, yet all this is no more important to the final result than the proper co-ordination of a great network of manufacturing sources meshed with the operation of these stores. . . .

"The small manufacturer standing alone has often lacked what it takes to duplicate the progress of his large competitor. He has lacked engineering and research talent—money for advertising and sales expense

Since we are talking of business leadership within an economic solidarity, we may properly begin by considering the distinctive role of the company or the businessman weighted with great size and/or strategic position. Certain industries and certain companies have put themselves or have been put into economically strategic positions where their actions have natural priority of influence or clearly discernible leverage value in the actual operation of our industrial society. Today we live in an automotive age. The automobile (including bus, truck, and tractor) determines where we live and how we work —and play. It shapes the geographical plan of our cities, influences the size and dispersion of our towns and villages, the location of our pleasure resorts, the mobility of our labor supply. It activates a gigantic program of road (and bridge) building, conditions the market

---

to displace some of his big competitor's goods from dealers' shelves. Probably most difficult of all, his manufacturing costs have been high because of the uncertain and spasmodic production schedules this situation forces on him. Just as the small dealer needs a powerful ally, which he finds in the large manufacturer to complete the sequence, so the small manufacturer needs an ally who can furnish what he lacks—acceptance by the public, expert product leadership, and assured volume. He finds this in the development of the large distributor. So, as I see it, we are developing two parallel systems, each having its place in the total economy of the country. On the one hand, the dominant, large manufacturers with their own branded lines, distributing their products through thousands of independent dealers—on the other hand, the mass distributor with his many and various branded lines, buying each of these lines from smaller manufacturers. In each case the production of goods is in the factory and the retail sale to the public is in a store, but in one case the manufacturer determines the character of product, i.e., its design, quality, prices and production schedules; while in the other case, these functions are assumed by the mass distributor. . . .

"It is not a case of the small merchant against the big chain, nor for that matter, the small manufacturer against the industrial giant. Surely neither system can, nor need replace the other. Surely this country will always need small manufacturers and small dealers. An attack on a large manufacturer is indirectly an attack on thousands of dealers: an attack on mass distributors is an attack on thousands of small manufacturers. . . ." T. V. Houser, Vice President, Sears, Roebuck and Co., New England Sales Managers Conference, Jan. 8, 1943.

for houses and apartments, alters our farming practices. Finally, the automotive industry wields a major influence in the petroleum, rubber, and steel industries (besides lesser lines of production) and very possibly has it in its power to contribute to the growth of business cycles or to mitigate their disastrous violence. Hence the prices at which automobiles, trucks, and tractors are offered to the public are going to be a major factor in determining the way in which peacetime business gets back to operation after the war and what its course will be thereafter. Three big, and half a dozen lesser companies provide the pattern of this great industrial empire.

If a low-price policy for automobiles is boldly inaugurated by General Motors, Chrysler, or Ford after the war, it would almost inevitably force low-price practices throughout the industry. This would contribute to enlargement of the market not merely for cars but for gasoline, tires, steel, and aluminum. If Firestone renews its ancient tradition of low prices, and if the petroleum companies display as much price competition as the independents brought into the industry in the twenties, this would make it possible for the impetus furnished by the assembling companies to attain full economic momentum for the automobile (and satellite) industries. If ALCOA follows the policies espoused in its recent advertising (see p. 334) rather than that by which it priced itself out of the automobile market of the twenties[2] and if the steel industry will follow policies conspicuously absent in the past, we should, through the action of some dozen companies, be assured that the industrial tempo of the postwar industrial age would be set well toward all-out peace operation. This would be

---

[2] See *Industrial Price Policies and Economic Progress*, pp. 205 ff.

effected by or lost without the initial motion of the automobile industry group.

But this is an electric age too. General Electric is in a hardly less strategic position than General Motors. The policies it follows become a factor in the cost of enlarging the network of electric generating stations and power line,[3] through which cheap light and heat and power may—or may not—be made available to the whole country after the war. To this end its efforts toward more adequate exploitation of our resources must, of course, be reinforced by complementary efforts of electric utility companies to wor kout rate structures that will give maximum encouragement to the use of more electric machinery in shops and on farms, more electric appliances in every home. How fast the market for electric current expands will in turn depend on how cheaply General Electric, Westinghouse, and a host of smaller companies can and will make electric refrigerators, fans, vacuum cleaners, washing machines, and stoves.[4]

This mention of articles which are supplied by very small as well as very large companies directs our attention to the fact that leadership does not necessarily come all from the side of the big companies. The policies and practices of small companies are likewise of indispensable

[3] Using copper or aluminum cable, depending on which is priced lower.

[4] Two other industries which naturally come to mind as being of great strategic significance are the chemical industry and the housing industry. In the former the importance of research and plant requirements contribute to putting major leadership in the hands of giant companies like the du Pont Company, the Allied Chemical and Dye Company, and United Carbon and Carbide Company, although there are many middle-size and small companies which are quite capable at times of assuming leadership as to particular articles or lines of output. The housing industry is, of course, very much less integrated but seems to have suffered from the lack of any dominating large-scale leadership more than it has gained from the supposed natural competition of a large number of small units.

importance, even if not fully equal influence, in maintaining the health and vigor of our economic system. One phase of the significance of the small company touches its very real ability to become a price competitor. This may be illustrated by the lighter forms of electric appliances just referred to, such as fans, toasters, vacuum cleaners, radios, washing machines. For such articles, the small factory or even "the little shop down the alley" may, with its light-running organization and the personalized interest, incentive, and inventiveness of its personnel become a minimum-cost producer and a significant factor in price making and job creation. If uninhibited and unimpeded, these small companies often set the pace of competition.

But the policies and practices of the rank and file of small companies also have other and wider significance in the total business process. Even when they do not become pacemakers or prime movers in starting business forward or in seeing that its rate of progress is maintained, it is quite clear that they play an essential, even if negative, role of followership, complementary to the leadership of the very big or most strategically placed companies. The mere undertaking or expansion of operations by a handful of giant companies assures an initial outlay of hundreds of millions of dollars and the provision of hundreds of thousands of jobs. This at once imparts a note of confidence to the whole business world as well as a substantial positive movement of funds and goods. But if these leadership concerns are to be able to produce at minimum cost and make a necessary margin of profit within the limit of price which can be secured for a volume of goods sufficient to employ the whole working force, every producer of goods that enter into automobiles, electric equipment, chemically derived materials and appliances, natural raw materials, and all the rest must be pursuing a real policy of translating potential efficiencies into low prices and abundant supplies.

Here we must bear in mind the distinction between mere size and the leverage value or strategic significance of a given industry or line of business. The American Telephone and Telegraph Company and Western Union are two of the biggest of the big, yet no sense of responsibility to the economy as a whole would make it possible for them to initiate business revival or significantly underwrite business stability through any conceivable reduction in the price of telephone calls or telegraphic messages. Similarly Procter and Gamble and Lever Brothers could not engineer business salvation even by doing everything they could about the price of soap or the number of people employed in soap making. But it is equally true that the great fabricators of finished products cannot achieve minimum cost and maximum volume unless they are able to get all their constituent goods and services at the lowest prices made possible by both full and efficient use of resources—down to the cost of their telephone calls and the soap they supply in their washrooms. Stated from the consumer's side, his purchasing power must be as little as possible drained away in supplying his needs for soap and shoes and breakfast cereal if he is to be in as good a position as possible to make the most of the market for automobiles, domestic air conditioning, and movie tickets. And active business in the amusement and luxury trades helps sustain the market for soap and telephone service and all the staples.

Thus we arrive at three conclusions as to the relation of low-price policy to the size of business units and the character and consequences of business controls. First, management must substitute the principle of carefully measured efficiency and necessary costs in place of tactical maneuvering and the search for individual security as a principle or technique of price making. Second, in following this approach, the issue of size must be allowed to settle itself as a consequence of market response to the prices achieved by the several companies in the light of the costs resulting from scale of operations and ratio of utilization of facilities attained by the several companies. Size would cease to be an instrument of power in the manipulation of market relations. Third, executives of companies, both large and small, would find it necessary to consider the strategic significance of their operations as well as the actual magnitudes involved. They would have to recognize that the success of business operations as an interrelated system depends equally upon the vigor and skill of the leadership and on the competence and sustained morale of the rank and file who must be depended upon to support and complement that leadership. Each is the reciprocal of the other.

THE "AMERICAN WAY"—FOR THE FUTURE

What has just been said about economic solidarity, business leadership, and the complementary practices of the rank-and-file outlines a system of business operation which to some people seems to imply a wide departure from accepted concepts of "the American way" of economic life. Since our opening chapter took preservation of "the American way" as the objective of our study, we must now check the positions summarized in this chapter against the traditional tenets of free enterprise, competition, and the profit motive.

Free enterprise—individual and group. The free enterprise which the Founding Fathers of the American economic system sought under the emancipated conditions of a new land was democratic or individual free enterprise. Under the pioneer conditions of a virgin continent and still within the technological anteroom of handicraft methods, it was easy to achieve this kind of individual free enterprise, and such a way of organized business life induced maximum or at least a very high level of total productivity and economic progress. It both stimulated and rewarded industry, ingenuity, and venturesomeness.

By the latter part of the 19th century, we had reinterpreted the doctrine of individual free enterprise so as to give like freedom of action to the quite unlike legal person—the business corporation. There is an obvious incompatibility between the democratic concept of real freedom of enterprise for the individual and the aristocratic concept of complete freedom of enterprise for the corporate business, allowed to grow with no external restraint and to use its pyramiding power as it may see fit, both against small corporate units and against the individual persons who contribute their productive efforts within the corporation itself.

For some fifty years now, we have been, cautiously and against much opposition, revising the laws under which corporate powers were granted and imposing regulatory restraints under government authority in the hope of retaining the advantages of large-scale organization without sacrificing the advantages which come from allowing each individual the fullest possible opportunity for exercising his own spirit of economic enterprise and of being rewarded in full proportion to the amount which such participation contributes to the total stream of production. These efforts are important, have been meeting with a certain measure of success, and should be continued further.

It is our belief, however, that no scheme of conferring legal powers and defining legal limitations upon the exercise of those powers is capable of insuring a satisfactory exercise of group enterprise. It is necessary to delegate a very large measure of authority to the administrative officers of business corporations if they are to have the stimulus of responsibility and the necessary flexibility for quick adaptation of general principles to rapidly changing and technically complicated situations. We have argued, therefore, that for the really successful operation of a system of free enterprise, the managerial staffs in whose hands these administrative functions come to a focus must abandon the aristocratic philosophy of concentrating the benefits of the system or the fruits of its operation upon a limited number of participants in certain titular positions or upon any class of participants whose function is conceived as more important than that of other participants. This is equally true whether the class in question be the capitalists, the managers, the technicians, the white-collar workers, or the operatives.

We believe that the attainment of what might be called "scientific" management of a system of private business would call for a systematic attempt to give all workers with hand or brain ample access to the use of natural resources and accumulated equipment at the place for which their capacities best fit them and to establish the closest approximation to an open market for the valuation of their productive contributions in these respective posts. This would lead us, in the complex technological and commercial situations of a modern industrial age, to the equivalent of freedom of individual effort (and its reward) which was embodied by Thomas Jefferson and Adam Smith in two notable documents in "the spirit of '76."

Some people dissent from such an interpretation of the principle of free enterprise, alleging that personal freedom would under such a scheme of operation have given place to private bureaucracy. They "do not see much of a case for having the business executive selected by the industry and paid by the industry if in fact his responsibilities are primarily to the public and are the same as they would be if he were selected and paid by the government." Admittedly this is not free individual enterprise in the sense of that "rugged individualism" whose harmful effects upon the economy have now been belatedly but generally recognized. As stated above, it is calculated to restore the participating position of all individuals, little as well as big, to a team system of private enterprise which seeks, by giving each his maximum opportunity, to evoke his maximum productive contribution and to reward it with a proportionate share of consumer goods.

To say, however, that the professional business manager administering his company under such an interpretation of the spirit of enterprise is "responsible primarily to the public" involves a serious confusion. His responsibilities are primarily to his company as a continuously functioning group within an industry which in turn is a sector of the whole economy. To realize that he promotes the real and abiding interests of the company as such only by considering it in this broad and long operational perspective is something very different from directing operations in the supposed interest of that undefined and undefinable entity—the public.[5]

[5] I have argued elsewhere (*American Economic Review*, March 1944) that the distinctive shortcoming of even the most well-intentioned form of statism is that there is no such thing as the "common *good*" which can be set up as a concrete and verifiable objective of bureaucratic action. On the other hand, it is possible for private business groups to identify real and tangible *interests* which must be achieved jointly if at all.

Competition—co-operatively organized. Competition is the manner in which enterprise, individual or group, expresses itself—more or less freely. We have noted that the idea of competition also has undergone notable changes with the progress of industrial development and has become involved in considerable ambiguities. Under strictly free individual enterprise with self-employed individuals or families, competition takes the form of each enterpriser seeking to improve his own situation by selecting the best location, the most desirable line of production, and the most suitable method of production. There is no sharp struggle amongst the several individuals. None of them has any appreciable influence on the price of the product. Each employs his labor and his resources as fully as he desires and as advantageously as he can toward enlarging his income. None of them throttles down production to boost prices and enhance his profits. Each simply shifts his efforts from the less remunerative to the more remunerative application.

But when large and powerful group organization enters, the competitive process takes on the substantially different character of inter-group rivalry. Furthermore, this rivalry becomes definitely a struggle centered on prices, which in varying degrees are subject to influence by the operative practices of organized groups within the market. The use of such power may have either of two possible outcomes.

In one direction, this powered competition may result in stimulating business enterprise to develop and introduce new efficiencies with the utmost vigor and skill, relying on superior product at lower price to increase market volume and secure the fullest stream of continuing rewards to those who lead in this scheme of economic progress. On the other hand, the powered competition of group enterprise may direct itself toward another type of price competition, namely the attempt to gain profits by supporting prices through the restriction of output below the level which would result from full utilization of labor and of capital resources. This restrictionist competition is practiced by the administrative agencies of both capital and labor. At its worst, it becomes a "donkey race" of economic stagnation in which contending groups try each to advantage itself by holding back productive effort rather than unleashing all forms of economic enterprise and finding workable ways of sharing in the enlarged and ever-enlarging flow of product. To the generally lowered state of business prosperity that comes from practices in restraint of production, the individual firm must, except in the occasional instance, itself fall a victim in the long run.

It is evident that both the expansionists' and the restrictionists' interpretations of business competition are exemplified in current business practices. But if we read the record of the last few decades, the restrictionist tendencies—under the slogan of "stabilization"—are so much in the ascendancy or are so little frowned upon or combated by responsible business leadership that they threaten again to involve us in deep and apparently incurable depression unless competition as one of the basic ingredients of the American way of economic life can be generally accepted and consistently practiced as a struggle toward superior efficiency, not merely in the qualitative sense of superior techniques but in the quantitative sense of economical and efficient utilization of the whole body of labor with efficient equipment.

Effective competition is not native to the modern system of corporate industry and trade, but prices may be so administered as to restore a calculated and more beneficent competition than that assumed to flow from automatic small-scale competition.

The profit motive—as maximum gain in the long run. The third doctrine traditionally accepted as a major ingredient of the American way of business is that the profit motive is the mainspring of economic life. That motive is commonly interpreted in terms of maximum profit to the capitalist partner in business enterprise. We accept this principle but interpret it in the light of the fact that a large proportion of the participants in industrial and mercantile life have, through technological necessity or advantage, been transferred from the position of independent enterprisers to a condition of working for wage or salary. To preserve the functional meaning of the profit motive requires that a substantial share of the increasing product be distributed in the real incomes of these persons. If they are not to lose the stimulus toward productive effort or adequate incentive to contribute to the enlargement of product, they must derive personal benefits from this increased productivity. Maximum total production must be maintained if profits are to attain their maximum total in the long run. The profit motive may defeat itself if so much of the proceeds of current operation is allocated to capital formation that the consumer market provided is not adequate to absorb the product of so large a plant. Without such absorption the new capital proves to be sterile or the earning power of both old and new capital is needlessly reduced.

These conclusions present a modern interpretation of the profit motive consistent with and dependent upon what has already been said about the interpretation of competition and free enterprise in a world of institutionalized business and professional administration. The whole system of prices of goods and services; wage rates, salaries, and bonuses; interest, dividends, surplus, and profit sharing must be brought into such relationship as will facilitate full use of resources, human and propertied, at as high a rate of efficiency as can be progressively maintained. This calls for proper weighing of the potential gains from new machinery against the need of providing for the physical and spiritual efficiency of workers through a pattern of income distribution which converts full production into full consumption.

Under a properly designed system of price relations, moderate rates of profit from sustained operations take the place of high profits during spurts of activity followed by dwindling profits or even losses during periods of sharp recession or more chronic low activity. There is no reason to suppose that a supply of new capital adequate to maintain technological progress could not be provided from the internal savings of companies so operated, together with the savings of salary and wage workers enjoying the standard of real income which would be permitted—indeed necessitated—by full utilization of our productive resources. And under such a scheme of prices and incomes the country's capacity to consume would be much more adequate to support the scale of market absorption needed to stabilize a profit-making situation for producers in general.

The doctrines of free enterprise, competition, and the profit motive here expounded represent a return, under the new conditions of modern industrialism, to the objectives sought and the criteria proposed under the American way as it was conceived in the early days of free America. If to any it should appear that the emphasis on the consumer as an object of concern and as a beneficiary of the system introduces a new plank in the platform of business thinking in the classic tradition, we may well recall Adam Smith's famous postulate:

> Consumption is the sole end and purpose of all production; and the interest of the producer ought to be attended to, only so far as it may be necessary for promoting that of the consumer. The maxim is so perfectly self-evident, that it would be absurd to attempt to prove it. But in the mercantile system, the interest of the consumer is almost constantly sacrificed to that of the producer; and it seems to consider production, and not consumption, as the ultimate end and object of all industry and commerce.[6]

RESPONSIBILITY IS THE BEST POLICY

The fundamental philosophy of price-and-production policy expounded in this volume has been hit off by one commentator as, "Be good, big boy, and let who will be high priced." A previous section of this chapter should, we think, make it clear that low-price policy is not a principle that applies merely or primarily to the "big boys." Strongly as we emphasize the leadership role of large and strategically-placed corporations, we stress no less the complementary importance of having the same general objectives and criteria of business understood and observed by the lesser groups who make up an equally important part of the complete and interrelated business machine.

But even more inept is the use of the phrase "be good" in connection with the principles of business management here expounded. The word "good" in its ethical sense is entirely irrelevant to the analysis presented in this book. The writer has purposely avoided the use of the words "ethical," "altruistic," or even "social." This is not because he is anti-social or because he

---

[6] Adam Smith, *An Inquiry into the Nature and Causes of the Wealth of Nations*, Edwin Cannan, ed. (1922), Vol. 2, p. 159.

believes that business is properly a battle of tooth and claw in which regard for others has no place. On the contrary, it is because he believes that all these considerations, instead of being placed in a separate category, must, for the successful operation of business, be integrated into the policy of the professional managers of the corporate business institution or the professional executives of other organized economic groups, such as the labor union or the trade association. It is much better for the businessman so to conduct his business as to promote the maximum economic welfare of all parties *in the process* than to conduct it in such manner that certain interests are forgotten or subordinated in the operative plan, and then introducing corrective or ameliorative measures according to some different set of "social" criteria.[7] Business is itself a social process and for its own success must be organized and conducted as a consistent, harmonious, and integrated whole. Maximum long-run prosperity of the individual firm can be attained only

[7] There is, of course, a large school of thought which holds that we cannot hope to make private business operate so perfectly as to produce even approximately satisfactory results for anywhere near all our people. It is therefore necessary that doles, income supplements, and relief measures be supplied as means of correcting or at least ameliorating the defects in the product of our economic process. Such is the situation when great fortunes are made from business and these fortunes are then distributed by their owners as subsidies to schools, hospitals, libraries, and all manner of eleemosynary institutions. There is a basic objection to this kind of distributive system in a democratic society whose members desire to get the full value of their productive contribution and exercise free choice in determining the types of consumption to which it shall be directed rather than having large lumps of the product amassed in the hands of a limited number of individuals who then decide how it shall be channeled into consumption. A democratic people resents sumptuary legislation, and extra-legal sumptuary control is no less distasteful.

It would seem to be at least premature to decide that we are not capable of devising a scheme of price relations under which technically correct division of product will be effected in the first instance rather than relying on the capricious redistribution of Lords and Ladies Bountiful or the politically determined redistributions of the Provident State. There was

within the structure of an economy functioning under conditions of sustained general prosperity. And to this general or total prosperity, the individual firm must, through suitable policies and practices, make its own peculiar contribution.

It may be responded that, even if all this be true in principle, business policies must be adopted and put in practice by the manager of the individual firm, and he cannot operate in ways which will promote maximum efficiency for the economy as a whole while the rest of the business world is operating on a very different principle. The preceding chapter considered strengths and weaknesses of the voluntary business association as an aid in propagating expansionist operating policies among their members. It is to be noted also that the operations of individual firms must be carried on within a structure of statute law, judicial interpretation, and administrative activity. Hence the role played by government in the economic field may be such as to stimulate and facilitate the following of broad and sound policies by private business enterprise. On the other hand, fiscal or taxation policies or specific regulatory measures and practices may interpose more or less serious barriers to the best functioning of private business.

The analysis of private business policy presented in

a time not so long ago when in our industrial processes we expected a casting, stamping, or broaching machine to turn out a product that only roughly approached the size specifications needed. We then added laborious hand chipping, filing, hammering, and grinding, to bring it within a still not very exact engineering tolerance. Today we turn out in the first process a product that meets physical specifications within one-one-thousandth or one-millionth of an inch, or chemical specifications precise to a second or third decimal, with only a small percentage of units found defective under inspection practices more rigorous than were even dreamed of in the days of early machine methods. Is it too much to hope that similar perfection of economic processes can be attained when we apply our minds with equal diligence to problems of that field?

this book must remain in some details incomplete until it is carried through the adjacent area of public policy and governmental action. Any such task, however, lies outside the scope of the present study. The writer is in part reconciled to this limitation by reason of his belief that the spontaneous and independent action of individual firms is capable of meeting the requirements of successful operation of our economy under a private enterprise system more fully and with less reliance on government aids or with much less fear of government constraints than is commonly supposed. Furthermore the allegedly hampering effects of government action are often advanced merely as an alibi by those who are unwilling to face squarely the issues of private business policy. The more fully self-discipline promotes sustained prosperity, the less will be the urge for regulatory action on the part of government, or for compensatory spending, programs of relief or income supplementation, and the reformatory taxation which accompanies these undertakings.

But if one suggests that this interpretation of private enterprise boils down to an admonition, "Be good, Mr. Businessman, and let who will be high priced,"[8] we reply: Maximum success for our business system demands "good" businessmen only in that common usage in which we refer to the good surgeon or to any good workman— he who knows his machine, its capacities and its limitations, how to adjust and how to feed it, how to make necessary repairs, how to use it skillfully to produce the finest quality and the maximum quantity of product. We

[8] The ineptitude of this phrase as a characterization of low-price policy is all the more evident if one recalls the original lines upon which it is a parody: "Be good, sweet maid, and let who will be clever." It has been a major purpose of this book to show that "clever" and "high-priced" are *not* synonymous.

would not think of asking a locomotive engineer to be good to his engine or the master mechanic to be good to his factory plant. What we expect of him is to be intelligent as to conditions of efficiency and responsible as well as skillful in complying with those conditions. Throughout the book we have reasoned that the manager of the individual firm is in fact the only one who can know the precise conditions as to the introduction of operative efficiencies or the availability of such efficiencies for introduction. He is thus in a position to make the necessary adjustments with the greatest precision and most exact timing. No external organization or bureaucratic regulation can supersede him in this role.

Such a formulation of business principles represents the second level of advancing economic literacy characteristic of the evolution of our industrial institutions. The first stage of this development has long been summed up in the business aphorism, "Honesty is the best policy." The individual handicraftsman often found it possible to disguise the defects of his materials or workmanship. The itinerant merchant might falsify the origin, quality, or cost of his wares or, by superior craft in bargaining, exact unwarranted prices from individual consumers. Lacking uniformity or even consistency as to their differences, prices exploited the ignorance or meekness of the buyer or the exigency of his position. The process was wasteful in the time it consumed in arriving at the terms of each particular sale and inefficient in that it failed to build up a dependable and expanding market for different qualities of goods among the clientele to which each was suited.

Mass production, branded merchandise, and certified standards have now superseded the old rule "let the purchaser beware" over a major part of the field of modern business. Broad general standards are defined under public authority, and infraction of these standards penalized by regulatory agencies and the courts. More specialized and refined standards covering quality, dimensions, containers, service, and business practices are further defined with scientific precision by voluntary business associations (notably the American Standards Association) and voluntary compliance secured among participants in the business because of the practical value of buying from a "certified," "reputable," or "ethical" producer or distributor. There will of course always remain an intractable fringe of avaricious or naturally lawless persons who will refuse this group discipline and seek to "live by their wits." But a great majority find that orderly social life yields better dividends in the long run.

Not merely do they find that honesty pays in the more obvious legal and commercial meanings of the term. They have given a whole new and higher range of meaning to "honest" wares and "honest" values to the consuming public that "buys with its eyes." If the family likes the color of the paint or the style of the upholstery, father doesn't even go through the motions of lifting the hood to check on the quality of the engine. He says, "You know you will get just what you pay for," or "No big manufacturer can stay in business if he does not deliver the goods."

A second—and, we hope, definitely emerging—plane of business evolution may well be paraphrased as "Responsibility is the best policy." In the early days of the factory system, the employer failed to realize that in taking over the direction of other people's money and other people's labor, he was as a class assuming responsibilities for maintaining the activity and efficiency of the business process in which these factors of production are employed—a process "clothed with a public interest" in the broadest sense of that term. The individual employer might for a time dodge this responsibility, but the evil birds of low-quality labor supply, wasted natural resources, impaired public health, inadequate markets, wage unrest, and cyclical depression or secular stagnation inevitably came home to roost.

It is a matter of common knowledge that businessmen by and large have accepted a greatly increased responsibility for furnishing safe and sanitary working conditions, protection of public health, and to some extent the maintenance of purchasing power after the wage-earning period and in times of unemployment. Some of this improvement has come through the voluntary action of employers as individuals or trade groups. Some of it has come through government action, often opposed by businessmen and business organizations but sometimes supported or even initiated by business interests.

We can only hope that the ultimate intellectual judgment of private businessmen will be not merely that responsibility is the best policy in the limited terms in which it has already been put in practice and validated by experience but also in that broader and more comprehensive interpretation of responsibility that requires the individual businessman to follow practices that sustain the sources of general business prosperity.[9]

[9] Numerous quotations from business leaders presented at various places in this book indubitably put business' best foot forward. Businessmen who hold a different view appear less inclined to be outspoken about it at the present time. One such voice has, however, sounded from a very high quarter recently: "Exactly defining the function of a business unit is becoming of extreme importance in these days when so many post-war worlds are being constructed with alternate bricks of fact and fancy. The fancies—and a whole social fabric is being woven out of them—conceive of the paraphernalia of production and distribu-

THE SEEN HAND AND GUIDING BRAIN

The writer has experienced some difficulty in seeking to convey the basic importance he attaches to low-price policy as a guide to business management without seeming to offer a panacea. Many independent factors enter into the total situations within which the process of business must be carried out. Some of them are stimulating, some retarding influences, while some merely are elements of change which may either stimulate or retard, depending on how they are dealt with. But I reiterate the position taken in the introductory chapter to the effect that all the organizational and technological and operative problems of business have price relations as their ultimate frame of reference and that price policy therefore becomes the highest common denominator of practically all business decisions. To set low-price policy as the master key for solving these managerial puzzles is simply to say that the business enterprise of all our

tion as constituting in themselves the source of prosperity. In times of general prosperity, it is true, the machinery of production and distribution goes into high gear and in so doing requires the employment of so large a number of human beings that nearly everyone who wishes work may find it at fairly satisfactory wages. This has brought about the widespread illusion that the whirring of the machinery causes the prosperity and the employment. From this illusion is deduced the theory that it is the social obligation of the owners of the machinery to keep it whirring and to preserve a high level of employment. . . . It is rather odd to discover that many of those who call themselves businessmen and are presumed therefore to be versed in commercial accounting, subscribe to the fundamental illusion that we can act as if we have large orders in hand when we have only small orders and therefore find no difficulty in solemnly averring that business has the responsibility of learning how to go forward while operating in reverse. . . Rather than talk glibly about accepting responsibility, let us try to fulfill the responsibilities which we have, in the faith that thereby we shall all learn the ways of a material organization in which every man gets what is squarely coming to him. By that I mean each gets the equivalent of what he produces—that is the American ideal." Enders M. Voorhees, chairman of Finance Committee, U. S. Steel Corporation, address, Controllers Institute of America, Sept. 21, 1943.

people cannot be most fully unleashed to use the knowledge that comes from advancing science to enlarge most greatly the wealth of the nation unless volume of production be accepted as the prime objective of economic life and price as merely the expression of trading ratios which conform to such full-scale activity.

It may be objected that to attach so much importance to a single principle in the operation of our business system is simply to revive the naive concept of the "Invisible Hand" from an earlier day, but in the midst of conditions to which it is even more palpably inapplicable. Such a possible objection may be answered very briefly.

While Adam Smith's doctrine of the Invisible Hand probably had deistic connotations, it did not mean that God whispered the answer in each man's ear whenever he had a decision to make. Instead, this professor of moral philosophy noted first that men in general were endowed by their creator with a spirit of ambition, a basic instinct of selfishness, and the common sense that enabled them to select the bigger of two apples. This being so, he reasoned that so long as everyone was free to make his own choices in situations as to whose personal values he was better informed than anyone else could be, the system would be highly active and move flexibly toward steadily greater satisfactions.

Adam Smith accepted self-interest as the basis of his economic philosophy. "It is not," he said, "from the benevolence of the butcher, the brewer, or the baker that we expect our dinner, but from their regard to their own interest." It was, moreover, a purely naive or automatic self-interest—hence universally to be depended upon under a system of complete *laissez faire*. Today the conditions of business life have become more complex with the growth of the arts and the development of large group organizations as the prevailing pattern of business life. Many persons have the range of their personal decisions very much circumscribed, whereas a few have power to make decisions of the most far-reaching consequences to others. It is the attempt to discharge these over-all functions of business direction on the plane of intuitive reactions of immediate self-interest that causes many of the frictions and partial breakdowns of contemporary economic life.

Adam Smith's recognition of self-interest as a perennial and dependable spring of human conduct is as true today as it was in his time. But the operation of self-interest on the part of officials of a highly organized economy must be on the basis of truly enlightened self-interest if the system is not to destroy itself—and hence its administrators. It must be advanced through promotion of the common interest, not at the expense of others' interests. Along with centralizations of decision making, there must go a development of great professional competence and disciplined responsibility so that power shall be used to promote democratic economic opportunity, high production, and high-level consumption.

The hand that directs such activity is seen and very human. The process is conscious and must be guided by sincere study of the principles of economic production, not merely the tricks of personal acquisition.

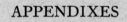

APPENDIXES

APPENDIX A

THE ROLE OF PRICE POLICY IN BUSINESS MANAGEMENT[1]

While, of course, the conditioning environment imposes rigorous limitations on the price administrator's freedom of action[2] in a capitalistic society dedicated to "free enterprise," he devises and implements business plans in ways broadly similar to those of military command. A general must operate within the limitations of the terrain on which he fights and of the personnel and material at his disposal—to say nothing of meteorological conditions. But at the same time, much depends too on the strategy which he and the high command devise and the specific tactics by which he and his officers seek to carry it out. It seems appropriate, therefore, to discuss price policy in terms of business strategy and tactics.

PRICE POLICY AND BUSINESS STRATEGY

Perhaps the simplest distinction that leaps to the mind to elucidate the relationship between price strategy and price tactics is that the former concerns the price *level* for the given firm or industry and the latter its price *structure*. This, however, is rather too simple. Price level is only a statistical artifact

[1] Excerpted from an article, "The Meaning of Price Policy" published by the author of this book in the February 1941 issue of the *Quarterly Journal of Economics*.

[2] The introductory part of this article, which is here omitted, considered the earlier background of institutionalism and statistical studies of price "behavior." It suggested that while these deterministic factors were not to be neglected, our analysis of the price-making process needed to be rounded out by taking account of the personal factor introduced by the business executive as "rationalistic innovation."

and is not a concept that is much used in actual business administration. In some raw material or semi-finished product industries, "base" prices do reflect the price level idea. But for a great number of diversified producers, particular lines of goods, particular outlets, and particular transactions or operating periods crowd the foreground of the business stage. Even in such concerns, operating under conditions of monopolistic competition or oligopoly, there are questions of grand and lesser strategy to be decided which, beyond their bearing on the profitableness of the firm's operations, affect in important ways the functioning of the economy.

In broadest terms, it may be said that businessmen have only one policy, and that is to make money. It could be said with equal truth that a commander and his staff have only one policy, and that is to achieve victory. But given a general objective, policy must devise its grand strategy as a program for attaining that end. This involves determination of the general types of goods to be produced, the range of styles or models, financing, and organization of the business. On their price side, these operating policies converge on certain major and relatively long-run decisions which affect the general scale of prices to be charged by the company as the theoretical and experimental solution of a problem whose factors involve the twin issue of volumes of output and spread between price and costs—"manufacturer's margin" or "distributor's margin." The problem of "margin" at once sets the executive and his cost accountants and production managers and research workers to considering a wide range of matters covering management efficiency, plant utilization, alternative techniques, economic size, location of plants, and degree of integration. These in turn raise issues of labor displacement, wage incentives, and investment needs. If he starts from the side of volume, he is concerned primarily with purchasing power and its distribution, relative response to sales pressure or to price appeal, and possibilities of segregating his market from others by any one of a variety of schemes of product or service differentiation.

Obviously the two halves of the profit question—volume and margin—are closely intertwined. This is true both in the businessman's sense that the number of units sold responds in various ways to the price charged and also in the economist's sense that the scheme of prices for the various economic goods will determine how fully society's resources are utilized in supplying our wants. When important basic industries—steel, copper, automobiles, electric power, food products—are dominated by a few very large corporations, the price decisions of a small number of executives, accompanied by compendent decisions as to wage rates, volume of employment, capital accumulation, choice of technique, amount and timing of investment, and the like, are the basic determinants of the manner in which the whole economy is to function. As military strategy can be broadly divided into defensive and offensive, so major price strategy falls naturally under two heads, adaptive and creative. In the former, the executive uses his own brains and the resources of his organization to work out the best adjustment of his prices to existing conditions of technique, both physical and organizational. In the second he carries the war into the enemy's country and attempts to advance the fortunes of his firm by improvements in technique or organization which will permit of constructive changes in the price structure. Today, the impact of scientific advance is so great as to make this latter type of price policy characteristic of a large part of the industrial scene. In so far as this offensive rather than defensive strategy is adopted, in so far as price policy becomes creative rather than adaptive,

. . . industrial price-making . . . instead of passively accepting the market's pricing of a supply subject to no central control . . . sets a price objective and directs a controlled productive mechanism toward attainment of that price level. With this change the price-making executive takes over from the "Unseen Hand" as guide and regulator of the economic process in a considerable part of our business world. He takes upon himself the responsibility for the standard of living for an ever-larger proportion of our people. Much as he generally hates the phrase, he becomes in fact the economic planner of our society rather than merely the adapter of his personal affairs as best he can to a largely automatic price mechanism.[3]

At this point, however, the objection may be raised that the business executive is not a free agent but that decisions nominally his are in fact dictated by his banker, the machinery of his trade association, or the officials of some regulatory agency.[4] It is true, of course, that here we find one executive accepting the formulation of his price program by his commercial or investment banker. But there another executive may, like Ford, succeed in inaugurating an independent scheme of prices divergent from the existing pattern but expressing an internally coherent strategy of price, technique, investment, employment, wage rates, and purchasing power.[5] If, in a given case, the decision is that of the banker (or of the trade association, or the regulatory agency), this does not negative the idea of policy as a price-making factor. It simply modifies the chart of dispersion of this function. It sets us to examining the rationale according to which the banker or counsellor or commissioner decides that maintenance of wide margins or restricted volume is desirable, or that investment in labor-saving machinery shall be expanded, or settles other similar matters. Furthermore, questions of price policy, instead of being shifted to functionaries above the titular top executives of the company, may be shifted downward also to minor executives or to employees of relatively minor rank. In a general way, this is true of matters which fall below the level of grand strategy to those of minor strategy and of commercial tactics. We shall pass on, therefore, to survey briefly

[3] E. G. Nourse and H. B. Drury, *Industrial Price Policies and Economic Progress*, pp. 253-54.
[4] Or by other factors in his business environment, and hence that executive discretion is only a sort of higher behaviorism.
[5] Theoretical examination of the nature of monopolistic competition has been useful in showing the range of choices open to a firm on the assumption of certain forecasts of the course which other firms will pursue in given situations. To be complete, the theory must examine the way in which alternative courses are discovered and explored as a basis of choice and must study the *a priori* prospects and *a posteriori* results of policies which undertake constructive alteration of the market situation through a comprehensive price-production-investment policy.

these other gradations in the hierarchy of price policies.

After a military high command has decided whether it is to wage an offensive or a defensive war, *blitzkrieg* or war of attrition, it must proceed to matters of minor strategy—particular objectives, time schedules, the use and co-ordination of branches of the service, and particular implements of warfare. Similarly, after the major questions of price maintenance versus maximum technical progress and price reduction, price or non-price competition, and the like have been decided, management must proceed to minor questions of price strategy, such as the exclusion of all unprofitable lines or the intention of maintaining itself in a position to serve all the needs of a certain clientele, the eschewing of discriminatory prices or the use of some scheme of purposive differentials, the exercise or the acceptance of price leadership or the adoption of some studied course of individual pricing. Just where the line between minor strategy and major tactics begins, it would be difficult to say and probably fruitless to attempt to decide.

PRICE POLICY AND COMMERCIAL TACTICS

That we recognize at least a qualitative difference between broader decisions which establish general principles to be followed over a wide area and a considerable period of time and *ad hoc* actions to meet particular situations of great variety and others, which, though not unique, are constantly changing, is fairly evident. Particular tactics however good do not add up to a strategy or render a general plan superfluous. Good tactics in the specific situation, however, are essential to the success of the grand strategy.[6] Similarly, the price administrator cannot be content with an answer merely to what his general pricing principles should be. With plants distributed in a given way, a wide range of productive techniques and marketing practices open to him, with consumers dispersed in various income categories, and with varying tastes, attitudes, and spending habits and propensities, the attainment of a given level of prices will

[6] Sir Edward Hamley makes the distinction: "The theater of war is the province of *strategy;* the field of battle is the province of *tactics.*"

be influenced greatly by the shrewdness and ingenuity of his commercial tactics in devising schemes of quality differentiation, sales and service procedure, and settlement terms. The list of pricing practices in this broad sense which are amenable to policy decision is long. The details of differential pricing, instalment or other credit selling, seasonal patterns, full-line forcing, and a great variety of matters of advertising, high or low-pressure salesmanship, and various quality, service, and premium adjuncts recall the more familiar categories. In its ultimate development as minor tactics, pricing comes down to the thousands of individual prices of parts sold by a machinery company, the preparation of the thousand-page catalogue of a great mail-order house, the writing of price tags and planning of "sales" in a store or shop, and the making of particular deals by traveling salesmen.[7]

Here the distinction is very fine between positive price policy and routine pricing procedure. In a large corporation, with possibly thousands of individual quotations to be promulgated, it is of course quite out of the question for any top executive or group of upper flight men to give personal attention to the calculation of these myriad prices. What, then, shall be the scheme of price ingredients and the general rules of compila-

[7] This involves the somewhat curious point made by Mason (*American Economic Review*, Supplement, March 1933, p. 61) that it "serves no useful purpose to attribute a price policy" unless the seller or buyer "customarily conducts his operations by means of a quoted price." Certainly the prices quoted in the Sears Roebuck catalogue faithfully reflect whatever price policy the company has, but the quotations of an iron and steel company are practically meaningless if it is the policy of the company to meet competition in such a way as "to get its share of the business" or to use price as a weapon for expanding its position. Similarly, quoted prices in the sense here used are not possible for a firm doing contract or custom work and yet it may have a very definite and conscious price policy. His point that one who sells "at the market" cannot have a price policy emphasizes the external form of the transaction rather than its inner character. Such a transaction does not mean that the seller will release his entire product or the buyer supply his whole need regardless of market fluctuations. The order is for *a given quantity* "at the market," reflecting the policy of the buyer or seller to make transactions of that amount regardless of such small change in price as he believes the market may make before his transaction is consummated.

tion by which the final catalogue of prices shall be derived from base prices, extras, service charges, cost allocations, and what not? And what delegations of price-making authority shall be made to minor executives, of what sort of education and experience, of what professional titles and personal predilections, and under what rules or principles of discretion? These matters of procedure will influence in important ways the manner in which a policy formulated in general terms at the top comes ultimately to express itself in prices actually realized in the market.[8] It will determine too in no small degree the impression which top executives will derive as to the consequences—in terms of buyer response or plant operation—that flow from a given course of action.[9]

In sum, then, the discretionary factor in price-making shows at times or places a high degree of concentration and at other times or places a great amount of diffusion. The way in which carefully devised strategies are implemented through consistent local action and the way in which well- or ill-conceived major policies are wrecked or are mitigated by the considered or casual divergence of subordinates' pricing practices, all are strands weaving together into the full fabric of business policy as a factor in price determination.

SCOPE AND METHOD OF BUSINESS PRICE POLICY STUDIES

This general description of the field covered by business price policy may be illuminated by considering the scope and methods of the research program by which policy aspects of the price-

[8] R. A. Gordon discusses the relation of corporate structure to the development and execution of business policies. *Business Leadership in the Large Corporation* (in press).

[9] A particular phase of the question of delegation of price-making authority relates to the administrative scheme of a large corporation having numerous subsidiaries or branch plants. Shall basic price policy be decided at the central administrative headquarters (with or without participation by local executives) with some or no leeway given in local application? Or shall the initiation and character of price changes be left to local authority subject to review or veto at headquarters? The difference in the weighting given to considerations of investment, change in operative organization, consumer peculiarities, and other pertinent factors under the several procedures is obvious.

making process can be brought within the ambit of the economist's attention and understanding. Here the task divides, as in the case of price behavior, into two general divisions—first, portrayal; second, analysis.

If the task is to be reduced to manageable form and subjected to workmanlike processes of study, the task of portrayal can be docketed under three heads. First there must be an array of the actual prices to be considered. The only comment needed here is that in such work we are not dealing with index numbers, prices in the mass, or published quotations, which make up the typical raw material of price behavior studies. For our purposes, we must have price realization in specific transactions or clearly defined situations.[1] Second, we must relate the price realization to the scheme of quotation, base prices, extras, allowances, discounts, "deals," attendant services, and what not by which the whole structure of prices as between buyers and over seasonal or other significant time periods is made up. Third, we must make explicit the scheme of thinking of all the parties, superior and subordinate, who exercise judgment, formulate a rule, or accept a routine of procedure by which these particular prices are given this precise character in the face of the total market situations which form their setting.[2]

It is the devising of methods capable of producing results in the third phase of this task which presents to us the greatest challenge.[3] The task of "capture and recording" is rendered particularly difficult because of the vast amount of ephemeral data involved, and the hypersensitivity of businessmen in general to outside scrutiny. The businessman has a rich but weedy field of experiential data, a wealth of shrewd knowledge of

[1] And even here, only those sets of prices for which we can secure also those other types of data which are essential for the analytical process toward which portrayal is only the first step.
[2] The portrayal of this setting itself, though not a part of price policy studies as such, is a necessary preliminary to the analytical phase of the task.
[3] The second phase, though important and interrelated, is more baldly factual in character, and the first is shared by many types of price investigators.

behavior both of consumers and of his fellow producers and distributors, but also intuitive rather than analytical habits of dealing with this experience and a heavy load of prejudices and fallacious notions about economic cause and effect. He may or may not give evidence of an appreciation of the possibility and usefulness of making his particularized experience accessible to scientifically trained analysts. The realistic economist and the sophisticated businessman will have to work out more mutual respect and forbearance before we can array from this field the empirical data needed in the formulation of realistic and adequate generalizations.

Early theory cramped itself by using in its analysis of atomistic competition an unreal and oversimplified "economic man." Current theory is no less weak in its attempts to explain oligopoly and monopolistic competition in terms of "the entrepreneur" vaguely sketched and naïvely conventionalized beyond recognition in the business world. We need to add realism and detail to this picture. The content of the executive's thinking, his personality, and the organization in which and through which he operates become matters of deep significance. Seeking objective study of this category of subjective factors in price-making, we cannot pursue our goal by making case histories of the training and business experience of executives en masse, get formal expositions of their views as to how the economic system works, and supplement these by personality tests and perhaps a psychiatrist's analysis. Though all these would be the scientifically indicated procedure, we must be content with less intensive examination of selected samples. Much light may be derived from careful study of a moderate number of careers of outstanding leaders and conspicuous atavists. Further analysis of the problem might suggest a manageable number of types, or a scheme of sampling might be devised which would give us, at the very least, a basis for understanding the part played by the policy-making executive much truer and more illuminating than anything we now have.[4]

[4] Biographical studies of Rockefeller, Carnegie, Ford, Chrysler, and Sloan afford some materials of value. But these were written by journal-

Business leaders are steadily becoming more articulate, and the growing literature of business management includes considerable transcripts of the economic and business philosophy of such men as Sloan, Weir, Kendall, Batt, Prentiss, and Chester.[5] Obviously such public utterances, though they give side-lights on the thinking of these leaders, are not adequate for our purpose. They do not follow such an outline of analysis as the economist would propose. Nor are they always to be taken at face value. Thus, the president of a great tire company uses large advertising space to announce a sweeping reduction in tire prices made possible by improvement in production methods. On closer reading, it appears that the cut in quotations is in part an expression of a revision in dealer relations. How much it will mean in price realized for the manufacturer will become clear only after detailed study.

Company announcements, annual reports, public addresses, autobiographies, however, are all "human documents" which by their defects and omissions as well as by their positive contributions give us essential elements of the knowledge we seek, their evidential value depending upon the skill and rigor of the methods developed for their interpretation. In our sister disciplines, sociology and psychology, attention is being given to this

---

ists for the popular reader or by a historian and their authors did not ask the right questions for the economist's purpose. Miss Beard's *A History of the Business Man* missed a glorious opportunity and Barnard's *The Functions of the Executive* became lost in sociological conceptualism. Furthermore, other executives, big and little, would need to be added to fill in the picture, give it geographical and time perspective.

[5] Henry S. Dennison, besides the collaboration with an economist already referred to, collaborated with three fellow industrialists, Morris Leeds, Ralph Flanders, and Lincoln Filene on a volume, *Toward Full Employment*, published in 1938. Edward A. Filene published *The Way Out* in 1925 and *Successful Living in This Machine Age* in 1931, and a posthumous collection of his speeches and articles appeared in 1939 under the title, *Speaking of Change*. Some twenty business executives, along with an attorney and a business college dean, contributed chapters to a volume *The New Outlook in Business* which appeared in 1940. Important material for studies of price policy as well as price behavior has been made available in connection with the hearings and related investigations of the T.N.E.C.

problem of the use of "human" or personal documents in the social sciences in that vague but indispensable field of probative values which lies beyond the realm of objective evidence amenable to statistical or abstractly logical checking. Perhaps principles of analysis and rules of evidence will be developed which will enable us to derive insights from such studies not less important than the "proofs" that the more ardent devotees of quantification believe they derive from statistical methods. In view of the admitted inaccuracy of such documents in their raw state, it is worth remembering that most of the basic data to which the statistician must resort are notoriously inaccurate and inadequate as documentation of the facts sought.

In investigating the thought and purpose of the executive as a phase of the price-making process, we must not forget the point already made that this rationalistic factor is widely diffused throughout the business structure and that significant innovations in the lower ranks may negative the purely behavioristic response of top executives. Or, vice versa, constructive efforts emanating from the top may be paralyzed or distorted by cross-currents of thought and effort elsewhere in the organization or simply stalled by friction developing at these points. Students of price policy, therefore, will need to cover this whole gamut of the executive function. Of particular concern must be the recent but increasing development of research on price and related problems which has appeared in many of our industrial organization.[6] Sometimes it is specialized in a particular division, sometimes scattered among cost accounting, marketing, or even operative departments. Not merely must the content and method of such investigational work within the corporate structures be studied but, likewise, the extent to which and the manner in which results so developed become influential in the thought and action of officials and employees clothed with some measure of price-making authority.

Attempting, as we have, to delineate the portrayal phase of

[6] The National Resources Planning Board has recently published a study on this subject under the title: *Research—A National Resource. III. Business Research.*

price policy studies, we pass almost insensibly over to the analysis phases. For we cannot discover and set forth the thinking, the prejudice, and the conventionalization which characterize the executive's role in choosing or creating a line of price action without such selection and grouping of material as implies some analytical consideration of the economic processes which form the context of these data. On the foundation laid by industrious and skillful portrayal of price action and its rationale in the executive hierarchy, price policy studies should proceed to the most rigorous examination of the actual effects of such relief, reasoning, or experimentation upon the functioning of the price system and its relation with and influences upon the rest of the economic system.[7] In the metaphor of price as the nervous

[7] Edward Mason warns against dangers in this realm, particularly the attempt to trace the effect upon the price maker of a sleepless night, a good meal, or his domestic relations. But this good counsel is overdone if it urges us to fall back upon deterministic studies of "market situations" in whose fell grip the executive is conceived as but a robot. Mason himself, while using the phrase "price policy," has a habit of linking it in the joint phrase "price behavior and price policy"—as in "damn-yankee." Price policy to him evidently means only that executive action which has become stereotyped. This is the behavioristic fringe of what I would call pricing practice to distinguish it from constructive or innovating policy. Mason makes approach to price policy studies through "classification of [deterministic] market situations," saying:

"The statistical approach [sic!] to price policy starts with an examination of price behavior and then proceeds to correlate various measures of price change with changes in other economic variables . . . an adequate analysis of price and production policies requires consideration of (a) the influence of the organization of a firm on the character of the firm's reaction to given market situations; and of (b) elements of market structure which include many more things than numbers and product differentiation. It goes without saying that a realistic treatment of these questions necessitates the use of analytical tools which are amenable to empirical application. The problem, as I see it, is to reduce the voluminous data concerning industrial organization to some sort of order through a classification of market structures. Differences in market structure are ultimately explicable in terms of technological factors. The economic problem, however, is to explain, through an examination of the structure of markets and the organization of firms, differences in competitive practices including price, production, and investment policies. . . . No doubt Messrs. Ford and Firestone set the impress of their personalities on the policies of their respective industries, but the larger problem for economists to consider is the impress of large-system within the body economic, we recognize that there are in that nervous system many motor reflexes which are not under the control of reason or volition, but we are here concerned with that aspect of the nervous system of economic life which centers in the organizational equivalent of the brain or at most the subordinate control centers analogous to the higher nerve ganglia.

Price policy studies should show the way in which the factor of rationalistic guidance fits into the operation of business concerns within the structure provided through institutions created and undergoing modification in response to public price policy. This involves several fields of analytical specialization such as the relation of price policy to techniques, to the classes of goods produced in order to tap demands of various income groups, to the wage level and wage structure as related to the adjustment of purchasing power, to investment as related both to the progress of technique and the provision of savings out of operating revenue, or the determination of their magnitude and direction through the channel of individual voluntary savings, and finally to the volume and character of employment growing out of these interrelated adjustments. Having started from study of the sources and composition of price policy and proceeded through examination of its operational manifestations, we must follow these specific courses of action through to their effects upon the fortunes of the given firm and the well-being of the economy of which it is a functional part.[8]

---

scale business organizations on the character and functioning of the management groups that are called to control positions. . . . While the personality of Firestone, plus the fact that his firm is admittedly a low cost producer, has no doubt been an important factor, it seems probable that if Firestone, like God in another context, had not existed the structure of the tire market would have created him." *American Economic Review*, Pt. 2 (Supplement) March 1939, pp. 65, 66, 68, 71.

[8] All these analyses must include consideration of the youth or maturity of the firm whose policy is being studied and the character of the product, new or old, producer's or consumer's good.

APPENDIX B

DEMOCRACY AS A PRINCIPLE OF BUSINESS[1]

Throughout the decade before the war broke out, the democracies were being told by the protagonists of other patterns of political organization that democracy does not work in the economic sphere. Foreign dictators taunted us in those prewar years with our excessive unemployment and the want which existed amidst the plenty of our productive resources. Though their own systems may even now be tottering toward their fall, there has been a widespread fear even among ourselves that we must renounce the democratic way in the struggle to defeat anti-democracy. It has been alleged that besides being too slow in action, democracy conduces to hoarding that capital which is the life-blood of modern industry, that democracy is wasteful of resources—both natural and human—that democracy is planless and clumsy.

Such aspersions upon the economic system we have built within the framework of democracy have aroused in the minds of many Americans a consuming resentment, in the minds of others a confusing doubt. On how solid ground, then, does the faith of the faithful rest? And do the doubts of the uncertain stem from weakness in the democratic principle or from our own shortcomings in reducing it to practice?

In putting the special questions that the economist asks of democracy we focus attention first on the problem of how relatively scarce resources, both human and natural, can be administered to produce for the whole mass of a society—a nation functioning within the structure of its international relations—the largest possible amount of such material goods and services as its people crave. This requires such an economic organization as will draw out the largest and most effective labor contribution

[1] This appendix appeared as an article in the *Yale Review*, Spring Number, 1942. It is reproduced here (with very slight editorial changes) with the kind permission of the editors of the *Review*.

from the whole population. It demands also such property relationships as will put natural resources and tool equipment fully at the disposal of this labor force, but in such ways that they will be both skilfully and providently employed for the general welfare.

THE DEMOCRACY OF LABOR

Let us inquire first into the labor aspect of the economic problem. It seems axiomatic that if the productivity of a society is to be brought to full tide, we must draw out our whole labor force. Particular concern is directed toward discovering and placing at strategic posts persons of relatively rare qualities. Such are the scientist, the administrator, the salesman, the promoter, the leader of men. But equally indispensable in an economic scheme of labor utilization are the operatives who possess a wide range of distinctive proficiencies based on manual dexterity, accuracy, or speed rather than superior mental ability or flair for directing human relations.

For the most effective recruitment of our labor force, we must go from top to bottom of our population. We must sift it clear through for all those people who have distinctive qualities which are needed to realize the productivity of the complex mechanism which is modern economic life. One thing that the history of the human family has shown and that the researches of science have confirmed and illuminated is that the Lord of Creation was genetically democratic. He scattered physical endowments, mental aptitudes, and artistic genius with a fine impartiality. The record of great scientists, artists, statesmen, musicians, inventors, and executives who have come from the home of the peasant or working man is too impressive to be forgotten. It would seem that, at least in America, this part of the democratic lesson has been well learned though we still must better our means of identifying distinctive abilities and aptitudes of our youth at an early age.

Even after the discovery of special kinds of labor fitness has been made, there still remains the problem of training—not only the specialized training of those who may go on to the top but also the other kinds of training for those who stop at stations all along the way. Broader and more general training than we now have for the great mass of the population is necessary that these people too may be equipped to develop fully their native capacities.

From the beginning in America, we have been working consistently to put this lesson of democracy of labor into practice, and we are still extending the area of its application. The excellent start made under our system of universal free public education extended rapidly beyond the elementary stage to embrace high schools, secondary trade schools, state and municipal universities with their professional schools, free or low-cost instruction in art and music, free lectures and concerts, and a wide variety of types of adult education. Our military service has had a considerable amount of technical training infused into it, and, in the last decade, the C.C.C. camps have been developed into agencies for improving physical fitness and giving vocational training instead of permitting physical deterioration and character demoralization during periods of unemployment.

To the economist these developments must in general commend themselves as an economical way of conserving valuable human resources and of utilizing the economies of standardization and specialization in preparing these raw materials for use in the process of production. . . . But if, with this promising basis for economic democracy in its labor phase, we are to rear a fully democratic system, not only must labor capacity be developed but also labor opportunity must be made available. This brings us back to consideration of what in fact is meant today by freedom of economic enterprise.

As the phrase was used in the period of Colonial settlement and early national expansion before the growth of modern industrialism, it voiced a demand that each individual should be allowed to embark on farming, trade, or handicraft production without let or hindrance from some feudal lord or other holder of exclusive right or restrictive franchise. This kind of free enterprise was readily attainable in a land of unexploited natural resources and with techniques of production still so little industrialized that new producers could gain a footing with only their small individual resources.

That sort of free enterprise is no longer possible over a substantial part of our economy. But the democratic principle of economic enterprise, with inevitable modifications in form, has survived the shift from the individual proprietorship or small partnership to the giant corporation. Top-flight executives and technicians today are characteristically those who as young men started at the bottom, without inherited wealth or special advantages outside the system of free public schools and subsidized universities. For the most part, they have been selected, promoted, and finally entrusted with posts of greatest opportunity and responsibility because "they had what it takes." Profit-seeking business cannot afford to be run on any other principle.

It is not strange that these children of success should have their minds so filled with the satisfactory and effective aspects of the system through which they rose that they are inclined to ascribe to it the qualities of perfection. They feel that the condition under which a lad could start from scratch, with nothing but talent and ambition, and win his way to the top of our business organization should not be destroyed by any scheme of hereditary power or political bureaucracy. And in this position every economist must stand squarely with them. But when they assume that this is all that is needed for a satisfactory personnel system—instead of being merely one indispensable ingredient of it—then they and the economist must part company. He must insist on some procedure that provides not merely for the exceptional few but equally well, according to their capacities, for the less richly endowed many.

The freedom of enterprise which permits the gifted home-town boy to "make good" has abolished the monopolistic aristocracy of birth and to a large extent the aristocracy of amassed wealth. It has substituted a competitive aristocracy of talent and aggressiveness. That is a step in the right direction, but it is not the achievement of full economic democracy in its labor aspect. A further condition to the achievement of full labor democracy would be that those who fall below the level of executive rank still should have the chance of some active participation in the life of business.

In his search for efficiency of labor use, the economist has long stressed such division of labor as will distribute specialized tasks according to the native endowments and training of the workers. But even this good principle may be carried to a self-defeating extreme. I suspect that just this result follows when the voices of only one or two per cent of the personnel may be heard in business management. The prevailing aristocratic theory of organization implies that the labor personnel have only strong backs and nimble fingers to bring to the service of the business and that all the strong minds and nimble wits are in the upstairs office. This water-tight separation leads to two bad results—it impairs the morale of labor and it gives a partial and lop-sided view to management.

There is no need to press the point that labor is not the same as equipment, to be turned on or off by an electric switch or a steam throttle. If the sense of business enterprise gives man an indispensable stimulus to industry and ambition, as we are told and as we believe, is it not important to diffuse that vitalizing force as fully as possible through the ranks of labor? It is a bit puzzling to find businessmen who loudly extol the stimulating value of business enterprise, saying with equal certainty that the majority of those who form the actual population of the business domain should be denied even an advisory part in the making of decisions that deeply concern their welfare.

There seems a trace of inconsistency when those who have "arrived" by the process of promotion from the ranks vaunt the soundness of their own qualities and the brilliance of their achievement and yet repudiate the idea that they could profit by the counsel of their fellows who are still in the ranks. Do they not consider that they themselves had good intelligence and sound ideas before the day of their preferment? Instead of allowing labor to sink to the level of unpalatable routine, would it not be more sensible to invigorate it with a greater sense of personal enterprise? Is not the worker likely to be a better operative if he is not completely divorced from the thrill, the enlightenment, the worry that come from even small-scale management?

But even if it be conceded that a wider application of the doctrine of economic enterprise would be good for the worker, would it not be hard on the business? Perhaps it might be good for it. The ready argument that labor is not sufficiently intelligent or well informed to have a tenable judgment on the questions that confront management is somewhat offset by the fact that rather glaring mistakes of judgment are often made by executives themselves.

The making of sound business policies is a complex task which involves a wide variety of considerations. Good judgment about these widely varied aspects of the complete business problem can be developed only on the basis of intimate knowledge of all the facts at first hand. The safe executive is one who buttresses his own opinion with the counsel of all the persons who are in a position to have pertinent observations. The president or manager in his office can get a bird's-eye view of many large considerations beyond the ken of travelling salesmen, office worker, or plant employee. But the latter can get a close-up view of many minute details which together have a tremendous impact on efficiency and profitableness—details inevitably hidden from the remote executive—remote not only from such details but also from sight and understanding of such important facts as workers' attitudes, aspirations, and frustrations.

Let us suppose some representative system is devised by which all who are actively interested shall be able to participate in business enterprise. Perhaps less importance is to be attached to the bits of information and understanding the president or directors might thus get from the workers than to the wisdom that might be borne back from them to workers. If all those whose livelihood is dependent on the success of a business be given opportunity to discuss situations and problems freely together, there is hope of mutual understanding of how everyone's bread is buttered. Representative spokesmen of wage earners returning from such conference would make for sound and conservative attitudes among their fellows when the rabble rouser who sometimes takes the place of intellectual leader in the hierarchy of union organization, would seek to lead labor on paths of self-destruction.

If working people are left in ignorance as to the true needs of business, that ignorance will express itself no less actively and probably somewhat more dangerously in the action that they take through their unions and through their endorsement of politicians and political proposals than it would if they were participating in a comprehensive discussion of business problems within the administrative system of the business on which they are dependent.

Some employers have already moderated the aristocratic claims of management and are seeking through a democracy of business enterprise to bring thoughtful and constructive participation to the masses, disfranchised under the predominant interpretation of free enterprise in business. Do they find labor so organized and thinking along such lines of economic democracy as would make for harmonious and effective attack on the basic problem of maximum production? Too often, no.

THE ARISTOCRACY OF LABOR

While labor organization has set greater democracy in the distribution of wealth as its goal, it has also kept its face turned backward toward aristocratic patterns of procedure. Faced by the opposition of the hard-boiled school of business which has asserted that policies are no concern of labor, the union movement has concentrated its efforts on an acquisitive struggle rather than the constructive possibilities of a business partnership. Militant unionism has run true to the non-democratic tendency of all fighting bodies. Notoriously has this been the case with the railroad brotherhoods, and it is broadly true in building trades, printing trades, and the whole hierarchy of skilled crafts. Workers of higher skills, greater education, or less patience organized themselves into groups to exploit whatever "scarcity value" their distinctive talents had or to create a strategic scarcity by the very devices of their organization.

While a few of the younger leaders have attained a broader vision of their task in terms of economic statesmanship, the older men still conceive of themselves as war lords of the labor battalions, indulging in local jurisdictional brawls, collecting war chests for major future campaigns, or conducting guerilla warfare which has frequently endangered the success of enterprises which all knew were essential to the economic health of the country, or even its safety after war came.

With the partial transition from trade unions to labor unionism, a great stride has been taken toward equal concern for the economically weaker members of the labor force. But this rise of industrial unionism has itself developed rival factions within the labor field, with a struggle of leaders for personal prestige and power intermingled with a clash of ideologies that threatens to submerge the welfare of the rank-and-file worker. As an economic institution, the union should exist for the worker, not the worker for the union. Members should have the right of free speech (without fear) in the councils of both local and central unions and the secret ballot as a means of registering their personal views on policy, finances, and action.

Since their own incomes must in the last analysis be closely identified with the total productivity of the economic system, workers must not allow themselves to be drafted to blind support of whatever strategy of force may be advocated by leaders who rely on power politics rather than policies constructively conceived in the general interest. Permanent economic adjustment, rather than an endless succession of costly strikes and fragile settlements, demands that such "leaders" be removed or converted to new lines of effort.

Such change of leadership should be followed by comprehensive examination of basic issues. What determines the demand for labor, what are the facts as to its supply both quantitative and qualitative, and how must it be priced if the market is to be developed to its maximum possibilities? Labor leaders, not less than executive managers, may have their perspective impaired by remoteness from the hopes and fears and aspirations of the actual worker—a defect for which democratic reconsideration of basic facts and economic principles is the indicated remedy.

In economic principle quite as much as democratic theory, labor rewards should be differentiated as closely as possible in accordance with ascertainable or measurable differences in the productivity of the respective workers. I strongly suspect that, under the prevailing mixture of labor autonomy and management autocracy, the range in payments for services is considerably too wide for a smoothly functioning economy. Differentials are probably too great between certain skilled trades and other proficiencies neither less difficult to acquire nor less important in determining productivity of industrial processes. The so-called employer is generally himself a white-collared worker as well as a capitalist or deputy for capital. Are the salary rates of top-flight executives—in unions as well as corporations—soundly based on personal contributions to productivity as compared with results due to the efforts of minor but indispensable supervisory agents? And what of the productive value of men of scientific training and inventive ability, whose salaries are meager in comparison with those of the upper executive hierarchy?

There is something essentially non-democratic in policies or programs that produce high wage rates for those in strategic positions to protect their own employment while leaving many of the less well situated out of jobs. The attaining of employment for all who want to work would be a major objective of any truly democratic union movement. If such an end is to be attained, labor must be offered in the market at prices at which employers can afford to use it. If the labor of the aristocracy of the building trades is forced up to twelve or fifteen or eighteen dollars a day and the volume of construction shrinks, unemployment is forced upon semi-skilled workers and common laborers clear down the scale of dependent industries to the lowliest mine helper or saw mill laborer. But if such a structure of wages and salaries is to be set up as will promote full employment, the process of education and group consultation already touched upon in our discussion of labor's relation to management must be enlarged and intensified from the labor side.

Under compete freedom of speech we have not merely permitted but have done much to promote continuous re-examination of all the questions of public policy, taste, or morals in which an alert and intelligent people become interested. Many specialized groups have developed professional associations for periodic or continuous consideration of the technical problems of their craft. Though a beginning in economic education has been made by some unions, nowhere has provision been made for a great system of adult schools in which the mass of thinking work people could continuously apply their minds to the solving of their own problem.

Here the problem for workers is to learn how to conduct themselves individually and through their organization so as to promote the greatest long-run production for the economic system, to study what changes to ask of management, what proposals to espouse and which to reject in the political and governmental sphere. To labor schools or forums devoted to the rank-and-file study of these problems the best minds from the business management group, from academic ranks, and from government—both legislative and administrative personnel—could well afford to come—to learn and to teach. In fact, they could not afford to stay away.

But even if labor were organized to seek by democratic study and to promote by democratic effort the great basic purposes of making the opportunity to work available to everyone according to his labor capacities, this is but one side of the problem. Workers must have full access to the capital equipment accumulated from their past labor or that of others who have gone before. This brings up the second major problem in our inquiry. How, one may ask, does capital's performance square with the democratic theory of free enterprise?

IS CAPITAL INHERENTLY ARISTOCRATIC?

From one point of view, it would seem that we have dealt in truly democratic fashion with the problem of capital accumulation and use. Our basic law has recognized and protected the right of the individual to set aside any part of his income he may desire in a savings fund in which his rights of property and free disposition are guaranteed. Furthermore, we have set up devices both elaborate and ingenious whereby such savings, from the largest to the smallest in amount, may be accumulated and administered. Drawn from those who cannot employ them profitably in their own work, these savings are channeled through to other points, where large outlays must be made or facilities provided for using the labor of other persons, selected for their working proficiencies rather than their ability to bring the capital needed for their own equipment.

So far, so good. The system has a commendable degree of flexibility. It preserves the inducement to save by rewarding the saver out of the wealth which his saved capital produces when converted into machinery or other forms of equipment. With the development of our blue-sky laws and the S.E.C., the government has shown an intention to provide this high-powered vehicle of finance with such safety devices as will safeguard it from the undue risks which in the past have often interfered with its proper working. But, here, we come to a difficult and controversial issue in the working of our economic mechanisms. A question arises as to whether the principles of democracy need in this area to be somewhat abated in order to produce an effectively operating system.

Certainly the administration of capital funds, once they were accumulated—and accumulated by a widely democratic system —has been distinctly aristocratic. The great democratic mass who contribute through savings banks, insurance companies, bond houses, or brokerage firms to the bonded loan funds or the equity interests represented by stock have a participation in policy-making or control which in practice has been reduced almost to zero. This is a matter of common knowledge which has been illuminatingly documented by Ripley, Berle and Means, and others.

Whether practical remedies for this situation could be devised, and, if so, what these new business devices would prove to be, would involve technical questions of great difficulty far beyond the scope of this article. There would be no occasion to take the trouble necessary for drafting initial measures or securing their adoption and application in practice unless we were as sure as human judgment could make us that greater democracy in our handling of capital relations is desirable in the sense of making for a more productive economic system. Here the most we can do is to look sympathetically but candidly at capitalism as it now operates—that is, before global war engulfed ordinary business.

In the decade of the 1930's we saw enormous amounts of capital which had been accumulated at great sacrifice and which were capable of great addition to our national productivity, lying idle or being given only intermittent or partial employment. The reason for this novel phenomenon ascribed by those who had in their hands the administration of such capital was that the funds could not be so used as to secure a proper rate of return or enjoy necessary security. This assertion, it should be noted, involves two issues—one as to *how* capital may be used, and the other the criterion by which to decide *whether* it shall be used. Can the democratic principle be involved in either of these questions? It lies, in fact, at the very heart of both.

As to how capital is used to promote the highest productivity of a society, the facts of life as lived in an industrial age are, in broad outline, known to everyone. Capital nourishes research, implements invention, provides giant equipment, finances far-flung and intricate systems of integrated production and market distribution. It works while the consumer sleeps, toiling unseen and without reward for one, five, perhaps ten years to bring forth a new or better product to satisfy the wants of men, perhaps only dimly realized in their own minds, but rich in delight and benefit once the wants have been made capable of satisfaction.

The daring and skill with which this process of capitalist free enterprise has raised the standard of living during the last century and a half is plain to anyone who will look about him. The technological triumph has won general acclaim, at times even been overdrawn in such phrases as "miracles of science" and "magic of modern manufacture." But these advancing technologies can come to expression in the service of mankind only through the economic system. Here the record is brilliant but erratic, compounded of both achievement and frustration.

The man on the street who exaggerates his praise of technological "miracles" and "magic" exaggerates too his complaint over the frequently seen shortcomings of business performance, in such phrases as "breakdown of the economic system," "stalled engine," and "business paralysis." The fact, however, remains that enormous amounts of capital already invested in plant and equipment have often worked at low capacity and high cost. Capital funds, whose only excuse for being saved is that they might be invested in productive operations, for long periods (before the present flood of war activity) lay sterile in the banks, investment houses, and insurance companies. Meanwhile, a quarter of the nation's labor force was unable to employ itself or be employed, and a quarter of the wants for which we have the means of satisfaction went unsatisfied. A postwar recrudescence of the problem will come in the form of questions as to how to convert the gigantic defense capacities to the uses of peace.

It is not strange nor is it improper that, in such situations, we look to the capitalist exponents of free enterprise for the answer to our problem of partially unfulfilled opportunity. They answer in all good faith that at times they find no way for the fuller use of these capital resources. Here, however, counsel is divided. While some have advocated digging in and accepting the immobilization of trench warfare, and some have insisted that even retreat is necessary, others have found, and in their own sector have carried out, a policy of aggressive advance. But, whatever their course of action, all these captains of industry, as they have marshalled plants, mobilized workers, and organized selling campaigns, have had at the heart of their strategy a theory and practice of price making.

PRICES FOR THE *DEMOS*

In the peacetime situation most widely characteristic of free business enterprise under private capitalism, corporate executives (with the counsel or subject to the veto of large stockholders, directors, and bankers) "administer" a price system. In so doing they face a dilemma. Prices must be high enough so that operating costs may be recouped and capital continue to answer the mating call of profits. They must be low enough so that consumers' purchasing power shall be able to take all the product that is turned out. The mere mechanics of a working balance require that technological gains be passed on, and the price route is the one by which this can be done most widely and hence effectively.

Thus giving more goods for less money has been the cause and measure of the tremendous advance we have made since the Industrial Revolution. In this country the widespread application of this democratic principle has put good food on the workman's table, smart and durable clothes on his family's backs, a radio in his living room, an electric refrigerator in his kitchen, and a car—luxurious according to the standards of yesterday—waiting at the curb to take him and "the wife" to the movies. Under modern industrial conditions costs are brought down by the use of the labor-saving devices that go with automatic machines, routine operation, mass production. To achieve the economies of mass production, we must have an economy of mass consumption. Democracy thus becomes the life of the market.

But not less amazing than the extent and speed of the achievement already made was the fact that in the prewar years the free enterprise of private capitalism seemed to falter, even at a time when so substantial an area of clearly expressed wants was still unsatisfied, with a great body of capable labor not merely available but eager—even restive, plants operating below capacity, and funds seeking in vain for new investment. In so far as larger output is obtained by putting idle plant capacity into use, it is not difficult to perceive how the fall in unit costs that results from full operation makes possible larger service to the consumer without loss—indeed even with added profit— to the producer. Only one step more remote lies the truth that the absorption of idle labor, by reducing the cost of relief, crime, ill-health, and public disorder, lowers public costs and every-body's tax bill, which in turn means cheaper goods and more consumer purchasing power to absorb them. The leaders of American enterprise have demonstrated that over a large area, the lowering of prices through daring and patient enterprise in mass production has linked the democracy of mass production with expanding profits for producers.

But it would be fatuous to suppose that this is a one-way street. Profits do not increase endlessly through the application of this principle. Indeed, to suppose that such an end would even be desirable reflects a serious lack of understanding of the or-ganic nature of the capitalist economy. It is essential that this member of the productive partnership be rewarded well enough but not too well, be sufficiently well fed and systematically exer-cised as to be always in the pink of condition and dependably rendering his best performance. He must be the lean athlete or the hard-muscled laborer, not the pampered glutton. Hence, if we accept the view that capitalistic enterprise, in order to follow a course which gives maximum employment to both capital and labor, must find ways of pricing product within reach of the purchasing power of a fully employed people, we are brought back to our earlier inquiry as to what the criterion is upon which the decision is made whether or not to give capital the "go" signal.

Here is a problem of the utmost difficulty but of basic importance to the success of our economic system. It is not only natural but perhaps most enlightening to look at it first not in personal terms of the wealthy individual but institutionally in terms of the investment banker, the financier, the specialist who has been entrusted with responsibility as administrator of the funds of others. These people have put in his hands as trustee savings which represent the deprivation of past consumer wants and the hope of future return of principal and interest to provide for their old age or the needs of their dependents. He is bound in fiduciary honor not to release capital except when in his judgment these conditions of safety and proper return have been met.

Under the somewhat favorable conditions of the developmental phase through which capitalism in this country was passing prior to the First World War and with a second blooming that was nipped by the frost of 1929, this control over and responsibility for capital could be delegated by the democratic mass to the aristocratic few with a high measure of success and satisfaction to both parties. But during the decade preceding the Second World War a conjunction of less favorable circumstances brought us to a virtual impasse. We saw a great volume of equipment standing idle and billions of dollars in funds unemployed, funds which would have provided for the maintenance, replacement, and enlargement of this plant and furnished the working capital complementary to it. For such plant and funds to be unemployed meant being unrewarded so far as its owners were concerned, unproductive so far as the nation was concerned. On the other hand, we saw millions of men swelling the ranks of the unemployed—the unproductive—because the system did not give them access to the capital equipment with which they could unleash their labor power to the filling of their unsatisfied wants.

This dilemma cannot be escaped by merely putting blame on the short-sighted policies of organized labor discussed earlier in this article or by charging that labor legislation of recent years has been economically ill-advised or administration of the acts partisan in character. The problem runs deeper than this—down to the most fundamental issues of capitalism and the profit motive. The thought suggests itself that perhaps it was the aristocratic character of twentieth-century capital administration which revealed its weakness in the times of stress after the First World War. With this in mind, it may be well to re-examine the democratic ingredients which functioned efficiently under simpler conditions and which might with careful study and skilful application be made useful even in our complex modern system.

It is sometimes asserted that one of the dangers of large-scale corporation growth in this country is the magnitude of the responsibility which devolves upon the head of a giant concern, creating a tendency to divide responsibility, "pass the buck," and paralyze action. So much is at stake that effort concentrates on not doing anything which might prove to be a mistake rather than on doing those things which, often by their very originality and daring, make for success and progress. It seems quite possible too that those who have taken delegated responsibility for large blocks of amassed capital have adopted rules of necessary reward and safety which are too strict for the vigorous functioning of a capital economy and are in fact higher than those which would be set by the great mass of workers whose savings, direct or indirect, are the actual source of these funds.

One point, so simple that it is perhaps likely to be overlooked, is that the basic reason why capital is accumulated at all is that labor may be more productive. If, then, we withheld capital from use because of paralyzing fears that it may become impaired, or because we think the wage it could earn would be too low, we are defeating that basic purpose and demonstrating the unworkability of such methods of handling private capitalism.

Let us look for a moment at the much simpler conditions of private capitalism and free enterprise which are found at the agricultural and handicraft level of development. At that level the thrifty worker holds down his consumption to the point where there is a margin of savings for the specific purpose of buying a machine or animal, erecting a building, or installing drains, wells, or fences which will increase the productivity of the proprietor's labor and that of his family or work people. If, by any chance, he has on hand any accumulated savings, he is not likely to hesitate to put them into the business because the expected rate of return is one or even several per cent below some ideal standard which he has set in his mind. Nor will he on occasion boggle at taking a substantial risk if it appears to him that by avoiding that risk he will hamper himself or his dependents in their opportunity to work. To protect capital saved from past work at the expense of continued employment which keeps up the stream of wealth production is in this simple situation a palpable case of being "penny wise and pound foolish."

The key to the direct and effective handling of the inter-related problem of capital and labor by farmer or handicraftsman is to be found in the fact that here the responsibility for the labor force and for the capital fund is one and indivisible. The same individual is capitalist, manager, and laborer. In our modern practice of private capitalism and free enterprise the trend has been, in large measure, to divest those who administer the capital fund from responsibility for the employment and material well-being of the labor force as a whole. When this tendency goes far enough, the two parts of the economic process fall apart and its functional integrity is lost. Restoration to this process, as fully as possible, of that democracy of participation, counsel, and control which were found when business units were still relatively small offers the best prospect of regaining the organic wholeness of a society of free enterprise for all.

DEMOCRATIC OBJECTIVES ARE BEST ATTAINED BY DEMOCRATIC METHODS

The process by which such a democratic integration can be accomplished is large and complex. I have sought simply to set forth the nature of the objective and to mark out in broad outline a few of the major paths of adjustment by which it would have to be approached. The actual devising of practical measures, putting them in operation, and revamping them as further experience showed the need would be the continuing task of many men, managers, operatives, legislators, administrators. In stressing democracy as the central theme of such a broadly efficient restoration of private enterprise in the postwar period, I have been speaking in the purely objective terms of economic science. The argument has none of the subjective ardor of the nationalistic patriot who shouts, "Give me liberty or give me death." It is akin rather to the attitude of the engineer who, studying a sputtering engine, a creaking machine, says, "How can these straining efforts, wasteful of power, meager of product, be so released, so freed of avoidable frictions, that output may be most greatly enlarged?"

The economist, with eye single to the achieving of the greatest material well-being for the people as a whole, must reject whatever aristocratic pretentions have survived from earlier master-and-servant attitudes or have grown up amid the militant activities of swift and splendid industrial conquest. The power of our economic machine comes from the working contribution, physical and mental, of all its individual participants. Efficiency demands that we draw this power forth. But all these individuals are centers of personal interest as well as productive capacity. They coalesce in corporate companies, interest groups, economic classes, nationalistic political bodies aligned in every instance between "haves" and "have nots." Rival interests must be compromised to the common good. Democracy is a major biologic principle of economic life because it bases the health of the whole organism on the appropriate nourishment, stimulation, and co-ordination of every cell in its structural and functional relationship, whether it be of bone, tissue, or organ.

Our greatest hope for the end of this war is that world economy may be established on the basis of healthy organic relations among the several nations. We are pleased to talk of this as a federal union of democracies or—to use the older British phrase—commonwealths. But, as the latter term suggests, the strength of such a union will depend largely on the internal strength of its members—the extent to which they are able to settle for their own people the basic problems of class and group interest and to gain full strength through utilizing the resources of all their individual citizens.

APPENDIX C

STATISTICAL TABLES

INDEX NUMBERS OF MONEY WAGES AND WHOLESALE PRICES, 1801–1942
(1926 = 100)

Year	Money Wages[a]		Wholesale Prices[b]		Year	Money Wages[a]		Wholesale Prices[b]	
	Annual Index	3-Year Moving Average	Annual Index	3-Year Moving Average		Annual Index	3-Year Moving Average	Annual Index	3-Year Moving Average
1801..	11.0	—	111.8	—	1851..	17.0	17.0	64.5	63.1
1802..	10.1	10.7	91.8	99.2	1852..	17.0	17.1	62.5	64.5
1803..	11.0	11.3	93.9	95.7	1853..	17.4	17.4	66.4	65.9
1804..	12.9	12.7	101.5	99.9	1854..	17.9	17.9	68.8	68.0
1805..	14.2	13.6	104.2	102.6	1855..	18.3	18.2	68.9	68.9
1806..	13.8	13.9	102.2	100.8	1856..	18.3	18.5	68.9	68.8
1807..	13.8	13.3	96.0	97.4	1857..	18.8	18.6	68.5	66.5
1808..	12.4	13.6	93.9	96.2	1858..	18.8	18.8	62.0	63.8
1809..	14.7	13.8	98.7	100.1	1859..	18.8	18.8	61.0	61.3
1810..	14.2	13.9	107.7	103.8	1860..	18.8	18.8	60.9	61.1
1811..	12.8	13.9	104.9	106.3	1861..	18.8	19.0	61.3	64.6
1812..	14.7	—	106.3	—	1862..	19.3	—	71.7	—
1813..	14.7	—	123.6	—	1863..	22.0	—	90.5	—
1814..	13.8	—	154.6	—	1864..	25.2	—	116.0	—
1815..	14.2	—	121.5	—	1865..	28.0	—	132.0	—
1816..	14.7	—	103.5	—	1866..	29.8	—	116.3	—
1817..	15.1	14.7	104.2	103.3	1867..	30.7	—	104.9	—
1818..	14.2	14.2	102.2	98.7	1868..	31.2	—	97.7	—
1819..	13.3	13.4	89.7	89.5	1869..	32.6	—	93.5	—
1820..	12.8	13.3	76.6	79.8	1870..	33.0	—	86.7	—
1821..	13.8	13.1	73.2	75.0	1871..	33.0	33.0	82.8	84.7
1822..	12.8	13.8	75.2	73.4	1872..	33.0	33.0	84.5	83.7
1823..	14.7	13.9	71.8	72.7	1873..	33.0	32.7	83.7	83.1
1824..	14.2	14.2	71.1	71.6	1874..	32.1	32.1	81.0	80.8
1825..	13.8	13.5	71.8	71.3	1875..	31.2	31.2	77.7	76.9
1826..	12.4	13.6	71.1	71.6	1876..	30.3	30.0	72.0	72.4
1827..	14.7	13.5	71.8	70.4	1877..	28.4	28.7	67.5	67.1
1828..	13.3	13.8	68.3	69.2	1878..	27.5	27.8	61.7	62.7
1829..	13.3	13.5	67.6	67.2	1879..	27.5	27.5	58.8	61.9
1830..	13.8	13.9	65.6	67.9	1880..	27.5	28.0	65.1	62.8
1831..	14.7	14.5	70.4	69.0	1881..	28.9	28.6	64.4	65.2
1832..	15.1	15.0	71.1	70.6	1882..	29.4	29.5	66.1	65.0
1833..	15.1	15.3	70.4	69.0	1883..	30.3	29.8	64.6	63.7
1834..	15.6	15.3	65.6	70.2	1884..	29.8	30.0	60.5	60.6
1835..	15.1	15.3	74.6	74.6	1885..	29.8	29.8	56.6	57.7
1836..	15.1	15.1	83.5	80.3	1886..	29.8	30.0	56.0	56.3
1837..	15.1	15.1	82.8	81.9	1887..	30.3	30.3	56.4	56.6
1838..	15.1	15.3	79.4	81.9	1888..	30.7	30.6	57.4	57.1
1839..	15.6	15.6	83.5	78.0	1889..	30.7	31.0	57.4	57.0
1840..	16.1	15.8	71.1	75.0	1890..	31.7	31.5	56.2	56.5
1841..	15.6	15.9	70.5	69.1	1891..	32.1	32.1	55.8	54.7
1842..	16.1	15.8	65.7	66.0	1892..	32.6	32.0	52.2	53.8
1843..	15.6	15.8	61.8	63.2	1893..	31.2	31.1	53.4	51.2
1844..	15.6	15.8	62.1	62.2	1894..	29.4	30.4	47.9	50.0
1845..	16.1	16.1	62.6	63.2	1895..	30.7	30.1	48.8	47.7
1846..	16.5	16.4	64.8	64.1	1896..	30.3	30.4	46.5	47.3
1847..	16.5	16.5	64.9	63.8	1897..	30.3	30.4	46.6	47.2
1848..	16.5	16.5	61.8	62.3	1898..	30.7	30.9	48.5	49.1
1849..	16.5	16.7	60.1	61.4	1899..	31.7	31.7	52.2	52.3
1850..	17.0	16.8	62.3	62.3	1900..	32.6	32.6	56.1	54.5

INDEX NUMBERS OF MONEY WAGES AND WHOLESALE PRICES,
1801–1942—*Continued*

Year	Money Wages[a]		Wholesale Prices[b]		Year	Money Wages[a]		Wholesale Prices[b]	
	Annual Index	3-Year Moving Average	Annual Index	3-Year Moving Average		Annual Index	3-Year Moving Average	Annual Index	3-Year Moving Average
1901..	33.5	33.5	55.3	56.8	1922..	87.2	90.1	96.7	98.3
1902..	34.4	34.7	58.9	57.9	1923..	94.0	92.4	100.6	98.5
1903..	36.2	35.6	59.6	59.4	1924..	95.9	95.9	98.1	100.7
1904..	36.2	36.5	59.7	59.8	1925..	97.7	97.9	103.5	100.5
1905..	37.2	37.3	60.1	60.5	1926..	100.0	98.9	100.0	99.6
1906..	38.5	38.7	61.8	62.4	1927..	99.1	99.7	95.4	97.4
1907..	40.4	39.3	65.2	63.3	1928..	100.0	99.9	96.7	95.8
1908..	39.0	39.9	62.9	65.2	1929..	100.5	97.9	95.3	92.8
1909..	40.4	40.8	67.6	67.0	1930..	93.2	92.3	86.4	84.9
1910..	43.1	42.2	70.4	67.6					
					1931..	83.1	81.2	73.0	74.7
1911..	43.1	43.4	64.9	68.1	1932..	67.4	72.0	64.8	67.9
1912..	44.0	44.3	69.1	67.9	1933..	65.6	68.5	65.9	68.5
1913..	45.9	45.4	69.8	69.0	1934..	72.6	72.1	74.9	73.6
1914..	46.3	46.5	68.1	69.1	1935..	78.0	78.0	80.0	78.6
1915..	47.2	48.3	69.5	74.4	1936..	83.5	84.1	80.8	82.4
1916..	51.4	—	85.5	—	1937..	90.8	85.7	86.3	81.9
1917..	57.8	—	117.5	—	1938..	82.8	87.5	78.6	80.7
1918..	70.2	—	131.3	—	1939..	88.8	88.6	77.1	78.1
1919..	81.2	—	138.6	—	1940..	94.2	98.4	78.6	81.0
1920..	95.9	—	154.4	—					
					1941..	112.1	112.4	87.3	87.9
1921..	89.0	—	97.6	—	1942..	130.9	—	97.7	—

[a] Index numbers for money wages, 1801–1926 from H. G. Moulton, *Income and Economic Progress*, pp. 181–82. Figures for 1926–42 computed from U. S. Bureau of Labor Statistics, *Handbook of Labor Statistics* (1941), Vol. II (Wages and Wage Regulation), Bulletin No. 604, pp. 16–17, and current issues of *Monthly Labor Review*. Since 1926 the index shows the trend of average weekly earnings in manufacturing and mining. For earlier years, the index is based on a much more comprehensive coverage of wage earners. (See Barron's *National Financial Weekly*, Oct. 23, 1933.) The index prior to 1913 is apparently more representative of hourly than of weekly earnings, since the figures do not seem to reflect the decline in hours worked per week, at least during the period 1840 to 1913. (See index numbers of wage rates per hour, 1840–1926, published in U. S. Bureau of Labor Statistics, *History of Wages in the United States from Colonial Times to 1928*, Bulletin No. 499, p. 521.)

[b] Figures for wholesale prices are the "All Commodity" index compiled by the U. S. Bureau of Labor Statistics. Data for 1801–1941 are from *Handbook of Labor Statistics*, (1941), Vol. I, (All Topics Except Wages), Bulletin No. 694, p. 715. The average for 1942, based on figures for January to June, from current issues of the *Monthly Labor Review*.

INDEX NUMBERS OF HOURLY EARNINGS IN MANUFACTURING AND
WHOLESALE PRICES OF MANUFACTURED PRODUCTS, 1900–41
(1926 = 100)

Year	Hourly Earnings[a]			Wholesale Prices[b]	
	In Cents	Annual Index	3-Year Moving Average	Annual Index	3-Year Moving Average
1900	16.3	29.8	—	57.6	—
1901	16.5	30.1	30.6	56.6	58.2
1902	17.4	31.8	31.6	60.3	58.8
1903	18.0	32.8	32.3	59.6	59.9
1904	17.6	32.2	32.7	59.8	60.3
1905	18.1	33.0	33.3	61.4	60.6
1906	19.0	34.6	34.7	60.7	62.5
1907	20.0	36.5	35.2	65.5	63.5
1908	18.9	34.4	35.4	64.4	65.9
1909	19.3	35.2	35.4	67.9	67.6
1910	20.1	36.7	36.3	70.5	67.7
1911	20.3	37.1	37.5	64.6	68.1
1912	21.2	38.7	38.8	69.2	67.7
1913	22.2	40.6	40.0	69.4	68.8
1914	22.3	40.7	40.6	67.8	68.7
1915	22.2	40.6	43.1	68.9	73.0
1916	26.4	48.1	—	82.3	—
1917	31.6	57.7	—	109.2	—
1918	39.7	72.4	—	124.7	—
1919	47.7	87.0	—	130.6	—
1920	58.9	107.4	—	149.8	—
1921	50.7	92.5	—	103.3	—
1922	47.7	87.0	91.5	96.5	99.7
1923	52.0	94.9	93.8	99.2	97.3
1924	54.5	99.5	97.9	96.3	98.7
1925	54.4	99.3	99.6	100.6	99.0
1926	54.8	100.0	100.0	100.0	98.5
1927	55.2	100.7	101.0	95.0	97.0
1928	56.0	102.2	102.1	95.9	95.1
1929	56.6	103.3	102.1	94.5	92.8
1930	55.2	100.7	99.4	88.0	86.5
1931	51.7	94.3	92.9	77.0	78.4
1932	45.8	83.6	87.0	70.3	72.6
1933	45.5	83.0	88.4	70.5	73.0
1934	54.1	98.7	94.6	78.2	77.0
1935	55.9	102.0	101.2	82.2	80.8
1936	56.4	102.9	106.9	82.0	83.8
1937	63.4	115.7	111.7	87.2	83.8
1938	63.9	116.6	116.6	82.2	83.3
1939	64.4	117.5	118.8	80.4	81.4
1940	67.0	122.3	124.7	81.6	83.7
1941	73.6	134.3	—	89.1	—

ᵃ Hourly earnings. To obtain a continuous series over the entire period three sources have been used: (1) United States Bureau of Labor Statistics *Handbook of Labor Statistics, (1941), Vol. II, Wages and Wage Regulation* (Bulletin No. 694), p. 10, and current issues of *Monthly Labor Review:* (2) Paul Douglas, *Real Wages in the United States, 1890–1926*, p. 101; and (3) H. G. Moulton, *Income and Economic Progress*, p. 185. The Bureau of Labor Statistics figures covered the years 1909, 1914, 1919, and 1923–41. Figures for other years, adjusted to the B.L.S. levels, were obtained by simple interpolation. Data from Paul Douglas were used for years prior to 1919 and the index published in *Income and Economic Progress* was used for 1920–1922.

ᵇ Wholesale prices of manufactured products, formerly called index of finished products. The entire series is based on data compiled by the Bureau of Labor Statistics. For 1913–41 the figures are from *Handbook of Labor Statistics, 1941 Edition, Vol. I, All Topics Except Wages* (Bulletin No. 694), p. 733. The trend from 1900–12 is based on comparable data for 70 manufactured commodities published in *Wholesale Prices, 1890 to 1921* (Bulletin No. 32), p. 44.

APPENDIX D

THE INDUSTRIAL "FAMILY" OF PRICES[1]

E. Stewart Freeman
Budget Controller, Dennison Manufacturing Company

The scientific pricing of an industrial product should, I think, involve three steps:

First, somebody with market information and experience must estimate what quantities can be sold at a variety of possible prices.

Second, somebody with cost and budgetary training must estimate what the cost and investment would be for each of these possible quantities and hence what the profit in relation to capital would be for each such price level.

Third, somebody should compare the sales revenue, cost, resulting profit, and required capital for each level of volume and select the price likely to yield the most profit in relation to capital over the long or short run.

JUDGING THE MARKET

Often, but not always, the number of units which can be sold will tend to vary inversely with the price per unit. Hence the first step is to estimate the effect of the price on the volume of sales.

If the product is already being sold by others, the pricer should find out what they are charging. If it differs only slightly from what others are selling, he should judge what the difference is likely to be worth to a buyer.

[1] This discussion of pricing as the industrial man sees it was presented at the Twentieth International Cost Conference held in Atlantic City, New Jersey, June 26-29, 1939 and appears under the title, "Pricing the Product" in the National Association of Cost Accountants *Yearbook 1939*, pp. 21-38. It is reproduced here through the courtesy of the author and the National Association of Cost Accountants.

If the product is to be sold to consumers, the pricer should compare it with other articles serving similar purposes or which are likely to make substitute appeals for the same class of consumers' dollar. He must consider the type of people to whom he expects to sell and how many will be likely to think they can afford to buy the product at various possible prices.

If the product is a raw material, the pricer must compare its value with the materials with which it is expected to compete and consider what the difference, if any, is worth to the buyer's customers. If the product is a manufactured part, he will consider, also, what it would cost the buyer to make it for himself. If it is a new machine, he must figure how much it will be worth to the buyer in terms of reduced cost or increased sales. . . .

EFFECT OF VOLUME ON COSTS

The second step in pricing is to judge the effect of the volume on the various costs and hence on profit. This effect may be either very large or very small, depending upon the circumstances and the way in which these circumstances are controlled by management. A larger volume sometimes makes possible lower material costs. It gives greater bargaining power and the larger machine runs or shipments may reduce the costs of the supplier. On the other hand, a rapid increase in the demand for a raw material might tend to bid up its price, except as and until the supply also can be increased.

In addition, volume can affect manufacturing costs. It may permit more automatic larger-scale production as, for example, in steel mills and the straight-line assembly of automobiles. Also, improvements in technique since the existing plant was built might permit the construction of a far more efficient plant for the additional output and thus make the average cost per unit lower for the enlarged plant than for the existing one. Under other conditions a rapid increase of output might necessitate the use of less efficient equipment and labor.

The costs most affected by volume are, of course, the indirect costs, especially the costs of marketing. These are to a large extent the costs of providing the capacity to make and sell rather than the costs of actually making or selling any given volume. Hence, when the capacity provided is not fully utilized, larger quantities can be made or sold without any increase in the expenditure for capacity. In addition, costs per unit can be reduced by spreading the cost of machine setups, dies, jigs, design, research, sampling, advertising, selling and management over a larger number of units of product.

Yet increases of volume do not always reduce overhead costs per unit. Much depends upon when and where the increase comes, how long it lasts and upon other attendant circumstances. A distinction must be made between increases of volume which fill up the valleys of idle capacity and increases which raise the peak loads, cause shorter runs to meet delivery dates or require the introduction of some new equipment or technique. Also, the mere fact that there is spare capacity in equipment does not necessarily mean that there is an equivalent spare capacity in personnel.

The real distinction in overhead costs is not so much between variable and fixed as it is between quickly moving and lagging. When changes in volume come quickly, the lagging costs do not move as far or as fast, but in the course of time the same relationship as before may be re-established. While the variable costs slide up and down on an inclined plane or ramp, the so-called fixed costs move up a step at a time and do not slide back so easily. What we call fixed costs are commonly costs which are merely temporarily maladjusted to the existing volume of business. . . .

RELATION OF SELLING PRICE TO COST

. . . selling price and cost are each both cause and effect of the other. When supply is in excess of demand, competition drives prices downward and exerts a downward pressure on profits, material prices, wages, rents and other costs. When demand is in excess of supply, the seller is able to get a good profit and also the downward pressure on the costs themselves is relieved so that raw material prices, wages, rents and other costs tend to rise. In the long run the shifting balance between supply and demand will sometimes force the seller and sometimes the buyer each to yield something to the other.

Thus the selling price is most likely to be a compromise of some sort between the cost-plus-profit which the seller would like to get and some different price which the buyer is willing to pay. Even when the seller has a free choice of the price per unit, the buyers collectively still have the right to decide how many units they will buy at the price he asks.

The relation between selling price and cost is an elastic one. It will vary with the business cycle, with the efficiency of the seller, and with the nature and age of the product. Yet there are certain general rules which should govern this relation.

The selling price of any product or order should cover at least the differential cost which can be saved by not making and selling it. In addition, it should contribute toward paying for the joint costs as much more as the market value permits. Furthermore, when operations are near capacity, no product or order should be sold at a price which contributes less toward paying for the joint costs than the amount which would be contributed by any other product or order which could be substituted for it.

WHEN FACTORY CAPACITY EXCEEDS SELLING CAPACITY

Now let us ... consider how these principles should be applied when the capacity of the factory exceeds the capacity of the sales organization. The proportion of the manufacturing and order-filling costs which can be saved when orders are not accepted will depend somewhat upon the expected duration of the below-capacity production. If it is only temporary, the direct costs can be saved but very little of the indirect costs will be, probably only those expenses which vary automatically or are very closely controlled with the volume of output. An individual order may therefore show a marginal profit if the price more than covers the [direct and the quickly variable factory] costs.

That, of course, is not the same as saying that one should quote that low. There is no need of quoting any lower than is necessary to get the order. Likewise, at times it may pay to risk losing the order rather than to take any action which may result in a permanent lowering of the prices quoted by competitors. If the low level of sales is to be of longer duration, it may be cheaper to reorganize down to the volume of business which can be obtained than to continue to spend money which cannot be recovered in the selling price. Over a sufficiently long period of time without orders, very nearly all of the indirect costs of manufacturing and order filling can be saved. Even the cost of equipment is savable when the time for replacement arrives. Hence the longer a price is to remain in effect or to influence the future price level, the larger should be the proportion of the cost which the price should cover.

Ordinarily, no part of the costs for soliciting orders will be saved if an individual order is rejected. These are costs for developing and maintaining customers over the long run, rather than costs for individual orders. In fact, a large part of the expense, usually more than half, is the cost of trying to get orders which are not, in fact, obtained. The larger part of the remainder is a joint cost in the nature of overhead. The actual direct cost of the single order is usually relatively small and it is water over the dam by the time any single order is offered for acceptance. Order-getting expenses are, to a large extent, speculative investments made before it can be known what sales will result. When prices are made for an entire season a considerable part of the selling cost may still be savable, but the pricing of individual orders is primarily a salvaging operation. The only choice is between taking what one can get toward paying for the selling cost, or taking nothing at all.

Yet, on the average, the prices obtained from marginal customers ought to cover at least any differential cost which could be saved by eliminating such customers.

Probably no saving would be realized if calls on only a few customers were eliminated. But if enough calls were cut out, the travel plans might be rearranged so as to reduce the number of salesmen and thereby yield a substantial saving. The cost of selling is of course reduced very much less than pro rata when the number of calls is reduced. But the sales also are reduced very much less than pro rata because the marginal calls are the least productive. Therefore, if the potential market has been very thoroughly canvassed, it will sometimes be possible to reduce the selling expense in proportion to the reduction in sales.

Hence, on the average, although not necessarily on every order, the selling price should cover all of the costs [publicity and sampling and the marginal cost of salesmen's calls on customers for the marginal product plus part of the cost of calls on customers for products sold in combination].

WHEN FACTORIES AND SELLING CAPACITIES BALANCE

Let us now . . . consider how the situation differs when the factory and selling capacities are more nearly in balance.

At such times there is no idle capacity of any importance and hence there is no substantial reduction of unit costs to be gained by an increase in the volume of sales. The cost of providing the existing capacity would not be saved if volume falls off, but on the other hand no substantial increase in volume is possible without an increase in capacity. Hence, if necessary, it would pay to curtail volume until prices more than cover all the costs which an increase in capacity would involve.

Under such conditions the price on every order should cover at least the complete cost of executing the sales contract. . . . Generally the price should also cover almost all of the cost of soliciting sales contracts. . . .

WHEN SELLING CAPACITY EXCEEDS FACTORY CAPACITY

Now let us suppose that the factory gets behind on its orders. Before expansion of either facilities or organization is considered, the price quotations probably should stiffen to prices which would warrant an increase of capacity.

While the costs of providing capacity are thought of as fixed, they are 100 per cent savable before the capacity is increased. Moreover, the fixed costs of a depression are largely determined by the extent of expansion during the preceding prosperity.

Hence, before any expansion is actually undertaken, there

should be evidence of an ability during the next minor cycle to get a price per unit for the added capacity which would cover the complete cost per unit and a fair profit on the investment in added capacity. . . .

Let us suppose, however, that the increase of sales is believed to be temporary only, perhaps likely to last only during the cyclical peak. Instead of increasing capacity, it would probably be better to permit sales to be limited by the capacity of the various parts of the factory. Under such conditions the wisest policy for the long pull might be to take care of the regular customers first regardless of immediate profit. But suppose that after this need is met there remains capacity for customers who buy less regularly. The plan then would ordinarily be to use such remainder of the limited capacity so as to get the largest possible margin of gross profit above the cost of executing the order.

During ordinary times it is customary to figure the gross profit as a percentage of the sales dollar or of the total factory cost. This custom makes no distinction between a profit on the relatively large investment in factory capacity and a profit on the relatively small investment in material. So long as the price is determined by market conditions, it is well to follow the custom of the industry in this respect. But when the capacity of the factory sets the limit to sales, there are advantages in figuring the gross profit as a rate per factory machine hour. At such times no order should be taken at a lower profit per machine hour than could be obtained for any other order which could be substituted for it. This would mean, in effect, auctioning the limited hours of each machine to the highest gross profit bidders.

CONTRIBUTION OF PRODUCTS TOWARD JOINT COSTS

Let us now . . . discuss the relationship of prices to costs by products over a relatively longer range of time.

Orthodox accounting has, as a rule, provided for only two types of products, main products and by-products. Sometimes the difference between products may be so great as to make this classification valid. When, however, a considerable variety of products is handled and the complete cost is used instead of the factory cost only, this distinction is likely to prove arbitrary and unrealistic. The distinction between the various products is not like that between snow white and jet black but more like that between various shades of gray. Also, the relationship of one product to another is not constant. The by-products of today may become the main products of tomorrow and the change is likely to come not suddenly but by imperceptible degrees. This is a field of cost accounting in which more exploration should be undertaken.

If a company is handling only one product it must make that product pay or its capital will in time be depleted. The situation is somewhat different when many products are being made and sold jointly with other products. There are then many costs which are common to more than one product. As a matter of accounting these costs can be prorated to the several products on the basis of dollar sales, orders, physical units or some other factor. But if one of the products is eliminated, the costs so allocated will not be saved, but instead must merely be shifted so as to increase the costs of the remaining products. The costs of a traveling salesman selling, say, ten products, or of a delivery wagon delivering such products are joint costs of this nature. If 10 per cent of the products are discontinued the saving in such costs may not exceed perhaps 2 per cent. Many general expenses of the factory are also of this nature.

The usual reason for incurring joint costs is that two or more products can be made or sold cheaper in combination than separately. Suppose, for example, that two products which cost $200 when made and sold separately, would cost only $150 if made and sold together. For accounting purposes it might be considered reasonable to divide the $150 by two and say the cost of each was $75. Yet only $50 could be saved if one were abandoned and, in case of abandonment of one, the other would then cost $100. Suppose one can be sold for only $60, whereas the other can sell for $110. The combined selling price is then $170 or $20 more than the combined cost of $150. If we drop one of the products, we reduce the profit from $20 to $10.

Hence it is obviously more profitable to sell both than only one even though one is sold at a price below the $75 average cost.

The rule is that each product and each group of products should pay for at least as much cost as could be saved by its elimination, but should not be forced to pay for more of the cost than it would have to pay if it were made and sold separately or in combination with some more profitable product which competitors would be able to combine with it. In the example used above this gives a range from the $50 savable to the $100 cost of making and selling separately. The possibility of combining with a substitute product might narrow this range. Subject to this qualification, any cost accounting system which attempted to establish a more precise cost at some point between these extremes could be more or less unrealistic. The important factor is the marginal contribution of each product toward the total profit. The seller may get more profit in the aggregate by collecting whatever marginal contribution he can get, when and where he can get it, than by trying to make each product pay for some particular portion of the joint cost.

THE INDUSTRIAL FAMILY

The joint costs of an industry are no more divisible according to any set plan than are the joint costs of a family. In fact, an industry which is handling a variety of products to a variety of customers has many elements of resemblance to a human family.

Products, like humans, pass through a life curve from the early development of childhood through the expanding period of youth to the critical stages of middle age and thence downward to the dotage of obsolescence. Also, products, like members of a family, are subject to illness, owing perhaps to an epidemic of public fickleness or to insufficient nourishment (research, redesign, advertising) and they may be temporarily disabled by fights with neighbors (price wars, patent suits, etc.) Hence they cannot be judged entirely by the contribution they make during any single year. It may be as unreasonable to expect all products to pay a like share of this year's costs as it is to expect the baby, young sister, older brother, and grandparent to contribute alike toward the household expenses. Some are relics of the past still worth preserving, some are the sustenance of the present, while others are the hope of the future.

The prosperous family is one which develops a lot of big strong brothers; yet, even in the prosperous family, all cannot be big brothers. We can save money today by not having any children, but when the present products approach obsolescence there may be none to replace them. On the other hand, balance is very important. No family or business can survive if at any given time it has too large a proportion of infant or infirm members to support. Likewise, it will be in a continuous state of unstable equilibrium so long as it depends too much on the contribution of a relatively few members. Such members might become sick or be attacked by competitors who have no weak sisters for their big brothers to support.

Over the short run, the test is not so much whether one is making the profit which one should on every line of merchandise as it is whether the selling prices are properly adjusted to the market and the costs are under proper control. Hence, in my opinion, there really is no need for the accounting system to distribute all the joint costs by products currently.

For the longer run, I prefer to make cost and profit analyses independent of the accounts(but, of course, using data supplied by the accounts). Instead of trying to allocate joint costs according to some routine plan which at the best can satisfy only one point of view, I prefer to determine what proportion of the joint cost each product is capable of contributing. The products can then be classified according to their respective contributions and each studied accordingly from many points of view.

The classification, of course, does not in itself furnish any answers to the question of what should be done, but it does furnish leads as to the method of approach. It helps to focus the attention and direct the thinking of the organization. For this purpose I have invented the family designations of "big brother," "self supporting," "weak sister," and "problem child." . . . I could, instead, use the terms "very good," "good," "bad," and "very bad," but the more novel family terms have helped to explain the ideas and attract attention to the problem.

SELF-SUPPORTING AND BIG-BROTHER PRODUCTS

What I call a "self-supporting" product is one which sells at a price capable of contributing a pro rata share of the joint cost. Such a price would probably be considered about right on a cost-plus basis with the joint costs distributed in accordance with the conventional methods used for factory overhead costs.

A "big-brother" product is one which sells at a price which contributes more toward the joint costs than would be expected of a "self-supporting" product. Among the factors which might make this possible are (1) the ability to manufacture or market more cheaply than competitors, (2) the ability to manufacture a product better than competitors in quality, design or some other feature, (3) the ability to keep ahead of competitors in research, invention, or the command of limited resources, (4) the existence of model or habitual prices in the market which might make prices slower to move than costs, (5) the possibility that competitors with a varied line might be ignorant of their costs for the specific product, and (6) the possibility that competitors also might be in need of big brothers to recoup losses on other products.

In the case of big brothers, even more than with other products, the possibility that more profit can be obtained by selling a larger quantity at a lower price, must never be neglected.

When a company keeps ahead of its competitors in efficiency or when, as a result of research, invention or enterprise, it risks its capital in bringing out a new or improved product, it probably is entitled to a substantial margin of selling price above current costs. The customer is pleased to have something new and different and is more willing than he will be later to pay a price which is high in relation to cost. Also, when a product is new it may be too much of a gamble in equipment or require more than the available capital to jump into quantity production at once. Likewise the inability to foresee the effect of a change in price with certainty may often make for conservatism in reducing price.

If, however, competitors are likely to copy the product, one must beware of trying to get a high profit for too long a period. After a product has proved itself profitable, capital will be more eager to enter the field and therefore in the course of time competition will be bound to increase and customers will shop around for lower prices. Thus a business must usually either keep ahead of its competitors in reducing costs or in improving the value offered at a given price, or else it must in the course of time reduce its selling price faster than its cost, thereby accepting a lower margin of profit per unit. The maintenance of a more-than-necessary margin above cost is like holding an awning or umbrella over the head of prospective competitors while they go through the high-cost period of breaking into a new market and learning how to produce efficiently.

WEAK SISTERS AND PROBLEM CHILDREN

A "weak sister" is a product, the selling price of which contributes more than the savable costs, but not enough of the joint cost to rank it as self-supporting. Such sisters are helpful and decorative in the home. They pay for their own clothes and outside meals, but they are unable to contribute their pro rata share of the joint household expenses.

A "problem child" is a product, the selling price of which fails, perhaps only by a small margin, to cover the costs which might be saved by its elimination.

Some of the types of products which might not pay a pro rata share of the joint costs and the problems in connection with each are as follows:

1. The fairly well-known by-products of manufacturing and the much more numerous by-products of marketing, which either could not be made or sold profitably by themselves or if so made or sold would require a cheaper technique.

2. Loss savers which it would not pay to make or sell at all were it not for the existence of unused manufacturing or market-

ing capacity. While loss savers can be valuable during a depression, they should be discontinued by the time normal volume is regained. Otherwise they are likely to disguise the need of reorganization downward and may even be the cause of an automatic increase of capacity.

3. New products of reasonably certain promise which are expensive to develop and promote but are expected to be very profitable later. The logical cost accounting procedure would be to defer part of the early cost of these until subsequent years but this is not yet a generally accepted method of accounting.

4. More speculative products. Most concerns must speculate to some extent but few can afford to get in too deeply at any one time. Hence speculative products ought to be launched on a scale which would limit losses to what can be afforded as experimental expense. A good plan might be to limit speculation of this sort to some revolving fund with a time limit on its use for any one product.

5. Items which are said to be necessary to complete the line. It may be worth while to carry a full range of sizes, colors or designs in order to get dealers to handle the line even though many of these items cannot pay their pro rata share of the costs. To a lesser extent the same principle may apply in respect to related products which customers are in the habit of buying from the same sources.

If a reasonable profit is made on the aggregate sales to a given customer, it may not for the moment make any difference how that profit is distributed among the products which he buys. The current profit might not be changed by charging him less for the big brothers and more for the weak sisters. This may hold true as long as a balance between the two classes of products is maintained with each class of customer. One possible objection to charging different markups on different products is that the products with the higher markup may be more vulnerable to competition. The customer may in time find he can buy the big brothers cheaper from suppliers who ask only a self-supporting price. There may then be fewer and fewer big-brother sales to help support the weak-sister sales. This may tend in time to turn the profit on such customers into a loss.

Another difficulty in respect to weak sisters is that once in the line they may be sold to customers who buy very little else.

When a program of standardization and simplification is impractical, the next best thing is to try to maintain a balance in the sales to each class of customer.

6. Products facing a saturated market due to over-expansion in the industry or a decline in the demand for the product. In a short period of time, such as a depression, it might be difficult to distinguish between temporary and permanent difficulties of this nature. If a concern dropped every item which was in temporary difficulty, it might end up with nothing left. On the other hand, if it keeps on carrying losses indefinitely, it may permit its life-blood to be drained away.

7. Products which for some reason are not being made or sold as efficiently as by competitors or which are inferior in value to what competitors offer. All weak sisters and problem children should be suspected of this kind of guilt until they are proved innocent. If the concern is reasonably efficient in other respects it may be that it is trying to handle a line for which its organization or equipment is not adapted. If the efficiency cannot be improved within a reasonable time, consideration should be given to discontinuing the product.

WHAT TO DO ABOUT IT

After we have classified our products according to their respective contributions toward the joint costs and discovered the reasons for the small size of the contributions of some, the next step is to decide what to do about it. Usually this requires the combined effort of different types of minds. Some should be challenged and stimulated to study the market angle and others to study the cost aspect.

Sometimes the spread between selling price and cost can be increased over a period of time by a change in market conditions or an improvement in the value of the product with a less than a pro rata change in cost.

The ideal way is to have new products in the course of development so that they can from time to time be substituted for products which have passed the prime of life. When no substitute is available, aging products can be dropped during a period of expansion, such as the upward movement of the business cycle. At such times, the growth in the contribution of other lines can replace the contribution of the dropped line, while the actual overhead expense is held constant.

If none of these solutions seem possible, then careful consideration must be given to reorganizing downward so as to save the costs formerly charged against the product to be dropped. This may be very difficult during a period of depression, but there is more opportunity for it when other parts of the business are improving.

THE NEED FOR SPECIAL COST ANALYSIS

Ordinary standard or average costs are of little use in determining what can be saved when a product is dropped. Such figures show what the cost should average under existing conditions but do not show the effect on cost of a change in the conditions themselves.

The proper way, I think, is to make definite plans as to precisely what should be done to make the business more profitable. Then several complete budgets should be set up, one showing what the costs and profit would be if no change were made and the others showing what they would be under each of the proposed plans. Overhead rates should not be used for this purpose, but instead every item of indirect cost should be examined to see how it actually would be affected by each change under consideration. If any of the proposed plans are adopted, the person in charge of the budget should follow it up to see that the expected savings in cost are in fact realized.

Often it will take two or three years and sometimes longer to get the full cost effect of a reorganization required by the elimination of a product. The comparative budgets should therefore show not only what the effect on profit would be for the first year, but also what it would be after all proposed changes have had time to become fully effective.

ORGANIC AND DYNAMIC COST ACCOUNTING

So long as cost accounting was content to deal with only part of the cost, that is, factory cost alone, it could retain the simplicity of one dimension. The substantial margin between selling price and cost was sufficient to cushion the error in this treatment of the relatively few joint costs of manufacturing. But when cost accounting extends its jurisdiction over the whole of the cost, including the predominantly joint costs of marketing, it can no longer retain both simplicity and realism.

The principles of overhead distribution which worked well enough when applied to an amount equal to perhaps 10 per cent of the sales are not likely to prove so satisfactory when applied to an amount equal to, say, 50 per cent of the sales. A cost which contains only a small element of the theoretical may be practical, whereas a cost which is one half or more theoretical may be impractical and misleading.

When all of the costs are allocated according to the orthodox methods of overhead distribution, the accounts are likely to show that from 20 to 40 per cent of the sales are made at a price below cost. Yet when we eliminate products which contribute anything at all toward the joint costs which are not saved by such elimination, the result must be to reduce the aid given the remaining products from something to nothing. Logically, the elimination of products which are sold at a loss should benefit the business. Actually, the elimination of products which an over-simplified accounting merely says show a loss, may be as likely to hurt the business as to help it. The figures must tell a more dependable story than this if they are to be a real guide to action.

Too many of us have fallen into the error of thinking of cost accounting primarily as a method of slicing up the costs so that each slice can be treated as if it represented a separate and static business. Yet the parts of a modern business are in fact not so separated and unrelated. The selling price per unit affects the volume of sales and the volume of sales affects the cost per unit. Also the manufacture and marketing of one product in combination with another affects the cost of both and hence the price of each.

Cost accounting must develop methods of diagnosis better adapted to the organic and dynamic businesses of today. Its theories must become more profound so that its practice can become more realistic. We must have a more thorough understanding of our costs before we can make much progress in pricing.

APPENDIX E

PROPOSAL FOR A NATIONAL MARKET-BUILDING ASSOCIATION[1]

John E. Webster
Formerly General Works Engineer, Westinghouse
Electric and Manufacturing Company

If some individuals or some industries refuse to operate their business so that prices may be adjusted to sustained full employment, they will have to be brought in line by some authority. If the government is this authority, we no longer have the free enterprise system; it becomes some form of state capitalism. The only authority that can bring the offenders in line and still retain the free enterprise system, would be the authority of a voluntary organization of all business units. Business leaders never felt so frustrated as now. They would welcome an escape from bureaucracy and regimentation which is smothering them. In spite of the frequently made statement that businessmen would not submit to group control, there is reason to believe that they yearn for strong, sound, constructive leadership.

ORGANIZING BUSINESS FOR SELF-DISCIPLINE

To save Free Enterprise we must have an over-all business association dedicated to the task of building and protecting a market that will continuously absorb near full employment production. This association, in order to solve the problem of unemployment, must have the authority to require each producer and each industry to do its part. We must give up individual play for team play, always remembering that under team disci-

[1] Excerpts from an article, "Free Enterprise Must Save Itself," in *Advanced Management*, July-September 1942, pp. 118 ff.

At the time of publishing this article, Mr. Webster referred to his proposal as a National Price Limiting Association but has subsequently changed this to "National Market-Building Association" and it is thus referred to in Chapter XIII.

pline the individual as well as the whole team has the greatest opportunity for success. Freedom and discipline are not contradictory terms. Our most cherished freedoms are based on individual and group self-discipline. Team play requires an umpire and the umpire must act instantly in accordance with accepted rules. In our games the rules are formulated and accepted by the players. Business is our greatest and most interesting game. Impartial decisions, made in conformity with rules formulated by business leaders to promote their own and therefore the public's advantage, would be rarely disobeyed. Sound self-imposed rules require few administrators. The administration of arbitrary government rules require large growing bureaucracies.

Let us call this voluntary but authoritative body the National Price-Limiting Association. If this association is to succeed those who found and administer it must subscribe to a body of principles something like the following:

1. The success of Free Enterprise requires high mass prosperity. This mass prosperity must be *earned* by the participation of our people in the production, transportation, selling and servicing of the products of our industries.

2. The creation of mass prosperity is as much a responsibility of business as is the production and distribution of the products of our industries.

3. The market of the product of each industry is largely determined by the price and sales policy of every other industry. Therefore the managers of each industry are not "minding their own business" unless they concern themselves with the price and sales policy of every other industry. This may effectively be done through their representation in the National Association.

4. Any producer or any industry that absorbs more of the effective national buying power than it currently releases is detrimental to the interests of all other producers.

5. There is nothing that the owners of business, as a group can do to promote their own long pull advantage which will not also promote mass prosperity.

The success of the National Price-Limiting Association would depend on the soundness of the rules adopted. To date neither our business nor our economic leaders have agreed on what these rules should be. No one has ever written a definition of a fair wage or a fair price. We only know that prices and wages must be so set that they will encourage, not restrict, production.

This association, in my opinion, should have power and authority to clamp down on persistent offenders but most of its purposes can be achieved through friendly consultations. Industry must be put on its honor before the court of public opinion and its self-appointed umpire to obey its rules to preserve its own existence. The essential thing is that business get together and establish prices that will move full employment production. The details of how it is done are unimportant. I, however, merely as a suggestion will present a form that the "get-together" might take.

A convention of men who believe in the above principles would formulate a code substantially like the following:

Industrial Code
A. Objective. Continued full capacity production of wanted goods and services.
B. A uniform base wage scale.
C. A uniform price-making policy. All prices to be based on costs at full capacity production with markups as uniform as possible. (Consideration must be given to variations in efficient marketing costs but slight consideration should be given to costs of high-pressure selling.)
D. The margin of allowed prices above full capacity costs to be gradually lowered until 96 per cent to 98 per cent of all potential workers are working efficiently. At this point full capacity production might be considered to have been attained.
E. Uniform accounting methods.
F. Honesty in advertising.
G. Strict rules governing deferred payment selling—the pur-

pose being to keep interest rates low and outstanding obligations uniform.

H. Goods produced under this code to be so advertised and labeled.

I. No penalty of any kind to be attached to selling at prices lower than those authorized by the Association. Free enterprise demands free markets.

This code is an attempt to outline the simplest possible working rules for American industry that will attain the stated objective.

The suggested Association would be composed of representatives of all present business and trade associations. The number of voting members of the national group would be proportional to the total employes in each group plus the total investment in dollars divided by a suitable constant. The voting members would elect a governing board or single administrator having powers similar to those of Judge Landis in baseball or Will Hays in the motion picture industry. All meetings would be open to the public, including representatives of the government, the press, organized labor and consumer groups.

The Association executive would request each trade association to submit a break-even chart similar to the one shown here, of enough of the most efficient units in the line to cover at least 75 per cent of the capacity, also a composite break-even chart of these units. A comparison of the above reports would show how far various prices were out of line and the variations in the cost of distribution.

Balanced prices are the first essential to inter-industrial cooperation and the only yardstick that can be impartially used in equalizing prices is the full capacity cost of the products of each industry. Based on the full capacity costs [as shown by a break-even chart], the Association would publish suggested price adjustments needed to equalize all prices. Before these suggested prices were made official, public hearings would be held in which the representatives of each industry would be given the novel opportunity of studying and protesting prices suggested for other industries as well as for their own. The representatives of each industry would insist on being assured that they would be compensated for accepting *reduced* prices for their goods by an increased volume which would result from similar price adjustments on all other goods.

After these hearings, a corrected list of price adjustments would be published giving the percent reduction each industry would be required to make in its average price. Each industry would assume the responsibility of making the detailed price changes needed to bring the average of the line to the desired level. While these detailed price changes can be easily made by the industries with their own men, any outside agency would require an enormous staff of clerks and accountants. Outside control would result in endless bickering, delay and court trials which would nullify the control. As stated by Professor Slichter, effective control must act instantly at the first evidence of need. Some price adjustments requested by public service commissions have been before the courts for ten years!

The NPLA should be organized before the war is won. There is real danger that we will be lured into a state of false security by a postwar boom that is liable to result from an artificial market that is now being created. . . . The NPLA would be a powerful factor in preventing inflation during and after the war. Postwar prices of consumer goods, durable goods and housing should be kept at a level that will quickly bring these industries to maximum prewar production. As a guide, the NPLA administrators would then set up a schedule of re-employment, based on the estimated maximum rate that plants can be organized and men trained. When approximately full employment is obtained, the industrial productive payroll will be the vital index. This payroll is always proportional to the volume of goods in production, which is the volume purchased. Hence, this payroll, with a constant wage rate, is the index of employment, production, and purchasing power. An estimate could be made of the rate that this payroll should be increased to absorb the inefficient workers in other lines and to provide for population increase. Any failure of this payroll to meet this estimated increase would be a signal to lower prices. An effective control functions instantly at the first evidence of need. By self-disciplined teamwork, business leaders and business leaders only, can make prices the perfect instrument for maintaining full employment.

ADVANTAGES AND OBJECTIONS

The average investor will profit by the adoption of uniform pricing policies that will result in full capacity volume in all his corporations. There should be a national organization of stockholders which should recommend to its members that they petition the directors of their companies asking them to participate in the formation of the National Price-Limiting Association. In sending their proxies, stockholders should assure themselves that their stock will be voted for directors who favor this industrial co-operation. Security holders are fast losing control of their properties. Only through co-operation can they regain and retain control. They have more at stake than the individual managers.

The formation of a National Association based on the code proposed here would create favorable conditions for the formation of new enterprises by new groups or by individuals. These new entrepreneurs would and should take full advantage of any evidence of staleness in the old organizations. The market would be always open to those who could make better goods at lower cost.

The big test of the National Price-Limiting Association as outlined here is: can it be kept open-shop or non-monopolistic? We would need to depend on the following:

A. The purpose of the NPLA, as outlined in the code, is to obtain full employment by the establishment of low prices.

B. The code requires that there be every encouragement to those who can and will sell at prices below those authorized.

C. All meetings are to be open to the press, labor leaders, government agents and consumer groups. At the first signs of agreements in restraint of trade the antitrust laws would swing into action.

D. The owners of industry, as a group, have all to gain by maintaining non-monopolistic policies. This is due to the fact that their income is determined by production and production is determined by mass prosperity and managerial efficiency. Maximum managerial efficiency can be obtained only if the posts of management are open to any who show superior qualifications. A closed shop self-perpetuating group of managers will soon become stale and production will suffer. This is why the self-perpetuating managerial group, as described by Mr. Burnham in *The Managerial Revolution*, would have to suppress the masses and take over all political power. Only a suppressed people will submit to state monopolies. All rights of private ownership would also be eliminated. Stockholders should, through a national organition, insist in the managerial co-operation in market building.

E. Even the managers, not necessarily as individuals but as a group, will profit more under open-shop Free Enterprise control as there is more profit and greater security in leading a free prosperous people than there can be in bossing a suppressed poverty-stricken people.

F. There is every reason to believe that Free Enterprise, freed from production limiting prices and special privilege, can provide full employment or near enough full employment to regain and keep popular support. Our workers must be convinced, through proper publicity, that full employment under Free Enterprise is a far different thing from full employment under the despotic rule of bureaucratic government. In the one case the workers will have the opportunity to work as many hours as they wish with the most efficient tools and management to produce the goods they want as their wants are expressed in free open markets. In the other cases, they will work as long as they are told and where they are told with a large part of their labor going to production of guns and monuments instead of consumer goods.

APPENDIX F

TOTAL SECURITY
A Challenge to Business Management[1]

Charles E. Wilson
President, General Electric Company

Tonight I should like to invite your constructive consideration of a program—and of a proposal for an American Free Enterprise System constitutional convention, if you will. These I shall submit in the belief that with the support of this serious minded body of citizens, this program and proposal could result in a worthy contribution to the solution of the exceedingly complicated problem of preserving our democratic way of life and our Free Enterprise System in the dark decades ahead. In this statement, I am anxious to have you see evidence of an ambition to serve America—and you—rather than to seek support of a particular plan.

In the course of this presentation, I may seem, at times, to express some thoughts which might be interpreted as a criticism of industry. Therefore, at the outset, I should like to establish understanding on that point. My whole career has been in industry, and, fortunately, the character of that career has been such that I have been brought into intimate association with almost every form of industrial and commercial enterprise. Out of these associations, there has grown a tremendous pride in the accomplishments of industry, as well as an intense admiration and respect for the progressive citizens who, in the preponderant majority, compose it—the conscientious citizens in the shops and offices—in the drafting rooms—and in positions of management of every degree and kind, who, operating as organizations in enlightened enterprises, have given employment and enjoy-

[1] An address before the American Institute of Electrical Engineers, Philadelphia, January 1941.

514

ment to millions of people, while providing America with the highest degree of economic security and the highest standard of living in the world. Therefore, in anything which I may later say which seems to suggest shortcomings, I hope you will see in my comments not a presumptuous inclination to criticize, but, instead, a positive indication of my infinite confidence in the ability of industry to do an even better job in the building of an ever better America—a confidence which is coupled with a driving desire to have industry, as an integrated entity, go forward faster and more fruitfully than it ever has before. . . . I shall speak rather emphatically, assured that you will accept my words for what they really are—words which are merely the earnest expression of the convictions of some of your fellow-citizens who are concerned, above all else, with their country's welfare—the carefully considered words of fellow-countrymen of yours who seek the collaboration of the splendid minds which comprise this body in finding the most effective means of preserving individual initiative and private enterprise as the mainstays of our economic life. . . .

The world is immersed in more than a war of historically conventional character. Our own beloved nation is involved in more than a temporary emergency, from which, after a few years, it will emerge, and return to "normal" living in a "peaceful" world—a world made "peaceful" by the fact that some "national leaders" had gained military ascendancy over others and had thus forced the signing of some papers. Instead, the world—our nation included—is passing through what history may later record as the second stage of a revolutionary movement of the masses—a movement born during World War I and likely to last, with intermittent armistices of one kind or another, for two or three decades more. We must fully realize that this is a movement based upon a sense of frustration—an emotional manifestation frequently approaching unreasoning, sacrificial hysteria—and we must see that, as such, it can be turned to a course of reason only by reasonable and sacrificial actions of a character which appeal to the emotions and the aspirations of the masses more than do the actions and the appeals to which they are now responding. Today, hundreds of millions of people throughout the world have been persuaded, to the point of evangelistic conviction, that the capitalistic system is the cause of the economic insecurity of the common man and that, as the root of his economic ills, this system must be drastically modified, or failing that, destroyed.

Recognition of the revolutionary character of this world conflict will also lead to a fuller realization of the fact that Stalin, Mussolini, Hitler, and the Japanese army leaders are but symbols of this movement. . . . Should these symbols meet the disaster or the death so widely and so earnestly wished upon them, this revolutionary movement, most probably, would suffer no more than temporary confusion while substitute symbols were being elevated to leadership. As a world movement, the scope of this conflict extends beyond the sphere of these symbols. In the Central and South American countries, manifestations of it have been and continue to be common, and this is equally true of many parts of the British Empire.

While political freedom has happily been preserved in the British Isles, in its associates in the Commonwealth, and in the United States, it is important to remember that in these countries many economic controls have been willingly granted to government by the masses of the people in exchange for promises and for performances serving the mass revolutionary aim— more economic freedom and security. Hence, while, in this country, so far, we have had no more than an acceleration of the evolutionary process—rather than the revolutionary process— it should be borne in mind that the aim of the majority of the American people, as evidenced by their insistence that this acceleration continue, has been substantially that of the revolutionaries.

What more can the Free Enterprise System do, in the face of this world revolutionary movement, heretofore unmatched, either in extent, or in emotional intensity, or in destructive potentialities? How, in the midst of this dynamic world disorder, shall the capitalistic system—or what we, in this country, call the American Free Enterprise System—which, parenthetically, I should like to call the capitalistic system in its most constructive form—How shall this system of ours be sustained in its most useful form—the form in which it can be the primary provider of economic security for all of the people at all times—in times of peace and plenty—in times of depression—in times of national emergency—and in times of war? How may an ever broadening bulwark of public faith be built to protect this Free Enterprise System against its communistic and totalitarian enemies, as it seeks to serve this purpose? How may we control and conquer the causes of suspicion and condemnation which too often create breaches in this bulwark of public faith upon which the protection of the system depends?

Basically, the answers to these questions seem simple. Practically, the solution of the problems they present is most difficult. The financial and managerial components of our Free Enterprise System must prove, by deeds as well as by words, their full comprehension of their social responsibilities—their deep sense of public service—and their unmatched capacity to positively plan—to put into effect—and, if you will, to police, by self-imposed rules, a constitution for industrial and commercial progress acceptable to the majority of our people. This action must be prompt and positive, and of a character which will demonstrate, beyond the chance of successful challenge, that the public-spirited people administering private enterprise inherently and actually excel the people comprising political organizations —no matter how sincere the intentions of the latter may be— as instrumentalities for insuring an ever increasing measure of economic freedom and security for all of the people—save the indolent—all of the time.

Never before has the American Free Enterprise System been confronted by such a serious challenge. And never before has there been—and perhaps never again will there be—such an opportunity —or such an obligation—to prove the full worth of this system as an efficient, economical and trustworthy servant of society. Moreover, in these dark days we may be sure that, as the American Free Enterprise System sees this enlarged opportunity—as it assumes this greater obligation—and as it proves still more fully its worthiness, it will re-establish emotional bonds of mutual regard and respect between all elements of our economy—the bonds of national unity which will serve as a firm foundation of our moral security—the first fortification of our political and economic freedom.

Now, I should like to present the program I mentioned at the outset—a program which attempts to establish a general pattern of the stages and steps I consider essential to the further fortification of our political freedom and the extension of economic freedom to our whole society through the instrumentality of the people who comprise the American Free Enterprise System acting in close, cordial, and constructive co-operation with the people who comprise the Government of the United States. While the steps under the various stages will be set before you in what appears to be the approximate order of their importance, I am sure it will be apparent that each is not a distinct, successive step. Obviously, some require continuity from the time of their initiation—and these I shall try to identify as I go along. Others are overlapping in various degrees. And still others are temporary. Nevertheless, their interrelation will be clearer, I think, if you have the relativity of their importance in mind. Connected with the relativity of these stages and steps, in terms of importance, I should also like to emphasize the importance of timing the actions I shall propose by stages. This I consider extremely important, because some of these steps, taken too soon or too late, could very easily have an effect contrary to that sought.

Also, it will be evident that some of the elements of this pattern are logically within the province of government—that others are logically within the province of private enterprise—and that still others are of an uncertain category. The point to be re-emphasized in this connection—and it is a point requiring very special emphasis—is that the components of the private enterprise system should take the initiative in defining the obligations the whole system can and will positively assume —while, collaterally and co-ordinately, it defines those obligations which it will actively support government in assuming.

In this suggestion, I present no thought of arm's-length co-operation, overshadowed by suspicion between government and business. Instead, I seek arm-in-arm concord and co-ordinated effort in the common good—the kind of concord and effort which can, in my judgment, eliminate the causes of conflict, competition, and confusion between government and business.

For our economic security then, upon which our cherished democratic way of life and our dynamic Free Enterprise System may depend for survival during the coming dangerous decade, I submit this program:

The first period in this program I identify as the "recovery stage." This is the stage in which we are now, and in which I believe we shall remain until the Federal Reserve Board Index of Industrial Production (Unadjusted) averages 140 during a two months' period. This figure roughly represents the absorption of 90% of all employables and approximately the same percentage of all effective production capacity now available.

In this recovery stage we need:

(1) First—a sincere, determined, and unswerving devotion to democracy—coupled with a clear understanding of and infinite patience with its deliberative processes—and need I say that this is a primary and everlasting essential?

(2) Next—universal respect for the rules which the people, through their freely chosen representatives, establish for the protection of their rights—which is, of course, only another way of saying, universal respect for the sanctity and the spirit of the laws of our land—quite obviously an eternal essential.

(3) Next—a wholly free and enterprising system of free enterprise—another continuing necessity.

(4) Next—full-time employment of all employables—and, of course, this, too, is always essential to total economic security.

(5) Next—the free flow of all goods, purchasing power, and enterprise capital for production.

(6) Next—the encouragement and development of new inventions, accompanied by aggressive pioneer product promotion. This, too, is a continuing necessity.

(7) Next—rural electrification, and the industrialization of agriculture, to the end that a strong agricultural economy and contented people on our nation's farms may be the constant companions of and constructive contributors to a strong industrial economy comprised of contented people.

(8) Finally, in this stage—development of hemispheric self-sufficiency, through the development of South America as a source of raw materials—a development which should be subsidized, if necessary. Clearly, this, too, is a continuing necessity, as I shall later try to emphasize in connection with another reference to our relations with South America.

These, then, are the requirements of the recovery stage.

Now we come to what I label the "stabilization stage"—the period immediately after the Federal Reserve Board Index of Industrial Production (Unadjusted) has averaged 140 for two months. The necessities in this stage are—

(1) First—credit and price control against inflation—against long-term commitments of durable consumer goods purchases—and against nonessential personal loans.

(2) Next—maintenance of a full supply of normal needs of a nondurable character to all strata of society—still another continuing necessity.

(3) Next—an acceleration of the modernization of industry—including within that identity all utilities—power, transportation, communication, etc. Again a continuing necessity, to the end that we may always be in a position to provide more goods and services for more people at less cost.

(4) Next—gradual reduction in governmental activities, expenditures, and loans connected with all nondefense purposes in the conventional field of private enterprise.

(5) Next—taxation to balance the nondefense budget—a

step which, with the one just passed, you will notice I place in the second stage of this program because we want no restraints upon employment and increased purchasing power in the first.

(6) Next—industrial development of the Temperate Zone of South America— another continuing necessity, which should be aided by subsidy in the degree necessary . . . not commercial exploitation of the character which, too often, has created hemispheric discord.

Now we come to what may be called the "backlog building stage"—the stage during which we undertake to dam up a part of the demand for goods, in order that we may have a reservoir of nonessential unfilled wants in reserve for the days ahead, when employment connected with defense could diminish in a degree sufficient to be dangerous to our economy and to our way of life. This is the stage which will be reached when the Federal Reserve Board Index of Industrial Production (Unadjusted) has averaged 145 for two months. In this stage we shall require:

(1) First—further credit and term restraints upon durable consumer goods purchases, and nonessential personal loans.

(2) Next—the encouragement and expansion of individual, industrial, and governmental reserves in cash or its equivalent. This we may accomplish through—

(a) Personal savings, induced by the active promotion and sale of Government Savings Stamps and bonds of small denominations—stamps and bonds which serve the additional purpose of providing the people at large with a means of sharing in the financial support of our national defense effort.

(b) Increases in the amounts of payment, the extension of coverage, and the extension of the time period under our unemployment insurance laws.

(c) Increases in the amounts of payment and the extension of coverage under our social security laws.

(d) Medical and hospitalization insurance on a national

scale for the people of our country whose insufficient incomes do not permit them to purchase this protection from private organizations.

(As I propose larger commitments under our unemployment and social security laws as a socially desirable form of accumulation against adversity —and as I invite the initiation of a national insurance plan to cover medical and hospitalization expenses, for the underprivileged, I, at the same time, propose that all of these activities be jointly supported by contributions from every individual prospective beneficiary under these plans—by all employers—and by the government.)

(3) Next in this stage—drastic curtailment of all governmental activities, expenditures, and loans connected with all nondefense purposes in the conventional field of private enterprise.

(4) Next—restraints on business expansion loans for nondefense purposes.

(5) Next—taxation for reduction of the National Debt.

(6) Finally—the diversion of the major portion of sales promotion and advertising expenditures to the speculative promotion of pioneer products.

Now I come to the final stage—the stage when the private enterprise system will meet its most serious challenge—and therefore the stage which we may very consistently call the "Free Enterprise System Challenge Stage." This is the period after the Federal Reserve Board Index of Industrial Production (Unadjusted) has declined—mark this word "declined" —to an average of 150 for two months.

Then, indeed, at this time when our future economic security is at stake, we must call upon all of our vision and imagination— upon all of our resources—upon all of our ingenuity—and, above all, upon the same deep sense of service that now motivates us, as we move forward in providing the materials for our physical security—to the end that all employables will be kept employed—and that the preponderant majority will find employment on the payrolls of the private enterprise system.

With these thoughts in mind, then, these are the needs in this most critical stage:

(1) Here I submit, in all seriousness, as a first step—prayer and the wholehearted practice of the Golden Rule—and this, I hardly need say, is a continuing, compelling, and comforting requirement—and, happily, that fact is gaining greater force with each passing day as a bedevilled and bewildered world seeks the solace of divine inspiration from the source of all righteousness and all human rights.

(2) Next—Passing from this sublime step to one more material—liberal credit and term expansion, as a strong stimulant to purchases of all kinds.

(3) Next—More goods and more services for more people at less cost—first of all, more and better housing for more people at a price they can afford to pay—then, more and better furnishings of every kind for these houses, to the end that, within the means of their occupants, these houses may be converted into comfortable, convenient, and happy homes—then, more consumer goods of every character at lower cost—and, finally, low-cost distribution as a means of filling the people's wants at the least possible cost. Of course, more goods and services for more people at less cost is another continuing necessity.

(4) Next—Intensive sales promotion and advertising.

(5) Next—Intensification of industrial and utility modernization.

(6) Next—Conversion of surplus defense plants on private property to the production of goods for the normal needs of the Nation.

(7) And, finally, permanent government public works.

With this outline of the requirements of our most challenging stage, I conclude my presentation of the stages and steps—with the reminder that, as heretofore stated, all of the foregoing is an attempt to first present a realistic view of the forces underlying the world conflict, and then to provide a specific basis for discussion, to the end that, together, we may find the

way to best insure our moral, physical and economic security—
the total security I feel we must have if, amidst the destructive
forces flooding the world with false philosophies, the democratic
process and the American Free Enterprise System are to be
preserved in their most useful form.

This, then, leaves only a suggestion pertinent to an earlier
statement that "the components of the private enterprise system
should take the initiative in defining the obligations the whole
system can and will positively assume—while, collaterally and
co-ordinately, it defines those obligations which it will actively
support government in assuming."

This proposal is that, with this whole presentation as a starting
point, public-spirited leaders in finance—in industry—and in
commerce consider what kind of a program they can develop,
to which they can gain the whole-hearted support of those elements representing 70 per cent of the financial, industrial, and
commercial power of the private enterprise system. Then, having established the obligations of business—the manner in which
these obligations would be discharged, and the manner in which
business would exercise internal self-discipline, they should urge
equally enlightened leaders in labor and agriculture to proceed
to the same end. Then, finally, after all factors have reconciled
their differences and reached an agreement upon the responsibilities they would jointly discharge, government—the servant
of all of the people—could have a clearer definition of the public
service the Free Enterprise System could be definitely relied
upon to supply. And, collaterally, government could be constructively presented with a clear definition of the province
within which it could operate in the common interest, with the
firm and full support of all elements of the private enterprise
system, as well as with the support of the general public.

This suggestion is made with a deep realization of the difficulties involved—but it is also made with a comprehension of
the fact that the private enterprise system is faced with two
alternatives—either private decisions will be made and enforced
by public-spirited and fully supported leaders in finance, industry, commerce, labor, and agriculture—or public decisions will

be made and enforced by the government of the whole people for the whole people. Therefore, it must be seen that, if no way can be found to make and enforce the first kind of decisions, there can be little justification for resistance to the second kind.

And at this point let us recall to mind some impressive lessons of history.

The Magna Charta was the work of a few wise and courageous men whose minds and hearts were brought into concord by their common zeal for service in the common good. This, too, was true of our own Declaration of Independence—and of our cherished Constitution. Yes—these historic guides to greatness were the work of a few men whose words and ideas, falling like a pebble in the center of the pool of world thought, set up ever widening circles of acceptance and support. Now, as I propose the gathering together of a few wise and courageous men from the ranks of free enterprise—men whose minds and hearts are in concord because of their common zeal for service in the common good—men whose work could be the composition of a constitution for the Free Enterprise System—I remind you of the process whereby progress is made.

And as I do so, I also assert that it is the duty of the American Free Enterprise System to fully recognize the advent of a new and dangerous era, and, recognizing that fact, to adjust itself in a manner which will permit it to freely exercise its full potentialities for service to the public, while preserving its entirely consistent purpose of producing a profit.

The call to the people who comprise the American Free Enterprise System today is the call that all Americans must heed—no matter what their walk of life may be. It is a call best expressed in the words of John Milton, recently quoted by a famous American editor. Milton's cry was—

"Awake—arise—or be forever fallen."

Tonight, as I repeat that challenging call to you, I am certain that we shall meet it—and I shall conclude this lengthy presentation with a statement of the conviction upon which this certainty is based.

First—I am completely confident that, notwithstanding the difficulties and dangers before us, the public-spirited citizens who preponderantly comprise the American Free Enterprise System will see in this new era, not an occasion for disheartenment and despair, but, rather, an inspiring and challenging opportunity to regain both the full faith of the common people and the cordial, constructive support of the servant of all of the people—the Government of the United States.

Further—it is my firm conviction that my enlightened associates in industry, commerce, and labor will seize this challenging opportunity with a clear, deep, and broad conception of the social obligations of the American Free Enterprise System—the system upon which all of us rely in some way or another, no matter what our occupation may be.

Holding this conviction, I am equally certain that, with this complete comprehension of our opportunities—of our obligations—and of the character of the challenge confronting us, we shall all play our full part—earnestly, enthusiastically, and effectively.

And, finally, my most positive and most comforting conviction is that, as we thus play our full part in sustaining the dynamic character of our democracy, we shall have the soul-stirring satisfaction of knowing that we have done our full duty—the duty of providing our noble nation with the solid foundation of moral, physical, and economic security—the solid foundation of total security upon which we, as a free, friendly, and united people, shall continue to courageously construct an ever greater and grander America.

DISSENTING COMMENT BY CHARLES O. HARDY

(With rejoinders by the author)

I agree with Mr. Nourse's appraisal of the consumer as an object of concern whose interests should take precedence over those of all producer groups—whether capitalists, wage workers, or independent farmers and businessmen. I agree also that in general the gains of progress can be disseminated through society by a gradual process of price lowering better than through increases of wages and business profits. I have, however, considerable reservations as to some of the argument by which he supports this conclusion.

A major point of disagreement comes out most clearly in the arithmetical illustration of the results of different price policies (pp. 276-84). The model case starts with the installation of machinery which reduces the work of producing a year's output of consumer goods by 800,000 man-hours, figured at 50 cents an hour; no additional capacity being involved. It is pointed out correctly, that if the capitalist thus increases his profits by $400,000 and spends it all, whether on consumer goods or on additional capital, he re-employs as much labor outside his business as has been displaced from it. It is argued, however, that a series of such distributive cycles could not be carried through successfully, because if the capitalists invest their incomes in new capital the future output of this capital will not be balanced by new community income to buy it; and if they try to consume their growing incomes they will reach the limit of their power to consume.

First, as to the output resulting from investing the new profit in new capital goods. Mr. Nourse says: "Since . . . no wages have been raised and no more current employment created, the sources of such a consumer market would have to be found among those whose incomes had been increased by the retention of profits from the preceding increase of efficiency and those who draw income from the new plant." With respect to the first of these sources of demand, we may concede even more than Mr. Nourse claims. No market for the new consumer goods will be found in the incomes that were increased by the preceding increase of efficiency, since that income has already been used to buy the equivalent of the "old" goods that were diverted from the employees who lost their jobs, thus maintaining the "old" level of activity in other industries. But why are "those who draw income from the new plant" passed over so lightly? Utilization of the new plant does not proceed in a vacuum. It involves the disbursement of wages and other income in the process of operation, and that income is sufficient to buy the new output, if the income recipients spend it, just as the old income was sufficient to buy the old output.

> Mr. Hardy seems to ascribe complete and continuing success to the all-to-capital allocation of technological gains because, as is evident, any single such operation could be carried through successfully under the simple assumption "*if* they spend it." But the validity of this assumption is precisely what I am attacking. Thus, in the last analysis, the whole issue comes down to the question of whether a capitalist class, limited in numbers as they are under the present distribution of wealth (or even with less concentration), can consume the whole increase of physical product that our technologies make available.
>
> The issue is not one between black and white—complete breakdown of the economic process *versus* perfect functioning. (See page 277, lines 9 to 12.) I argue that as we approach an all-to-capital distribution of technological gains, there is a progressive tendency toward retardation of economic progress. If I understand Mr. Hardy, he denies that there is any such retardation. The fundamental disagreement between us on this point is evident from his next statement.

As to the inability of profit recipients to consume the gains of progress, the dilemma is remote. Pioneers in extravagance have blocked out great areas of potential consumption which have yet to be explored, and the average capitalist has hardly crossed their frontiers.

I cannot conceive that "pioneers of extravagance" could teach recipients of profits how to consume the increment due to technological gains as fast as it could be created in an advanced industrial society. Furthermore, experience shows that the relatively wealthy people on whom such incomes would progressively converge are too thrifty or too eager for growing financial power thus to dissipate their incomes.

Mr. Nourse's picture of the results of rising profits ends with "congested consumption, hoarded savings, and unutilized plant capacities, all three of these situations resulting in unemployment or wasted labor." (p. 279; see also p. 325.) Of these alternatives it is only the hoarded savings that result in unemployment. "Suits, shoes, and hats in the closet, fleets of automobiles standing idle much of the time, and houses standing largely untenanted" *are* the equivalent of goods promptly worn out by persons of modest means, so long as the recipients of income prefer them to hoarded cash. The existence of consumer goods or capital goods in excess of those in active use is not a cause of unemployment, though in the case of capital goods it is a necessary accompaniment of wide-scale unemployment. A wealthy community has far more instruments than its labor force can utilize simultaneously; such a reserve of excess capital actually facilitates full employment by making productive programs more flexible.

> "So long as the recipients of income prefer them to hoarded cash." But my point is precisely that they will not prefer them to hoarded cash indefinitely. Mere ownership of such goods involves carrying charges—housing, protection, service—which act as a brake on their indefinite acquisition just as non-use operates restrictively on their rate of replacement. Of course this custodial care provides some employment but relatively little compared with that furnished as a result of active use. Congested consumption slows market absorption, market retardation leads to partial disuse of plant, excess plant capacity encourages hoarding of funds. I agree that hoarding is the ultimate manifestation of the conditions that lead to unemployment. But it is not causally independent of idle plant and inactive consumption; each in turn underlies it and is therefore of progressively more fundamental importance. Consumption is the ultimate spring of economic activity.

The author's comparison of wage rate advances with price lowering as a method of distributing gains of progress is not wholly convincing. It is true, as stated (p. 280) that "wage raises as such create no jobs for displaced workers," except as the savings of those whose wages are raised furnish capital with which to equip the unemployed. Otherwise, previously unemployed capital may be found and put into use if additional jobs are to be created. But exactly the same thing is true of the price-lowering solution. Starting with an investment which saves labor but provides no capacity for increased output, price lowering puts consumers in possession of purchasing power which they may seek to expend. But no added goods come forward to meet this added demand except as capital is provided from new savings or previously unemployed capital is put to work.

> Converting the labor-saving improvement into higher wages for a smaller number of employees creates no jobs for displaced workers because it brings about no increase in the total payroll and thus no increase in total market demand. Diverting some of this higher per capita income of the wage-earner group to invest- ment in capital goods facilitates new jobs rather than creating them —this inevitably depends upon demand for consumer goods in the market. If, on the other hand, prices are lowered, the unconsumed purchasing power remaining in the hands of consumers becomes an immediate demand for additional products and hence creates additional jobs. If the capital necessary to equip these workers is not forthcoming from idle sources, a part of the savings in the hands of consumers will obviously have to be diverted to this pur- pose (except as the new "goods" might be services, for whose render- ing no capital equipment was required). Here again the difference is relative rather than absolute. The wage-raising method seems to me to get the cart before the horse.

So far as I can see, Mr. Nourse's case for low prices as a preventive of unemployment boils down to an apprehension that high prices will lead to high profits which, because they go to the wealthy, will be saved and not invested. This objection to high profits is simply a special case of the present-day standard objection to all inequality of income distribution. High profits are equally objectionable, irrespective of their origin. If a low-price policy is more profitable in the long run than a high-price policy (pp. 425, 438), then it is more objectionable in the long run, because it increases the share of income that goes to the wealthiest fraction of society.

> NO. Low-price policy means an ultimately *larger absolute amount* of profits, derived from a *smaller share* in an *enlarged total product*. As to the question of inequality of present wealth distribution, this is a factor in my argument, but Mr. Hardy's statement considerably overemphasizes its importance. In fact, his comment places emphasis at the wrong spot. Those who have past wealth and current control which they use in quest of high profit *rates* restrain production and withhold investment below the levels possible in the state of our resources. This faulty functioning of our capitalistic system would not necessarily be remedied by a more equal distribution of wealth. The smaller capitalists or the administrators of the financial agencies by which their small savings are cumulated might follow the same philosophy as present owners (and their agents). On the other hand, if low price and low *rate*-of-profit policies were followed by present owners, the relative inequality would be progressively lessened. But this would be primarily by bringing up the real income position of persons in the lower and middle income brackets.

Moreover, the remedy suggested by Mr. Nourse is not the most practical one. The manager is not under the necessity, as is the economist, of relying for guidance on a generalized propensity of a whole economic class. If the difficulty is serious enough to justify corporate managers in basing price policy on it, the managers should inform themselves as to the wealth and consuming propensities of their own stockholders and adjust their prices accordingly, seeking high profits if their stockholders are, on the whole, poverty stricken or extravagant, and low profits if they are wealthy and thrifty.

> Such quarrel as I have with the bare mechanics of this argument has already been indicated on page 529. But when such a proposal is advanced as the "most *practical*" means of dealing with the problem, I must ask: (a) How could corporate managers inform themselves as to the spending and savings propensities of each stockholder and synthesize these findings into a general index?

(b) Can there be any possible doubt as to the state of facts today as to stockholders as a class compared to the mass of consumers? Perhaps, however, it was not intended that this proposal should be taken seriously.

Limitations of time and space prohibit discussion of a number of scattered points of difference such as the following:

1. The extent of control actually exercised by professional managers, as compared with both investors and consumers, which seems to me to be exaggerated.

2. The implication (p. 108) that it is any more "fatal" to freeze or hoard profits than to do the same with any other kind of income.

> I see no implication that it is "more" fatal. I simply was not talking about "other kinds of income" whose hoarding would likewise be deleterious or "fatal" to the best functioning of the system.

3. The statement that high wage rates, established by monopolistic bargaining, "no doubt" promote efficiency (by the financial pressure they put on the employer). No doubt the same effect has sometimes been achieved by exorbitant interest rates, or railway rates, or alimony allowances, but such by-product values should be given no weight in appraising extortionate practices.

> No doubt. But here too I was talking about the influence of this factor, not other possibly similar ones.

4. The discussion of the market effects of price cutting in a depression (pp. 293, 295) which, I think, generalizes a relatively infrequent type of market behavior.

5. The implication (p. 304) that wage rates do not, except for union pressure, tend to rise sharply as business approaches full scale. (At such time there are indeed "possibilities of substituting lower-priced labor or labor-saving methods"—but not more than at any other time.)

> I did not intend so to imply. Union pressure is not the only wage-raising influence at such a time, but the situation then favors its exercise. And, of course, "*possibilities* of substituting low-priced

labor or labor-saving methods" are equally present at other times—but more likely to be resorted to at times when wages are advancing.

6. The statement (p. 422) about anticipated burdens of disuse of capacity (obsolescence reserves). The point is valid only in so far as reserves are accumulated in cash balances, and to that extent it applies to *all* depreciation allowances. What will be the consequences if obsolescence and depreciation are not provided for?

> To present this broad issue as synonymous with obsolescence reserves must rest on a theory that any plant which is not profitable at the bottom of a depression—its earning power not to be restored by subsequent recovery—is obsolescent (or obsolete?). I make a distinction between depreciation as a technical fact and obsolescence as an economic contingency. Of course disaster will follow if depreciation reserves are not provided against physical deterioration due to use or against value shrinkage because of changes in taste, technique, population distribution, or the like. But these costs incidental to normal operation are very different from the non-use of technically and commercially acceptable machinery for which there is an available labor supply and a potential market if this labor is simply allowed to use this equipment. I argue that the attempt to erect protection against such non-use becomes a factor in bringing it to pass.
>
> Somewhat obscured by the obsolescence issue in Mr. Hardy's comment is the question whether reserves (even reserves against the costs of non-use) have a harmful effect only if kept as cash balances. I would deny this. Investing such reserves in plant capacity in excess of that being profitably used at the peak of the boom is on the whole more harmful in that it postpones the beginning of readjustment and puts capital in a form in which it is less available for remedial uses after recession has taken place.

7. Finally, I find nothing in the book which justifies the conclusion (pp. 439, 446) that high-price policy affords the key to an understanding of the cause of the business cycle, and that under a low-price policy "sustained operations" would replace the alternation of spurts of activity and periods of recession.

> I should have been most happy if I could have written this whole book without a single allusion to business cycles or cycle

theory. But, as stated on page 291, that would have been to turn my back upon reality. I am sorry if others besides Mr. Hardy gained the impression that I believe "high price policy affords the key to an understanding of the cause of the business cycle," or that low-price policy would cure all cyclical disturbances. It could not change the weather or human tastes and propensities. It would not arrest or greatly alter the course of scientific and technological progress nor control our financial institutions and fiscal antics. "Spurts of activity and periods of recession" we shall doubtless always have *in some degree*. What I intended to say, and what I strongly believe, is that high-price policy operates to aggravate such aberrations of business, and low-price policy would operate in the direction of mitigating disturbances and helping to sustain operations on a higher average level. (See page 306.)

INDEX

Group enterprise. *See under* Enterprise

Harvard Graduate School, 236n.
Harlow, Rex F., 381
High-price policy. *See under* Price policy
High wages. *See under* Wages
Hoffman, Paul G., 72, 74, 101n., 341-42
Homan, Paul T., 384n.
Hook, Charles R., 28
Houser, T. V., 239n., 426n.
Housing industry, 162, 189, 429n.
Humphrey, Don D., 148

Incentives in business, 20, 31, 78, 88, 96ff., 275, 285ff., 301, 317, 322, 419, 424, 434ff.
Income elasticity, 211, 269.
See also under Demand
Income, types of, 83ff.
Individual bargaining. *See under* Bargaining
Individual enterprise. *See under* Enterprise
Individual firm,
policy of, 287, 320, 323, 326, 330, 349n., 361-62, 395, 410, 442
Individual,
responsibility of. *See under* Responsibility
Industrial concentration. *See* "Big Business"
Industrial Revolution, 31, 37, 39, 264
Industry, age of, 184, 259
Institutions,
business. *See* Business, institutionalized
economic, 18, 51
evolution of, 7, 23, 88
Investments,
timing and
volume of, 14, 90, 269, 277, 298, 302ff., 314, 321, 323ff. *See also* Capital, formation of

Invisible Hand, 19, 51, 448
Iron and Steel Institute, 75

Johnston, Eric A., 344, 346, 409n.
Joint demand. *See under* Demand
Judgment, mechanized, 194, 206, 287, 382ff.
Justice, Department of, 240, 414

Kaiser, Henry J., 408
Knapp, J. G., 252n.
Knight, Frank H., 60n., 79n.
Kreps, Theodore J., 155n.

Labor saving, 39, 265, 275ff., 300, 326ff., 349, 376, 445
Labor unions, 8, 11, 45, 46n., 65
officials of, 44. *See also* Union officials
Laissez faire, 12, 30, 31, 33n., 34, 49, 51, 448
Large-scale business. *See* "Big Business"
Leadership,
business. *See* Responsibility, of business leaders *and* Strategic factor in price making
Logan, John A., 159n.
Low income groups,
and elasticity of demand, 215. *See also under* Demand
Low-price policy. *See under* Price policy

Machinery and Allied Products Institute, 179
Mail order houses, 156, 158, 159n., 236, 237, 250n., 426n. *See also* Sears, Roebuck and Co.
Management,
professional, 37, 66, 80, 88, 91, 98, 143, 364, 438, 441. *See also* Business, institutionalized
Market,
analysis, 216, 365ff.